# MACROECONOMICS
A Mathematical Approach

# MACROECONOMICS
# A MATHEMATICAL APPROACH

**ANITA GHATAK**
Principal Lecturer
Department of Economics
De Montfort University
LEICESTER (U.K.)

**CONCEPT PUBLISHING COMPANY, NEW DELHI 110059**

ISBN 81-7022-478-0

First Published 1994



*Published and Printed by*
Ashok Kumar Mittal
Concept Publishing Company
A/15-16, Commercial Block, Mohan Garden
NEW DELHI 110059 (India)

*Lasertypeset by*
Printing Express
H-13, Bali Nagar
NEW DELHI 110015

# CONTENTS

# MACROECONOMICS
# A MATHEMATICAL APPROACH

The book discusses the evolution of macroeconomics around different schools of thought — classical, Keynesian, monetarist, new classical and new Keynesian. It highlights the central issues in the controversies between these schools, e.g., the relevance of centrally administered policies.

Classical macroeconomics relies on complete wage — price flexibility and absence of money illusion to derive the policy ineffectiveness result. Keynes introduces money illusion and wage rigidity and derives a consequent role for fiscal and monetary policy. Fiscal (monetary) policy is stronger (weaker) whenever interest elasticity of money is high and that of investment demand low. Classical macroeconomics is consistent with the optimising behaviour of economic agents whereas Keynesian economics lays the foundations of disequilibrium economics. Patinkin, Barro and Grossman contribute significantly to the exploration of disequilibrium economics.

Monetarists emphasise the dynamic effects of the government budget constraint ignored in static Keynesian macroeconomics. The financing of government budget introduces important wealth effects which make a significant difference between the short and the long-run effects of fiscal and monetary policies. In the monetarist model the rate of inflation is a function not only of the rate of unemployment but also of the expected rate of inflation, real money stock, interest rate, ratio of government debt to money stock, government spending, etc. The monetarists (Keynesians) hold that the net effect of a rise in debt-money ratio on the rate of inflation is non-positive (positive).

The neoclassical economists provide an alternative explanation of Friedman's natural rate hypothesis by replacing adaptive expectations by rational expectations hypothesis. Lucas, Sargent and Wallace derive the policy irrelevance result under rational expectations and continuous market clearing. Anticipated changes in policies are fully accommodated in the agents' expectations and therefore, do not affect the rate of output or unemployment. As shown in Phelp's "island" model business cycles are equilibrium phenomena. Policy irrelevance issue under rational expectations is challenged by Fischer in his explicit labour contract theory and this conclusion is supported by Phelps and Taylor. The latter show that monetary policy is effective even under rational expectations whenever wages and prices are predetermined.

Noting that some form of wage rigidity is required for policy effectiveness, new Keynesian economics attempts to provide the micro-foundations allegedly lacking in conventional presentations of Keynesian macroeconomics. The implicit labour contract theory and efficiency wage theory are two important ingredients of new Keynesian economics.

Finally the important macroeconomic issues for an open economy are explained in both a Keynesian and a monetarist framework. Exchange rate overshooting is explained with both adaptive and rational expectations. Dornbusch, Mussa, Barro and others' contributions are notable in this context. The microfoundations are discussed in terms of intertemporal utility maximisation subject to wealth constraints. It is concluded that both the real factors like trade and capital flows and monetary factors like money supply inflation and interest rates are important in explaining exchange rates and balance of payments fluctuation. The Keynesian and monetary approaches are, therefore, not rivals but complementary. Montiel and others' synthesis between the two approaches explains both short and long-run changes in balance of payments and exchange rates.

In view of the mathematical nature of the literature the book explains the mathematical tools and derives the mathematical proofs in the appendices to respective chapters.

ANITA GHATAK

# 1

# INTRODUCTION

Macroeconomic thought has evolved round a number of different schools, Classical, Keynesian, monetarist, new Classical and new Keynesian. While there are a large number of textbooks approaching macroeconomic theory in a descriptive and non-mathematical manner, there are relatively few adopting a mathematical approach. This book attempts to emphasise the increasing importance of mathematics in explaining macroeconomic problems and policy issues. Although the use of mathematics was rather limited in Classical and Keynes's own writings the pioneers of new Classical and new Keynesian economics could not do without fairly sophisticated mathematical techniques. Also, early supporters of Keynes like Blinder favoured macroeconomic model building. Ever since Hicks's contribution in 1937 the IS-LM interpretation of macromodels became a very popular and useful apparatus for any broader discussion of macroeconomic problems and policy issues. The simple IS-LM framework can also highlight a few important distinguishing features of Classical and Keynesian economics. This has, therefore, been discussed in Chapter 2.

The IS-LM model considers only the demand sides of output and money markets and assumes supply of output to be demand determined. Aggregate supply of output is explained in Chapter 3 with the help of three sector models comprising output money and labour markets. This also highlights a few distinctive features of classical and Keynesian economics — e.g., the dichotomy and the consequent neutrality of money in the Classical and the role of money illusion in Keynesian economics. Pigou's attempts to resolve Keynes's criticism of Classical economics is discussed in the same chapter. While these have been tackled in an aggregative framework, the need for embedding individual decision making into macroeconomic models has also been discussed at length in Section 3. Keynes was frequently criticised of ignoring the microfoundations of macroeconomics and attempts made by his supporters to provide such foundations have logically been included in the same chapter. The disequilibrium models of Barro-Grossman, Patinkin, Clower, Leijonhufund and others have been included.

A stable demand for money function lies at the heart of monetary economics. There are various theories of demand for money. Chapters 2 and 3 are based on a very simple version, viz, that the real demand for money depends positively on real income and inversely on the real rate of interest. The stability of the demand for money, however, depends also on a number of other considerations, like expectations, availability of alternative assets, etc. Such issues are important for a discussion of Keynesian's and monetarists' debate. Chapter 4 discusses various theories and empirical stability of demand and supply of money in closed and open economies. The supply of money is usually considered given or determined outside the private sector in simple macromodels like those considered in Chapters 2 and 3 of the present book. However it is also important to discuss the details of the mechanics and components of money supply and these are dealt with in section 4.

The endogeneity of money supply paves the path for a discussion of Keynesian *versus* monetarists' debate. This is sparked off by the inclusion of the budget constraint of the government sector and the consequent dynamic elements into the hitherto static macro frameworks of Keynesian and classical economics. The standard Keynesian economics is short-run while the monetarists' framework emphasises the long-run stability. The dynamics of government budget logically involves the consideration of wealth effects into individuals' consumption and money demand functions as budget deficits can be financed by bond sales as well as by printing money. Chapter 5 discusses a number of models including the government budget constraint and wealth effects and the relative effectiveness of fiscal and monetary policies. The debate between Keynesians and monetarists has been discussed mainly in terms of relative efficacy of fiscal and monetary policies. This is the approach favoured throughout the book. The long-run and short-run implications of government budget and wealth effects have both been discussed in very much detail and microeconomic considerations have been highlighted whenever possible in Chapter 5. Blinder and Solow, Tobin and Buiter, Turnovsky and a number of models including micro analysis of individual utility maximisation have been discussed.

The discussions of Chapters 2–5 assume a constant price level and full employment of labour, i.e., assume no inflation or unemployment. As any textbook runs in an ascending order of complexities, the problem of inflation and unemployment is discussed in Chapter 6. The discussion starts as expected with that of the Phillips curve and then gradually extends to the role of expectation adaptive and rational. As is well known, the rational expectation rule not only dominates the literature but it also constitutes an important ingredient of new classical economics. Lipsey-Parkin, Brechling, Friedman, Phelps and then a number of important models using the rational expectation rule have been critically examined in exploring the relation between inflation and unemployment and the consequent roles for policy. Lucas-Sargent-Wallace, Phelps and Taylor and Fisher's contributions on rational expectation and natural rate hypotheses have been discussed at depth and this discussion prepares the background for new classical macro-economics further explained in the next chapter.

The rational expectation rule is further explained as an integral part of new classical economics in Chapter 7. It also ties up the debate between Keynesians and monetarists by highlighting a few characteristics separating the two schools. In this context, Stein's model has been analysed in detail. In the new classical group, Lucas's pioneering work, and Phelp's "islands" model are discussed along with others. Finally the line of research known as new Keynesian economics is also outline in Chapter 7. This is based, like Keynesian economics, on wage-rigidity explained by implicit contracts between employers and employees. The well known contributions of Azariadis, Grossman and others have been discussed in this context.

The open economy models form the subject matter of Chapter 8. Once again a distinction in made between Keynesian and monetarist approaches towards the determination of exchange rates and to the theory of balance of payments. A number of important contributions including and without the role of expectations have been discussed in this chapter. Keynesian and monetarists features have been combined to explain both short and the long run fluctuations of exchange rates. Dornbusch, Mussa, Frenkel, Barro and others' models including micro analyses of individuals' utility maximisation in an open economy have been discussed in very much detail.

## Types of Macromodels

Macromodels discussed in the book are basically of two types : *static* and *dynamic*. A static model involves equations — behavioural technological or institutional in which all the variables pertain to the same time point, e.g., the simple IS-LM model of Chapter 2 and the three sector models of Chapter 3. A dynamic model involves equations in which the variables do not all belong to the same time point. In a dynamic equation, the current value of a variable depends on its own past values and, in some cases, on past values of other variables. For example, the current consumption expenditure may depend on past expenditure if there is inertia in consumers' behaviour and, it quite logically, may also depend on past as well as current income of the consumer. A dynamic equation can be stated in either a *discrete* period form or in a *continuous* time form. Accordingly, a dynamic model can be presented in either the discrete period form or the continuous time form. The present book considers dynamic models of both types. For example, the Ott and Ott model of Chapter 5 is in the discrete period form and Stein's monetarist model of Chapter 7 is in the continuous time form to name just one of each type. The discrete time period dynamic equation is a *difference* equation and the continuous time dynamic equations are *differential* equations. The appendix to this chapter discusses the principles on which the solution of each type of equation is based. In a dynamic equation the question of *stability* is important and it requires the variable explained by the dynamic equation under consideration to converge to its *equilibrium* value in the long-run. Equilibrium can be defined in various ways but essentially it means a situation from where there would be no tendency to change unless the factors assumed to be constant change.

The equilibrium value of an *endogenous* variable in a static model is automatically ensured by the economic theory underlying the model. For example the equilibrium values of real income and real interest rates in the simple two sector IS-LM model are derived from the conditions for equilibrium in the output and money markets. Under the ceteris paribus assumptions, the condition for equilibrium in a market is that aggregate supply becomes equal to aggregate demand in that market and a static model would include such equilibrium conditions for as many markets as are considered in the model. So, static models are equilibrium models. A static model, when solved, gives the equilibrium values of all the *endogenous* variables in terms of the *exogenous* variables and *parameters* of the model. An endogenous variable is the variable which is to be determined from within the model and an exogenous variable is given or determined outside the model. For example, in the simple IS-LM model of Chapter 2, money supply, government spending, exports, price level, etc., are treated as exogenous variables. A model to be determinate should have as many equations as endogenous variables. A convenient method of solving for endogenous variables in a static model is *Cramer's Rule*. This is explained in the appendix to this chapter. The state of equilibrium does not necessarily imply an ideal state; all it means is that it is a state, which if attained, will perpetuate itself unless the given conditions change. The equilibrium value of a variable explained by a dynamic equation is, accordingly, derived by putting the past, present and future values equal to one another. This is explained in the Appendix, 1.A.3 and 1.A.4.

All the models considered in the book have been analysed by the comparative statics method. This method studies the change in the equilibrium value of each endogenous variable as a result of a change in any one exogenous variable at a time. This method then necessarily involves the use of differential calculus. As only one exogenous variable is allowed to change at a time, the technique required is that of *partial differentiation*. The basic rules of partial and total differentiation requires that the exogenous variables are independent of one another. As the subsequent chapters will demonstrate, many of the these exogenous variables are important policy *instruments* which are changed from time to time by the policy makers to attain desired changes in endogenous *target* variables. For example, government spending and money supply are policy instruments and real income and real interest rates are targets in the simple model of Chapter 2. The partial derivatives are the respective policy multipliers.

Use of Cramer's rule has been made throughout the book to the relevant systems of simultaneous equations formulating the latter in terms of *determinants* rather than *matrices*. Determinants are somewhat easier to understand as they can be reduced to a scalar and interpreted easily. The rules of simple algebraic manipulation with determinants are also discussed in the appendix.

The appendix on mathematical techniques used in the book is by no means a complete explanation of the respective topics. It only attempts to explain the rules used in the subsequent chapters of the book beforehand. For a fuller understanding and proofs of such mathematics, the reader is advised to look at Chiang's *Fundamental Methods of Mathematical Economics*.

# APPENDIX TO CHAPTER 1

## NATURE OF MATHEMATICS USED IN THE BOOK

### 1.A.1 Solution of Simultaneous Equations by Cramer's Rule

*Theory of Determinants*

The methods of elimination and substitution get very tedious when more than two independent variables and, therefore more than two equations, are involved. Cramer's Rule is more convenient in such cases. The first step in applying this rule is to arrange the system of simultaneous equations in terms of *determinants* and *row* or *column vectors*. A determinant is a square arrangement of numbers in the form of rows and columns. So, by nature it always has the same number of rows as columns. The number of rows or columns gives the *order* of the determinant. A row (column) vector has only one row (column) and as many columns (rows) as the order of the vector. So, a determinant of the third order will have three rows and three columns and a row (column) vector of the third order will have one row (column) and three columns (rows). The following is a system of three independent equations in three unknowns, $x_1$, $x_2$, and $x_3$ where $a_{ij}$ are the known constant coefficients not all of which are zero and $A_i$ are known constants, $i, j = 1, 2, 3$.

$$a_{11}x_1 + a_{12}x_2 + a_{13}x_3 = A_1 \tag{1}$$

$$a_{21}x_1 + a_{22}x_2 + a_{23}x_3 = A_2 \tag{2}$$

$$a_{31}x_1 + a_{32}x_2 + a_{33}x_3 = A_3 \tag{3}$$

The above three equation model comprising equations (1) to (3) can be rewritten in the following form:

$$\begin{vmatrix} a_{11} & a_{12} & a_{13} \\ a_{21} & a_{22} & a_{23} \\ a_{31} & a_{32} & a_{33} \end{vmatrix} \begin{vmatrix} x_1 \\ x_2 \\ x_3 \end{vmatrix} = \begin{vmatrix} A_1 \\ A_2 \\ A_3 \end{vmatrix} \tag{4}$$

In equation (4), the square array of $a_{ij}$, $i, j = 1, 2, 3$, is a determinant of the third order and the other two vertical arrays are column vectors of order three. A determinant can be denoted by its typical element, meaning the element of the $i$-th row and the $j$-th column $\Rightarrow$ the coefficient determinant in (4) could be summarised as:

$$\left| \begin{matrix} a_{ij} \\ 3\times3 \end{matrix} \right|$$

*Properties of Determinants*

1. A determinant can be evaluated by expanding in terms of the *Cofactors* of any one row or any one column. This is called *Laplace expansion.* The cofactor of an element of a determinant is the smaller order determinant obtained by deleting the row and column in which that element belongs with the *proper sign* prefixed.

The cofactor of the element $a_{ij}$ is the determinant obtained by deleting the $i$-th row and the $j$-th column with its sign $(-1)^{i+j}$ prefixed. Referring to the determinant on the L.H.S. of equation (4) the cofactors of various elements are:

$$C_{12} = \text{Cofactor of } a_{12} = -\begin{vmatrix} a_{21} & a_{23} \\ a_{31} & a_{33} \end{vmatrix}$$

$$C_{23} = \text{Cofactor of } a_{23} = -\begin{vmatrix} a_{11} & a_{12} \\ a_{31} & a_{32} \end{vmatrix}$$

$$C_{11} = \text{Cofactor of } a_{11} = -\begin{vmatrix} a_{22} & a_{23} \\ a_{32} & a_{33} \end{vmatrix}$$

and so on.

The value of the determinant then can be obtained as:

$$|a_{ij}| = a_{11}C_{11} + a_{12}C_{12} + a_{13}C_{13}$$

or as $$|a_{ij}| = a_{21}C_{21} + a_{22}C_{22} + a_{23}C_{23}$$

or as $$|a_{ij}| = a_{11}C_{11} + a_{21}C_{21} + a_{31}C_{31}$$

and so on

It is important to note that such Laplace expansion can be continued until one gets an $1 \times 1$ determinant. However, it is more convenient to bear in mind that a $2 \times 2$ determinant can be simply evaluated as the cross product connected by a negative sign:

$$\begin{vmatrix} a_{22} & a_{23} \\ a_{32} & a_{33} \end{vmatrix} = a_{22}a_{33} - a_{23}a_{32}$$

*Example 1*

$$\begin{vmatrix} 3 & -8 & 7 \\ 2 & 5 & 4 \\ 1 & 2 & 1 \end{vmatrix}$$

Expanding by the cofactors of the first row:

$$= 3\begin{vmatrix} 5 & 4 \\ 2 & 1 \end{vmatrix} - 8(-1)\begin{vmatrix} 2 & 4 \\ 1 & 1 \end{vmatrix} + 7\begin{vmatrix} 2 & 5 \\ 1 & 2 \end{vmatrix}$$

$$= 3(5-8) + 8(2-4) + 7(4-5)$$

$$= -9 - 16 - 7 = -32$$

The same result would be obtained if it were expanded by the Cofactors of the elements of say, the second column. Expanding by the cofactors of the elements of the second column:

$$= -8(-1)\begin{vmatrix} 2 & 4 \\ 1 & 1 \end{vmatrix} + 5\begin{vmatrix} 3 & 7 \\ 1 & 1 \end{vmatrix} + 2(-1)\begin{vmatrix} 3 & 7 \\ 2 & 4 \end{vmatrix}$$

$$= 8(2-4) + 5(3-7) - 2(12-14)$$

$$= -16 - 20 + 4 = 4 - 36 = -32$$

and so on.

2. The value of a determinant is reduced to zero if expanded by alien cofactors i.e., by cofactors of another row or another column:

$$a_{11}C_{21} + a_{12}C_{22} + a_{13}C_{23} = 0$$

With reference to the previous example, this property can be proved easily. Multiplying the elements of first row by the cofactors of the elements of the second row, one obtains:

$$3(-1)\begin{vmatrix} -8 & 7 \\ 2 & 1 \end{vmatrix} - 8\begin{vmatrix} 3 & 7 \\ 1 & 1 \end{vmatrix} + 7(-1)\begin{vmatrix} 3 & -8 \\ 1 & 2 \end{vmatrix}$$

$$= -3(-8-14) - 8(3-7) - 7(6+8)$$

$$= 66 + 32 - 98 + 0$$

3. The value of a determinant remains unchanged if any multiple of a row (a column) is added to or subtracted from another row (another column).

With reference to the previous example, this property can be proved as follows. Multiply the first column by 2 and subtract the result from the third column. The resulting determinant becomes

$$\begin{vmatrix} 3 & -8 & 1 \\ 2 & 5 & 0 \\ 1 & 2 & -1 \end{vmatrix} = 3(-5) + 8(-2) + (4-5)$$

$$= -15 - 16 - 1 = -32$$

This property is often used to reduce the labour of calculation.

4. The value of a determinant remains unchanged if its rows and columns are interchanged. The determinant so obtained is called the *transpose* of the original determinant.

Interchanging rows and columns, the determinant of our example becomes:

$$\begin{vmatrix} 3 & 2 & 1 \\ -8 & 5 & 2 \\ 7 & 4 & 1 \end{vmatrix} = 3(5-8) - 2(-8-14) + (-32-35)$$

$$= -9 + 44 - 67 = 44 - 76 = -32$$

Using a single letter for a determinant, the transpose is denoted by a prime over it:

$$\text{If} \quad |A| = \begin{vmatrix} a_{11} & a_{12} & a_{13} \\ a_{21} & a_{22} & a_{23} \\ a_{31} & a_{32} & a_{33} \end{vmatrix}$$

$$\Rightarrow \quad |A'| = \begin{vmatrix} a_{11} & a_{21} & a_{31} \\ a_{12} & a_{22} & a_{32} \\ a_{13} & a_{23} & a_{33} \end{vmatrix}$$

5. A determinant changes its sign if any two rows (columns) are interchanged. It is therefore obvious that the value of the determinant will remain unaltered by interchanging rows (columns) an even number of times. A simple proof is provided below with reference to our previous example.

Interchanging the first two rows, the determinant becomes:

$$|B| = \begin{vmatrix} 2 & 5 & 4 \\ 3 & -8 & 7 \\ 1 & 2 & 1 \end{vmatrix} = 2(-8-14)-5(3-7)+4(6+8)$$

$$= -44+20+56=32$$

Interchanging the last two rows of the determinant $|B|$, one obtains:

$$|C| = \begin{vmatrix} 2 & 5 & 4 \\ 1 & 2 & 1 \\ 3 & -8 & 7 \end{vmatrix} = 2(14+8)-5(7-3)+4(-8-6)$$

$$\Rightarrow \quad |C| = 44-20-56=-32$$

6. The value of a determinant changes $K$-fold if any *one* row (or *one* column) gets multiplied by a scalar $K$. Similarly a constant can be factored out of any *one* row (or *one* column).

The first part of the property can be proved with reference to the example 1. Multiplying the third row by 2 and then expanding by the cofactors of the first row, one obtains:

$$|D| = \begin{vmatrix} 3 & -8 & 7 \\ 2 & 5 & 4 \\ 2 & 4 & 2 \end{vmatrix} = 3(10-16)+8(4-8)+7(8-10)$$

$$= -18-32-14 = -64 = 2\times(-32)$$

For proving the second part the determinant $|D|$ can be reused as follows: Taking the common factor out of the third row of $D$ one gets the value of the original determinant of example 1.

7. The value of a determinant is reduced to zero if any two rows (or columns) are identical or multiples of each other, i.e., linearly dependent.

*Example 2*

$$|E| = \begin{vmatrix} 3 & 5 & 7 \\ 1 & 2 & 3 \\ 1 & 2 & 3 \end{vmatrix}$$

Expanding by the cofactors of the elements of the first row:

$$|E| = 3(6-6)-5(3-3)+7(2-2) = 0$$

To prove the second part consider the determinant in Example 3.

*Example 3*

$$|F| = \begin{vmatrix} 2 & 5 & 4 \\ 7 & 8 & 9 \\ 14 & 16 & 18 \end{vmatrix}$$

The elements of the third row of $|F|$ are those of the second row multiplied by 2. To prove that the value of $|F|$ is zero, one can use property 6 and the first half of property 7.

Using property 6,

$$|F| = 2\begin{vmatrix} 2 & 5 & 4 \\ 7 & 8 & 9 \\ 7 & 8 & 9 \end{vmatrix} = 2\times 0$$

by property 7.

These seven properties should be sufficient to get through the application of Cramer's Rule in the book. Unless otherwise mentioned, each determinant will be expanded by cofactors of the first row.

## Multiplication Rule for Matrices and Determinants

$$\text{Let} \quad A = \begin{vmatrix} a_{11} & a_{12} & a_{1m} \\ a_{21} & a_{21} & a_{2m} \\ \vdots & \vdots & \vdots \\ a_{m1} & a_{m2} & a_{mm} \end{vmatrix}$$

$$\text{and} \quad B = \begin{vmatrix} b_{11} & b_{12} & b_{1m} \\ b_{21} & b_{21} & b_{2m} \\ \cdots & \cdots & \cdots \\ b_{m1} & b_{m2} & b_{mm} \end{vmatrix}$$

Then the product of the two $|AB|$ is:

$$\begin{vmatrix} a_{11}b_{11} & + & a_{12}b_{21} & + & \cdots & + & a_{1m}b_{m1}, & \cdots & a_{11}b_{1m} & + & a_{12}b_{2m} & + & \cdots & + & a_{1m}b_{mm} \\ a_{21}b_{11} & + & a_{22}b_{21} & + & \cdots & + & a_{2m}b_{m1}, & \cdots & a_{21}b_{1m} & + & a_{22}b_{2m} & + & \cdots & + & a_{2m}b_{mm} \\ \cdots & \cdots & \cdots & \cdots & \cdots & \cdots & \cdots & \cdots & \cdots & \cdots & \cdots & \cdots & \cdots & \cdots & \cdots \\ a_{m1}b_{11} & + & a_{m2}b_{21} & + & \cdots & + & a_{mm}b_{m1}, & \cdots & a_{m1}b_{1m} & + & a_{m2}b_{2m} & + & \cdots & + & a_{mm}b_{mm} \end{vmatrix}$$

The sum of the products of the elements of the first row of $A$ with those of the first column of $B$ gives the member of the first row and first column of $AB$; the sum of the products of the elements of the first row of $A$ with respective elements of the second column of $B$ give the member of the first row and second column of $AB$; and so on. Similarly, the sum of products of respective elements of second row of $A$ and first column of $B$ gives the second row and first column of the product $|AB|$; and so on.

Although applying this rule is not so important in the case of determinants (as each determinant has the same number of rows and columns and it can be reduced to a scaler by means of Laplace's expansion), it should be noted that the number of columns of $|A|$ must be equal to the number of rows in $|B|$ if $|A|$ has to premultiply $|B|$. In applying Cramer's rule, which is discussed in the next section, the idea of premultiplication and confirmability is required in the simplest possible sense, for instance in representing a system of equations as in (1) – (3), a determinant of the 3rd order premultiples a column vector of order three.

In matrix multiplication confirmability must be observed as the product of two matrices [$A$] and [$B$] is not necessarily equal to the product of the same two matrices taken in the reverse order: [$B$] and [$A$].

[$AB$] $\neq$ [$BA$] except in a few cases. The discussion of matrix algebra is not intended here.

*Cramer's Rule*

First it is very important to check whether the determinant formed by the coefficients of the variables in the system of equations is non-zero. From properties 6 and 7 of determinants it should be clear that the determinants of coefficients would be zero if any two equations are identical or linearly dependent on each other.

For example, the following equations are linearly dependent.

$$2x_1 + 3x_2 + x_3 = 10 \tag{5}$$

$$4x_1 + 6x_2 + 2x_3 = 20 \tag{6}$$

So even if a third equation is added to the above set (5) and (6), the system cannot be solved for $x_1$, $x_2$ and $x_3$.

Once one is sure that the coefficient determinant is non-zero, it is evaluated in the way explained above and by Cramer's Rule, the variables are solved as follows.

$$x_1 = \frac{1}{|A|}\begin{vmatrix} A_1 & a_{12} & a_{13} \\ A_2 & a_{22} & a_{23} \\ A_3 & a_{32} & a_{33} \end{vmatrix} \tag{7i}$$

$$x_2 = \frac{1}{|A|}\begin{vmatrix} a_{11} & A_1 & a_{13} \\ a_{21} & A_2 & a_{23} \\ a_{31} & A_3 & a_{33} \end{vmatrix} \tag{7ii}$$

and $$x_3 = \frac{1}{|A|}\begin{vmatrix} a_{11} & a_{12} & A_1 \\ a_{21} & a_{22} & A_2 \\ a_{31} & a_{32} & A_3 \end{vmatrix} \tag{7iii}$$

In equations (7), the solutions are easy to understand in the sense that $x_i$ is obtained by the determinant with the $i$-th column of coefficients replaced by the column vector of constants divided by the coefficient determinant, $i = 1, 2, 3$ (as the coefficients of $x_i$ appear in the $i$-th column of the determinant of coefficients). The proof is given in any textbook of linear algebra. Here the rule is illustrated with the following simple system of simultaneous equations:

$$3x + 5y + z = 10 \quad (8i)$$

$$x + 2y + 3z = 15 \quad (8ii)$$

$$2x + 3y + 4z = 16 \quad (8iii)$$

Representing the system of equation (8) in the determinant and vectors:

$$\begin{vmatrix} 3 & 5 & 1 \\ 1 & 2 & 3 \\ 2 & 3 & 4 \end{vmatrix} \begin{vmatrix} x \\ y \\ z \end{vmatrix} = \begin{vmatrix} 10 \\ 15 \\ 16 \end{vmatrix} \quad (9)$$

Evaluating the coefficient determinant one obtains:

$$3(8-9) - 5(4-6) + 1(3-4)$$

$$\Rightarrow \quad = -3 + 10 - 1 = 6 \quad (10)$$

The numerator of the solution for $x$ is the determinant

$$\begin{vmatrix} 10 & 5 & 1 \\ 15 & 2 & 3 \\ 16 & 3 & 4 \end{vmatrix} = 10(8-9) - 5(60-48) + (45-32)$$

$$= -10 - 60 + 13 = -57 \quad (11)$$

$$\Rightarrow \quad x = \frac{-57}{6} = -9.5$$

The numerator of the solution for $y$ is the determinant

$$\begin{vmatrix} 3 & 10 & 1 \\ 1 & 15 & 3 \\ 2 & 16 & 4 \end{vmatrix} = 3(60-48) - 10(4-6) + (16-30)$$

$$= 36 + 20 - 14 = 42 \quad (12)$$

$$\Rightarrow \quad y = \frac{42}{6} = 7 \quad (13)$$

Similarly $z$: The numerator is:

$$\begin{vmatrix} 3 & 5 & 10 \\ 1 & 2 & 15 \\ 2 & 3 & 16 \end{vmatrix} = 3(32-45) - 5(16-30) + 10(3-4)$$

$$= -39 + 70 - 10 = 21 \quad (14)$$

$$\Rightarrow \quad z = \frac{21}{6} = 3.5 \qquad (15)$$

The complete solution is then:

$$\begin{vmatrix} x \\ y \\ z \end{vmatrix} = \begin{vmatrix} -9.5 \\ 7 \\ 3.5 \end{vmatrix} \qquad (16)$$

## 1.A.2 **Rules of Differentiation used in the Book**

As in the case of Cramer's Rule, no mathematical proofs will be provided for various rules as these are given in any textbook of Differential Calculus. Only simple illustrations of each rule will be discussed.

*Functions of a Single Variable*

1. *Product Rule*

The product of two functions is to be differentiated in the following way:

Let $y = f(x) \cdot g(x)$ (17)

where $f(x)$ and $g(x)$ are continuous and differentiable functions of $x$. Then, the derivative of $y$ with respect to (w.r.t.) $x$ is:

$$\frac{dy}{dx} = f'(x)g(x) + g'(x)f(x) \qquad (18)$$

where $f'$ and $g'$ are the first-order derivatives of $f$ and $g$ respectively w.r.t. $x$.

2. *Quotient Rule*

Let $z = [f(x)/g(x)]$ (19)

then, $$\frac{dz}{dx} = \frac{g(x)f'(x) - f(x)g'(x)}{\{g(x)\}^2} \qquad (20)$$

Alternatively one can look at $z$ as the product:

$z = f(x) \cdot 1/g(x)$ (19)′

and apply the product rule. But in order to do that one has to apply the Chain Rule and partial differentiation rule explained below.

3. *Chain Rule*

The chain rule is also referred to as the function of-a-function rule or as the composite function rule.

Let $v = f(y)$ where $y = g(x)$ (21)

then, $\frac{dv}{dx} = \frac{dv}{dy} \cdot \frac{dy}{dx} = f'(y)g'(x)$ (22)

This chain rule has to be applied almost on every occasion in the comparative static analysis of the macromodels in the subsequent chapters. The chain rule can be extended to any number of functions:

If $v = f(y)$ where $y = g(x)$ and $x = h(w)$ then

$$\frac{dv}{dw} = f'(y)g'(x)h'(w) \quad (23)$$

In addition to the above the following simple rules are also stated below.

4. *Power-Function Rule*

Let $f(x) = kx^n$ where $k$ and $n$ are constants.

Then $f'(x) = knx^{n-1}$ (22)

5. *Constant-Function Rule*

If $f(x) = k$, a constant

then $f'(x) = 0.$ (23)

It is a special case of rule 4. The function in (23) means $n = 0$ as (23) can be rewritten as:

$$f(x) = kx^0 \quad (23)'$$

Applying rule (22)

$$f'(x) = k.0.x^{-1} = 0$$

6. *Sum Rule*

Let $y = f(x) + g(x) + h(x) + \ldots..$

then $\dfrac{dy}{dx} = f'(x) + g'(x) + h'(x) + .....$ (24)

7. *Difference Rule*

Let $y = f(x) - g(x) - h(x) - .....$

then $\dfrac{dy}{dx} = f'(x) - g'(x) - h'(x) - .....$ (25)

8. *Logarithmic Function Rule*

Let $y = \log x$ then $\dfrac{dy}{dx} = \dfrac{1}{x}$ (26)

9. *The Exponential Function Rule*

Let $y = e^{ax} \quad \Rightarrow \dfrac{dy}{dx} = ae^{ax}$ (27)

10. *Inverse Function Rule*

If the function $y = f(x)$ is such that there exists a unique value of $y$ for each unique value of $x$ then the function, $f$ will have an inverse function:

$$x = f^{-1}(y)$$

In this case of one-to-one correspondence,

$$\frac{dx}{dy} = \frac{1}{dy/dx} \qquad (28)$$

*Example 1*

$$y = 2x + 3$$

For each value of $x$, there exists a unique value of $y$. So an inverse function can be obtained for $x$:

$$x = (y - 3)/2$$

Applying rules 4 and 5 to the original function,

$$\frac{dy}{dx} = 2$$

Applying the same rules to the inverse function

$$\frac{dx}{dy} = \frac{1}{2}$$

*Example 2*

$$y = (2x+3)(5x^2+1)$$

Applying product rule and the power function rule

$$\frac{dy}{dx} = 2(5x^2+1) + (2x+3)10x$$

$$\Rightarrow \quad \frac{dy}{dx} = 10x^2 + 2 + 20x^2 + 30x = 30x^2 + 30x + 2$$

*Example 3*

$$y = \frac{5x-3}{x-1}$$

Applying quotient rule and the power function rule

$$\frac{dy}{dx} = \frac{(x-1)\,5 - (5x-3)\cdot 1}{(x-1)^2}$$

$$\Rightarrow \quad \frac{dy}{dx} = \frac{5x-5-5x+3}{(x-1)^2} = \frac{-2}{(x-1)^2}$$

*Example 4*

$$v = 3y^2 \quad \text{where } y = 2x-3$$

Applying Chain rule and power function rule

$$\frac{dv}{dx} = \frac{dv}{dy}\cdot\frac{dy}{dx} = 6y(2) = 12y$$

$$\Rightarrow \quad \frac{dv}{dx} = 12(2x-3) = 24x - 36$$

*Example 5*

$$v = (4y+2)^2 \quad \text{where } y = \log x = h(x)$$

Putting $z = 4y + 2 = g(y)$

$$v = z^2 = f(z) = f[g\ \{h(x)\}\ ]$$

$$\Rightarrow \quad \frac{dv}{dx} = \frac{dv}{dz} \cdot \frac{dz}{dy} \cdot \frac{dy}{dx} = f' \cdot g' \cdot h'$$

$$\Rightarrow \quad \frac{dv}{dx} = 2z(4)\frac{1}{x} = \frac{8}{x}(4\log x + 2)$$

*Example 6*

One can derive the quotient rule from the product rule and applying chain and power function rules. Rewrite (19)′ as the product:

$$z = f(x) \cdot \frac{1}{y} \quad \text{where } y = g(x)$$

$$\Rightarrow \quad z = f(x) \cdot h(y) \quad \text{where } h(y) = \frac{1}{y}$$

$$\Rightarrow \quad \frac{dz}{dx} = f'(x)h(y) + f(x)h'(y)\frac{dy}{dx}$$

applying product and chain rules.

Applying power function rule to $h(y)$

$$h'(y) = -\frac{1}{y^2} = -\frac{1}{\{g(x)\}^2}$$

$$\Rightarrow \quad \frac{dz}{dx} = f'(x)h(y) - [f(x)/\{g(x)\}^2]\ g'(x)$$

$$\Rightarrow \quad \frac{dz}{dx} = [f'(x)/g(x)] - \frac{f(x)g'(x)}{[g(x)]^2}$$

$$\Rightarrow \quad \frac{dz}{dx} = [f'(x)g(x) - f(x)g'(x)]/\{g(x)\}^2$$

as given in (20)

*Example 7*

$$v = \log y \quad \text{where } y = x^2 + 5x + 3$$

$$\frac{dv}{dx} = \frac{dv}{dy} \cdot \frac{dy}{dx} = \frac{2x+5}{x^2+5x+3}$$

*Functions of More than One Variable*

In the subsequent chapters one will encounter functions of more than one variable for example in the production function (3.1), quantity of output is a function of the inputs of capital and labour; the real demand for money is a function of real income and real rate of interest, etc. For differentiating functions of more than one variable, one needs to apply the rules of partial differentiation. These are illustrated below.

*Rules of Partial Differentiation*

1. If a variable $z$ is a function of two variables $x$ and $y$, then there would be two partial derivatives of $z$ — one w.r.t. each variable and the total change of $z$ will depend on the change owing to the change in each variable.

Referring back to the production function example, quantity of output will change if either the input of capital or that of labour or if both inputs change. The change in output due to change in capital (labour) alone is obtained by holding input of labour (capital) constant and varying the input of capital (labour). This gives rise to the partial derivation of output w.r.t. capital (labour).

If $\quad z = f(x, y)$ (29)

then the total change in z is given by the *total differential*, $dz$ where,

$$dz = \frac{\delta z}{\delta x} \cdot dx + \frac{\delta z}{\delta y} \cdot dy \tag{30}$$

Where $\delta z/\delta x$ and $\delta z/\delta y$ are the partial derivatives of $z$ w.r.t. $x$ and $y$ respectively and $dx, dy$ and $dz$ give the total changes in $x$, $y$ and $z$ respectively. Each partial derivative gives the rate of change of the dependent variable as it changes itself, treating the other variable as constant. So, $\delta z/\delta x$ will be obtained by differentiating $f(x, y)$ w.r.t. $x$ alone treating $y$ as a constant. Similarly, $\delta z/\delta y$ will be obtained by differentiating

$f(x, y)$ w.r.t. y treating x as constant. Sometimes these partial derivatives are denoted as $f_x, f_y$. In deriving $f_x$ or $f_y$, the above rules of differentiation explained for functions of a single variable will continue to apply.

*Example 8*

$$\dot{z} = 3x^2 + 2xy + y^2 \quad \Rightarrow \quad \delta z/\delta x = 6x + 2y$$

treating $y$ as a constant and applying power function rule. Similarly,

$$\delta z/\delta y = 2x + 2y$$

treating $x$ as a constant and applying power function rule.

The chain rule and partial differentiation would be required (more) often than any other rule) in the comparative static analysis of the macromodels in the subsequent chapters. For example, the partial derivative of the equilibrium condition of the labour market w.r.t. the fiscal policy instrument, viz, government spending, $G$, will be required. This is explained below. Assuming both the demand and the supply of labour, $N^d$ and $N^s$ respectively as functions of real wage, $W/P$, the equilibrium condition can be written as

$$N^d(W/P) - N^s(W/P) = 0$$

To differentiate this partially w.r.t. $G$, one has to apply the difference rule, the chain rule the product or quotient rule and the partial differentiation rule. This yields, step by step,

$$N^{d'} \frac{\delta}{\delta G}(W/P) - N^{s'} \frac{\delta}{\delta G}(W/P) = 0$$

$$\Rightarrow \quad [N^{d'} - N^{s'}] \left[ \frac{\delta W}{\delta G} \cdot \frac{1}{P} - \frac{W}{P^2} \frac{\delta P}{\delta G} \right] = 0$$

Similarly, differentiating the equilibrium condition in the money market w.r.t. the fiscal parameter, $G$ would yield

$$L'_Y(Y, r)\, \delta Y/\delta G + L'_r(Y, r) \frac{\delta r}{\delta G} = \frac{1}{P} \frac{\delta M}{\delta G} - M/P^2\, \delta P/\delta G$$

Where $L(Y, r)$ is the real demand for money and $M/P$ is the real money supply of which the nominal money supply $M$ is fixed exogenously. In the simple comparative static analysis of Chapters 2 and 3, $M$ is treated as independent of $G$ implying $\delta M/\delta G = 0$. So the equilibrium condition of the money market when differentiated partially w.r.t. $G$ would yield

$$L'_Y \delta Y/\delta G + L'_r \delta r/\delta G + M/P^2 \delta P/\delta G = 0$$

*Jacobian Determinants*

A Jacobian determinant $|J|$ is composed of the first order partial derivatives of the dependent (endogenous) variables w.r.t. all the independent (exogenous) variables of a system of equations (models) arranged in a chosen order. For example

If $z_1 = f(x, y)$ and $z_2 = g(x, y)$

then $|J| = \left|\frac{\delta(z_1, z_2)}{\delta(x, y)}\right|$ $\Rightarrow$ $|J|$ is a determinant of

the 4th order:

$$|J| = \begin{vmatrix} \frac{\delta z_1}{\delta x} & \frac{\delta z_2}{\delta x} \\ \frac{\delta z_1}{\delta y} & \frac{\delta z_2}{\delta y} \end{vmatrix} \tag{31}$$

Jacobian determinants are useful in testing for functional dependence — linear or non-linear in the equations of a model. A zero value of the Jacobian implies that the equations constituting the model are not all independent which, in turn, implies that no unique solution exists for all the dependent (exogenous) variables of the model. In addition, when equations are given in the general forms, e.g. as $f(x, y)$ or $g(x, y)$ rather than in specific forms like $z_1 = 2x + 3y$ or $z_2 = 5x^2 + 2xy + 3y^2$ one has to use the Jacobian determinants to apply Cramer's rule to solve for the partial derivatives. In the economic models of Chapter 3 onwards, all the equations are given in general form and Jacobian determinants are applied for comparative static analyses of the models. In the economic models, Jacobian determinants are applied under a few simplifying assumptions. These will be explained in due course. First a simple example.

*Example 9*

$$z_1 = 3x^2 + 2y^2$$

$$z_2 = 5x + 1$$

To test for functional dependence the Jacobian is obtained as:

$$|J| = \begin{vmatrix} \frac{\delta z_1}{\delta x} & \frac{\delta z_2}{\delta x} \\ \frac{\delta z_1}{\delta y} & \frac{\delta z_2}{\delta y} \end{vmatrix} - \begin{vmatrix} 6x & 5 \\ 4y & 0 \end{vmatrix}$$

$\Rightarrow \quad |J| = -20y \neq 0 \quad \Rightarrow \quad$ one can obtain unique solutions for $x$ and $y$.

*Example 10*

$$z_1 = 2x + 3y$$

$$z_2 = 4x + 6y$$

$z_1$ and $z_2$ are not independent as it is evident that $z_2 = 2z_1$. So one cannot obtain unique solutions for $x$ and $y$. This could alternatively be checked by evaluating the Jacobian.

$$|J| = \begin{vmatrix} 2 & 3 \\ 4 & 6 \end{vmatrix} = 2\begin{vmatrix} 1 & 3 \\ 2 & 6 \end{vmatrix} = 2 \times 3\begin{vmatrix} 1 & 1 \\ 2 & 2 \end{vmatrix}$$

$= 0$ applying properties 6 and 7.

However in the example 10, functional dependence was of a very simple, linear type. So one need not have taken the trouble of deriving the Jacobian to check that no solution exists. It may not be so obvious in the following example.

*Example 11*

$$z_1 = x + 2y = f(x, y) \text{ say}$$

$$z_2 = x(x + 4y + 1) + 2y(2y + 1) = g(x, y), \text{ say}$$

Simplifying $g(x, y)$:

$$z_2 = x^2 + 4xy + 4y^2 + x + 2y.$$

To check for functional dependence between $f$ and $g$, the Jacobian is derived as:

$$|J| = \begin{vmatrix} 1 & 2x + 4y + 1 \\ 2 & 8y + 4x + 2 \end{vmatrix} \tag{32}$$

The second row of the determinant, $|J|$ has a common factor 2 in its elements.

$$\Rightarrow \quad |J| = 2\begin{vmatrix} 1 & 2x+4y+1 \\ 1 & 2x+4y+1 \end{vmatrix} = 0$$

applying properties 6 and 7 of determinants.

$|J| = 0$ because $z_1$ and $z_2$ are not independent. In this case the nature of dependence is non-linear:

$$z_2 = z_1(z_1 + 1)$$

In the macroeconomic models with structural equations given in the general form, the Jacobian determinants are composed of the partial derivatives of *implicit functions*. It is useful to know the distinction between types of functions known as explicit functions and those known as implicit functions. The following section briefly explains these two types of functions and how to find the partial derivatives of implicit functions.

*Implicit Functions and Partial Differentiation*

The function $z_1 = x + 2y$ is an *explicit function* but the same function can be rewritten as $z_1 - x - 2y = 0$

$$\Rightarrow \quad F(z_1, x, y) = 0,$$

i.e., as an *implicit function*. An explicit function can be rewritten as an implicit function but not vice versa. For example, a function given in the general form can be written as an implicit function but not as an explicit function because the specific nature of dependence is not known. When an implicit function cannot be solved out explicitly for a variable in terms of the other variables, one can only derive and solve for the partial derivatives provided the latter exist and are continuous for the function in question. Throughout the book we assume that each implicit function has continuous first and second order partial derivatives. The existence and continuity of partial derivatives enables one to make use of the Implicit Function Theorem.

*The Implicit Function Theorem*

If a set of implicit functions:

$$F^1 (z_1, z_2, \cdots z_n; x_1, x_2, \cdots x_m) = 0 \qquad (33i)$$

$$F^2 (z_1, z_2, \cdots z_n; x_1, x_2, \cdots x_m) = 0 \qquad (33ii)$$

$$F^3 (z_1, z_2, \cdots z_n; x_1, x_2, \cdots x_m) = 0$$

$$\cdots\cdots\cdots\cdots\cdots\cdots\cdots\cdots\cdots\cdots\cdots\cdots .$$

$$F^n (z_1, z_2, \cdots z_n; x_1, x_2, \cdots x_m) = 0 \qquad (33iii)$$

possess continuous partial derivatives w.r.t. all the $z$ and $x$ variables, then it is possible to define the following set of implicit functions:

$$z_1^* = f^1(x_1^*, \quad x_2^* \cdots x_m^*) \qquad (34i)$$

$$z_2^* = f^2(x_1^*, \quad x_2^* \cdots x_m^*) \qquad (34ii)$$

$$z_n^* = f^3(x_1^*, \quad x_2^* \cdots x_m^*) \qquad (34iii)$$

in the $m$-dimensional neighbourhood of $(x_1^*, x_2^* \cdots x_m^*)$ provided the $(n \times n)$ Jacobian determinant

$$|J| = \begin{vmatrix} \delta F^1/\delta z_1 & \delta F^1/\delta z_2 & \cdots & \delta F^1/\delta z_n \\ \delta F^2/\delta z_1 & \delta F^2/\delta z_2 & \cdots & \delta F^2/\delta z_n \\ \cdot & \cdot & & \cdot \\ \cdot & \cdot & & \cdot \\ \cdot & \cdot & & \cdot \\ \delta F^n/\delta z_1 & \delta F^n/\delta z_2 & \cdots & \delta F^n/\delta z_n \end{vmatrix} \neq 0 \qquad (35)$$

at the point $(z_1^*, z_2^* \cdots z_n^*; x_1^*, \cdots x_m^*)$.

The theorem therefore means that the set of $n$ equations

$$F^1 = 0, F^2 = 0 \cdots F^n = 0$$

can be solved for the $n$ variables $z_1, z_2 \cdots z_n$ at least in the implicit form provided the partial derivatives exist and the Jacobian determinant is non zero.

### *Comparative Static Analysis, Implicit Functions and Jacobian Determinants*

In most of the macro models in this book, the equations are given in the general forms, which can be conveniently put in the implicit functions form. The endogenous variables are treated as the $z$-variables and the exogenous variables (and the parameters if any) are to be treated as the $x$-variables in sets (33) and (34). For example, the equilibrium condition in the output market:

$$Y - C(Y - T) - I(r) - G = 0$$

can be rewritten as:

$$F^1(Y, r, T, G) = 0 \tag{36i}$$

as $T$ and $G$ are treated as exogenous policy parameters. Similarly the equilibrium condition in the money market:

$$L(Y, r) - M/P = 0$$

can be rewritten as

$$F^2(Y, r, M, P) = 0 \tag{36ii}$$

as in the simple IS-LM model, $P$ is fixed and $M$ is an exogenous policy parameter. The comparative static derivatives are derived to find the effects of fiscal and monetary policies on real income and real interest rate. The first step is to obtain the Jacobian. The Jacobian is:

$$|J| = \begin{vmatrix} \delta F^1/\delta Y & \delta F^1/\delta r \\ \delta F^2/\delta Y & \delta F^2/\delta r \end{vmatrix} \tag{37i}$$

$$\Rightarrow \quad |J| = \begin{vmatrix} 1 - C' & -I' \\ L'_Y & L'_r \end{vmatrix}$$

$$\Rightarrow \quad |J| = (1 - C')L'_r + I'L'_Y \neq 0 \tag{37ii}$$

By virtue of the implicit function theorem, one can now write the equilibrium solutions for $Y$ and $r$ as:

$$Y^* = f^1(T^*, G^*, M^*, P^*) \tag{38i}$$

$$r^* = f^2(T^*, G^*, M^*, P^*) \tag{38ii}$$

Equation set (37) ensures that the fiscal and monetary policy multipliers can be found at the equilibrium values. Also, the advantage in such policy applications is that only one exogenous variable is allowed to change at a time. So, in finding the fiscal policy multipliers w.r.t. government spending, $T$, $M$ and $P$ are treated as constants. Such multipliers can be obtained either from the set (36) or from the set (38). When the implicit forms (38) are not known specifically, one has to differentiate the form (36).

Differentiating (36i) and (36ii) partially w.r.t. $G$, one obtains (39i) and (39ii) respectively.

$$\frac{\delta F^1}{\delta Y}\cdot\frac{\delta Y}{\delta G}+\frac{\delta F^1}{\delta r}\cdot\frac{\delta r}{\delta G}+\frac{\delta F^1}{\delta T}\cdot\frac{\delta T}{\delta G}+\frac{\delta F^1}{\delta G}=0$$

$$\Rightarrow \quad (1-C')\frac{\delta Y}{\delta G}-I'\frac{\delta r}{\delta G}-1=0 \tag{39i}$$

$$\frac{\delta F^2}{\delta Y}\cdot\frac{\delta Y}{\delta G}+\frac{\delta F^2}{\delta r}\cdot\frac{\delta r}{\delta G}+\frac{\delta F^2}{\delta M}\cdot\frac{\delta M}{\delta G}+\frac{\delta F^2}{\delta P}\cdot\frac{\delta P}{\delta G}=0$$

$$\Rightarrow \quad L'_Y\frac{\delta Y}{\delta G}+L'_r\frac{\delta r}{\delta G}=0 \tag{39ii}$$

The set of equations (39) can be rewritten as:

$$\begin{vmatrix} 1-C' & -I' \\ L'_Y & L'_r \end{vmatrix}\begin{vmatrix} \delta Y/\delta G \\ \delta r/\delta G \end{vmatrix}=\begin{vmatrix} 1 \\ 0 \end{vmatrix} \tag{40i}$$

$$\Rightarrow \quad |J|\begin{vmatrix} \delta Y/\delta G \\ \delta r/\delta G \end{vmatrix}=\begin{vmatrix} 1 \\ 0 \end{vmatrix} \tag{40ii}$$

Cramer's rule can now be applied to solve for the multipliers $\delta Y/\delta G$ and $\delta r/\delta G$.

### 1.A.3 Solution of Differential Equations: Single and Simultaneous Differential Equations in Single Variables

Such equations will arise in continuous time analysis. They can be solved by direct integration or by other methods.

*Basic Rules of Integration*

Integration is the inverse process of differentiation. For example, the result of integrating $2x$ w.r.t. $x$ will be $x^2+c$ where $c$ is any constant as the derivative of $(x^2+c)$ w.r.t. $x$ is $2x$. A few simple rules of integration are given below. The notation of integration is an elongated $S$.

*Rule 1: The Power Function Rule*

If $f(x)=kd^n$ where $k$ and $n$ are constants and $n\neq-1$,

$$\int f(x)dx = k\int x^n dx = k \cdot \frac{x^{n+1}}{n+1} + c \tag{41i}$$

*Rule 2: The Constant Function Rule*

As in the case of differentiation the integration of a constant follows the general power-function rule (41i) above.

The constant function as in (23) can be rewritten as

$$f(x) = k = kx^0 \tag{23$'$}$$

$$\Rightarrow \quad \int f(x)dx = \int kdx = kx + c \tag{41ii}$$

which is obtained by putting $n = 0$ in (41i)

*Rule 3: The Logarithmic Function*

Following the inverse process of the result (26):

$$\int \frac{1}{x}dx = \log x + c \tag{42}$$

*Rule 4: The Exponential Function Rule*

Following the inverse process of (27)

$$\int ae^{ax}dx = e^{ax} + c \tag{43i}$$

$$\Rightarrow \quad \int e^{ax}dx = \frac{e^{ax}}{a} + c \tag{43ii}$$

*Rule 5: The Sum/Difference Rule*

$$\int [f(x) \pm g(x) \pm h(x)]dx = \int f(x)dx \pm \int g(x)dx \pm \int h(x)dx \tag{44}$$

*Example*

$$\int (x^2 + 4x + 1)dx$$

$$= \int x^2 dx + 4\int x dx + \int dx$$

$$= \left[\frac{x^3}{3} + c_1\right] + \left[4\frac{x^2}{2} + c_2\right] + x + c_3$$

$$= \frac{x^3}{3} + 2x^2 + x + c \qquad (45)$$

Where $c$ is the combined constant of integration: $c_1 + c_2 + c_3$.

*Rule 6: The Chain Rule*

Let $v = f(y)$ where $y = g(x)$ as in (21)

$$\int v dx = \int \left[f(y) \cdot \frac{dy}{dx}\right] dx = \int f(y) dy \qquad (46)$$

*Rule 7: The Product Rule: Integration by Parts*

$$\int \frac{dy}{dx} \cdot dx = \int [f'(x)g(x)]dx + \int [g'(x)f(x)]dx$$

$$\Rightarrow \quad \int dy \cdot = \int g(x)df(x) + \int f(x)dg(x) \qquad (47)$$

$\therefore$ the total differentials of $u = f(x)$ and $v = g(x)$ are, respectively, $du = f'(x)dx$ and $dv = g'(x)dx$.

Putting $y = uv$, (47) can be rewritten as:

$$\int duv = \int vdu + \int udv$$

$$\Rightarrow \quad uv = \int vdu + \int udv \tag{48}$$

$$\Rightarrow \quad \int vdu = uv - \int udv \tag{49i}$$

or,

$$\Rightarrow \quad \int udv = uv - \int vdu \tag{49ii}$$

(49i) and (49ii) are known as integration by parts.

*Definite Integrals*

All the integrals discussed so far are indefinite integrals. They are all functions of a variable and do not possess definite numerical values. That indefinite integrals possess no definite values is amplified by the presence of the constant of integration which has no definite value. In case of differential equations, as will be demonstrated later, the constants of integrations are to be evaluated by initial conditions.

Definite integrals have specific numerical values. They have important applications in Economics, especially as the area under a curve can be interpreted as a definite integral. Definite integrals can be obtained by choosing two values of the variable $x$ in a domain, e.g. $a$, $b$ where $a < b$ and evaluating the integral of the function of $x$ between these two values of $x$:

$$\int_a^b f(x)dx = [\Phi(x)+c]_b^a \tag{50}$$

where $\Phi'(x) = f(x)$

The definite integrals are written in the form (50) and evaluated as:

$$[\Phi(b)+c] - [\Phi(a)+c]$$

$$= \Phi(b) - \Phi(a) \tag{51}$$

*Example*

$$\int_0^5 x^2 dx = \left[\frac{x^3}{3} + c\right]_0^5$$

$$= \left[\frac{125}{3} + c\right] - c = 125/3$$

*Solution of First-Order Differential Equations*

Only first-order differential equations will be needed for this book. Differential equations arise, as already pointed out, in the continuous time analysis of economic models. So instead of using $x$, the following discussion is based on '$t$' as the independent time variable.

Differential equations of the first-order involve only the first order derivatives. They can be of two different types — homogeneous and non-homogeneous. The degree of a differential equation will be given by the highest power attained by the derivative.

The following is a linear non-homogeneous differential equation of the first-order.

$$\frac{dy}{dt} + yf(t) = g(t) \tag{52}$$

If $f(t)$ is a constant and $g(t)$ is identically zero, then (52) reduces to a homogeneous equation, (53):

$$\frac{dy}{dt} - ay = 0 \tag{53}$$

The solution of a non-homogeneous differential equation like (52) is broken down into various parts:

*Step 1:* Find a general solution for the homogeneous part (53) either by integration or by the other method. This is called the *complementary function.*

*Step 2:* Find a particular solution to the entire non-homogeneous equation. This is called the *particular integral.*

*Step 3:* Obtain the complete general solution by adding the results obtained in steps 1 and 2.

*Step 4:* Obtain the complete definite solution by evaluating the constant of integration at the initial time point, $t = 0$.

*Step 5:* Resubstitute the definite value of the constant to obtain the complete definite solution. The steps are illustrated below.

*Example:* Solve the equation (54) given that $y(t)=5$ for $t=0$.

$$\frac{dy}{dt}+2y=4 \tag{54}$$

(54) is a non-homogeneous equation. The homogeneous part of (54) is:

$$\frac{dy}{dt}+2y=0 \tag{55}$$

To solve (55) by integration, rewrite (55) as:

$$\frac{dy}{y}+2dt=0$$

Integrating, $\int\frac{dy}{y} 2\int dt=0$

$$\Rightarrow \quad \log y+2t=c$$

$$\Rightarrow \quad \log y=c-2t$$

$$\Rightarrow \quad y=e^{c-2t} \tag{56}$$

Without any loss of generality one can write $c=\log A$, where $A$ is another constant. Then (56) becomes:

$$y=e^{\log A-2t}$$

$$\Rightarrow \quad y=Ae^{-2t} \tag{57}$$

$$:: \quad e^{\log A}=A$$

(57) is the general solution of the homogeneous part.

As a particular solution to (54) one can try a constant

$$y=\bar{y} \quad \Rightarrow \frac{d\bar{y}}{dt}=0$$

This is where the concept of the equilibrium value comes in. This will be discussed later. Putting $y=\bar{y}$ in (54), one obtains:

$$0+2\bar{y}=4 \quad \Rightarrow \bar{y}=2 \tag{58}$$

Adding (57) and (58) the complete general solution for (54) can be written as:

$$y=Ae^{-2t}+2 \tag{59}$$

Now, the initial value of $y$ is given as 5. Substituting $y(0)=5$ and $t=0$ in (59),

$$5 = A + 2 \quad \Rightarrow A = 3$$

Resubstituting the value of $A$ in (59) the complete solution of (54) is

$$y = 3e^{-2t} + 2 \tag{60}$$

*An Alternative Method of Solving Differential Equations*

This method has been used in most of the dynamic models in the continuous form discussed in the book. The first step in this method is to define the concept of an equilibrium value in a dynamic equation.

The equilibrium value of $y = y(t)$ is that value which once attained will be repeated forever. Let $y^*$ be the equilibrium value of $y$ in a dynamic equation:

$$\frac{dy}{dt} + ay = b \tag{61}$$

where $a$, $b$ are constants.

In equilibrium

$$\frac{dy}{dt} = 0 \quad \Rightarrow y^* = b/a \tag{62}$$

Now, (61) can be rewritten as:

$$\frac{dy}{dt} = a(y^* - y) \quad \Rightarrow \quad \frac{d(y - y^*)}{dt} + a(y - y^*) = 0 \text{ as } \frac{dy^*}{dt} = 0. \tag{63}$$

$y - y^* = Z$ can be interpreted as the deviation of $y$ from its equilibrium value. So, the given non-homogeneous differential equation (61) can be rewritten as a homogeneous differential equation in $Z$:

$$\frac{dZ}{dt} + aZ = 0 \tag{64}$$

Try $Z = e^{\lambda t}$

as a solution and note that if $e^{\lambda t}$ is a solution to (64), then so is $Ae^{\lambda t}$, where $A$ is any constant.

If $e^{\lambda t}$ satisfies equation (64), then one has

$$\lambda e^{\lambda t} + ae^{\lambda t} = 0 \tag{65}$$

Equation (65) is called the *Characteristic equation* of (63).

Putting $Z = Ae^{\lambda t}$, (64) yields $A\lambda e^{\lambda t} + aAe^{\lambda t} = A(\lambda e^{\lambda t} + ae^{\lambda t}) = 0$ if $e^{\lambda t}$ is a solution to (64). Trying $Z = e^{\lambda t}$ as a solution to (64) $\lambda$ can be solved from the characteristic equation (65) as:

$\lambda = -a$. So, the general solution for (64) is $Z = A e^{-at}$ which is the same as that obtained by direct integration. The solution can be made definite by evaluating $A$ from the given initials values. If $y(0)$ is given, they $Z(0)$ is obtained from definition:

$$Z(0) = y(0) - y^* \quad \Rightarrow \quad Z(0) = Y(0) - b/a$$

$$Z(0) = A \quad \Rightarrow \quad A = y(0) - b/a \tag{66}$$

Finally the solution for $y$ is obtained as:

$$y(t) = Z(t) + y^*$$

$$\Rightarrow \quad y(t) = [y(0) - b/a]e^{-at} + y^* \tag{67}$$

Equation (67) gives the dynamic time path of the variable $y$.

*Stability of a Dynamic Variable*

An important issue in dynamic models in economics is whether the time path converges to a stable equilibrium value.

If it does then the model is said to be stable. For instance, in the simple case of (61), one is concerned with the issue: if the equilibrium is disturbed once whether $y$ can converge to its equilibrium value as time goes on. Stability of a dynamic equation can be defined in the following way: The dynamic equation (61) will be stable if $y(t)$ tends to its equilibrium value, $y^*$ as defined above in the limit as time, $t$, tends to infinity. Symbolically it is written as:

$$\operatorname*{Lt}_{t \to \infty} y(t) = y^* \quad \Rightarrow \quad \operatorname*{Lt}_{t \to \infty} Z(t) = 0$$

The time path $y(t)$ as given in (67) will be stable if

$$[y(0) - b/a]e^{-at} \to 0 \text{ as } t \to \infty$$

Accordingly the condition for stability requires the exponent to be negative. This will be ensured is a positive. However if a were negative instead, then the exponent gets larger and larger as time goes on implying that the time path (67) diverges more and more away from equilibrium. So, the condition for stability for the dynamic equation in the continuous form (61) is $a > 0$.

*Simultaneous Differential Equations*

The method of solving dynamic equations in more than one variable is based on the same principles as discussed in the previous section. Changing the symbols for time derivatives to dots over respective variables:

$$\frac{dx}{dt} \equiv \dot{x} \; \frac{dy}{dt} \equiv \dot{y}$$

a simultaneous differential equation system can be written as:

$$a_{11}\dot{y} + a_{21}\dot{y} + b_{11}x + b_{21}y = B_1 \qquad (68i)$$

$$a_{12}\dot{x} + a_{22}\dot{y} + b_{12}x + b_{22}y = B_2 \qquad (68ii)$$

The set (68) consists of two first-order linear differential equation in two dynamic variables.

The equations can be rewritten in the compact form

$$\begin{vmatrix} a_{11} & a_{21} \\ a_{12} & a_{22} \end{vmatrix}\begin{vmatrix} \dot{x} \\ \dot{y} \end{vmatrix} + \begin{vmatrix} b_{11} & b_{21} \\ b_{12} & b_{22} \end{vmatrix}\begin{vmatrix} x \\ y \end{vmatrix} = \begin{vmatrix} B_1 \\ B_2 \end{vmatrix} \qquad (69i)$$

$$\Rightarrow \quad J\begin{vmatrix} \dot{x} \\ \dot{y} \end{vmatrix} + M\begin{vmatrix} x \\ y \end{vmatrix} = \begin{vmatrix} B_1 \\ B_2 \end{vmatrix} \qquad (69ii)$$

Both $|J|$ and $|M|$ have to be non-zero.

Assuming that simultaneous equilibrium exists at $x = x^*$ and $y = y^*$, the equation (68) can be written in respective deviation variables $z_1 = x - x^*$ and $z_2 = y - y^*$. So, the equation (68) and (69ii) can be rewritten respectively as (70i), (70ii) and (71).

$$a_{11}\dot{z}_1 + a_{21}\dot{z}_2 + b_{11}z_1 + b_{21}z_2 = 0 \qquad (70i)$$

$$a_{12}\dot{z}_1 + a_{22}\dot{z}_2 + b_{12}z_1 + b_{22}z_2 = 0$$

$$J\begin{vmatrix} \dot{z}_1 \\ \dot{z}_2 \end{vmatrix} + M\begin{vmatrix} z_1 \\ z_2 \end{vmatrix} = \begin{vmatrix} 0 \\ 0 \end{vmatrix} \qquad (71)$$

The equilibrium values can be solved easily from substituting $\dot{x}^* = \dot{y}^* = 0$ and $x^*$, $y^*$ for $x$ and $y$ in (69ii)

$$\Rightarrow \quad J\begin{vmatrix}0\\0\end{vmatrix}+M\begin{vmatrix}x^*\\y^*\end{vmatrix}=\begin{vmatrix}B_1\\B_2\end{vmatrix} \tag{72}$$

Solving (71) by Cramer's rule

$$x^* = \frac{\begin{vmatrix}B_1 & b_{21}\\ B_2 & b_{22}\end{vmatrix}}{|M|} \tag{73i}$$

$$y^* = \frac{\begin{vmatrix}b_{11} & B_1\\ b_{12} & B_2\end{vmatrix}}{|M|} \tag{73ii}$$

The solution of (70) can be obtained by extending the method discussed above to the case of two variables. The trial solutions can be written as:

$$z_1(t) = A_1 e^{\lambda t} \quad \text{and} \quad z_2(t) = A_2 e^{\lambda t}.$$

Substitution of trial solution in (70) yields

$$A_1\lambda a_{11}e^{\lambda t} + A_2\lambda a_{21}e^{\lambda t} + A_1 b_{11}e^{\lambda t} + A_2 b_{21}e^{\lambda t} = 0 \tag{74i}$$

$$A_1\lambda a_{12}e^{\lambda t} + A_2\lambda a_{22}e^{\lambda t} + A_1 b_{12}e^{\lambda t} + A_2 b_{22}e^{\lambda t} = 0 \tag{74ii}$$

Equations (74) when simplified will yield the characteristic equation of the model. It is important to note that the characteristic equation in simultaneous differential equation involving two variables is a quadratic although the given equations are of the first-order. (75i) and (75ii) can be written in the compact form (76): First, simplifying (74i) and (74ii)

$$(\lambda a_{11} + b_{11})A_1 e^{\lambda t} + (\lambda a_{21} + b_{21})A_2 e^{\lambda t} = 0$$

$$(\lambda a_{12} + b_{12})A_1 e^{\lambda t} + (\lambda a_{22} + b_{22})A_2 e^{\lambda t} = 0$$

$$\Rightarrow \quad \begin{vmatrix}\lambda a_{11}+b_{11} & \lambda a_{21}+b_{21}\\ \lambda a_{12}+b_{12} & \lambda a_{22}+b_{22}\end{vmatrix}\begin{vmatrix}A_1\\A_2\end{vmatrix}e^{\lambda t} = 0 \tag{76}$$

As $e^{\lambda t} \neq 0, \quad A_1 \neq 0, \quad A_2 \neq 0,$

one obtains the characteristic equation as:

$$|\lambda^2 J + M| = 0 \tag{77}$$

$$\text{Where}\quad \lambda^2 J = \begin{vmatrix} \lambda a_{11} & \lambda a_{21} \\ \lambda a_{12} & \lambda a_{22} \end{vmatrix} \tag{78}$$

Expanding the L.H.S. of (77) the quadratic characteristic equation is obtained as (79):

$$(\lambda a_{11} + b_{11})(\lambda a_{22} + b_{22}) - (\lambda a_{21} + b_{21})(\lambda a_{21} + b_{12}) = 0$$

$$\Rightarrow \quad \lambda^2(a_{11}a_{22} - a_{12}a_{21}) + \lambda[(a_{11}b_{22} + a_{22}b_{11}) - (a_{21}b_{12} + a_{12}b_{21})] +$$

$$(b_{11}b_{22} - b_{12}b_{21}) = 0 \tag{79}$$

$\Rightarrow \quad a\lambda^2 + b\lambda + c = 0$ where $a, b, c$ are given in (81).

$\Rightarrow$ The two roots of the quadratic (79) will be given by (80)

$$\lambda_1, \lambda_2 = \frac{-b \pm \sqrt{b^2 - 4ac}}{2a} \tag{80}$$

Where $a = a_{11}a_{22} - a_{12}a_{21}$ (81i)

$$b = (a_{11}b_{22} + a_{22}b_{11}) - (a_{21}b_{12} + a_{12}b_{21}) \tag{81ii}$$

$$c = b_{11}b_{22} - b_{12}b_{21} \tag{81iii}$$

Now the condition for real roots is $b^2 - 4ac \geq 0$ as the square root of a negative quantity yields a complex number. The equation (79) will have complex roots if $b^2 - 4ac < 0$. The solution to the equation (71) can be written as:

$$\begin{vmatrix} z_1 \\ z_2 \end{vmatrix} = \begin{vmatrix} A_{11}e^{\lambda_1 t} + A_{12}e^{\lambda_2 t} \\ A_{21}e^{\lambda_1 t} + A_{22}e^{\lambda_2 t} \end{vmatrix} \tag{82}$$

Where $\lambda_1$ and $\lambda_2$ are given as in (80). The constants $A_{11}$, $A_{12}$ and $A_{21}$, $A_{22}$ can be obtained by solving (76) once $\lambda$'s are known. As there are two roots, i.e., two values of $\lambda$ so to say, one gets two sets of constants by solving (76) for $A_1$ and $A_2$. Substituting $\lambda_i$ for $\lambda$ in (76) one obtains $A_1 = A_{1i}$ and $A_2 = A_{2i}$ where $i = 1, 2$.

$$(\lambda_i a_{11} + b_{11})A_{1i} + (\lambda_i a_{21} + b_{21})A_{2i} = 0 \tag{83i}$$

$$(\lambda_i a_{12} + b_{12})A_{1i} + (\lambda_i a_{22} + b_{22})A_{2i} = 0 \tag{83ii}$$

from which one can solve for the $i$-th set $A_{1i}$ and $A_{2i}$. This explains why the solution for each dynamic variable involves two constants in (82).

*The Condition for Stability*

Stability requires that the time paths of both $x(t)$ and $y(t)$ tend to stationary equilibrium values $x^*$ and $y^*$ respectively as time goes on. Stability therefore requires $z_1$ and $z_2$ to tend to zero as time goes on. The exponential nature of solution for $z_1$ and $z_2$ in (82) imply that $z_1$ and $z_2$ will tend to zero if and only if the exponent is negative. Stability therefore requires $\lambda_i < 0$ for

$$i = 1, 2 \tag{84}$$

## 1.A.4. **Solution of Difference Equations**

*Single Variable/Single Equation*

Difference equations arise in discrete time period analysis. In this case, a dynamic equation involves the values of a variable at different time points. This book discusses dynamic macroeconomic models involving first and second-order difference equations in single and simultaneous equations systems. These are discussed below in turn. In what follows the subscript, $t$ stands for the value of the variable in question at time point, $t$.

*First-Order Difference Equations*

A linear first-order difference equation in a single variable can be written as:

$$x_t + ax_{t-1} = c \tag{85i}$$

where $a$ and $c$ are constants. If $c = 0$, then the equation is homogeneous and if $c \neq 0$, the equation is called non-homogeneous. As might be gathered, a difference equation is similar in nature to a differential equation as $x$ is deemed as a function of time, $t$ in each case. The time path of $x$ is obtained therefore in a very similar manner. The steps are:

1. Find a general solution to the homogeneous part:
   $$x_t + ax_{t-1} = 0 \tag{85ii}$$
   This may even be called the complementary function.
2. Find a particular solution to the entire equation (85i) and call it the particular integral if you like.

3. Add the solutions obtained in steps 1 and 2 to obtain a general complete solution to the non-homogeneous equation (85i).
4. Find the specific complete solution to (85i) by evaluating the constant term of the general complete solution from given initial value of $x$.

Because of the importance of the concept of stationary equilibrium in economics, the solution will be discussed by defining the equilibrium and deviation from equilibrium. The equilibrium value of $x_t$ is such that if it is attained once, it will *b* repeated forever.

Let $\cdots x_{t-2} = x_{t-1} = x^* = x_t = x_{t+1} \therefore$ Substituting this in (85i),

$$x^* + ax^* = c \quad \Rightarrow \quad x^* = \frac{c}{1+a} \tag{86}$$

An equilibrium value exists if and only if $|a| < 1$ if $a < 0$.

By virtue of (86), one can rewrite (85i) as:

$$x_t + ax_{t-1} = (1+a)x^*$$

$$\Rightarrow \quad x_t - x^* + a(x_{t-1} - x^*) = 0$$

$$\Rightarrow \quad Z_t + aZ_{t-1} = 0 \tag{87}$$

Where $Z_t = x_t - x^*$

Equation (87) is a homogeneous difference equation. The trial solution for linear difference equations is $\lambda^t$. Trying $Z_t = \lambda^t$ as a solution.

$$\lambda^t + a\lambda^{t-1} = 0 \tag{88}$$

As $\lambda \neq 0, \lambda^{t-1}$ can be factored out.

$$\Rightarrow \quad \lambda + a = 0 \quad \Rightarrow \quad \lambda = -a$$

Equation (88) is the characteristic equation for (85i). Next step is to note that if $Z_t = \lambda^t$ is a solution then so is $A\lambda^t$. So, the general solution to (87) is $Z_t = A\lambda^t$ where the constant, $A$, has to be obtained from given initial values. Writing the solution for $Z_t$.

$$Z_t = A(-a)^t \quad \Rightarrow \quad Z_0 = A \quad \Rightarrow \quad x_0 - x^* = A$$

$$\Rightarrow \quad A = x_0 - \frac{c}{1+a}$$

$$\Rightarrow \quad x_t = x^* + \left[x_0 - \frac{c}{1+a}\right](-a)^t \tag{89}$$

Equation (89) gives the time path of the variable $x_t$.

*Condition for Stability*

Stability of the model requires $x_t$ to tend to its own equilibrium value, after a departure at some time point, as time goes on. The condition for stability therefore has to ensure that $\text{Lim}\, x_t \to x^*$. Equation (89) clearly demonstrates that the condition for stability is $a > 0$ as then $(-a)^t$ reduces its value as $t$ increases.

*Second-Order Difference Equations*

A linear second-order difference equation involves a two period lag in the dynamic equation as in (90i):

$$x_t + a_1 x_{t-1} + a_2 x_{t-2} = c \tag{90i}$$

Once again, an equilibrium value can be defined as $x^*$ which once attained will be repeated forever. Substitution for $x^*$ in (90i) yields:

$$x^*(1 + a_1 + a_2) = c$$

$$\Rightarrow \quad x^* = \frac{c}{1 + a_1 + a_2} \tag{91}$$

For equilibrium to exist $1 + a_1 + a_2 \neq 0$ and for economic meaningfulness of equilibrium $1 + a_1 + a_2 > 0$. Using (91) (90i) can be rewritten as:

$$x_t + a_1 x_{t-1} + a_2 x_{t-2} = (1 + a_1 + a_2)x^*$$

$$\Rightarrow \quad x_t - x^* + a_1(x_{t-1} - x^*) + a_2(x_{t-2}) - x^* = 0$$

$$\Rightarrow \quad Z_t + a_1 Z_{t-1} + a_2 Z_{t-2} = 0 \tag{92}$$

Where $Z_t = x_t - x^*$

Trying $Z_t = \lambda^t$ as a solution to (92) the characteristic equation is obtained as (93) $\lambda^t + a_1\lambda^{t-1} + a_2\lambda^{t-2} = 0$. Dividing through by $\lambda^{t-2} \neq 0$,

$$\Rightarrow \quad \lambda^2 + a_1\lambda + a_2 = 0 \tag{93}$$

The roots of (93) are given by:

$$\lambda_1, \lambda_2 = \frac{-a_1 \pm \sqrt{a_1^2 - 4a_2}}{2} \tag{94}$$

The condition for real roots are $a_1^2 - 4a_2 \geq 0$

The general solution for

$$Z_t = A_1\lambda_1^t + A_2\lambda_2^t \tag{95}$$

Where $A_1$ and $A_2$ have to be evaluated from given initial values. There must be two such values for a second order difference equation, e.g., $x_0$ and $x_1$. $A_1$ and $A_2$ are obtained from (96).

$$x_0 - x^* = A_1 + A_2 \tag{96i}$$

$$x_1 - x^* = A_1\lambda_1 + A_2\lambda_2 \tag{96ii}$$

Now the complete specific solution is obtained for $Z_t$ and, therefore, for $x_t$

$$x_t = x^* + A_1\lambda_1^t + A_2\lambda_2^t \tag{97}$$

Where $x^*$, $\lambda_1$, $\lambda_2$, $A_1$ and $A_2$ are given as in (91), (94) and (96) respectively.

*Condition for Stability*

The question of stability is if $x_t$ departs from its equilibrium value $x^*$ at some time point, whether it can ever return to equilibrium in the long-run.

Stability requires $\lim\limits_{t\to\infty} x_t = x^*$, i.e., it requires $\lambda_1^t$ and $\lambda_2^t$ to tend to zero as $t \to \infty$. This will be ensured if $|\lambda_i| < 1$ as then $\lambda_i^t$ diminishes as $t$ increases.

If each root is less than one, then so must be their product. Thus the condition for stability of equilibrium can be restated as $\lambda_1 \lambda_2 < 1 \quad \Rightarrow$ from (94),

$$a_1^2 - a_1^2 + 4a_2 < 4 \Rightarrow \quad a_2 < 1 \cdots \tag{98}$$

*Iterative Method of Solving Difference Equations*

This is popular mainly in time-series models in Econometrics. But otherwise it is considered too laborious. Iterative method means that the equation, e.g., (85ii) is written out for value of $x$ at each time point.

$$x_t = -ax_{t-1}$$

$$x_{t-1} = -ax_{t-2} \quad \Rightarrow \quad x_t = -a(-ax_{t-2})$$

But $x_{t-2} = -ax_{t-3} \quad \Rightarrow x_t = -a^3 x_{t-3}$ and so on.

If $x_0$ is given, then the solution for $x_t$ can be written as:

$$x_t = x_0(-a)^t$$

*Solution of Simultaneous Difference Equations*

Consider the simplest case of simultaneous difference equations involving only two dynamic equations:

$$x_t + a_{11}x_{t-1} + y_t + a_{12}y_{t-1} = c_1 \tag{99i}$$

$$x_t + a_{21}x_{t-1} + y_t + a_{22}y_{t-1} = c_2 \tag{99ii}$$

Rewriting equation (99) in the deviation forms

$$Z_{1t} + a_{11}Z_{1t-1} + Z_{2t} + a_{12}Z_{2t-1} = 0$$

$$Z_{1t} + a_{21}Z_{1t-1} + Z_{2t} + a_{22}Z_{2t-1} = 0$$

Where $Z_{1t} = x_t - x^*$

and $Z_{2t} = y_t - y^*$

and the equilibrium set $x^*, y^*$ is given by Cramer's rule applied to the system.

$$\begin{vmatrix} 1+a_{11} & 1+a_{12} \\ 1+a_{21} & 1+a_{22} \end{vmatrix} \begin{vmatrix} x^* \\ y^* \end{vmatrix} = \begin{vmatrix} C_1 \\ C_2 \end{vmatrix} \tag{100}$$

$$\Rightarrow \quad x^* = \frac{C_1(1+a_{22}) - C_2(1+a_{12})}{(1+a_{11})(1+a_{22}) - (1+a_{12})(1+a_{21})} \tag{101i}$$

and

$$y^* = \frac{C_2(1+a_{11}) - C_1(1+a_{21})}{(1+a_{11})(1+a_{22}) - (1+a_{12})(1+a_{21})} \tag{101ii}$$

Once again the solution method is very similar to that discussed in the case of simultaneous differential equations. Because of that and because simultaneous difference equations have not been used much in the book, details of such solution are not discussed any further in this appendix.

### 1.A.5 **Taylor's and Maclaurin's Series**

*Single Variable*

According to Taylor's theorem a function $f(x)$ the exact form of which is unknown can be approximated by the form (102) provided its value at a point $x = x_o$ is known.

$$f(x) \simeq \left[\left[\frac{f(x_0)}{0!}\right] + \left[\frac{f'(x_0)(x-x_0)}{1!}\right] + \left[\frac{f''(x_0)(x-x_0)^2}{2!}\right] + \left[\frac{f'''(x_0)(x-x_0)^3}{3!}\right] + \cdots\cdots\right] \tag{102}$$

The series on the R.H.S. of (102) expanded up to a finite order is known as Taylor's series.

The higher the order of derivatives taken into account the closer will be the approximation. Such approximation is very useful in Economics in linearising a non-linear function. In linearisation one takes into account only the first-order derivative. For example, the production function has been linearised around the full employment level in Chapter 6 by using Taylor's series rule (102).

Maclaurin's series is a special case of Taylor's series which assumes $x_0 = 0$:

$$f(x) \simeq f(0) + f'(0)x + \frac{f''(0)x^2}{2!} + \cdots\cdots \tag{103}$$

# 2

# THE SIMPLE IS-LM MODEL

## 2.1 INTRODUCTION

Soon after the publication of Keynes's General Theory (1936), J.R. Hicks (1937) provided a very useful and convenient apparatus to summarise Keynes's thought. This is the well known IS-LM model which has since been very widely used in applied macroeconomics. The IS-LM model analysed in this chapter is of the simplest type and it considers only the goods and the money markets. The model has both "Keynesian" and "Classical" features. Emphasis on the demand side only of each market and the assumption that the supply of output and the supply of money merely adjust to respective demands are well known as the Keynesian elements. Another characteristic typically associated with Keynes is the speculative component of the demand for money. However, as will be explained in Chapter 3, these elements can be accommodated in a classical model as well. It is how the supply side of the output market is explained that the Keynesians and the classics disagree on. In the demand-oriented model of the present chapter, the disagreement between the Keynesian and Classical systems will come to light only when some parameters of the model will be assigned certain critical values. This will be observed in due course. For now, the basic features of the present model can be noted. First, it is assumed that in the output market, whatever is demanded is produced and supplied and is equal to the net national product. In the money market, the money supply is determined by the monetary authorities and, therefore, treated as exogenous. Only the demands for output and money are explained in detail and for equilibrium in respective markets, demand equals supply.

## 2.2 THE MARKETS: OUTPUT AND MONEY

In a closed economy with government activity there are there components of demand placed on the country's output — consumption, $C$; investment, $I$, and government demand, $G$. In an open economy there is an additional component of demand placed on a country's output — viz., exports, $X$ or the foreigners' demand for the home-country's outputs; on the other hand, the home-countries demand for foreign goods, imports, $Im$, is a demand away from home produced goods. A closed economy is one with no foreign trade or other transactions with the rest of the world and an open economy is one which trades with other countries of the world. So, the total demand on a country's output is the sum of $C$, $I$, $G$ and $X$ net of import demand $Im$. The condition for equilibrium in the output market of an open economy is that the aggregate demand for output equals the aggregate supply $Y$:

$$Y = C + I + G + X - Im \tag{2.1}$$

Real consumption demand is assumed to depend on real disposable income or take-home pay, i.e., the income after deducting all taxes and other mandatory contributions paid and adding all social security payments received. A consumption function can be written as:

$$C = a + bY_d, \quad a > 0, \quad 0 < b < 1 \tag{2.2}$$

where the disposable income:

$$Y_d = Y - T \tag{2.2a}$$

In some of the models to follow, the net payment to the exchequer in real terms, $T$, will be assumed to be independent of income. For the present, $T$ is assumed to be a simple linear function of income:

$$T = t_0 + t_1 Y, \quad t_0 < 0, \quad 0 < t_1 < 1 \tag{2.3}$$

The consumption function (2.2) means that there is an autonomous part which is independent of income, e.g., the minimum necessary consumption of the bare necessities of life and this is given by the parameter '$a$'. The other part '$bY_d$' is the induced demand which shows that consumption increases with disposable income but not by as much. The slope of the consumption function $b(1 - t_1)$ is defined as the marginal propensity to consume, MPC and it is assumed to be positive but less than 1. The autonomous consumption '$a$' is the positive intercept implying that even at zero income this demand has to be met. The real taxes equation (2.3) has a negative autonomous part explained by transfer payments exemption limit etc., which are assumed to outweigh positive lump-sum taxes, license fees etc. The slope of the tax function is the marginal rate of tax, $dT/dY$.

Investment demand, in this simple model, is assumed to depend inversely on the real rate of interest, $r$:

$$I = A + dr, \quad A > 0, \quad d < 0 \tag{2.4}$$

In the investment function (2.4), $A$ is autonomous investment and the negative coefficient, '$d$' indicates an inverse relationship between investment and the real rate of interest. The latter incorporates the discounted present value criterion. This criterion selects all investment projects whose discounted present value are at least equal to the initial costs. The discounted present value, $PV$, of a project is the value obtained by discounting all the expected future yields of the project at a suitable rate of discount, say, the average real rate of interest. Then

$$PV = \frac{R_1}{1+r} + \frac{R_2}{(1+r)^2} + \frac{R_3}{(1+r)^3} + \cdots + \frac{R_n}{(1+r)^n} \tag{2.5}$$

where $R_t$ is the expected yield of the project in the year $t$ and the life of the project is $n$ years. If $X_0$ is the initial cost of the project, then:

$$PV > X_0$$

implies the project is viable:

$PV = X_0$ implies a net present value of zero for the project and if $PV < X_0$, the project is not viable. From the above expression for the $PV$ of a project, it is clear that a rise in the rate of interest will tend to reduce the $PV$ for a given stream of net yields and thereby would make some projects that were formerly viable no longer so. Therefore, as the rate of interest rises, the number of projects having a positive net present value will fall so that the amount of investment undertaken by the firm will fall implying $d < 0$.

The home-country's demand for foreign goods is assumed in this simple model, to depend on real income:

$$Im = mY, \quad 0 < m < 1, \quad m < b \tag{2.6}$$

The import demand function is written in the proportional form implying the impossibility of any imports at a zero income. Also, the marginal propensity to import, $m$ is likely to be smaller than the marginal propensity to spend on domestic output.

The government demand and the overseas demand for exports are assumed exogenous. The import and export demands will be explained in more detail along with theories of balance of payments in Chapter 8.

For the simple IS-LM model the output market is described by the equations (2.1) – (2.6).

### *The IS Curve*

The IS curve is the locus of all combinations of real income and the real rate of interest which keep the output market in equilibrium. From the explanation given above, the equation to the IS curve can be derived by substituting all the demand equations (2.2) – (2.6) into the equilibrium condition for the output market (2.1):

$$Y = a + b[Y - t_0 - t_1 Y] - mY + A + dr + G + X$$

$$Y\{1 - b(1 - t_1) + m\} - dr = a - bt_0 + A + G + X \tag{2.7}$$

Equation (2.7) passes through all combinations of $Y$ and $r$ which are consistent with equilibrium in the output market and it is the IS curve in the present model. Now the nature of the relation between $Y$ and $r$ concerns how equilibrium is maintained in the output market when either of the variables changes. If real output, $Y$ rises, the extra output cannot be completely absorbed in extra consumption demand because $b(1 - t_1) - m < 1$; therefore investment must rise to maintain equilibrium; the required increase in investment can be brought about by a fall in real rate of interest. This implies that the IS curve is negatively sloped in the $(Y, r)$ axes.

It is shown in Fig. 2.1. mathematically the slope can be derived by differentiating (2.7) w.r.t. $Y$ and solving for $\frac{dr}{dY}$:

$$\left(\frac{dr}{dY}\right)_{IS} = \frac{1 - b(1 - t_1) + m}{d} < 0 \tag{2.8}$$

Given the signs of the parameters $b, t_1, m$ and $d$ it follows that the slope is negative.

### *The Money Market*

The real demand for money by the households is given by:

$$\frac{M^d}{P} = L_0 + \alpha Y + \beta r, \quad \alpha > 0, \beta < 0, L_0 > 0 \tag{2.9}$$

The positive sign of $\alpha$ means that the transactions and precautionary demand rise with real income and negative sign of $\beta$ implies an inverse relationship between the real rate of interest and the real demand for money. This is also known as liquidity preference. Money holders as speculators compare money as an asset with other available financial assets — Bonds, i.e., the gilt-edged securities or Equities i.e., the industrial shares — . Idle money is the most liquid asset but it does not entitle the holder to an yield or a capital gain. As the rate of interest rises, the opportunity cost of holding idle money increases in terms of foregone interest income. This is the time when bonds are attractive; their prices fall when the rates of interest rise[1]; the reverse happens when the rate of interest is low-bonds are sold to take advantage of the capital gains. So, the demand for idle money increases when the rate of interest falls. Hence the inverse relationship between the two. $L_0$ is an autonomous component of the demand for money-representing the psychological attitude of the money holder. The nominal money supply is controlled by the monetary authorities and it is assumed exogenous in the models discussed in Chapters 2 and 3. In an open economy balance of payments situation can affect the domestic money supply and such effects will be considered in Chapter 8. A part of money supply also depends on the size of the government budget deficit and this will be considered in Chapter 5. For the purpose of this simple model, the nominal money supply is assumed exogenous and the condition for equilibrium in the money market is that demand for and supply of money are equal:

$$M^d = M^s = M \qquad (2.10)$$

Equations (2.9) and (2.10) describe the money market. After substitution, the condition for equilibrium in the money market can be derived in terms of $Y$, $r$ as

$$\alpha Y + \beta r + L_0 = \frac{M}{P} \qquad (2.11)$$

Equation (2.11) traces the *LM curve* in the $(Y, r)$ axes. The LM curve is defined as the locus of all combinations of real income and real rate of interest which will keep the money market in equilibrium. The slope of the LM curve can be derived from (2.11) as

$$\left(\frac{dr}{dy}\right)_{LM} = -\frac{\alpha}{\beta} > 0 \tag{2.12}$$

The positive slope implies an upward sloping LM curve. This is what ought to be expected. As income rises, the transactions and precautionary demands for money rise with it and with an unchanged money supply and an unchanged price level, the speculative demand has to fall to maintain equilibrium and to bring this about, the rate of interest must rise.

## 2.3 THE OUTPUT AND MONEY MARKETS: THE IS-LM MODEL

For simultaneous equilibrium in both output and money markets the values of real income and real rate of interest have to lie on both the IS and the LM curves. Since the former represents the equilibrium combinations required for the real sector and the latter represents those required for the monetary sector of the economy. The equilibrium combination $(Y^*, r^*)$ of real income and real interest rate is shown in Fig. 2.1 by the point of intersection between the IS and the LM curves. The equilibrium value of each in terms of the parameters and exogenous variables can be obtained by solving the IS and LM model. An explained before the model consists of the two equations (2.7) and (2.11) representing the IS and the LM equations respectively.

*The IS-LM Model*

$$Y[1 - b(1 - t_1) + m] - dr = a - bt_0 + A + G + X \tag{2.7}$$

$$\alpha Y + \beta r = \frac{M}{P} - L_0 \tag{2.11}$$

Since the two equations represent respective equilibrium the values of $Y$ and $r$ consistent with simultaneous equilibrium are the solution of the above two-equation model. Instead of following the simple method of elimination I shall introduce the method of Cramer's rule widely used in macroeconomic models. The simple method of elimination can be tedius in cases involving more than two endogenous variables. Cramer's rule is a convenient way of solving a system of linear equations.[2] To apply

Cramer's rule, the coefficients of the endogenous variables $Y$ and $r$ are collected from the two equations to form a determinant, $\Delta$ such that the coefficients of $Y$ and $r$ in (2.7) constitute the first row and those of $Y$ and $r$ in (2.11) the second row of $\Delta$. Then, the system of equations can be rewritten as:

$$\Delta \cdot \begin{vmatrix} y \\ r \end{vmatrix} = \begin{vmatrix} a - bt_0 + A + G + X \\ \frac{M}{P} - L_0 \end{vmatrix} \tag{2.12a}$$

$$\text{where} \quad \Delta = \begin{vmatrix} 1 - b(1 - t_1) + m & -d \\ \alpha & \beta \end{vmatrix} \tag{2.12b}$$

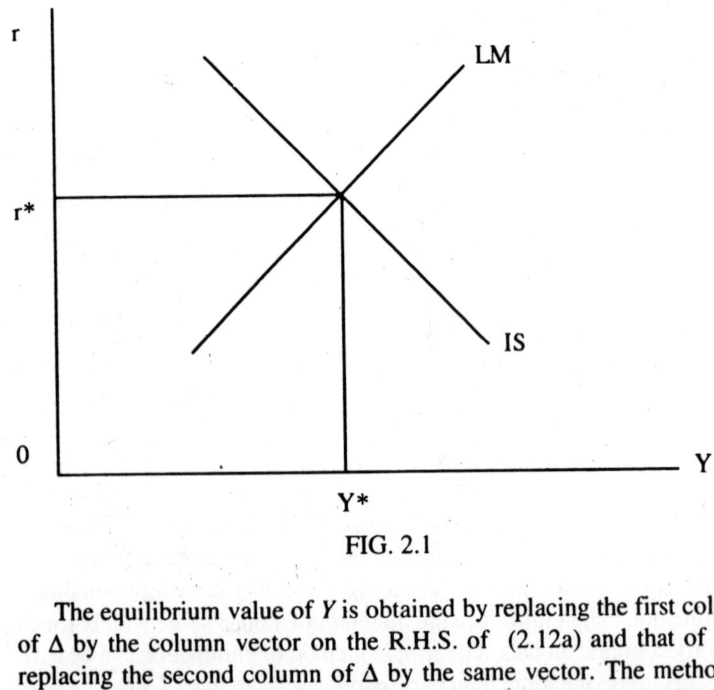


FIG. 2.1

The equilibrium value of $Y$ is obtained by replacing the first column of $\Delta$ by the column vector on the R.H.S. of (2.12a) and that of $r$ by replacing the second column of $\Delta$ by the same vector. The method of Cramer's rule is therefore an alternative to that of matrix inversion. The equilibrium values of $Y$ and $r$ in this simple model are given by Cramer's rule as:

$$Y^* = \frac{1}{\Delta}\begin{vmatrix} a - bt_0 + A + G + X & -d \\ \frac{M}{P} - L_0 & \beta \end{vmatrix} \tag{2.13a}$$

and $$r^* = \frac{1}{\Delta}\begin{vmatrix} 1 - b(1 - t_1) + m & a - bt_0 + A + G + X \\ \alpha & \frac{M}{P} - L_0 \end{vmatrix} \tag{2.13b}$$

The solutions (2.13) exist only if $\Delta \neq 0$. Expanding $\Delta$ by the cofactors of the elements of the first row:

$$\Delta = \beta\{1 - b(1 - t_1) + m\} + d\alpha \tag{2.14}$$

Substituting for $\Delta$ in (2.13)

$$Y^* = \frac{\beta(a - bt_0 + A + G + X) + d(M/P - L_0)}{\beta\{1 - b(1 - t_1) + m\} + d\alpha} \tag{2.15a}$$

and $$r^* = \frac{(M/P - L_0)\{1 - b(1 - t_1) + m\} - \alpha(a - bt_0 + A + G + X)}{\beta\{1 - b(1 - t_1) + m\} + d\alpha} \tag{2.15b}$$

It follows from previous discussion on the signs of various parameters, viz., $\beta < 0$, $0 < b(1 - t_1) - m < 1$, $d < 0, \alpha > 0$ etc., that the determinant $\Delta$ in (2.14) is negative. This in turn, implies that $Y^*$ in (2.15a) must rise with $G, X$, real money supply etc., and that $r^*$ must fall when real money supply increases and rise when government spending, exports etc., increase. Rises in $G$ and $X$ and in $M$ lead to shifts of the IS and LM curves respectively since these exogenous variables are intercepts of these equations. Government spending, money supply etc. are viewed as important to lead to important policy instruments of the government and changes in them are initiated desired effects on certain target variables, e.g., real income and real rate of interest in this model.

The equilibrium values such as those given in (2.15) are called static equilibrium values and the effects on them of an initial change in any one policy or other exogenous variable at a time are called the Comparative Statics of a model. Such comparative Statics have to deal with shifts of the IS and LM curves in response to policy and other changes, the consequent changes in the equilibrium values of the endogenous variables of the model and ascertaining the magnitude of such changes.

## 2.4 FISCAL AND MONETARY POLICIES IN THE SIMPLE IS-LM MODEL: COMPARATIVE STATICS

### *The Multipliers*

In comparative static analysis, one examines the effects of a change in any one exogenous variable at a time on the equilibrium values of all the endogenous variables of the model. Such effects can be studied from the relevant multipliers. A multiplier can be defined as the ratio of the induced change in the equilibrium value of an endogenous variable to the initial change in the selected exogenous variable. Such multipliers have important policy implications. For example, if one wanted to know the impact of a rise in government spending on real output and the real rate of interest in the economy, one would derive the fiscal policy multipliers $\frac{\partial Y}{\partial G}$ and $\frac{\partial r}{\partial G}$ respectively. The impact of monetary policy, on the other hand, would be derived from the multipliers $\frac{\partial Y}{\partial M}$ and $\frac{\partial r}{\partial M}$.

Fiscal policy refers to an attempt by the government to change real output, real rate of interest (the endogenous variables of the present model) in the required way by changing government spending and taxation. Monetary policy refers to an attempt to change these variables by changing the nominal money supply. In reality, the fiscal and monetary policies are interdependent but in this simple model without a government budget equation, they are treated as independent of one another. The policy variables like $G$, or $M$, a change in which is supposed to affect real output, etc., are called *instruments* and the variables which are sought to be altered are called *targets*. In this simple model, $Y$, $r$ are target variables and $G$, $M$ are the instruments. The role and effectiveness of fiscal and monetary policies can be judged by deriving the relevant policy multipliers in the present model. In this context, only $G$, $M$, $X$ and $P$ are exogenous but $T$ is endogenous. So there would be four sets of multipliers for each of the endogenous variables: $\frac{\partial Y}{\partial G}, \frac{\partial Y}{\partial M}, \frac{\partial Y}{\partial P}, \frac{\partial Y}{\partial X}$ and $\frac{\partial r}{\partial G}, \frac{\partial r}{\partial M}, \frac{\partial r}{\partial P}$, etc. In the comparative static analysis of multipliers, it is important to note that only one exogenous variable is allowed to change at a time. So, in deriving, say $\frac{\partial Y}{\partial G}$

$\frac{\partial r}{\partial M}$, $\frac{\partial G}{\partial M}$ and $\frac{\partial P}{\partial M}$, and $\frac{\partial X}{\partial M}$ are assumed to be zero. And so on.

*The Fiscal and Monetary Policy Multipliers in the Simple IS-LM Model*

These can be derived in two ways:

(a) by differentiating the IS and the LM equations partially w.r.t. the selected exogenous variable and then solving for the two multipliers simultaneously by applying Cramer's rule to the differentiated equations;

or

(b) by differentiating the equilibrium solutions as derived from the IS and LM equations in (2.15) partially w.r.t. the chosen exogenous variable.

*Method* (a):

For the fiscal policy multipliers, differentiate the IS and the LM equations partially w.r.t. $G$ and obtain:

$$\frac{\partial Y}{\partial G}[1-b(1-t_1)+m]-d\frac{\partial r}{\partial G}=1 \tag{2.16}$$

$$\alpha\frac{\partial Y}{\partial G}+\beta\frac{\partial r}{\partial G}=0 \tag{2.17}$$

Collect the coefficients of $\frac{\partial Y}{\partial G}$ in (2.16) and (2.17) in the first column and the coefficients of $\frac{\partial r}{\partial G}$ in (2.16) and (2.17) in the second column of a determinant, $J$ and rewrite the system of equations (2.16) and (2.17) as:

$$J\cdot\begin{vmatrix}\dfrac{\partial Y}{\partial G}\\[2ex]\dfrac{\partial r}{\partial G}\end{vmatrix}=\begin{vmatrix}1\\[2ex]0\end{vmatrix} \tag{2.18}$$

Where $$J=\begin{vmatrix}1-b(1-t_1)+m & -d\\ \alpha & \beta\end{vmatrix} \tag{2.19}$$

$J$ is called the Jacobian determinant or Jacobian for short. The Jacobian of a model is obtained from the coefficients of the first-order partial derivatives of the endogenous variables w.r.t. any one selected exogenous variable of the model. So the Jacobian is invariant with the choice of exogenous variables of a model. The test of functional dependence of a system of equations can be made easily by checking whether $J = 0$. The system of equation is independent and determinate only if the Jacobian of the system $\neq 0$. The Jacobian (2.19) has already been evaluated in (2.14). By Cramer's rule the fiscal policy multipliers are:

$$\frac{\partial Y}{\partial G} = \frac{1}{J}\begin{vmatrix} 1 & -d \\ 0 & \beta \end{vmatrix} = \frac{\beta}{J} \tag{2.20a}$$

and
$$\frac{\partial r}{\partial G} = \frac{1}{J}\begin{vmatrix} 1-b(1-t_1)+m & 1 \\ \alpha & 0 \end{vmatrix} = \frac{-\alpha}{J} \tag{2.20b}$$

Substituting for $J$ from (2.14)

$$\frac{\partial Y}{\partial G} = \frac{\beta}{\beta(1-b(1-t_1)+m)+d\alpha} \tag{2.21a}$$

and
$$\frac{\partial r}{\partial G} = \frac{-\alpha}{\beta(1-b(1-t_1)+m)+d\alpha} \tag{2.21b}$$

From the sign restrictions already discussed, it follows from (2.21) that a rise in government spending leads to a rise in real output as well as in the real rate of interest i.e., both $\frac{\partial Y}{\partial G}$ and $\frac{\partial r}{\partial G}$ positive. While the former being positive implies that fiscal policy is expansionary the rise in the real rate of interest following a rise in government spending may lead to a fall in private investment. This is known as the crowding out effect of fiscal policy where a rise in public spending can crowd private spending out to some extent. The strength of the crowding-out effect on private investment depends on the interest-sensitivity of private investment, judged by the value of the parameter, '$d$' in the present model. The size of the multiplier $\frac{\partial Y}{\partial G}$ depends directly on $\beta$ but inversely on $d$. The higher the value of $\beta$ (and the lower the value of $d$) the larger will be the expansionary effect on real income. In Fig. 2.2, a rise in $G$ is shown by a rightward shift of the IS curve from $IS_1$ and $IS_2$ and its consequences are a rise in income and interest rate from $OY_1$ to $OY_2$ and from $Or_1$ and $Or_2$ respectively. A shift to the right of the IS curve can be caused by a rise in exports also in the present model. This will raise real income by the same multiple. The foreign-trade multiplier $\frac{\partial Y}{\partial X}$ is also given by (2.21a). This result is, however dependent on the assumption that the import contents of all exogenous expenditure are the same.

The monetary policy multipliers, following the same method are obtained by differentiating the IS and the LM equations partially w.r.t. *M* and writing them as

$$J\begin{vmatrix}\dfrac{\partial Y}{\partial M}\\[2ex] \dfrac{\partial r}{\partial M}\end{vmatrix}=\begin{vmatrix}0\\[2ex] \dfrac{1}{P}\end{vmatrix} \tag{2.22}$$

Solving (2.22) by Cramer's rule again, the multipliers are:

$$\frac{\partial Y}{\partial M}=\frac{d}{P\cdot J}>0 \tag{2.23a}$$

and $$\frac{\partial r}{\partial M}=\frac{1-b(1-t_1)+m}{P\cdot J}<0 \tag{2.23b}$$

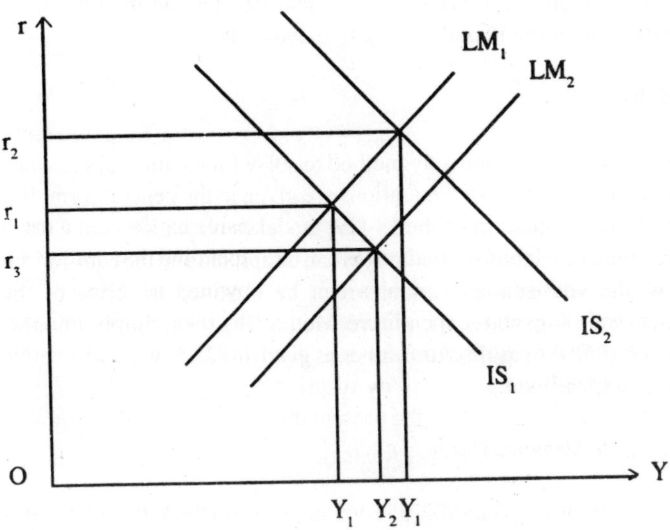


FIG. 2.2

The signs imply that monetary policy is expansionary on real output and a rise in the stock of money leads to a fall in the real rate of interest. A rise in the quantity of money with no change in price level implies a rightward shift of the LM curve as shown in Fig. 2.2 and as a result income and interest change to $OY_3$ and $Or_3$ respectively. It is easy to check that a fall in the price level with no change in money supply will have the same effects on income and interest rate. An increase in the real quantity of money supply leads to an excess supply of real balances; to restore money market equilibrium at the initial level of income the interest rate has to decline to induce people to hold more speculative balances. Alternatively at each interest rate real income has to be higher to induce people to hold more transactions and precautionary balances. A point in favour of using monetary policy vis-a-vis fiscal policy is that the former is expansionary but it does not lead to a crowding out effect on private investment through a rise in the rate of interest. This point which constitutes the centre of the debate between Keynesians and monetarists will be taken up later on in this Chapter and in more detail in Chapter 5. For now it can be noted from (2.23a) that the size of the expansionary effect on real income of a rise in money supply depends inversely on '$d$' and '$\alpha$', i.e., on the interest — sensitivity of investment and speculative demands.

*Method* (b)

The above method (a) is the only method to solve for the multipliers when all behavioural and structural equations are given in the general form. But in the present formulation of the IS-LM model the equations are written in explicit linear form and so method (b) can be applied and the equilibrium values of the endogenous variables can be obtained in terms of the parameters and exogenous expenditure. Method (b), then, simply amounts to differentiating the equilibrium values as given in (2.15) w.r.t. respective exogenous expenditure.

*The Aggregate Demand Curve*

In this demand oriented model, it is of interest to check the effect of a change in the price level on the demand for real output. This is given by the derivative $\frac{\partial Y}{\partial P}$. Following the same method:

$$\frac{\partial Y}{\partial P}=\frac{1}{J}\begin{vmatrix} 0 & -d \\ -\frac{M}{P^2} & \beta \end{vmatrix}=\frac{-dM/P^2}{J}<0 \tag{2.24}$$

The negative sign implies that in the $(Y, P)$ axes, the aggregate demand curve is downward sloping.

*The IS-LM Model in the General Form*

Substituting for the individual demand functions in the condition for equilibrium in the output and money markets the IS-LM model in the general form can be written as:

$$Y-C(Y-T)-I(r)+Im(Y)=G+X \tag{2.29}$$

$$L(Y,r)=\frac{M}{P} \tag{2.30}$$

For simultaneous equilibrium in money and output markets, both (2.29) and (2.30) have to be satisfied. The equilibrium values of the two endogenous variables $Y$ and $r$ can be obtained only in the general form[3]:

$$Y=Y(P,G,T,M,X) \tag{2.30a}$$

and $$r=r(P,G,T,M,X) \tag{2.30b}$$

The effectiveness of fiscal and monetary policies can be obtained as before from the respective multipliers. Differentiating the IS and LM equations, first w.r.t. $G$ one obtains

$$\frac{\partial Y}{\partial G}(1-C'+Im')-I'\frac{\partial r}{\partial G}=1 \tag{2.31}$$

and $$L_1\frac{\partial Y}{\partial G}+L_2\frac{\partial r}{\partial G}=0 \tag{2.32}$$

So, the Jacobian, in the general form is obtained by replacing the row and columns of that in (2.19) by the respective parameters in the general form:

33. You may use a tax equation also in the general form: $T=T(Y)$ with $0<T'<1$ as the marginal rate of tax. But here they are treated as a fiscal instrument.

$$J = \begin{vmatrix} 1-C'+Im' & -I' \\ L_1 & L_2 \end{vmatrix}$$

$$J = L_2(1-C'+Im') + L_1 I' < 0 \tag{2.33}$$

Applying Cramer's rule.

$$\frac{\partial Y}{\partial G} = \frac{L_2}{J} > 0 \tag{2.34a}$$

and $$\frac{\partial r}{\partial G} = \frac{-L_1}{J} > 0 \tag{2.34b}$$

Differentiating the IS and LM equations w.r.t. other exogenous variables by turn and solving for the multipliers by Cramer's rule yields

$$\frac{\partial Y}{\partial M} = \frac{I'}{P \cdot J} > 0 \tag{2.35a}$$

$$\frac{\partial r}{\partial M} = \frac{1-C'+Im'}{P \cdot J} < 0 \tag{2.35b}$$

$$\frac{\partial Y}{\partial X} = \text{R.H.S. of (2.34a)}$$

and $$\frac{\partial r}{\partial X} = \text{R.H.S. of (2.34b)}$$

Finally, the slope of the aggregate demand curve is obtained as

$$\frac{\partial Y}{\partial P} = \frac{-\frac{M}{P^2} \cdot I'}{J} < 0 \tag{2.35}$$

The signs of all these multipliers and of the slope of the demand curve have been explained before.

## 2.5 A QUICK LOOK AT KEYNES VERSUS: THE CLASSICS DEBATE

At this stage, the following aspect of the debate can be noted. The classical economists believed in the interest-elasticity of saving and investment implying $S'(r)$ or $I'(r)$ or '$d$' always non-zero; also the classical economists did not believe in the demand for idle money balances. Keynes, unlike the Classics, emphasised a very low interest elasticity of saving and investment and a very high interest elasticity of the demand for money.

In the limiting case $I'(r)=0$ and $L_2=-\infty$. The policy implications[4] of these two are important. First, these make the expansionary effect of fiscal policy on real output the strongest. The value of the multiplier $\frac{\partial Y}{\partial G}$ becomes $\frac{1}{1-b(1-t_1)+m}$ or $\frac{1}{1-C'+Im'}$ when $I'(r)=0$ and/or $L_2=-\infty$. This also is the value of $\frac{\partial Y}{\partial G}$ in the absence of the money market. In other words, the monetary policy cannot affect the real output or the real rate of interest. Also, no "crowding out" occurs because $\frac{\partial r}{\partial G}=0$ in these two cases.

The interest in elasticity of investment demand implies a vertical IS curve since $\frac{(dr)}{(dY)_{IS}}=-\infty$ if $I'(r)=0$. The other case, $L_2=-\infty$ implies $\frac{(dr)}{(dY)_{LM}}=0$ or, a horizontal LM curve. This situation is well known as the liquidity trap. At a critical, low, rate of interest, the speculative demand for money is infinitely elastic; bond prices are considered too high and all bonds are converted back into idle money to realise the high capital gains.

Finally, in these cases, the aggregate demand curve ceases to be downward sloping. $\frac{\partial Y}{\partial P}=0$ if $I'(r)=0$ or if $L_2=-\infty$ which implies a vertical aggregate demand curve.

To sum up: When investment *demand is insensitive to* changes in the rate of interest and in the presence of a *liquidity trap*, monetary policy is totally ineffective and the fiscal policy has the most expansionary effect on real income.

The Pigou effect [Pigou (1943) and Patinkin (1957)] and the light it throws on the Keynes-Classics debate will be explained in later chapters. The open economy macro models will be discussed in Chapter 8. For the next few chapters various macroeconomic problems will be dealt with in the context of a closed economy. The simple IS and LM equations for a closed economy are easily obtained from the respective equations above by assuming no exports and imports. The implications for the equilibrium values and the multipliers are:

$$X = Im = Im' = 0 \tag{2.36}$$

The IS and LM equations subject to the closed-economy assumptions will form the basis of the following analysis up to Chapter 8.

---

44. The students are required, to derive these results by substituting $I'(r)=0$ and $L_2=-\infty$ in all the relevant multipliers already obtained in this chapter.

# 3

# THREE SECTOR MODELS OF AGGREGATE DEMAND AND AGGREGATE SUPPLY IN THE SHORT-RUN

## 3.1 SUPPLY CONSIDERATIONS

### Supply of Output

The simple IS-LM model of Chapter 2 is based on the demand considerations alone. It assumes the supply of output as given. In this chapter, the supply of output is considered as determined by the input of labour, input of capital and by the state of technology in the economy. In the short-run, capital stock and technology are assumed constant and the quantity of output varies because of changes in the level of employment of labour alone. So, the short-run supply of output is given by the production function:

$$Y = F(N, \overline{K}, \overline{\Omega}) \tag{3.1}$$

where $N$ is the level of employment, $\overline{K}$, the given stock of capital and $\overline{\Omega}$ stands for the state of technology. $K$ and $\Omega$ are allowed to change in the long-run dynamic growth models. Because $K, \Omega$, are treated as constants, (3.1) can be rewritten as a function of $N$ alone:

$$Y = Y(N) \tag{3.2}$$

The short-run production function (3.2) is usually subjected to the law of diminishing marginal productivity of labour. When capital and technology are constant, the quantity of output rises with employment but at a diminishing rate: That is,

$$(Y' \equiv)\frac{\delta Y}{\delta N} > 0 \quad \text{and} \quad (Y'' \equiv)\frac{\delta^2 Y}{\delta N^2} < 0 \tag{3.2a}$$

Now, employment (and, therefore, the supply of output) is to be determined by the demand and supply conditions of the labour market.

## The Labour Market

### *The Demand for Labour*

The employers demand labour such that the net revenue from selling the output that the labour produces is maximised. The net revenue is defined as total sales revenue minus all costs. This is also the definition of total profit, $\pi$. A simple profit equation can be written for the short-run as:

$$\pi = PY(N) - W \cdot N - FC \tag{3.3}$$

where $W$ is the money wage rate and $FC$ are total fixed costs. It is only under perfect competition in both the product and the factor markets that $P$ and $W$ do not vary between employers. So, under perfect competition, $N$ is the only variable in the profit equation (3.3), which the employer is supposed to maximise. The first-order or, the necessary condition for maximum profits is:

$$\frac{d\pi}{dN} = 0 \quad \Rightarrow \quad PY' - W = 0 \quad \Rightarrow \quad Y' = \frac{W}{P} \tag{3.4}$$

(3.4) is the well-known marginal productivity condition for optimum employment. In this single-input short-run case, the second-order or, the sufficient condition for maximum profits is satisfied by the diminishing marginal productivity assumption. In perfectly competitive labour and output markets, the firms maximise profits by employing labour to the point where the marginal productivity of the last unit of labour equals the real wage rate. Since $Y$ and $Y'$ are functions of $N$, one can derive a demand function for labour from the profit maximising rule (3.4), viz.

$$N^d = N^d\left(\frac{W}{P}\right) \tag{3.5}$$

such that $N^{d\prime} < 0$ or, that as the real wage rate rises, employment falls.

Under imperfect competition in the product market, a firm faces a downward sloping demand curve for its product — more can be sold at a lower price and less at a higher price. So, price cannot be treated as a constant but as a function of the product demand:

$$P = P(Y) \tag{3.3a}$$

such that $P' < 0$.

Under imperfect competition in the labour market, money wage is also endogenous. In the case where there is perfect competition on both the buyers' and the sellers' sides of the labour market, the firm faces a perfectly elastic labour supply curve at the given wage $W$. But if there is imperfect competition, say, on the buyers' side, e.g., a monopsony, the employer of labour faces an upward-sloping labour supply curve implying that the wage rate he pays for his labour is an increasing function of the quantity he hires. In order to attract additional units of labour, the monopsonist must offer a higher wage rate. So, under imperfect competition[1] in the labour market,

$$W = W(N^s) \tag{3.3b}$$

with $W' > 0$.

Assuming perfect competition in the labour and imperfect competition in the product markets, the necessary condition for profit maximisation is derived by putting the first-order derivative of

$$\pi = P(Y) \cdot Y(N^d) - W \cdot N^d - FC \tag{3.6}$$

w.r.t. $N^d$ equal to zero. So, the necessary condition becomes:

$$\frac{d\pi}{dN} = P\frac{\delta Y}{\delta N^d} + Y\frac{dP}{dY} \bullet \frac{\delta Y}{\delta N^d} - W = 0$$

$$\Rightarrow \quad PY' + YP'Y' - W = 0 \tag{3.7}$$

Recalling the definition of the price elasticity of demand in the continuous formulation:

$$e \equiv \frac{dY}{dP} \cdot \frac{P}{Y} \quad \Rightarrow \quad \frac{1}{e} = \frac{P'Y}{P} \quad \Rightarrow \quad P'Y = P\frac{1}{e}$$

Substituting in (3.7).

$$\Rightarrow \quad \frac{d\pi}{dN} = P\left(1 + \frac{1}{e}\right)Y' - W = 0$$

$$\Rightarrow \quad \left(1 + \frac{1}{e}\right)Y' = \frac{W}{P} \tag{3.8}$$

(3.8) gives the modified form of the marginal productivity rule of optimum employment under imperfect competition in the product market alone.

---

1. For a detailed description, see David Sapsford [1981].

Finally, the necessary condition for maximum profits under imperfect competition in both markets is given by:

$$\frac{d\pi}{dN} = P\left(1+\frac{1}{e}\right)Y' - W - W'N = 0 \tag{3.8}$$

assuming $N^d = N^s = N$

that is, by,

$$P\left(1+\frac{1}{e}\right)Y' - W \cdot \frac{1}{\eta} - W = 0$$

where $\eta$ is the elasticity of labour supply w.r.t. $W$ defined as

$$\frac{dN}{dW} \cdot \frac{W}{N} \quad \Rightarrow \quad \frac{1}{\eta} = W'\left(\frac{N}{W}\right)$$

So, under imperfect competition in both labour and product markets, the necessary condition for maximum profits becomes:

$$\left(1+\frac{1}{e}\right)Y' = \left(1+\frac{1}{\eta}\right)\frac{W}{P} \tag{3.9}$$

It is evident from (3.4), (3.8) and (3.9) that whatever may be the form of competition in the product or factor markets, the necessary condition for profit maximisation always implies that the marginal product of labour, $Y'$ is some function of the real wage, $\frac{W}{P}$. From this, a general demand function for labour can be written as in (3.5) which can include (3.4), (3.8) and (3.9) as special cases.

*The Supply of Labour*

The supply counterpart follows from an exercise of utility maximisation on the part of the workers. A macro utility function for the workers is written as

$$U = U(Y, l) \tag{3.10}$$

where $Y$ is the real income and $l$ is the amount of leisure enjoyed by the workers. (3.10) is to be maximised subject to the real income and leisure constraints:

$$Y = \frac{W}{P} \cdot N^s \tag{3.11a}$$

and

$$l = H - N^s \tag{3.11b}$$

where $H$ is the total fixed number of hours available to work. A simple way to derive the results of this constrained utility maximisation is to substitute for $Y$ and $l$ from (3.11a) and (3.11b) in (3.10) and rewrite

$$U = U\left(\frac{W}{P}N^s, H - N^s\right) \tag{3.12}$$

the necessary condition for maximising utility is

$$\frac{dU}{dN^s} = 0 \quad \Rightarrow \quad U_1\frac{W}{P} + U_2(-1) = 0$$

$$\Rightarrow \quad \frac{W}{P} = \frac{U_2}{U_1} \tag{3.13}$$

In (3.13), $U_1$ and $U_2$ are, respectively $\frac{\delta U}{\delta Y}$ and $\frac{\delta U}{\delta l}$ and both $Y$ and $l$ depend on $N^s$. So the necessary condition for utility maximisation shows that the supply of labour too depends on the real wage rate:

$$N^s = N^s\left(\frac{W}{P}\right) \tag{3.14}$$

For an aggregate labour supply function like above, $N^{s\prime} > 0$ implying that a rise in real wage raises the labour supply and a fall reduces it. But in an individual worker's income-leisure choice, the net effect of a change in real wage rate on his labour supply depends on the relative strength of the income and substitution effects. As the real wage rate rises, the worker has to work a smaller number of hours to protect his real income and therefore the income effect tends to reduce the supply of labour as the real wage rate rises. On the other hand, a rise in real wage increases the opportunity cost of leisure and this prompts the worker to substitute work for leisure. Thus the substitution effect of a rise in the real wage rate tends to increase the labour supply. For an individual worker, therefore, a rise in real wage increases his supply of labour only if the substitution effect dominates over the income effect.[2] When the income effect dominates over the substitution effect one gets a backward bending supply curve of labour at a higher real wage. For the aggregate supply function of labour

---

2. For the micro implications in detail, the interested reader may look at Greenaway and Shaw [1983] and Levaeic and Rebman [1982].

considered here, we rule out the possibility of a backward bending supply curve of labour and assume $\frac{dN^s}{d\left(\frac{W}{P}\right)} > 0$ i.e., an upward sloping supply curve of labour.

*Equilibrium in The Labour Market*

The condition for equilibrium in the labour market is:

$$N^s = N^d = N \tag{3.15}$$

Now once $N$ is determined by the interaction of supply and demand of labour, the forthcoming supply of output is known by substituting for $N$ in the production function (3.2).

*Supply of Money*

This is still assumed to be fixed by the monetary authorities and therefore, treated as exogenous in the following 3-sector models of aggregate demand and aggregate supply.

## 3.2 A THREE-SECTOR CLASSICAL MODEL OF AGGREGATE DEMAND AND AGGREGATE SUPPLY

Making the labour supply depend on real, rather than money wage is well known as an assumption of the classical model of full-employment equilibrium. In this model involuntary unemployment is impossible. The only cause of unemployment is real wages being set at a level higher than that required for an equilibrium in the labour market. So, unemployment can be remedied, or, employment can be raised, by a general wage-cut. But Keynes argues that even a general wage-cut cannot restore full-employment equilibrium if investment demand is insensitive to the rate of interest or if the demand for idle cash balance becomes infinitely elastic. Pigou (1943) then replied to Keynes's attack on the classical system and showed that the real value of liquid assets, when included in the consumption function, would restore equilibrium in the classical model.

Ignoring the government spending and taxation from the output market, a simple classical model involving the output, money and labour markets can be summarised as

$$S(r) = I(r), \quad S' > 0, I' < 0 \tag{3.16}$$

$$\frac{M}{P} = kY, \quad k > 0 \tag{3.17}$$

$$Y = Y(N), \quad Y' > 0, Y'' < 0 \tag{3.2}$$

$$N^d\left(\frac{W}{P}\right) = N^s\left(\frac{W}{P}\right) = N, \quad N^{d\prime} < 0, N^{s\prime} > 0 \tag{3.18}$$

$$Y'(N) = \frac{W}{P} \tag{3.4}$$

Equation (3.16) summarises the condition for equilibrium in the output market. Real output or the real income[3] received by households is partly consumed and partly saved. That is:

$$Y = C + S(r) \tag{3.11a}$$

Real interest is the reward for sacrificing present consumption. As the rate of interest rises, consumption falls and saving rises. Saving does not take the form of hoarding but it means the supply of loanable funds. For equilibrium in the output market, investment demand has to equal saving. The demand for loanable funds or, the investment demand is inversely related to the rate of interest and the equilibrium rate of interest is determined where saving equals investment. In the classical model, both are highly elastic with respect to the rate of interest — an assumption challenged by Keynes.

Equation (3.17) is the Cambridge version of the quantity theory of money:

$$MV = PY$$

where $V$ is the velocity of circulation of money and $k$ is the reciprocal of $V^T$. So, the quantity theory is used in this context to explain the demand for money $\frac{M^d}{P}$, which is proportional to the individuals' real income. No individual wants money for its own sake but some money must be kept on hand for transactions purposes. This is necessary because of difference in the timing of receipts and disbursements. The classical economists did

---

3. The distinction between disposable and gross income is immaterial in this model since the government sector is not represented. That is, $G$, $T$ are virtually assumed zero.

not emphasise the demand for idle money balances — a feature given prominence by Keynes. The supply of money, $M^s$ is controlled by the monetary authorities. So, the money market in the simple classical model is summarised by

$$M^d = k\,PY, \quad k > 0$$

$$M^s = M$$

and $M^d = M^s = M$ in equilibrium. These three equations are condensed into (3.17) above.

The last three equations of the model (3.2), (3.4) and (3.18) summarise the supply conditions of the output market as determined by the production function (3.2) and employment which, in turn, is determined by the demand for and supply of labour. (3.2) is the short-run production function where output is determined by the labour input alone with a given capital stock and technology. The restrictions on the derivatives of the production function imply the law of diminishing marginal productivity. Full-employment — the most important feature of the classical model is guaranteed by equation (3.18). Equation (3.4) is the necessary condition for maximising profit, in perfectly competitive markets. Both the demand for and the supply of labour depend on the real wage rate as consequences of profit maximisation on the part of the employers and of utility maximisation on the part of the workers respectively.

## The Neutrality of Money or, The Classical Dichotomy

In the above model the only exogenous variable is $M$ and $Y$, $r$, $N$, $W$ and $P$ are the endogenous variables. The model is formulated in such a way that all the real variables, $Y$, $r$, $N$ and $\frac{W}{P}$ are determined completely within the real sector. The equations (3.18) and (3.4) determine employment, $N$, and the real wage rate, $\frac{W}{P}$. Once $N$ is determined, (3.2) yields the full-employment equilibrium level of output. The real rate of interest is solved out from equation (3.16). These are explained in the set of diagrams (a)–(e) of Fig. 3.1. Diagrams (a) and (b) explain full employment, the required real wage and the consequent level of output. Diagram (d) shows the equilibrium rate of interest and equilibrium levels of saving and investment. Fig. (e) determines consumption as the difference between income and saving. An exogenous increase in saving reduces consumption

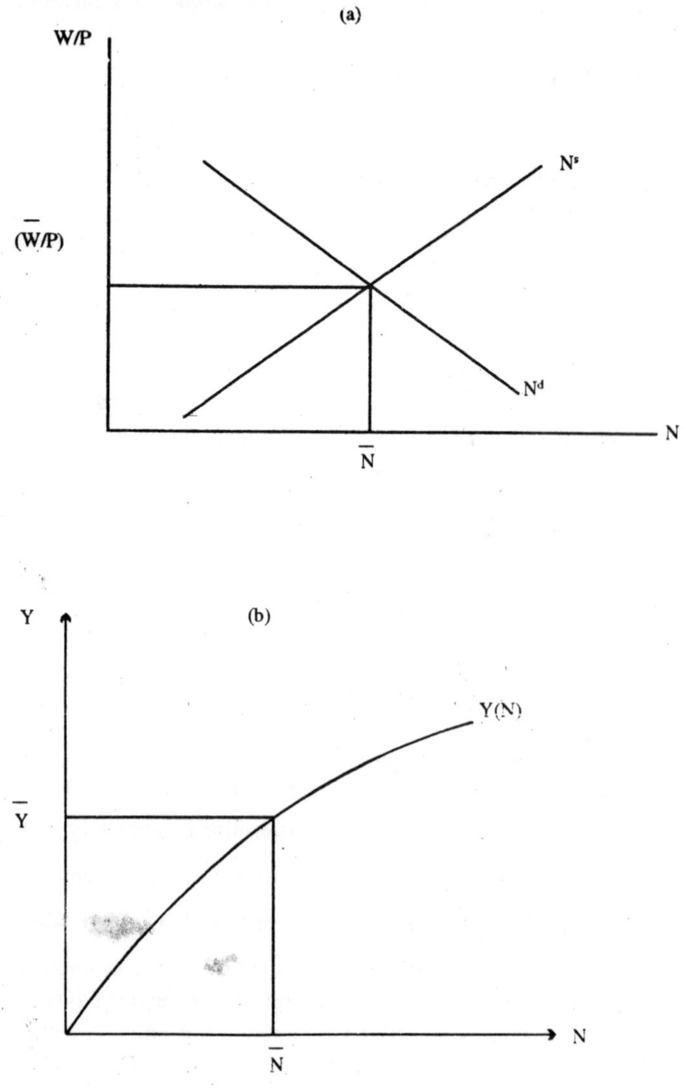


FIG. 3.1: The Real Sector of the Classical Model

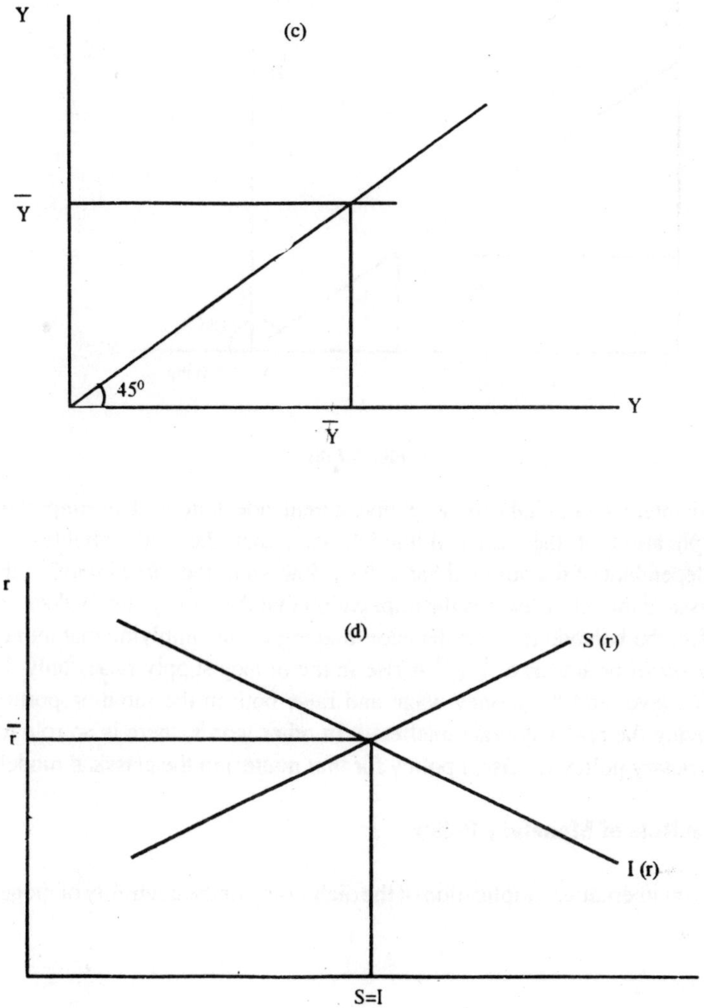


FIG. 3.1: The Real Sector of the Classical Model

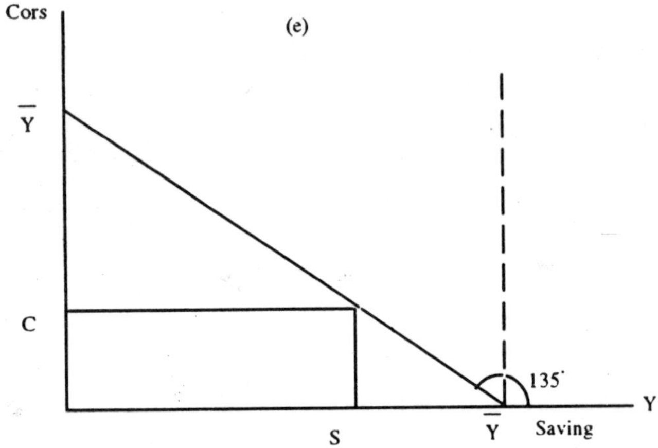


FIG. 3.1 (e)

and interest rate falls to raise investment adequately. This important implication of the classical model, viz., that the real variables are independent of the nominal variables is known as the '*dichotomy*' of the classical model; its twin is the implication that the money supply does not affect the behaviour of the decision-making agents implying that money is *neutral* or acts as a '*veil*'[4] A rise in the money supply raises only the price level and the money wage and raise both in the same proportion leaving the real wage rate unaltered. In other words, there is no role for monetary policy (or fiscal policy for that matter) in the classical model.

## The Role of Monetary Policy

The mathematical implication of the dichotomy or the neutrality of money is:

4. See A.C. Pigou (1943).

$$\frac{\delta Y}{\delta M}=\frac{\delta r}{\delta M}=\frac{\delta N}{\delta M}=\frac{\delta\left(\frac{W}{P}\right)}{\delta M}=0 \tag{3.19}$$

and $$\frac{\delta P}{\delta M}>0, \quad \frac{\delta W}{\delta M}>0 \tag{3.20}$$

(3.19) and (3.20) can be proved easily by differentiating the equations of the classical system w.r.t. $M$ and then applying Cramer's rule. So, the first step is to obtain, respectively,

$$(S'-I')\frac{\delta r}{\delta M}=0 \tag{3.21}$$

$$-\frac{M}{P^2}\frac{\delta P}{\delta M}-k\frac{\delta Y}{\delta M}=-\frac{1}{P} \tag{3.22}$$

$$\frac{\delta Y}{\delta M}-Y'\frac{\delta N}{\delta M}=0 \tag{3.23}$$

$$\frac{1}{P}(N^{d\prime}-N^{s\prime})\frac{\delta W}{\delta M}-\frac{W}{P^2}(N^{d\prime}-N^{s\prime})\frac{\delta P}{\delta M}=0 \tag{3.24}$$

$$Y''\frac{\delta N}{\delta M}-\frac{1}{P}\frac{\delta W}{\delta M}+\frac{W}{P^2}\frac{\delta P}{\delta M}=0 \tag{3.25}$$

Equation (3.21) shows that $\frac{\delta r}{\delta M}=0$ right away. Equation (3.24) readily demonstrates that $\frac{1}{P}\frac{\delta W}{\delta M}-\frac{W}{P^2}\frac{\delta P}{\delta M}=0$ which, in turn, implies that $\frac{\delta\left(\frac{W}{P}\right)}{\delta M}=0$[5] or, that a rise in money stock raises both $P$ and $W$ proportionately leaving the real wage rate unchanged.

Now to apply Cramer's rule, write the Jacobian of the model:

5. Not that

$$\frac{\delta\left(\frac{W}{P}\right)}{\delta M}=\frac{P\frac{\delta W}{\delta M}-W\frac{\delta P}{\delta M}}{P^2}=\frac{1}{P}\frac{\delta W}{\delta M}-\frac{W}{P^2}\cdot\frac{\delta P}{\delta M}$$

$$J = \begin{vmatrix} 0 & S'-I' & 0 & 0 & 0 \\ -K & 0 & 0 & 0 & -\frac{M}{P^2} \\ 1 & 0 & -Y' & 0 & 0 \\ 0 & 0 & 0 & \frac{1}{P} & -\frac{W}{P^2} \\ 0 & 0 & Y'' & -\frac{1}{P} & \frac{W}{P^2} \end{vmatrix} \tag{3.26}$$

Evaluate $J$ by expanding in terms of the cofactors of the elements of the first row. Then,

$$J = \frac{M}{P^2}(S'-I')\,Y''\frac{1}{P} < 0 \tag{3.27}$$

Solving for $\frac{\delta Y}{\delta M}$ etc., by Cramer's rule[6], one obtains

$$\frac{\delta Y}{\delta M} = 0, \quad \frac{\delta r}{\delta M} = 0, \quad \frac{\delta N}{\delta M} = 0 \tag{3.28}$$

$$\frac{\delta W}{\delta M} = \frac{(S'-I')\frac{1}{P}Y''\frac{W}{P^2}}{J} > 0 \tag{3.29}$$

and
$$\frac{\delta P}{\delta M} = \frac{(S'-I')Y''\frac{1}{P^2}}{J} > 0 \tag{3.30}$$

From equations (3.2), (3.4) and (3.18), the equilibrium solution of $Y$ is given solely in terms of the real wage implying that it is independent of the nominal price level or, that, the aggregate supply curve in the $(Y, P)$ axes is vertical, the horizontal intercept representing the full employment level of output. On the other hand, equation (3.17) can be interpreted as the aggregate demand curve for output where a rise in $P$ lowers $Y$ and a fall in $P$ raises it.[7] So, the aggregate demand curve is downward sloping; and the equilibrium price level is determined at the intersection of the aggregate demand and aggregate supply curves.

---

6. Solutions are given in the Appendix to Chapter 3.

7. From (3.17), $\frac{\delta Y}{\delta P} = \frac{1}{k}\left(-\frac{M}{P^2}\right) < 0$

This is shown in Fig. 3.2 where $O\overline{\overline{Y}}$ is the full-employment level of output and *AD* and *AS* are, respectively, the aggregate demand and the aggregate supply curves.

Once again, it is clear from (3.29) and (3.30) that the multipliers, $\frac{\delta W}{\delta M}$ and $\frac{\delta P}{\delta M}$ are both zero if $S' = I' = 0$.

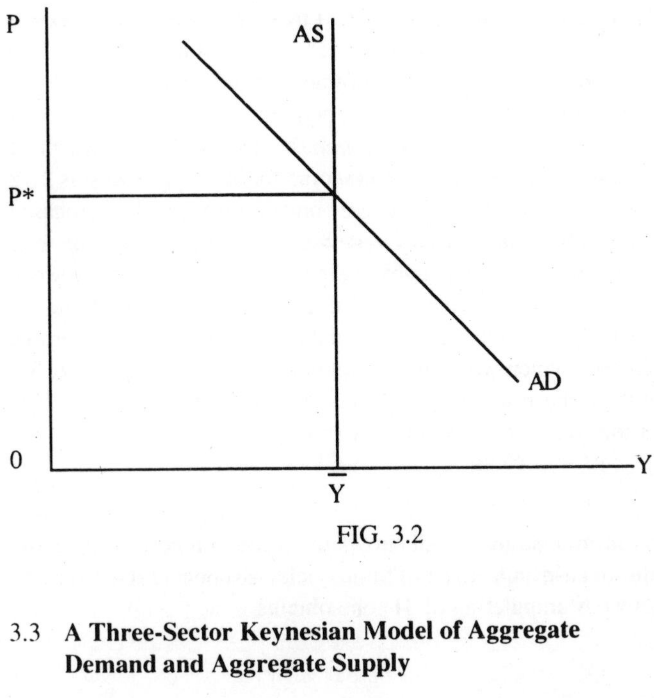


FIG. 3.2

## 3.3 A Three-Sector Keynesian Model of Aggregate Demand and Aggregate Supply

Keynes (1936) raised a number of points against the classical model. The main points on which Keynes disagreed with the classics are summarised below.

(a) Unlike the classics, Keynes emphasised the "idle" demand for money, i.e., the demand for money for speculative purposes. This demand goes up to avoid expected losses and goes down to take advantage of the expected capital gains in the bond market. Bond prices move inversely with the rate of interest meaning that capital gains[8] are expected to occur when the rate of interest is low and capital losses occur when the rate of interest is high. So, the demand for idle money varies inversely with the rate of interest. The inverse relationship between the rate of interest and the price of bonds is discussed in some detail below in the paragraphs enclosed within brackets. The reader may omit this bracketed section without losing continuity.

[Bonds are long-term financial assets which promise the holder an interest payment regularly per year until the year of maturity when the bond is repurchased by the issuer, e.g., Treasury 13 per cent 2000 is a government bond which entitles the holder an interest payment of £ 13 a year until the year 2000 when the government would repurchase the bond at the price of £ 100.[9] British Consols are perpetuities. These are the bonds which never mature, i.e., are never repurchased by the original issuer and the holder earns the specified interest income for ever, e.g., Consols 21/2 per cent pay £ 2.50 a year for ever. These bonds were originally purchased for £ 100 each when interest rates were very low. With rises in the rate of interest on other alternative assets, perpetuities can be traded between people at a price much lower than £ 100, e.g., if the average rate of interest on other assets is 10 per cent, people would be willing to buy the Consols at only £ 25 each which would ensure an interest at the average rate. So, for perpetuities, the price is the reciprocal of the rate of interest. It is derived for the simple example chosen above

$$P_B = \frac{£2.50}{1.1} + \frac{£2.50}{(1.1)^2} + \cdots\cdots \tag{3.31}$$

(3.31) is an infinite series which shows the price of a perpetuity as the present value of an infinite series of future yields discounted at the average rate of interest. Manipulating (3.31) one obtains

8. Capital gains means a rise in the value of bonds due to a rise in their price.
9. See Begg, Fischer and Dornbusch [1984, pp. 506-7].

$$P_B = \frac{£2.50}{1.1}\left[1 + \frac{1}{1.1} + \frac{1}{(1.1)^2} + \cdots\cdots\right]$$

$$\Rightarrow \quad P_B = \frac{£2.50}{1.1}\left[\frac{1-\left(\frac{1}{1.1}\right)^{\infty-}}{1-\frac{1}{1.1}}\right] = \frac{£2.50}{1.1}\left[\frac{1.1}{.1}\right]$$

$$\Rightarrow \quad P_B = \frac{£2.50}{.1} = £25 \tag{3.32}$$

This simple exercise shows that the price of a bond which pays the holder a fixed amount of money per year for ever is the reciprocal of the rate of interest].

To the speculative component varying inversely with the rate of interest, Keynes added transaction and precautionary demands for money. These two together constitute the demand for active balances varying directly with the households' real income. Adding all three components together, the total demand for liquidity is

$$\frac{M^d}{P} = L(Y, r), \quad L_1 > 0, \quad L_2 < 0 \tag{3.33}$$

The equilibrium condition in the money market as given in (2.10) now yields

$$L(Y, r) = \frac{M}{P} \tag{3.34}$$

Unlike in the classical model, equilibrium in the money market determines the equilibrium rate of interest at each given level of income. The speculative demand for money in the Keynesian system is thought to be highly interest elastic. At a low, critical, rate of interest the speculative demand for money can be infinitely elastic w.r.t. the interest rate. This is what Keynes called the 'liquidity trap'. At this critical rate of interest, no rise in the real money supply can bring the rate of interest down any further or make the monetary policy effective.

In Fig. 3.3, $r^e$ is the equilibrium rate of interest and $r^*$ is the critical rate which opens up the liquidity trap.

(b) Secondly, in opposition to the classics, Keynes argued that saving and investment are inelastic w.r.t. the rate of interest and in some cases, the rate at which saving and investment are equal may even be negative. The complete insensitivity of investment demand would imply $I' = 0$.

Keynes replaced the classical saving function $S(r)$ by $S(Y-T)$ with $0<S'<1$. This reflects Keynes's view on consumption which he made a stable function of disposable income:

$$C = C(Y-T), \quad 0 < C' < 1 \tag{3.35}$$

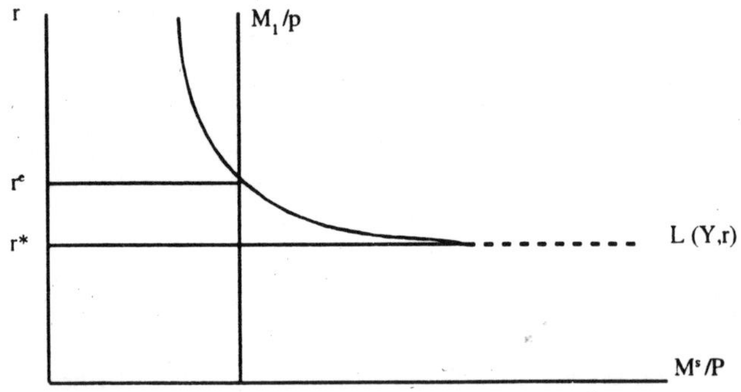


FIG. 3.3

(c) The most important difference between the Classical and the Keynesian models is regarding the cause of unemployment and the implied role of the money wage. In the classical theory unemployment is due to real wages being "too high" and in the Keynesian to aggregate demand being "too low". So the classics prescribed a reduction in real wages (or in money wages when the price level is fixed) and the Keynesians an increased public spending, tax-reduction etc. However, a formal analysis of the link between an insufficient effective demand in the output market and the demand for labour in the labour market did not come before Patinkin's (1956, 1965) contribution on the subject. In the conventional interpretation of the *General Theory* initiated by Leontief (1937) the major departure of Keynes from the classics was viewed as labour supply depending not on the real wage but on the money wage.[10] On this interpretation $N^s(W)$ replaces the Classical labour supply function $N^s(W/P)$ and destroys the classical dichotomy by establishing important links between the real and the monetary sectors of the economy. Like in the Classical model, demand for labour depends on the real wage. In this light, involuntary unemployment in the Keynesian model originally

10. Leontief, W. (1937), pp. 195-6.

caused by an insufficient demand for output persists due to the inflexibility of money wage in the downward direction. In the midst of unemployment workers refuse to accept a cut in their money wage but may not be reluctant to accept a cut in their real wage through a rise in the price level. A rise in the price level affects all workers in the same way but a fall in money wage can destroy some of the wage differentials previously enjoyed by the workers. A rise in government spending raises the price level and therefore raises thc demand for labour by lowering the real wage. This traditional interpretation of the Keynesian macro model will be discussed first in the following two sections. The theory of involuntary unemployment and the reinterpretation of the General Theory will be taken up in 3.6.2.

**The Keynesian 3-Sector Model without Involuntary Unemployment**

This model is obtained by maintaining the condition for equilibrium in the labour market along with the special features of the Keynesian system discussed so far.

$$Y - C(Y - T) - I(r) = G \qquad (3.36)$$

$$L(Y, r) - \frac{M}{P} = 0 \qquad (3.34)$$

$$Y - Y(N) = 0 \qquad (3.37)$$

$$Y'(N) - \frac{W}{P} = 0 \qquad (3.38)$$

$$N^d(W/P) - N^s(W) = 0 \qquad (3.39)$$

Equation (3.36) is the condition for equilibrium: $Y = C + I + G$ in the output market and therefore, it is the equation to the IS curve. Equation (3.34) is the equation to the LM curve.

The equation (3.39) restates the condition for equilibrium in the labour market incorporating the Keynesian labour supply function. Since, the demand for labour equals the supply of labour in equilibrium, we have only one endogenous variable, $N = N^d = N^s$ in equilibrium. The rest of the equations are the same as in the previous model. In the system of equations (3.36) down to (3.39), there are 5 endogenous variables, *Y, r, N, P* and *W* and 3 exogenous variables, *G, M* and *T*. Although the present model includes the labour market equilibrium and conditions (3.2) and

(3.4) of the classical system, it differs from the classical model of the section 3.2 in a few important respects: (a) It is no longer possible to dichotomise the model into a real and a monetary sector and, therefore, (b) real output, employment etc., are dependent on both fiscal and monetary policies; (c) interest-insensitivity of investment demand and/or infinite elasticity of the speculative demand for money still reduces (raises) the effectiveness of monetary (fiscal) policy to a minimum (maximum) and (d) most importantly, wage-price flexibility may not restore full-employment equilibrium. While it is easy to note point: (a) from the layout of the model, points (b)–(d) would be proved in the following sections. Equation (3.37), (3.38) and (3.39) can solve for $Y$, $N$ and $W$ for given $P$ and once $Y$ is known, (3.36) and (3.34) can yield $r$ and $P$. So, the real and the nominal variables ($W$ and $P$) are interdependent.

## 3.4 FISCAL AND MONETARY POLICIES IN THE KEYNESIAN MODEL

Keynesians assign a very important role to fiscal policy whereas the role of monetary policy is undermined by the existence of a liquidity trap. In the case of an infinitely elastic demand for money w.r.t. the rate of interest, a rise in money supply gets fully absorbed into speculative balances without raising output or employment. It is government spending which has expansionary effects on output and employment with some crowding out effects on private investment. But unlike in the classical model this is only a partial crowding out which leaves some expansionary effects on real output and employment.

The role of fiscal and monetary policies is explained below by working out the various multipliers from the 5 equations of the Keynesian model.

### *The Multipliers in the Keynesian Model*

Applying Cramer's rule to the system of equations

$$J \begin{vmatrix} \delta Y / \delta G \\ \delta r / \delta G \\ \delta N / \delta G \\ \delta W / \delta G \\ \delta P / \delta G \end{vmatrix} = \begin{vmatrix} 1 \\ 0 \\ 0 \\ 0 \\ 0 \end{vmatrix} \tag{3.40}$$

the fiscal policy multipliers are obtained as

$$\frac{\delta Y}{\delta G} = \frac{1}{(1-C') + I'\frac{L_1}{L_2} + I'\frac{M}{P^2}Y''\frac{N^{d'} - PN^{s'}}{P} \times \frac{1}{L_2 Y' N^{s'} \frac{W}{P^2}}} \tag{3.41}$$

$\Rightarrow \quad \frac{\delta Y}{\delta G} > 0$ and this expansionary effect is the strongest when $I' = 0$ or when $L_2 = -\infty$. In these cases, the multiplier reduces to $\frac{1}{1-C'}$, i.e., to the multiplier in the simple IS-LM model. To see the effect of fiscal policy on employment, work out the value of the multiplier, $\frac{\delta N}{\delta G}$. From the Appendix 3.A.2

$$\frac{\delta N}{\delta G} = \frac{1}{Y'\left[(1-C') + I'\frac{L_1}{L_2}\right] + I'\frac{M}{P^2}Y''\frac{(N^{d'} - PN^{s'})}{P} \times \frac{1}{L_2 N^{s'} \frac{W}{P^2}}} \tag{3.44}$$

$$\Rightarrow \quad \frac{\delta N}{\delta G} > 0$$

(3.44) implies that the value of $\frac{\delta N}{\delta G}$ is the highest when $L_2 = -\infty$ or, when $I' = 0$.

The important monetary policy multipliers are

$$\frac{\delta Y}{\delta M} = \frac{I' \times \frac{1}{P}}{L_2(1-C') + I'\frac{L_1}{L_2} + I'\frac{M}{P^2} \times \frac{N^{d'} - PN^{s'}}{P} \times \frac{1}{L_2 Y' N^{s'} \frac{W}{P^2}}} \tag{3.45}$$

$$\frac{\delta r}{\delta M} = \frac{-(1-C')\frac{1}{P}Y'\frac{W}{P^2}N^{s'}}{J} < 0 \tag{3.46}$$

Similarly, as shown in the appendix.

$$\frac{\delta W}{\delta M} = \frac{-I'\frac{1}{P}Y''N^{d'}\frac{W}{P^2}}{J} \tag{3.47}$$

and $$\frac{\delta P}{\delta M} = \frac{-I'\frac{1}{P}Y''N^{d'}\frac{1}{P}}{J} \tag{3.48}$$

(3.47) and (3.48) again imply that

$$\frac{1}{P}\frac{\delta W}{\delta M} - \frac{W}{P^2}\frac{\delta P}{\delta M} = 0$$

or that

$\frac{\delta\left(\frac{W}{P}\right)}{\delta M} = 0$, i.e., a rise in money supply raises money wage and the price level equi-proportionately.

### 3.5 KEYNES AND THE CLASSICS

So far we have noted a number of special features of the classical system viz., the dichotomy between the real and the monetary sectors implying the neutrality of money and no role of fiscal or monetary policy to alter the level of real output or employment. Full employment is guaranteed by complete flexibility of money wage and prices and equilibrium in the output market by a flexibility of the real rate of interest. These features are not due to the explicit exclusion of the government sector, or, the speculative demand for money, or, of the consumption function from the classical model. These Keynesian elements are trivial in the sense that their inclusion does not alter any of the conclusions of the classical model noted so far. The Keynesian elements which are vital and can alter the conclusions of the classical model are the assumptions of the money illusion in the labour supply function, and of the wage-price rigidity. It can be shown that as long as the labour supply still depends on the real wage and as long as wages, prices and interest rates are flexible both upwards and downwards, the classical model retains its conclusions of full-employment, dichotomy and ineffectiveness of fiscal or monetary policy to change real output and employment. The following 3-sector model is a modified classical model including some of the demand functions of the Keynesian model. Turnovsky (1979) has presented a very similar model to designate the classical system.

$$Y - C(Y-T) - I(r) - G = 0 \quad (3.36)$$

$$L(Y, r) - \frac{M}{P} = 0 \quad (3.34)$$

$$Y - Y(N) = 0 \quad (3.37)$$

$$Y'(N) - \frac{W}{P} = 0 \quad (3.39)$$

$$N^d\left(\frac{W}{P}\right) - N^s\left(\frac{W}{P}\right) = 0 \quad (3.18)$$

All these equations have been explained before. (3.18) is a restatement of the equilibrium condition in the labour market when both the demand for and the supply of labour depend on the real wage as explained in equations (3.5) and (3.14). Since demand and supply are equal in equilibrium, the system has only one endogenous variable, $N$, on account of employment. The classical model as presented above has 5 endogenous variables $Y$, $r$, $N$, $W$ and $P$ and 3 exogenous variables $G$, $M$ and $T$. The nominal variables, $P$, $M$ and $W$ do not affect the equilibrium values of the real variables $Y$, $r$ and $N$ because the labour market equations (3.42) and (3.18) determine $N$ and $\frac{W}{P}$ and then, the production function (3.37) determines $Y$; once $Y$ is known, $r$ is determined from the equilibrium condition in the output market, or, the IS equation (3.36). Once $Y$ and $r$ are known, the money market equilibrium condition determines $P$ in terms of $M$. With $P$ and $\frac{W}{P}$ both known, the money wage $W$ follows from the definition of the real wage rate. It is clear that the money supply $M$ or the price level, $P$, does not enter in the solution of $Y$ or $N$ directly. $Y$ depends on $N$ and, therefore, on, $\frac{W}{P}$, via $N$. But in the classical model, changes in $M$ affect $W$ and $P$ in the same direction and equi-proportionately—leaving the real wage rate unchanged. Through the IS equation, $r$ depends on $G$ such that a rise in $G$ raises the rate of interest and this crowds private investment out completely, leaving real output, $Y$ unchanged. Since these multipliers have been derived for very similar models above, the reader should verify the following results for himself.

In the classical model comprising equations (3.36) down to (3.18)

$$\frac{\delta Y}{\delta G}=0, \quad \frac{\delta N}{\delta G}=0, \quad \frac{\delta Y}{\delta M}=0, \quad \frac{\delta N}{\delta M}=0$$

$$\frac{\delta r}{\delta M}=\frac{-Y''\frac{M}{P^2}\cdot\frac{1}{P}(N^{d\prime}-N^{s\prime})}{J}>0$$

$$\frac{\delta P}{\delta M}=\frac{I'\frac{1}{P^2}(N^{d\prime}-N^{s\prime})Y''}{J}>0$$

$$\frac{\delta W}{\delta M}=\frac{I'\frac{W}{P^2}(N^{d\prime}-N^{s\prime})Y''\frac{1}{P}}{J}>0$$

where, $J$ is the Jacobian of the classical model and

$$J = I'(N^{d\prime} - N^{s\prime})Y''\frac{M}{P^2} \cdot \frac{1}{P} < 0$$

$$\frac{\delta W}{\delta G} = 0, \quad \frac{\delta P}{\delta G} = 0$$

The above multipliers show that the classical model retains all its conclusions noted in section 3.2. The aggregate supply curve is vertical as well.

### Unemployment and Wage-Price Flexibility

In the classical model, the only cause of unemployment is a high real wage rate and such unemployment can be cured by a general wage cut. To show the effect of a general wage reduction on employment, the money wage is assumed to be exogenous in the model and the equilibrium or the full-employment condition is dropped from the model. Kogiku (1968) presented a similar, but not identical model. If the money wage is assumed exogenous and supply of labour infinitely elastic at this wage rate, then employment or the demand for labour can be shown to increase with a fall in the money wage rate. This result is shown in the Appendix 3.A.3 in the context of a four equation model. With $W$ as exogenous one can determine the real wage once $P$ is known. So the number of endogenous variables reduces to four and the model comprises equations (3.36), (3.34), (3.37) and (3.38) where $N$ now stands for $N^d$ and $G$, $T$, $M$ and $W$ are the exogenous variables. The signs of the derivatives $\partial N/\partial W$ and $\partial P/\partial W$ shown in the Appendix 3.A.3.1 imply that a cut in money wage raises the demand for labour and leads to a fall in the price level.

The result in (3.49) also proves Keynes' argument that a wage-cut would fail to restore full-employment in the economy if either the investment demand is interest-inelastic or if the demand for money is infinitely interest-elastic.

### The Pigou Effect

Pigou (1943) tried to reinstate the classical model by introducing the *real balance effect* in the consumption function. A fall in the price level following the wage-cut increases the real value of liquid assets and this affects consumption positively. The new consumption function incorporating the Pigou effect:

$$C(Y-T, M/P)$$

in the classical model restores $\frac{\delta N^d}{\delta W}<0, \frac{\delta Y^d}{\delta P}<0$ etc., even when $I'=0$ or $L_2=-\infty$. Modifying the IS equation to

$$Y-C(Y-T, M/P)-I(r)=G \tag{3.50}$$

and leaving the rest of the equations unaltered, the crucial derivative.[11]

$$\frac{\delta N^d}{\delta W}=\frac{C_2'\frac{M}{P^2}\frac{1}{P}}{-Y'\frac{W}{P^2}\left(1-C_1'+I'\frac{L_1'}{L_2'}\right)+Y''\frac{M}{P^2}(C_2'+I'/L_2')} \tag{3.51}$$

From (3.51), it follows that $\frac{\delta N^d}{\delta W}<0$ even if $L_2'=-\infty$ or $I'=0$. In these cases

$$\frac{\delta N^d}{\delta W} \text{ reduces to } \frac{C_2'\frac{M}{P^2}\frac{1}{P}}{Y''\frac{M}{P^2}C_2'-Y'\frac{W}{P^2}(1-C_1')}<0$$

From equation (3.50), it follows that the IS curve will shift to the right due to a rise in the real money balances. According to Keynes, the increase in real money balances only shifts the LM curve to the right which, in the presence of the liquidity trap, would fail to lower the real rate of interest and therefore would leave employment and real income unchanged. The Pigou effect shows that rises in real income and employment can be achieved quite independently of any interest rate effect. A proportionate fall in the price level following a general cut in money wages increases the real value of money balances and this will stimulate consumption spending of the private sector. So, providing wages and prices are both flexible downward, a continuous outward shift of the IS curve will generate a rise in real income and employment. The slope of the LM curve depends on the interest elasticity of the real demand for money and the slope of the IS curve on the interest elasticity of the real demand for investment. The higher the interest elasticity of the real demand for money the flatter will be the LM curve and when the liquidity trap is operating the LM curve is horizontal. When both the IS and the LM curves shift rightward due to the Pigou effect, real income and employment can rise even if the real rate of interest does not fall. This is shown in Fig. 3.3b.

---

11. This $Y^d$ means the aggregate demand for output.

In the horizontal range of the LM curve, i.e., in the presence of the liquidity trap a shift of the IS curve leads to a rise in the real income and when the LM is upward sloping the shifts of the IS and LM together lead to a partial crowding out and a rise in real income.

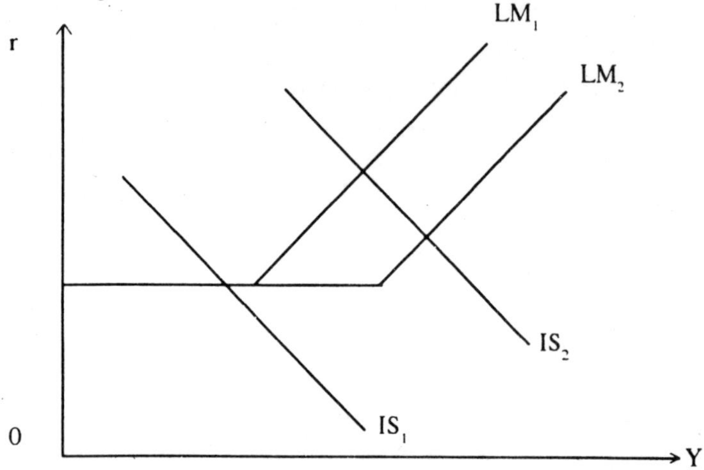


FIG. 3.3b: The Pigou Effect

In Leijonhufvud's view, the Pigou effect was not highlighted in the Keynesian model, not because of ignorance, but because of its irrelevance to the central issue of unemployment. Leijonhufvud and others presented an alternative interpretation of the General Theory, some traits of which will be taken up later on. According to Mayer (1959) the Pigou effect has limited empirical significance.

## 3.6 The Microfoundations of Classical and Keynesian Macroeconomic Systems

The discussion of the Macroeconomic System presented so far is based on the conventional interpretation of the Keynesian and the Classical theories. The interpretation of $N^s = N^s\left(\frac{W}{P}\right)$ as Classical and of $N^s = N^s(W)$ as Keynesian labour supply functions originated in Leontief's (1937) review of the General Theory. In Leontief's critical appraisal, the main difference between Classical and Keynesian theories is that the former assumes demand and supply functions of all commodities and labour to be homogeneous of degree 0 in prices whereas the latter drops this assumption for the labour supply function.[12] Homogeneity of degree 0 in prices implies that the demand and supply of commodities depend on relative prices and those of labour depend on the real wage rate. Dropping this assumption of homogeneity for labour supply function destroys the Classical dichotomy or the neutrality of money in the Keynesian model. Leontief added that the homogeneity postulate of the Classical theory followed from the rational optimising behaviour of economic agents whereas the Keynesian labour supply function was a denial of such behaviour. In the foregoing sections, the Classical labour supply function (3.14) was derived from a utility maximising behaviour of the workers whereas the Keynesian labour supply function in (3.39) reflected the assumption of money-illusion on the part of the workers.

This conventioanl interpretation of the two systems was accepted under the name of "neo-classical synthesis" till around the mid-sixties. Unemployment occurs in the Classical system only when the real wage rate exceeds the market clearing level, say, through trade union demands and the adjustment mechanism is that the unemployed workers bid down the money wage rate and thereby bring the economy back to full-employment equilibrium. The adjustment mechanism in the Classical economics is that prices rise (fall) in excess demand (supply) conditions and thereby equilibrium or demand-supply equality is restored. In this synthesis, Classical macroeconomic theory was shown to follow from an analysis of Walrasian general equilibrium.

In the conventional presentation of the Keynesian system, unemployment is not so easy to get rid of because of wage-price rigidity, liquidity trap, interest inelasticity of investment etc. So, Keynes's is one of the first recognitions that market clearing will not occur. This implication of Keynesian economics was highlighted and developed into a microeconomic analysis of general disequilibrium by Clower (1965), Leijonhufvud (1968), Barro and Grossman (1973). The Clower-Leijonhufvud work provided a choice-theoretic basis to Keynes's behavioural assumptions lacking in the previous interpretation of the General Theory. Whereas Clower developed the implications of involuntary unemployment for the demand for current output, Patinkin (1956, 1965) examined the implications of an insufficient demand for output for the

12. Addison, J. and Burton, J. (1982), p. 3.

demand for labour. In these attempts at reinterpretation of the General Theory, Keynesian economics is shown to fit the framework of a general disequilibrium process. A more recent appraisal of the General Theory is due to Tobin and Trevithick who not only reinterpret the labour supply function but also make important contributions to the Keynesian analysis of the dynamics of the wage-price process.

### 3.6.1 Walrasian General Equilibrium: Micro Foundations of Classical Economics

The distinctive feature of the Walrasian paradigm is interdependence of exchange. Agents exchange directly through a process of tatonnement and in the framework of a general equilibrium, the transactions and the demands are identical for each good and each agent. In other words desired trades are always realised.

*Walrasian Model without Money*

The most important result of a pure barter Walrasian economy is that there exists a set of $(m-1)$ relative prices for an $m$-good economy at which all markets will be cleared. It can be derived from an analysis of constrained utility maximisation on the part of each atomistic trader having a fixed initial endowment of the $j$th good. Let $i = 1, 2, \cdots n$ be the number of traders in the economy. Then, the utility function of the $i$th trader can be written as

$$V_i(q_{i1}, q_{i2}, \cdots q_{im}), \quad i = 1, 2, \cdots n \tag{3.52}$$

where $q_{ij}$ is the quantity of the $j$th good consumed by the $i$th trader. The utility function (3.52) is maximised subject to the budget constraint of the $i$th trader:

$$y_i = \sum_{j=1}^{m} p_j \bar{q}_{ij}, \quad i = 1, 2, \cdots n \tag{3.53}$$

where $y_i$, is the income of the $i$th trader and $p_j$ the price of the $j$th good. The excess demand of the $i$th trader for the $j$th good can be defined as

$$E_{ij} = q_{ij} - \bar{q}_{ij} \tag{3.54}$$

The income in (3.54) is understood in the sense of the amount of purchasing power the trader would have if he sold his entire endowment. Given the budget constraint, the value of total consumption must equal total income.

$$y_i = \sum_{j=1}^{m} p_j q_{ij} \Rightarrow \sum p_j q_{ij} = \sum p_j \bar{q}_{ij} \tag{3.55}$$

$$\Rightarrow \sum p_j (q_{ij} - \bar{q}_{ij}) = 0 \Rightarrow \sum_{j=1}^{m} p_i E_{ij} = 0$$

By virtue of (3.54), the utility function too can be rewritten in terms of excess demands:

$$V_i = V_i(E_{i1} + \bar{q}_{i1}, E_{i2} + \bar{q}_{i2}, \cdots \bar{q}_{im} + E_{im}) \tag{3.56}$$

(3.56) is to be maximised subject to the budget constraint (3.55). The Langrangaean is

$$L = V_i(E_{i1} + \bar{q}_{i1}, \cdots E_{im} + \bar{q}_{im}) - \lambda \sum_{j=1}^{m} p_j E_{ij} \tag{3.57}$$

(3.57) is a function of $E_{il}, \cdots E_{im}$ and $\lambda$.

Eliminating $\lambda$ from the first order conditions, the $m$ conditions for $i$th trader's equilibrium are given by

$$\frac{\left(\frac{\delta V_i}{\delta E_{ij}}\right)}{\left(\frac{\delta V_i}{\delta E_{ik}}\right)} = \frac{p_j}{p_k}, \quad j \neq k \tag{3.58}$$

and $$\sum_{j=1}^{m} p_j E_{ij} = 0 \tag{3.55}$$

In an $m - 1$ commodity economy there would be $(m - 1)$ equations like (3.58), and the original constraint (3.55) from which one could solve for the $m$ excess demands in terms of prices:

$$E_{ij} = E_{ij}(p_1, p_2, \cdots p_m) \tag{3.59}$$

An aggregate excess demand function for the $j$th good can be obtained by summing (3.54) over the $n$ traders, so,

$$E_j = \sum_{i=1}^{n} E_{ij}(p_1, p_2, \cdots p_m) = E_j(p_1, \cdots p_m) \tag{3.60}$$

For general equilibrium to exist all over the Walrasian economy, aggregate excess demand must equal zero for each of the $m$ goods:

$$E_j(p_1, \cdots p_m) = 0 \quad \text{for } j = 1, \cdots m \tag{3.61}$$

(3.61) must contain $m$ independent equations to enable the market clearing solution for each price variable. A market clears when excess demand equals zero in that market. That the system of $m$ equations like (3.61) contain only $(m-1)$ independent equations can be seen by summing the budget constraints (3.55) for all $n$ traders. These are the identities to be satisfied for any set of price.[13] Summing (3.55) over $n$

$$\sum_{i=j}^{n}\sum_{j=i}^{n} p_j E_{ij} = \sum_{j=1}^{m} p_j E_j = 0 \tag{3.62}$$

Since $\sum_{i=1}^{n} E_{ij}$ is the aggregate excess demand for the $j$th good, $E_j$. (3.62) is an identity called *Walras' Law*. For general equilibrium $E_j$ must equal zero for each $j$ but because of Walras' Law (3.62), if $E_j = 0$ for $j = 1, 2, \cdots m-1$, the remaining market must also be in equilibrium implying that one obtains only $(m-1)$ independent equations from the system (3.61). So, the $m$th equation is *redundant*. However this is not a problem because the number of variables can be reduced by 1 by expressing $E_j$ as functions of relative prices. Since the excess demand functions are homogeneous of degree zero in absolute prices, any one good can be chosen as a *numeraire* and

$$E_j = E_j\left(\frac{p_1}{p_j}, \frac{p_2}{p_j}, \cdots \frac{p_{j+1}}{p_j}, 1, \frac{p_m}{p_j}, \cdots \frac{p_m}{p_j}\right) \tag{3.63}$$

can be expressed as a function of $(m-1)$ relative prices. (3.63) can be completely solved for $(m-1)$ exchange ratios or relative prices under general equilibrium.

The above analysis shows that a set of $(m-1)$ relative prices consistent with Walrasian general equilibrium exists in this simple barter economy without money and without new production. The next question to answer is how this set of prices is arrived at. This is the job of a fictional *auctioneer*. The auctioneer tries alternative sets of prices until he finds the market clearing set of relative prices. This process by which the auctioneer groups towards the equilibrium set of relative prices and quantities is known as *tatonnement*. Trade occurs only at market clearing prices.

---

13. See Henderson, J.M. and Quandt, R.E. (1980, p. 235).

*Walrasian System Including Money*

Including money and time into the Walrasian economy implies that there is no need for an auctioneer because money performs as a medium of exchange. Including money in the $i$th trader's utility function (3.56) becomes

$$V_i = V_i(E_{i1} + \bar{q}_{i1}, \cdots E_{im} + \bar{q}_{im}, \quad E_{im+1} + \bar{q}_{im+1}) \tag{3.56}$$

where $\bar{q}_{im+1}$ is the initial money holding and $E_{im+1}$ the excess demand for money. The budget constraint (3.55) changes to

$$\sum_{j=1}^{m} p_j E_{ij} + E_{im+1} = 0 \tag{3.55}$$

since the price of money is 1.

Each trader is assumed to hold a quantity of money which is a fixed proportion, $k_i$ of the value of his initial endowment:

$$q_{im+1} = k_i \sum_{j=1}^{m} p_j \bar{q}_{ij} \tag{3.64}$$

Equation (3.64) is the micro counterpart of the quantity theory equation which can be derived by assuming all $k_i$ to be equal to $k$. The analysis of utility maximisation and general equilibrium can be carried out in the previous manner but these are not repeated here. General equilibrium can only be established when all markets, including the money market, are cleared. The economy can be separated into real and monetary sectors (the "classical dichotomy") if the excess demand functions for goods and money are homogeneous of degree 0 in prices and of degree 1 in money endowment.[14] The aggregate counterpart of (3.64) gives the total demand for money which must equal total initial money endowment:

$$\sum_{i=1}^{n} q_{im+1} = K \sum_{i} \sum_{j} p_j \bar{q}_{ij} = \sum_{i=1}^{n} \bar{q}_{im+1} \tag{3.65}$$

(3.65) determines the absolute price level and the aggregate excess demand equations for $m$ goods determine $(m-1)$ relative prices.

In principle the Walrasian pure exchange economy can also be translated into one with production. Traders are now divided into two classes — households and firms. The former own labour and services and

---

14. See Henderson, J.M. and Quandt, R.E. (1980, p. 252).

sometimes an ownership claim and firms own capital goods. The households sell labour to finance their consumption and firms hire labour and produce output with capital and labour. Both firms and households are price takers (the assumption of perfect competition in the classical model) in factor and output markets and the firms are assumed to maximise profit and households, utility at given prices and income. The households budget constraint is that the value of purchases plus money held at the end of a trading period must equal to total income from factor services and ownership rights plus the amount of money held at the beginning of the period. Clearly this is the "micro" or disaggregated version of the decision problem of a representative supplier of labour in the classical macro model analysed in 3.1 price. But this assumption is invalidated by a downward shift of the aggregate demand curve (or by the deflationary gap) in the output market. So, the demand function $N^d = N^d(W/P)$ undergoes a change in its form, though not in the variables. If the firms cannot sell all they want of a given good, they try to recover the shortage of their revenue by lowering the prices of other goods as well as of labour. The real wage rate offered for the same input of labour as before is less. The dynamic process of intermarket pressures is demonstrated by the following two Fig. 3.4(i) and 3.4(ii) — one for the commodity and the other for the labour markets.For the sake of convenience, we have drawn straight line demand and supply diagrams. The demand for labour associated with the aggregate demand curve $E_1$ and equilibrium output $Y_0$ is $N_0$ and it is consistent with full employment at equilibrium real wage $(W/P)^*$. If the demand for output falls and the curve shifts from $E_1$ to $E_2$, a deflationary gap, $d_1g_1$ is created. In this situation firms fail to sell their entire planned output $Y_0$ and, therefore are unable to pay for $N_0$ labour at the rate of $(W/P)^*$. So they either demand an input smaller than $N_0$ at the unchanged real wage $(W/P)^*$ or offer a rate lower than $(W/P)^*$ for the same input $N_0$. The demand for labour is no longer given by a point on $N^d(W/P)$. If, due to such dynamic intermarket forces, the firms are at a point like '*D*' on Fig. 3.4(ii), then the output produced would be $Y_2 = Y_2(N_2)$ and there would still exist an excess supply of output of $d_2g_2$. The same market pressure would lead the firms to demand an even smaller input of labour at the unchanged real wage rate. It is only when the demand for labour is reduced to $N_1$ with a corresponding reduction of output to $Y_1$ that the firms would be able to sell all they produce. Since $ABE^*N^d$ is no longer the demand curve for labour in the situation of an excess supply in the output market, the point $H$ in Fig. 3.4(ii) represents an excess supply of labour $HE^*$ at the unchanged real wage $(W/P)^*$. Thus, Patinkin provides the employers' side of the story in the situation of an involuntary unemployment. If the employers cannot sell all they want they cannot employ all they want. An excess supply in the output market manifests itself in an excess supply in labour market. The conventional Keynesian analysis concentrates mainly on the involuntariness of the workers — they are not receiving as much employment as they would like at the real wage rate $(W/P)^*$ but Patinkin shows a similar involuntariness on the part of the employers who are unable to provide as much employment as they would normally like at $(W/P)^*$. A major contribution of Patinkin was to change the static equilibrium framework into a dynamic framework of cyclical movements of real wage and employment. A fall in commodity demand leads to a fall in employment. If real wages fall in response to this then the decline in employment and that in real wages may go hand in hand during the downswing. But this is not the only possibility.[15] If, at some intermediate point, some action is taken to restore the demand for output, say from $E_2$ to $E_3$, this may lead to rising real wage and rising employment (or falling excess supply of labour) occurring simultaneously.

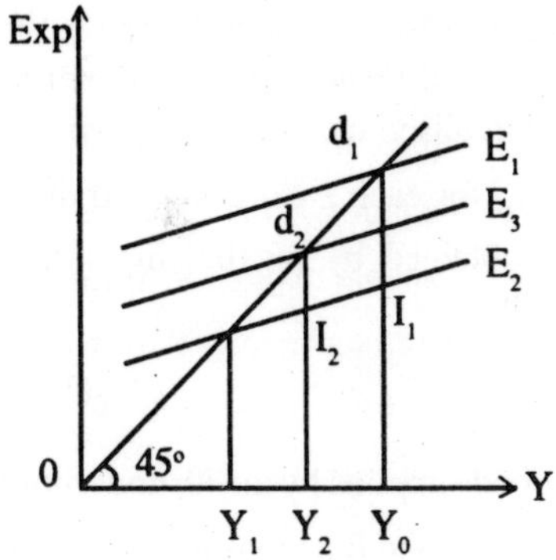


Output market

FIG. 3.4(i):

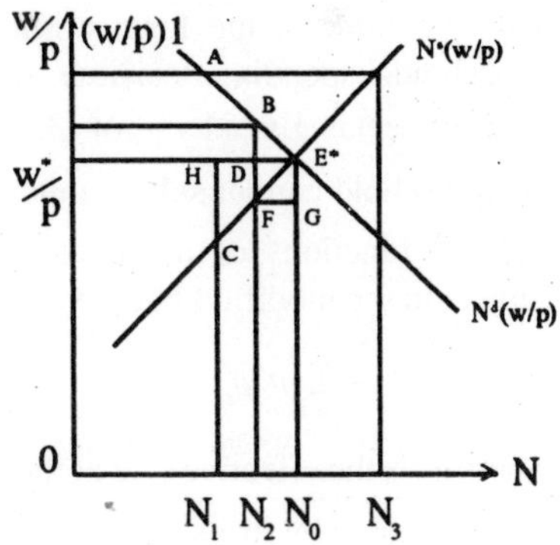


Labour market

FIG. 3.4(ii):

15. Barro, R.J. and Grossman, H.I. (1973, p. 87).

The disequilibrium analysis was subsequently developed in terms of the *notional* and the *effective* demand and supply by Clower, Barrow and Grossman, Benassy (1982) and others.

*Clower*

In Clower's reappraisal, "Keynesian economics is price theory without Walras' Law and price theory with Walras' Law is just a special case of Keynesian economics"[16] He demonstrates that in Keynesian theory market excess-demand functions include quantities as well as prices as explanatory variables and these functions do not satisfy Walras' Law except in the conditions of full employment.

In conditions of disequilibrium market transactions are the minimum of the planned market demand and the planned market supply. A logical implication of disequilibrium is that goods will accumulate or decumulate somewhere in the economic system. The development of a stock-flow analysis necessitates the introduction of assets as an additional variable in the market excess demand functions. More importantly, differences between planned and realised purchases and sales of households in the situation of disequilibrium should be developed in terms of a "dual-decision hypothesis". When involuntary unemployment exists households' realised current income is less than their notional current income and, accordingly, the former imposes an operative constraint on the households' spending decisions. The notional income of the $i$-th household (trader) is given by $y_i$ of (3.53) but realised income $\overline{y}_i < y_i$ because the household cannot sell as much as $\overline{q}_{ij}$ for each $j$. So the constrained demand functions of the households obtained by maximising utility subject to the modified budget constraint:

$$\overline{y}_i = \sum_{j=1}^{m} p_i q_{ij}^e \qquad (3.66)$$

where $q_{ij}^e$ is the effective sale of the $j$th good supplied by the $i$th household and demanded by firms. The constrained demand functions as derived by Clower depend on all the $m$ prices and income:

$$q_{ij}^{ed} = q_{ij}^{ed}(p_1, p_2, \cdots p_m, \overline{y}_i), \quad i = 1, 2 \cdots n \qquad (3.67)$$

16. Clower (1969, p. 295).

An effective demand function like (3.67) is Keynesian in the sense that it recognises the importance of current income flows in influencing demand for output and at the same time it is based on utility maximisation on the part of the workers or households. But the essential point of Clower's analysis is that this utility function has to be maximised subject to an employment constraint or a given effective demand for labour.

The complementary nature of Clower's and Patinkin's analyses can be shown by using a macro framework' Patinkin derived the effective demand for labour $N^{ed}$ for a given level of the aggregate demand for current output and Clower derived the effective demand for current output $Y^{ed}$ (for each worker) for a given level of demand for labour. In Patinkin's model, therefore, $Y^{ed} < Y$ where $Y$ is the notional supply of output and, consequently, the employer's problem is to select the minimum quantity of labour ($= N^{ed}$) necessary to produce $Y^{ed}$. The constraint $Y^{ed} < Y$ manifests itself in $N^{ed} < N$ implying, in turn, that the level of employment or the effective demand for labour is independent of the real wage (since $N^{ed}$ can vary even when the real wage is unchanged). Involuntary unemployment $(N - N^{ed})$ is due to not the real wage being too high (or above $(W/P)^*$ in Fig. 3.4(ii) but to the excess supply in the output market, i.e., to any factor responsible for the fall in the demand for output in the first place in Clower's model, households' realised income is $(W/P) \cdot N^{ed}$ and it is less than their notional income $(W/P) \cdot N$ which implies that their realised or effective demand for output would have to be less than if their notional income were fully realised. This situation in the commodity market when excess supply exists in the labour market i.e., when $N^{ed} < N$ is shown in Fig. 3.5.[17] Since money balances are included in the households' utility function, a rise in the general price level above the market clearing level $P^*$ can be used as a cause of the fall in the aggregate demand due to the real balance effect. The Fig. 3.5 supplements that of Patinkin in Fig. 3.4(ii).

The notional supply of commodities is a downward sloping function of the real wage since employment and therefore notional supply of output is higher at a lower real wage. The notional demand schedule like $Y^d(P^*)$ or $Y^d(P_1)$ is upward sloping because as real wage rises leisure becomes

17. Barro-Grossman (1973, p. 89).

more expensive and households work more and demand more commodities. A rise in the general price level from $P^*$ to $P_1$ leads to a fall in demand for commodities shifting $Y^d$ to $Y^d(P_1)$. $P^*$ and $W^*$ are the general equilibrium price level and real wage respectively. Point $E^*$ of Fig. 3.5 corresponds to that of Fig. 3.4(ii) and is consistent with the equilibrium of notional supply and notional demand in both labour and commodity markets. If $N^{ed} = N$, then $Y^{ed} = Y^d$, and if $N^{ed} < N$, then $N^{ed}$ and therefore $Y^{ed}$ is independent of the real wage and, of course, $Y^{ed} < Y^d$, as mentioned before, the higher price level $P_1 > P^*$ can be the cause of $Y^{ed} < Y^d$. Similarly points $A$, $B$, $C$, $D$, $H$ correspond to the same points in Fig. 3.4(ii) $Y^{ed}$ is vertical when $Y^{ed} < Y^d$. Points $H$, $C$, $A$ and $B$ are all associated with a price level $P_1$ higher than the equilibrium price level $P^*$. Point $H$ indicates notional equilibrium in the labour market but implies excess supply in the commodity market and, therefore, effective demand for labour being lower than the notional demand. Point $A$ is consistent with notional equilibrium in the output market but implies excess supply in the labour market.

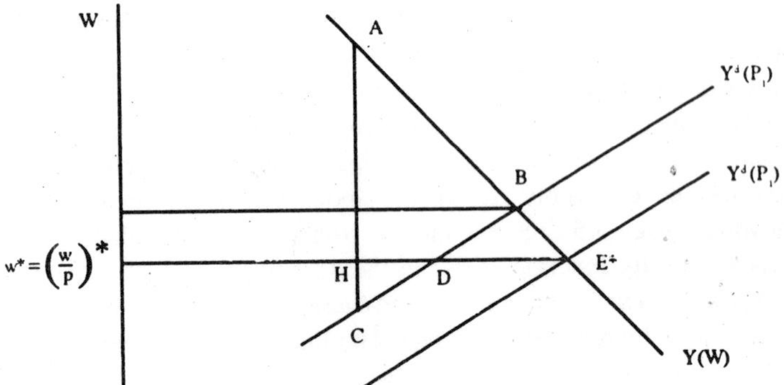


FIG. 3.5

### 3.6.2 *Barro and Grossman*

Barro and Grossman[18] analysed the complementary nature and the cyclical implications of Patinkin and Clower models and presented a general disequilibrium model of excess supply including both labour and commodity markets by joining the former two models. In addition, they derived a general disequilibrium model of an economy characterised by excess demands in labour and commodity markets. The essential ingredients of their model for a depressed economy obtained by joining Clower and Patinkin's analyses have already been given in the discussion above and in the Figs. 3.4(ii) and 3.5. The implications of the excess supplies in the two markets for real wage, price level, output and employment are explained in Figs. 3.6(i) and 3.6(ii).

Once again the points $A, B, C, E^*, H$ in Figs. 3.6(i) correspond to the same points in Fig. 3.4(ii) and 3.5. Only the price level $P^*$ and real wage $W^*$ are consistent with general equilibrium or are the market clearing prices. So, only $E^*$ indicates general equilibrium where all the vectors meet. The locus $N^d = N^s = N$ is horizontal because both depend on the real wage. Below this locus and to the right of $E^*$, there is excess supply in the labour market. $Y^d = Y^s = Y$ is upward sloping because $Y^d$ is a rising function of real wage and a falling function of the price level and $Y^s$??? is a following function of real wage. Above this locus and to the right of $E^*$, the effective demand for commodities is less than the notional demand when labour is in excess supply. Therefore, joining Clower's with Patkinkin's extends the region of excess supply in each market when there exists excess supply in the other market.

Fig. 3.6(ii) shows the determination of actual output and employment in the situation of excess supply in both markets. Let the existing real wage and price level be $W^*$ and $P_1$. Then the economy is at the point $H$ of Figs. 3.4(ii), 3.5 and 3.6(i). Effective demands for output and employment have to be consistent with both the firms and the households' behaviour under excess supply. Employment and output are given by

$$N = \min.[N^{ed}, N^s] \tag{3.68}$$

18. Barro, R.J. and Grossman, H.I. (1973, pp.82-93).

and

$$Y = \min . [Y^{ed}, Y^s] \tag{3.69}$$

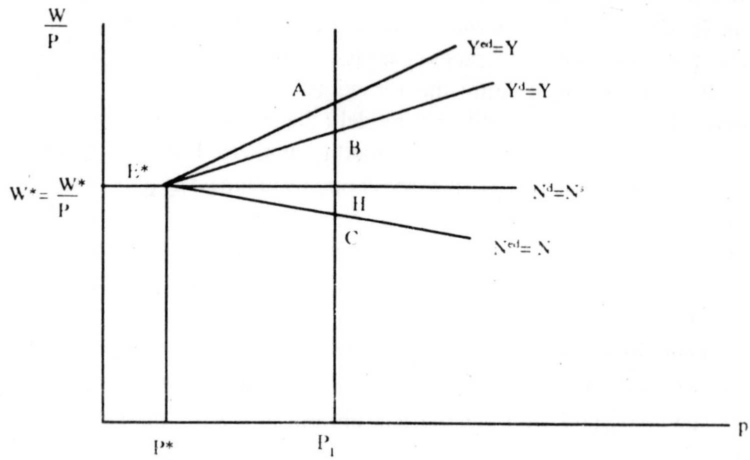


FIG. 3.6(i)

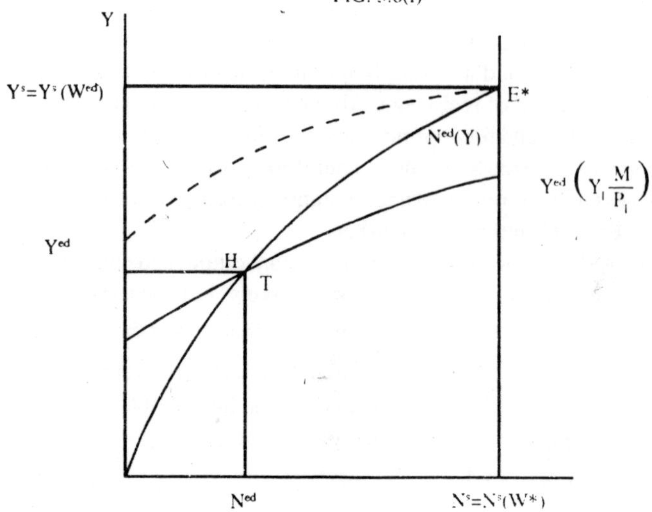


FIG. 3.6(ii)

respectively. Also,

$$N^{ed} = F^{-1}(Y)^{19} \qquad (3.7)$$

19

when the constraint on the output market is binding, i.e. for all values of

$$Y < Y^s \text{ and } Y^{ed} = Y^{ed}(Y, M/P_1) \qquad (3.71)$$

for all values of $Y < Y^s$. The intersection of the two loci (3.70) and (3.71) determine $Y$ and $N$. This is shown to be at point $H$ in Fig. 3.5(ii). Barro and Crossman considered the rise in the price level from $P^*$ to $P_1$ to be the cause of the fall in demand for output and, therefore, of the excess supply in the output market. So, a movement from $H$ back to full employment general equilibrium at $E^*$ would not be achieved by a fall in real wage but by restoring demand for output (and therefore employment) towards the equilibrium level $Y$ by, say, lowering the price level. This restoration of 1. $F(N) = Y$ is the production function as in (3.2) demand can even be accompanied by a rise in the real wage following upon the rise in the demand for labour.[20,21]

In the excess demand in each market the firms are willing to employ more labour than is available and the households are willing to purchase more output than is available. So, $N < N^d$ and $Y < Y^d$ in the respective markets. The unsatisfied demand in the commodity market may lead either extra money balances being held or increased consumption of the leisure on the part of the households or to some combination of the two. To the extent the households go for option two a fall in employment can result even in an excess demand situation. The point of this analysis is that an excess demand for labour can be caused not by a real wage being "too low" (i.e., below $W^*$) but by an excess demand for commodities. Also in this excess demand situation, employment can be lower than the full-employment level to the extent the households substitute leisure for work. The classical economists, by making labour supply a function of real wage alone disregard this possibility and relied on increased forced saving as the only form of reaction of the households.

---

19. $F(N) \equiv Y$ is the production function as in (3.2).

20. See 3.4.

21. Note that one of these relative wages = 1 .

*Tobin and Trevithick*

Tobin (1972) and Trevithick (1976, 1977) have provided a reinterpretation of Keynes's analysis of involuntary unemployment and some theoretical underpinning for the analysis of wage-price spiral. The latter aspect will be dealt with in Chapter 6.

Contradicting Leontief, Tobin and Trevithick argue that Keynes's labour supply function rests upon as analysis of utility maximisation as in the Classical model and that the worker's utility does not depend on money wage as assumed by Leontief but it depends on *relative* wage. The latter is a real variable and it is in this sense that one can explain why workers would accept a fall in their real wage resulting from a rise in the price level but resist to that resulting from a cut in money wage[22]; and more importantly, this is not due to money illusion on the part of the workers but to their concern for relative wages. So, in Tobin and Trevithick's interpretation, the *i*th worker's utility function is

$$V^i = V^i\left(q_{i1}, q_{i2}, \cdots q_{im}\frac{W_i}{W^1}\frac{W_i}{W^2}, \cdots \frac{W_i}{W^n}\right) \tag{3.72}$$

where $W_i$, $i = 1, \cdots n$ are the set of $n$ different wage rates in the economy. Trevithick (1976) draws textual evidence from the General Theory to explain the view that the downward money-wage rigidity is due to workers' preoccupation with relative wages and that such rigidity would disappear if wages fell uniformly everywhere. A rise in the general price level being the only neutral "economy-wide mechanism for altering all" real wages together can bring back full employment in the midst of downward rigidity.

Following the analysis of utility maximisation using (3.72), one can derive a labour supply function in the Keynesian system of the form:

$$N^{si} = N^{si}\left(\frac{W_i}{P}, \frac{W_i}{W_i}, \cdots 1, \frac{W_n}{W_i}\right) \tag{3.73}$$

Although (3.73) is rather similar to the Classical labour supply function including the assumption of "interdependence" in the labour market, Keynes's significant departure from the classical ideas is summarised by Trevithick in the two restrictions to be imposed on (3.73), viz,

22. Tobin (1972) p. 5.

$$\frac{\delta N^{si}}{\delta W_i} = \infty \tag{3.74a}$$

and $$-\infty < \frac{N^{si}}{P} < 0 \tag{3.76}$$

It is evident that Tobin and Trevithick reinterpret the Keynesian labour supply function by means of an interdependence postulate of the workers' behaviour. Dunesenberry (1949) used the same for explaining consumers' behaviour at the cross-section level in his Relative Income hypothesis (RIH). On RIH, an individual's saving (consumption) is an increasing (decreasing) function of his percentile position on the income ladder. Consumption behaviour is interdependent since one has to "keep up with the Joneses" next door. For aggregate time-series analysis, RIH used the irreversibility postulate where relative income is income relative to the previous peak.[23] However, this interpretation of Keynes's labour supply function by Tobin and Trevithick is hard to accept as "Keynesian" because it is inconsistent with Keynes's consumption function which is best described as an absolute income hypothesis.[24] Addison and Burton (1982) are of the view that despite their "appealing attempt", Tobin and Trevithick fail to provide a firm choice-theoretic underpinning of the wage spill over process and an analysis of Stagflation. The inclusion of relative wage variables in workers' utility functions is not sufficient to generate predictions about behaviour and the constraints subject to which the choice set is derived should also have been specified. In particular, this choice set crucially depends on the firms' behaviour explaining the demand side of the market. Tobin-Trevithick analysis does not specify "the influence of variations in employer resistance across sectors of the labour market".[25] The implications for stagflation would be dealt with in Chapter 6.

---

23. See Ghatak (1985) p. 7-13.
24. Leijonhufvud (1968) p. 97.
25. Addison and Burton (1982) p. 14.

## APPENDIX TO CHAPTER 3

3.A.1

(3.27) – (3.30) are obtained as follows. Expanding (3.26) in terms of the cofactors of the elements of the first row in each case

$$J = -(S' - I')\begin{vmatrix} -k & 0 & 0 & -\frac{M}{P^2} \\ 1 & -Y' & 0 & 0 \\ 0 & 0 & \frac{1}{P} & -\frac{W}{P^2} \\ 0 & Y'' & -\frac{1}{P} & \frac{W}{P^2} \end{vmatrix}$$

$$\Rightarrow \quad J = -\frac{M}{P^2}(S' - I')\left(-Y''\frac{1}{P}\right) = \frac{M}{P^2}(S' - I')Y''\frac{1}{P} \qquad (3.27)$$

$$\Rightarrow \quad J < 0$$

Solving for $\frac{\partial Y}{\partial M}$ by Cramer's rule,

$$\frac{\partial Y}{\partial M} = \frac{1}{J}\begin{vmatrix} 0 & S' - I' & 0 & 0 & 0 \\ -\frac{1}{P} & 0 & 0 & 0 & -\frac{M}{P^2} \\ 0 & 0 & -Y' & 0 & 0 \\ 0 & 0 & 0 & \frac{1}{P} & -\frac{W}{P^2} \\ 0 & 0 & Y'' & -\frac{1}{P} & \frac{W}{P^2} \end{vmatrix}$$

$$\Rightarrow \quad \frac{\partial Y}{\partial M} = \frac{0}{J} = 0$$

Similarly, $\frac{\delta r}{\delta M} = 0, \quad \frac{\partial N}{\partial M} = 0$

Now,

$$\frac{\partial W}{\partial M}=\frac{1}{J}\begin{vmatrix} 0 & S'-I' & 0 & 0 & 0 \\ -k & 0 & 0 & -\frac{1}{P} & -\frac{M}{P^2} \\ 1 & 0 & -Y' & 0 & 0 \\ 0 & 0 & 0 & 0 & -\frac{W}{P^2} \\ 0 & 0 & Y'' & 0 & \frac{W}{P^2} \end{vmatrix}$$

$$\Rightarrow \quad \frac{\partial W}{\partial M}=\frac{1}{J}\left[-(S'-I')\begin{vmatrix} -k & 0 & -\frac{1}{P} & -\frac{M}{P^2} \\ 1 & -Y' & 0 & 0 \\ 0 & 0 & 0 & -\frac{W}{P^2} \\ 0 & Y'' & 0 & \frac{W}{P^2} \end{vmatrix}\right]$$

$$\Rightarrow \quad \frac{\partial W}{\partial M}=\frac{1}{J}\left\{(S'-I')\left[\frac{1}{P}\begin{vmatrix} 1 & -Y' & 0 \\ 0 & 0 & -\frac{W}{P^2} \\ 0 & Y'' & \frac{W}{P^2} \end{vmatrix}\right]\right\}$$

$$\Rightarrow \quad \frac{\partial W}{\partial M}=\frac{(S'-I')\frac{1}{P}Y''\frac{W}{P^2}}{J}>0 \tag{3.29}$$

Proceeding in the same way and solving for $\frac{\partial P}{\partial M}$ by Cramer's rule, one obtains

$$\frac{\partial P}{\partial M}=\frac{(S'-I')Y''\frac{1}{P^2}}{J}>0 \tag{3.30}$$

3.A.2 **The Solutions of the Multipliers (3.41) − (3.48)**

First, the Jacobian of the model in Section 3.3 is

$$J = \begin{vmatrix} 1-C' & -I' & 0 & 0 & 0 \\ L_1 & L_2 & 0 & 0 & \frac{M}{P^2} \\ 1 & 0 & -Y' & 0 & 0 \\ 0 & 0 & Y'' & -\frac{1}{P} & \frac{W}{P^2} \\ 0 & 0 & 0 & \left(\frac{N^{d\prime}}{P}\right) - N^{s\prime} & -\frac{N^{d\prime}W}{P^2} \end{vmatrix} \quad (3.42)$$

$$\Rightarrow \quad J = [L_2(1-C') + L_1 I'] \begin{vmatrix} -Y' & 0 & 0 \\ Y'' & -\frac{1}{P} & \frac{W}{P^2} \\ 0 & \frac{N^{d\prime} - N^{s\prime}}{P} & -\frac{N^{d\prime}W}{P^2} \end{vmatrix}$$

$$-I'\frac{M}{P^2} \begin{vmatrix} 1 & -Y' & 0 \\ 0 & Y'' & \frac{1}{P} \\ 0 & 0 & \frac{N^{d\prime} - PN^{s\prime}}{P} \end{vmatrix}$$

$$\Rightarrow \quad J = [L_2(1-C') + L_1 I'] Y' \left[\frac{W}{P^2} \times \frac{N^{d\prime} - PN^{s\prime}}{P} - \frac{N^{d\prime}W}{P^2} \times \frac{1}{P}\right]$$

$$-I'\frac{M}{P^2} \times \frac{N^{d\prime} - N^{s\prime}P}{P} Y''$$

$$\Rightarrow \quad J = -[L_2(1-C') + I'L_1]\ Y'N^{s\prime}\frac{W}{P^2} - Y''I'\frac{M}{P^2} \times \frac{N^{d\prime} - PN^{s\prime}}{P} \quad (3.43)$$

$$\frac{\partial Y}{\partial G}=\frac{1}{J}\begin{vmatrix} 1 & 0 & 0 & 0 & 0 \\ 0 & L_2 & 0 & 0 & \frac{M}{P^2} \\ 0 & 0 & -Y' & 0 & 0 \\ 0 & 0 & Y'' & -\frac{1}{P} & \frac{W}{P^2} \\ 0 & 0 & 0 & \frac{N^{d\prime}-PN^{s\prime}}{P} & -\frac{N^{d\prime}W}{P^2} \end{vmatrix}$$

$$\Rightarrow \quad \frac{\partial Y}{\partial G}=\frac{1}{J}L_2\begin{vmatrix} -Y' & 0 & 0 \\ Y'' & -\frac{1}{P} & \frac{W}{P^2} \\ 0 & \frac{N^{d\prime}-PN^{s\prime}}{P} & -\frac{N^{d\prime}W}{P^2} \end{vmatrix}$$

$$\Rightarrow \quad \frac{\partial Y}{\partial G}=\frac{1}{J}L_2Y'\frac{1}{P}\frac{W}{P^2}(-PN^{s\prime})=\frac{-L_2Y'\frac{W}{P^2}N^{s\prime}}{J}$$

$$\Rightarrow \quad \frac{\partial Y}{\partial G}=\frac{1}{(1-C')+I'\frac{L_1}{L_2}+I'\frac{M}{P^2}Y''\frac{N^{d\prime}-PN^{s\prime}}{P}\times\frac{1}{L_2Y'\frac{W}{P^2}N^{s\prime}}} \tag{3.41}$$

$$\frac{\partial N}{\partial G}=\frac{1}{J}\begin{vmatrix} 1-C' & -I' & 1 & 0 & 0 \\ L_1 & L_2 & 0 & 0 & \frac{M}{P^2} \\ 1 & 0 & 0 & 0 & 0 \\ 0 & 0 & 0 & -\frac{1}{P} & \frac{W}{P^2} \\ 0 & 0 & 0 & \frac{N^{d\prime}-PN^{s\prime}}{P} & -N^{d\prime}\frac{W}{P^2} \end{vmatrix}$$

$$\Rightarrow \quad \frac{\partial N}{\partial G} = \frac{1}{J}\begin{vmatrix} L_1 & L_2 & 0 & \frac{M}{P^2} \\ 1 & 0 & 0 & 0 \\ 0 & 0 & -\frac{1}{P} & \frac{W}{P^2} \\ 0 & 0 & \frac{N^{d\prime} - PN^{s\prime}}{P} & -N^{d\prime}\frac{W}{P^2} \end{vmatrix}$$

$$\Rightarrow \quad \frac{\partial N}{\partial G} = \frac{1}{J}(-L_2)\begin{vmatrix} 1 & 0 & 0 \\ 0 & -\frac{1}{P} & \frac{W}{P^2} \\ 0 & \frac{N^{d\prime} - PN^{s\prime}}{P} & -N^{d\prime}\frac{W}{P^2} \end{vmatrix}$$

$$\Rightarrow \quad \frac{\partial N}{\partial G} = \frac{1}{J} L_2 \frac{W}{P^2} \cdot \frac{1}{P}(N^{d\prime} - PN^{s\prime} - N^{d\prime})$$

$$\Rightarrow \quad \frac{\partial N}{\partial G} = \frac{1}{Y'\left[(1-C') + I'\frac{L_1}{L_2}\right] + I'\frac{M}{P^2}Y''\frac{N^{d\prime} - PN^{s\prime}}{PL_2N^{s\prime}\frac{W}{P^2}}} \qquad (3.44)$$

$$\frac{\partial Y}{\partial M} = \frac{1}{J}\begin{vmatrix} 0 & -I' & 0 & 0 & 0 \\ \frac{1}{P} & L_2 & 0 & 0 & \frac{M}{P^2} \\ 0 & 0 & -Y' & 0 & 0 \\ 0 & 0 & Y'' & -\frac{1}{P} & \frac{W}{P^2} \\ 0 & 0 & 0 & \frac{N^{d\prime} - PN^{s\prime}}{P} & -N^{d\prime}\frac{W}{P^2} \end{vmatrix}$$

$$\Rightarrow \quad \frac{\partial Y}{\partial M}=\frac{1}{J}I'\begin{vmatrix} \frac{1}{P} & 0 & 0 & \frac{M}{P^2} \\ 0 & -Y' & 0 & 0 \\ 0 & Y'' & -\frac{1}{P} & \frac{W}{P^2} \\ 0 & 0 & \frac{N^{d\prime}-N^{s\prime}}{P} & -N^{d\prime}\frac{W}{P^2} \end{vmatrix}$$

$$\Rightarrow \quad \frac{\partial Y}{\partial M}=\frac{1/P}{J}\left(-I'Y'\frac{W}{P^2}N^{s\prime}\right)$$

$$\Rightarrow \quad \frac{\partial Y}{\partial M}=\frac{I'\frac{1}{P}}{L_2(1-C')+I'\frac{L_1}{L_2}+I'\frac{M}{P^2}\times\frac{N^{d\prime}-PN^{s\prime}}{P}\times\frac{Y''}{L_2Y'N^{s\prime}\frac{W}{P^2}}} \tag{3.45}$$

$$\frac{\partial r}{\partial M}=-\frac{(1-C')}{J}\frac{1}{P}Y'\frac{W}{P^2}N^{s\prime} \tag{3.46}$$

$$\frac{\partial W}{\partial M}=\frac{1}{J}\begin{vmatrix} 1-C' & -I' & 0 & 0 & 0 \\ L_1 & L_2 & 0 & \frac{1}{P} & \frac{M}{P^2} \\ 1 & 0 & -Y' & 0 & 0 \\ 0 & 0 & Y'' & 0 & \frac{W}{P^2} \\ 0 & 0 & 0 & 0 & -N^{d\prime}\frac{W}{P^2} \end{vmatrix}$$

$$\Rightarrow \quad \frac{\partial W}{\partial M}=\frac{1}{J}I'\frac{1}{P}\begin{vmatrix} 1 & -Y' & 0 \\ 0 & Y'' & \frac{W}{P^2} \\ 0 & 0 & -N^{d'}\frac{W}{P^2} \end{vmatrix}$$

$$\Rightarrow \quad \frac{\partial W}{\partial M}=\frac{-I'\frac{1}{P}Y''N^{d'}\frac{W}{P^2}}{J} \tag{3.47}$$

and
$$\frac{\partial P}{\partial M}=\frac{1}{J}\begin{vmatrix} 1-C' & -I' & 0 & 0 & 0 \\ L_1 & L_2 & 0 & 0 & \frac{1}{P} \\ 1 & 0 & -Y' & 0 & 0 \\ 0 & 0 & Y'' & -\frac{1}{P} & 0 \\ 0 & 0 & 0 & \frac{N^{d\prime}-PN^{s\prime}}{P} & 0 \end{vmatrix}=\frac{-I'\frac{1}{P}Y''N^{d\prime}\frac{1}{P}}{J}$$

(3.48)

### 3.A.3.1 The Effect of a Wage Cut on Employment in the Classical Model

The Jacobian of this model with 4 endogenous, variables, $Y$, $r$, $N$ and $P$, is

$$J_1=\begin{vmatrix} 1-C' & -I' & 0 & 0 \\ L_1 & L_2 & 0 & \frac{M}{P^2} \\ 1 & 0 & -Y' & 0 \\ 0 & 0 & Y'' & \frac{W}{P^2} \end{vmatrix}$$

$$\Rightarrow \quad J_1=-\frac{Y'W}{P^2}[L_2(1-C')+L_1I']+I'Y''\frac{M}{P^2}$$

$$\Rightarrow \quad J_1>0$$

Applying Cramer's rule,

$$\frac{\partial N}{\partial W}=\begin{vmatrix} 1-C' & -I' & 0 & 0 \\ L_1 & L_2 & 0 & \frac{M}{P^2} \\ 1 & 0 & 0 & 0 \\ 0 & 0 & \frac{1}{P} & \frac{W}{P^2} \end{vmatrix}\frac{1}{J_1}$$

$$\Rightarrow \quad \frac{\partial N}{\partial W}=\frac{I'\frac{M}{P^2}\bullet\frac{1}{P}}{J}<0 \tag{3.49}$$

Similarly,

$$\frac{\partial P}{\partial W}=\frac{1}{J_1}\begin{vmatrix} 1-C' & -I' & 0 & 0 \\ L_1 & L_2 & 0 & 0 \\ 1 & 0 & -Y' & 0 \\ 0 & 0 & Y'' & \frac{1}{P} \end{vmatrix}$$

$$\Rightarrow \quad \frac{\partial P}{\partial W}=\frac{-[(1-C')L_2+I'L_1]\,Y'\frac{1}{P}}{J_1}>0$$

3.A.3.2 **The Pigou Effect**

Differentiating the modified system of equations (3.50), (3.34), (3.37) and (3.42) w.r.t. $W$, one obtains

$$\frac{\partial Y}{\partial W}(1-C_1)+C_2\frac{M}{P^2}\frac{\partial P}{\partial W}-I'\frac{\partial r}{\partial W}=0$$

$$L_1\frac{\partial Y}{\partial W}+L_2\frac{\partial r}{\partial W}+\left(\frac{M}{P^2}\right)\frac{\partial P}{\partial W}=0$$

$$\frac{\partial Y}{\partial W}-Y'\frac{\partial N^d}{\partial W}=0$$

$$Y''\frac{\partial N^d}{\partial W}+\frac{W}{P^2}\frac{\partial P}{\partial W}=\frac{1}{P}$$

where $C_1 = C'$ of earlier models and $C_2=\frac{\partial C}{\partial(M/P)}>0$

The Jacobian is

$$J_2 = \begin{vmatrix} 1-C_1 & -I' & 0 & C_2\dfrac{M}{P^2} \\ L_1 & L_2 & 0 & \dfrac{M}{P^2} \\ 1 & 0 & -Y' & 0 \\ 0 & 0 & Y'' & \dfrac{W}{P^2} \end{vmatrix}$$

$$\Rightarrow \quad J_2 = [L_2(1-C_1) + I'L_1]\left(-Y'\frac{W}{P^2}\right) + I'\frac{M}{P^2}Y'' + C_2\frac{M}{P^2}L_2Y''$$

$$\Rightarrow \quad J_2 > 0$$

$$\frac{\partial N^d}{\partial W} = \frac{1}{J_2}\begin{vmatrix} 1-C_1 & -I' & 0 & C_2\dfrac{M}{P^2} \\ L_1 & L_2 & 0 & \dfrac{M}{P^2} \\ 1 & 0 & 0 & 0 \\ 0 & 0 & \dfrac{1}{P} & \dfrac{W}{P^2} \end{vmatrix}$$

$$\Rightarrow \quad \frac{\partial N^d}{\partial W} = \frac{L_2C_2\frac{M}{P^2}\frac{1}{P}}{-[L_2(1-C_1)+I'L_1]Y'\frac{W}{P^2} + I'\frac{M}{P^2}Y'' + C_2L_2Y''\frac{M}{P^2}}$$

$$\Rightarrow \quad \frac{\partial N^d}{\partial W} = \frac{C_2\frac{M}{P^2}\bullet\frac{1}{P}}{\left(1-C_1+I'\frac{L_1}{L_2}\right)\left(-Y'\frac{W}{P^2}\right) + C_2Y''\frac{M}{P^2} + \frac{I'}{L_2}Y''\frac{M}{P^2}} \tag{3.51}$$

$$\Rightarrow \quad \frac{\partial N^d}{\partial W} < 0$$

# 4

# THE DEMAND FOR AND THE SUPPLY OF MONEY

## 4.1 THE DEMAND FOR MONEY

An elementary account of the Classical and Keynesian theories of the demand for money has already been provided in Chapters 2 and 3. Microeconomic theory of demand tells us that various goods and services are demanded because they have *Utility*, i.e. the consumer derives some satisfaction from their consumption. The "utility" of money stems from the various functions that it can perform on behalf of the consumer. Money can be used as a medium of exchange, a store of value, a unit of account and as a standard of deferred payment.[1] Money can perform all these functions efficiently as long as its value is not eroded by inflation. This implies that the real demand for money must be distinguished from the nominal demand for money. The transactions demand for money arises from its medium of exchange and unit of account qualities whereas the asset demand obviously arises from its store of value and related functions.

### 4.1.1 **Theories of the Demand for Money**

*The Classical Theory.* It has been implied in Chapters 2 and 3 that the Classical theory of the demand for money emphasised only the transactions demand and, therefore, only the means of exchange function of money. The Cambridge equation of the demand for money as given in equation (3.17) was the first formal statement of a demand for money function and is obtained from the work of Pigou (1917).

---

1. The reader is referred to Greenaway and Shaw (pp. 75-77) for a detailed discussion of these functions.

Pigou's version of the *Quantity theory of money* assumes that an individual wishes to hold money because it can be exchanged for goods and services (transactions need) and his income, wealth, the rate of interest and expectations all exert important influences on the demand for money. But *Ceteris Paribus*, the nominal demand for money for each individual depends on his nominal income. From this we derived the Cambridge equation for the economy as a whole in (3.17).

Even before Pigou, the original version of the quantity theory emerged from the work of Irving Fisher (1911). Fisher's equation of exchange was more an identity than a theory of demand for money:

$$M^s V^T = PTR \tag{4.1}$$

where $M^s$ is the quantity of money in circulation assumed exogenous, $V^T$ is the transactions velocity of circulation, i.e. the number of times money changes hands and $TR$ the volume of transactions. All Classical economists believed in full employment and, therefore, the total volume of transactions was assumed to be constant. Fisher also treated $V^T$ as constant over short time periods.[2] Given these assumptions about $M^s$, $V^T$ and $TR$, the general price level, $P$ is determined by equation/identity (4.1).

Although the Cambridge and Fisher's versions of the quantity theory should be interpreted differently, they are closely linked. The Cambridge equation uses real income, $Y$ rather than the total volume of goods and services traded, $TR$, interprets the constant $K$ as the income velocity of circulation of money, i.e. its rate of circulation relative to the rate of production of real output. Treating $Y = TR$, $K = \frac{1}{V^T}$ one can derive the Cambridge equation from (4.1) by applying the equilibrium condition in the money market, but there are important differences in their interpretations:

(a) Pigou's equation (3.17) or the Cambridge equation

$$M^d = kPY \tag{4.2}$$

is a theory of the demand for money whereas Fisher's version (4.1) is an identity;

2. See Laidler, D.E.W. (1985) pp.44-47.

(b) Variables like the rate of interest, wealth and individuals' expectation about the future course of events are all assumed to influence the demand for money and one has to apply the *Ceteris Paribus* to the demand equation (4.2) but the constancy of $V^T$ etc is more easily obtained from satisfying Fisher's version (4.1).[3]

Friedman's brushing up on the quantity theory will be described shortly afterwards.

**Keynesian Theory**[4]

Keynes's theory of the demand for money has been discussed at length in Chapters 2 and 3. Keynes considered transactions and precautionary demands for money as functions of real income and speculative as a function of the real rate of interest and these components of the total demand for money as additive. So this demand function can be written either as in (2.9) or in the general from (2.28) for a long-run demand for money function of the Keynesian type, one should include the level of wealth, $V$, as well. So, on this extension a Keynesian demand for money function looks like

$$\frac{M^d}{P} = \alpha Y + L^2(r)V \tag{4.3a}$$

or, like $$\frac{M^d}{P} = L(Y, r, V), \quad L_1 > 0, L_2 < 0, 0 < L_3 < 1 \tag{4.3b}$$

In the extended IS-LM model incorporating the government budget constraint, we will use demand function of the type (4.3). In the short-run, the level of wealth can be assumed to be constant and, therefore, omitted from the demand for money function.

An important point of difference between the Keynesian and the Classical demand for money functions is that in the Keynesian function (2.9) or (2.28) or (4.3a), the transactions velocity is considered a variable and it changes in the opposite direction to the change in the quantity of money. A rise in $M$ gets completely absorbed in the speculative balances

3. See Laidler, D.E.W. (1985) pp. 47-50.
4. See Laidler, D.E.W. (1985) pp. 47-50.

(since the rate of interest falls) and this means a fall in the average velocity of circulation (since the velocity of circulation of idle/speculative balances is zero by definition).

In the Keynesian IS-LM model as explained in Chapter 2, a rise in money supply leads to a fall in the rate of interest leading to a rise in investment which, through the multiplier effect, leads to a rise in income. This transmission mechanism breaks down if investment demand is completely inelastic and the demand for money perfectly elastic to the rate of interest. Barring these two cases, there is a rise in equilibrium income following a rise in money supply but this equilibrium is reached in a cyclical fashion,[5] for, it creates feedback effects by raising transactions and precautionary demands for money leading to a rise in the rate of interest, and, therefore, to a fall in investment and income.

Leijonhufvud (1968) explained that in the Keynesian liquidity preference function the distinction between short- and long-term securities is important and that Keynes's definition of "money" included short-term securities as well as currency and sight deposits while that of "bonds" included only the long-term securities. So, the Keynesian demand for money function too implicitly pointed to a whole range of interest rates out of which the rate on long-term securities was "the rate" included specifically in the liquidity preference function. This long-term rate is closer to the concept of an expected rate than to that of the current rate. So, the speculative demand for money varies inversely with the current rate of interest only when there is no change in the "given state of expectations". In other words, the speculative demand depends on the relation between current rates of interest and the rates of interest expected to prevail in the future.[6] As will be shown later, following these basically Keynesian ideas, Tobin (1958) derived a range of critical rates of interest determining the portfolio choice and Friedman (1971) rewrote Keynesian demand for money function (4.3a) as

$$\frac{M^d}{P} = \alpha Y + L^2(r - r^e, r^e) \tag{4.4}$$

where $r^e$ is the expected rate of interest.

5. Dennis, G.E.J. (1981) pp. 82-89.
6. Keynes (1936) p. 168.

Considering equations (4.2) and (4.3) the difference between the Keynesian and monetarist positions can be reiterated as follows. The Keynesians assume $P = \overline{P}$ and therefore, a change in $M$ has to affect either $k$, or $Y$ or both. When liquidity preference is less than infinitely elastic, a change in $M$ changes $r$ and so $k$ can change along with the interest rate but the change in $r$ causes a change in $Y$ via the change in investment spending. But when liquidity preference is infinitely elastic w.r.t. the rate of interest, a change in $M$ causes no change in $r$ and, therefore, no change in the real income and $k$ has to absorb the entire impact without a change in the rate of interest. The monetarists argue that in the long-run, changes in the quantity of money may leave real income unaffected like Keynes believed but in the short-run changes in $M$ affect all three other variables — $k$, $P$ and $Y$ in (4.2).

More interestingly changes in $M$ and $k$ affect $Y$ in the same direction. So, one way to describe the monetarists' position would be as "money is all that matters for changes in *nominal* income and for *short-run* changes in real income" (Friedman, 1971, p. 27).

### *Modifications of the Keynesian Theory*

While the original Keynesian demand for money function implies a clear-cut distinction between the transactions demand depending on real income and the speculative or asset demand depending on the rate of interest, the works of Baumol (1952) and Tobin (1956, 1958) indicate the difficulty of maintaining such distinction. Baumol applied an inventory theoretic approach to show that the transactions demand for cash depends inversely on the rate of interest and it is proportional to the value of transactions. Tobin (1956) also shows that the transactions demand for cash depends inversely on the rate of interest and provides an important modification (1958) to the Keynesian theory.

Baumol derives a square-root rule of transactions demand for cash in two different cases:

(a) when an individual's disbursements precede receipts, and
(b) when his receipts precede disbursements. The value of transactions required per period of time is assumed to be exogenous and equal to, say, *TR*.

In case a, transaction needs are met by equal withdrawals (or, by borrowing) of $x_1$ units of money per time. So, the required number of withdrawals is $\frac{TR}{x_1}$ and, because withdrawals are spaced evenly, the individual's average moneyholding, for transactions purposes is $\frac{x_1}{2}$.[7] There are both interest and non-interest costs (e.g. broker's fees) of withdrawals (or borrowing) and the latter are assumed to be linearly related to or rise with the value of transactions. So, the total cost of withdrawal is:

$$\frac{r \cdot x_1}{2} + \frac{(a_0 + a_1 x_1) \cdot TR}{x_1}, \quad a_0 > 0, 0 < a_1 < 1 \tag{4.5}$$

The first term in (4.5) is the interest cost on average money holding — either on account of forgone interest income or the interest paid on the borrowed sum. $a_0 > 0$ stands for a fixed charge made by the brokers and the part $a_1 x_1$ rises with $x_1$. Assuming rational behaviour, the individual satisfies his transaction demand for cash at the lowest possible cost. The necessary condition for minimising the cost of withdrawal is obtained by setting the derivative of (4.5) w.r.t. $x_1$ equal to zero:

$$\frac{r}{2} - \frac{a_0 \cdot TR}{x_1^2} = 0 \quad \Rightarrow \quad x_1^2 = \frac{2a_0 \cdot TR}{r}$$

$$\Rightarrow \quad x_1 = \sqrt{\frac{2a_0 TR}{r}} \tag{4.6}$$

(4.6) gives the square-root rule between transaction demand for cash and the value of transactions and the rate of interest and this demand depends inversely on the rate of interest.

A similar rule can be derived for case (b). above as follows. When receipts precede expenditure the individual is assumed to invest any excess of receipts over his anticipated transaction needs, say, $IN$. During the period between receipts, the rest $(TR - IN)$ is used for transactions. The total transactions needed for the entire period being $TR$, the amount of

7. This can be seen by evaluating the definite integral:

$$\int_0^1 x_1(1-t)dt = \left[x_1 t - \frac{x_1 t^2}{2}\right]_0^1 = x_1 - \frac{x_1}{2} = \frac{x_1}{2}$$

cash $(TR - IN)$ can pay for $\frac{(TR-IN)}{TR}$ fraction of the period. As in case a. above, the interest and other costs of using this money for transactions can be worked out as

$$\frac{TR - IN}{TR} \bullet r \bullet \frac{TR - IN}{2} + (b_0 + b_1 IN)$$

$$= \frac{(TR - IN)^2 r}{2TR} + (b_0 + b_1 IN) \tag{4.7}$$

The first term in (4.7) is the interest or opportunity costs of withholding from investment and the second term is the non-interest cost of investing the sum $IN(b_0 > 0$ is the fixed broker's fee and $0 < b_1 < 1$ in the rate at which the fees rise with the amount invested). Still, there is the fraction $1 - \frac{(TR-IN)}{TR}$ remaining to be considered under case (b) For the remaining fraction of the period, $\frac{IN}{TR}$, the total cost can be worked out exactly as in case (a) above and, it is

$$\frac{x_1}{2} \bullet r \bullet \frac{IN}{TR} + (a_0 + a_1 x_1)\frac{IN}{x_1} \tag{4.8}$$

The total cost for the entire period in case (b) is obtained by adding the costs given in (4.7) and (4.8). So, when the individual receives income before he spends it, transaction demand for cash, $x_1$, is such that the sum (4.7) + (4.8) is minimised. First, the sum to be minimised w.r.t. $x_1$ is

$$\frac{r}{2TR}\{(TR - IN)^2 + x_1 IN\} + (b_0 + b_1 IN) + a_1 IN + \frac{a_0 IN}{x_1} \tag{4.9}$$

The necessary condition

$$\frac{rIN}{2TR} - \frac{a_0 IN}{x_1^2} = 0 \quad \Rightarrow \quad x_1 = \sqrt{\frac{2a_0 TR}{r}} \tag{4.10}$$

So, once again the individual demands cash in proportion to the square-root of the value of his transactions.

Tobin (1958), like Keynes, discusses two motives for holding cash balances — the transactions and the investment. But, unlike Keynes, he argues that both the transactions and the investment balances are held not only in the form of cash but partly in cash and partly in earning assets. So, even the transactions demand for cash would vary inversely with the rate of interest. Since this point has already been proved by Baumol, we go straight on to the investment demand or, what Keynes called the speculative demand. In the Keynesian theory, the individuals hold either just cash (when interest rates are low) or just bonds or monetary assets (when interest rates are high) for speculative purposes. In Tobin's model, cash is held for speculative purposes only because of (a) uncertainty about future interest rates and (b) inelasticity of expectations of future interest rates.

First Tobin derives a critical rate of interest $r^c$ below which no bonds and above which no cash is held by investors. This critical rate is derived by considering consols against which cash with a zero rate of return is compared. An individual investing £ 1 on consols can purchase $r$ consols. Then, his expected capital gain/loss on these is $r\left(\frac{1}{r^e}-\frac{1}{r}\right)$ where $r^e$ is the expected rate of interest. In the absence of uncertainty, the critical rate is derived by comparing the individual's total return on £ 1 worth of bonds with the zero return on £ 1 held in cash. So, a rational individual holds all speculative balances in consols if

$$r+r\left(\frac{1}{r^e}-\frac{1}{r}\right)>0,$$

i.e. if $$r+r\left(\frac{r-r^e}{rr^e}\right)>0$$

i.e. if $$r+\left(\frac{r}{r^e}-1\right)>0,$$

i.e. if $$r\left(1+\frac{1}{r^e}\right)>1,$$

i.e. if $$r>\frac{1}{1+\frac{1}{r^e}}$$

i.e. if $$r>\frac{r^e}{1+r^e} \tag{4.11a}$$

On the other hand, all speculative balances would be held in cash if

$$r + r\left(\frac{1}{r^e} - \frac{1}{r}\right) < 0$$

i.e. if $$r < \frac{r^e}{1 + r^e} \qquad (4.11b)$$

(4.11a and b) define the critical rate of interest as

$$r^c = \frac{r^e}{1 + r^e} \qquad (4.12)$$

A downward-sloping liquidity preference curve as given in Fig. 3.2 can be obtained as a part of Tobin's more general one by assuming different critical rates for different individuals. The critical rate of interest varies over individuals when they have different expectations about the future rate. If the minimum critical rate is $\min .r^c$ and the maximum critical rate is $\max .r^c$, then the speculative demand for assets varies inversely with the current rate of interest, $r$, between these two limits. So, the liquidity preference function has a negative slope for $\min .r^c \; r \; \max .r^c$. If $r > \max .r^c$, no cash and if $r < \min .r^c$, no bond will be held for speculative purposes, implying a vertical range of the speculative demand curve at either end. This is shown in Fig. 4.1. Tobin's curve is $B \max .r^c A D$. The segment of the curve lying between $\max .r^c$ and $A$ resembles the Keynesian curve.

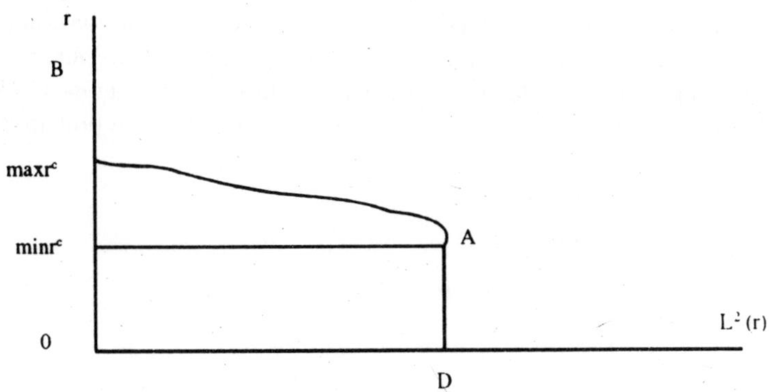


FIG. 4.1 Speculative demand for cash

In the situation of uncertainty expected returns and risks are discussed in terms of probability distributions. Capital gain or loss $cg$ is treated as a random variable distributed with a mean 0 and variance $\sigma g^2$. An inverse relation between the expected return on portfolio and the standard deviation of capital gain is derived by assuming that a proportion $0 \leqq A_1 \leqq 1$ of the speculative balances is held in cash and $0 \leqq (1 - A_1) \leqq 1$ in bonds.

Then the return on portfolio is

$$R = (1 - A_1)(r + C_g) \tag{4.13a}$$

Taking expectation of both sides,

$$\Rightarrow \quad E(R) = (1 - A_1)E(r) + E(cg) = (1 - A_1)r \tag{4.13b}$$

Taking standard deviation of (4.13a)

$$\sigma R = \sqrt{E[R - E(R)]^2} = \sqrt{(1 - A_1)\sigma g} \tag{4.13c}$$

Since $E(r) = r$ and s.d. $(r) = 0$

From (4.13b) and (4.13c) it follows:

$$E(R) = \frac{r}{\sigma g}\sigma R \tag{4.13d}$$

(4.13d) defines a linear constraint showing a trade-off between risk and portfolio return, which the investor has to satisfy in maximising the expected utility of portfolio return $E[U(R)]$. The standard deviation $\sigma R$ is a measure of dispersion of returns around their mean value and, therefore, it can serve as a measure of risk. The greater the risk undertaken, the higher would be the expected return. This analysis of constrained utility maximisation can be diagrammatically dealt with by means of indifference curves.[8] The necessary mathematics is shown below. Given the expectation and the standard deviation as in (4.13), the probability density function of $R$ can be written as

$$F(R; E(R), \sigma R).$$

Then, expected utility of $R$ is

$$E[U(R)] = \int_{-\infty}^{\infty} U(R)F\, dR \tag{4.14}$$

---

8. This is given in Greenaway and Shaw [1983, p. 91]. In this context, an indifference curve is the locus of all combinations of expected gain and risk yielding a constant expected utility.

If $R$ has a normal distribution with $E(R), \sigma R$ as mean and s.d. then, $NR = \frac{R - E(R)}{\sigma R}$ is a standard normal variate with zero excpectation and unit s.d. Normalising (4.14), Tobin obtains

$$E[U(R)] = \int_{-\infty}^{\infty} U[E(R) + \sigma R\ NR] F(0, 1) dNR \tag{4.15}$$

The expected utility maximisation subject to (4.13d) is carried out by assuming a quadratic utility function

$$U(R) = (1 + a)R + aR^2 \tag{4.16}$$

The coefficient, $a$ has to be such that marginal utility is non-negative. For

$$\frac{dU}{dR} \geqq 0, \quad 1 + a + 2aR \geqq 0$$

$$R \leqq -\frac{1 + a}{2a} \quad (4.17$$

A rational risk-averter undertakes higher risks only for higher expected return $-1 < a < 0$.[9] From (4.13a) and (4.17)

$$(1 - A_1)(r + Cg) \leqq \frac{1 + a}{2a} \tag{4.18}$$

Taking expectation of (4.16)

$$E[U(R)] = (1 + a)E(R) + aE(R^2)$$

$$\Rightarrow \quad E[U(R)] = (1 + a)E(R) + a[(\sigma R)^2 + \{E(R)\}^2] \tag{4.19}$$

[Since $\text{Var}(R) \equiv (\sigma R)^2 = E[R - E(R)]^2 = E(R^2) - \{E(R)\}^2 \quad \Rightarrow \quad E(R^2) = (\sigma R)^2 + \{E(R)\}^2$]

As well known from microeconomics, the slope of an indifference curve is derived such that there is no change in utility along the same curve:

99. For a risk-lover $0 < a < 1$ and $R \geqq -\frac{1+a}{2a}$. This case will not be discussed here.

$$dE[U(R)] = 0$$

$$\Rightarrow \quad (1+a)dE(R) + 2a[\sigma R\, d\sigma R + E(R)\, dE(R)] = 0$$

$$\Rightarrow \quad [1 + a + 2aE(R)]dE(R) + 2a\sigma R\, d\sigma R = 0$$

$$\Rightarrow \quad \frac{dE(R)}{d\sigma R} = -\frac{2a\sigma R}{1 + a + 2aE(R)}$$

$$\Rightarrow \quad \frac{dE(R)}{d\sigma R} = -\frac{\sigma r}{\frac{1+a}{2a} + E(R)} > 0 \tag{4.20}$$

The positive slope is what is to be expected for a risk-averter. Differentiating (4.20) once more, one can determine the curvature of the positively sloped indifference curve for a risk-averter in the presence of uncertainty.

$$\frac{d^2E(R)}{d\sigma R^2} = \frac{-\frac{1+a}{2a} - E(R) + \sigma R \frac{d}{d\sigma R}\left[\frac{1+a}{2a} + E(R)\right]}{\left[-\left\{\frac{1+a}{2a} + E(R)\right\}\right]^2}$$

$$\Rightarrow \quad \frac{d^2E(R)}{d\sigma R^2} = \frac{1}{-\frac{1+a}{2a} + E(R)} > 0 \tag{4.21}$$

Now the risk-averter maximises $E[U(R)]$ as given in (4.19) subject to the constraint (4.13d). Writing the lagrangean as

$$(1+a)E(R) + a[(\sigma R)^2 + \{E(R)\}^2] + \lambda\left[E(R) - \frac{r\sigma R}{\sigma g}\right]$$

the necessary conditions for maximisation are

$$(1+a) + 2aE(R) + \lambda = 0 \tag{4.22i}$$

$$2a\sigma R - \frac{\lambda r}{\sigma g} = 0 \tag{4.22ii}$$

and

$$E(R) - \frac{r\sigma R}{\sigma g} = 0 \tag{4.22iii}$$

Eliminating the lagrange multiplier $\lambda$ between (i) and (ii)

$$1 + a + 2aE(R) + 2a\sigma R\frac{\sigma g}{r} = 0$$

$$\Rightarrow \quad E(R) + \frac{\sigma R\,\sigma g}{r} = -\frac{1+a}{2a} \qquad (4.23)$$

Condition (4.23) is satisfied at the point of tangency between the highest indifference curve and the line given by (4.13d). Finally, substituting (4.13b and c) in (4.23) Tobin derives the inverse relation between the proportion of assets held in cash $A_1$ and the interest rate $r$:

$$(1-A_1)r + (1-A_1)\frac{(\sigma g)^2}{r} = -\left(\frac{1+a}{2a}\right)$$

$$\Rightarrow \quad (1-A_1)[r^2 + (\sigma g)^2] = r\left(-\frac{1+a}{2a}\right)$$

$$\Rightarrow \quad 1 - A_1 = \frac{r}{r^2 + (\sigma g)^2}\left(-\frac{1+a}{2a}\right) \qquad (4.24)$$

Differentiating (4.24) w.r.t. $r$

$$\frac{d(1-A_1)}{dR} = \frac{r^2 + (\sigma g)^2 - r \cdot 2r}{\{r^2 + (\sigma g)^2\}^2}\left(-\frac{1+a}{2a}\right)$$

$$\Rightarrow \quad \frac{d(1-A_1)}{dR} = \frac{(\sigma g)^2 - r^2}{\{r^2 + (\sigma g)^2\}^2}\left(-\frac{1+a}{2a}\right) \qquad (4.25)$$

(4.25) implies that $\frac{d(1-A_1)}{dR} > 0$

if $(\sigma g)^2 > r^2$. Therefore, a risk-averter increases the proportion of consols in his portfolio with $r$ for $r < \sigma g$. If $r$ exceeds $\sigma g$ however, then it must also exceed maximum possible capital gain the investor can think of for the proportion of consols to rise with $r$.[10]

Tobin's work is a significant improvement of the Keynesian liquidity preference theory and this has been further developed into a comprehensive theory of portfolio choice by the Yale school led by Professor Tobin himself.

10. For proof, see Tobin (1958, p. 79).

*The Revival of the Quantity Theory*

The quantity theory was revived in the writings of Friedman (1956, 1959) and his disciples known together as the "Chicago School". Professor Milton Friedman is also the leading critic of Keynesian economics. While Keynes believed in the all-important role of fiscal policy based on the stability of the multiplier (based, in turn, on $0 < MPC < 1$), the moneterists led by Friedman believed in the importance of non-interventionist monetary policy based on the stability of the velocity function. In the Keynesian system, the role of monetary policy is minimised by the existence of a liquidity trap whereas in the monetarists' view, monetary policy has powerful effects on the nominal variables such as the nominal aggregate demand, the price level, etc. Keynes was less than adequate on inflation and this deficiency was attacked by the monetarists. Full implications of this debate will have to wait till the dynamics of inflation have been explained. For now we continue with Friedman's theory of the demand for money.

Friedman lists a number of potentially important variables which can influence the demand for money and their relative importance is to be judged only from empirical investigation. He writes a general nominal demand function of money as

$$M^d = M^d\left(\frac{Yn}{r}, P, rb - \frac{1}{rb}\frac{drb}{dt}, re - \frac{1}{re}\frac{dre}{dt} + \dot{p}, h, \dot{p}e, t\right) \quad (4.26)$$

The nominal income $Yn$ is $P \times Y$ by definition. The ratio $\frac{Yn}{r}$ is included because the general[11] rate of interest, $r$, expresses the relation between the stock of wealth, $V$ and the flow of income from this wealth. Ideally, this stock should include both human and non-human wealth and income, $Yn$ should be interpreted in the broader sense of permanent or expected income rather than that of measured income. So,

$$V = \frac{Yn}{r} \quad (4.27)$$

11. By "general", one could imply a weighted average of all rates of interest on various types of assets.

There are a number of different rates of interest because it is necessary to distinguish between different forms in which wealth can be held. The wealth-owning units divide their wealth into different forms such that they can maximise the utility (of such wealth) subject to the total costs of converting one form of wealth into another.

Assuming money, bonds, equities and physical goods and services to be the forms in which assets can be held, one can justify the inclusion of the second, third and the fourth arguments in the demand for money function (4.26). The return on money is assumed to be only in kind-liquidity, convenience etc and, therefore, the price level, *P* represents the real return per £ 1 worth of asset kept in the form of money. Similarly, the real rate of return on £ 1 worth of bonds would be $\left(rb - \frac{1}{rb}\frac{drb}{dt}\right)$ where *rb* is the yield per year and $\frac{1}{rb}$ is the price and $-\frac{drb}{dt}\frac{1}{rb}$ is the gain or loss from the change in the price of bonds. The real rate of return on equity, in addition, would be adjusted for any change in the nominal price level $re - \frac{1}{re}\frac{dre}{dt} + \frac{\dot{P}}{P}$.

For assets held in the form of physical goods, the real rate of return is $\frac{\dot{P}^e}{P^e}$ or $\dot{P}^e$ or the expected rate of inflation. "*h*" stands for the ratio of income from non-human wealth to income from human wealth and *t* stands for all variables affecting tastes and preferences of the wealth-owner.

In the next stage a number of important assumptions are made about the general form (4.26). First, the general rate of interest, *r* is dropped as an additional variable because *rb* and *re* are enough to take its influence into account. Secondly, for the sake of simplicity, *rb* and *re* are assumed to be stable over time implying $\frac{drb}{dt} = \frac{dre}{dt} = 0$.

Thirdly, *Yn* is regarded as referring to the return to all forms of wealth except to that held in the form of money implying $\frac{Yn}{r}$ as referring to all forms of wealth other than money. Most importantly, the function derived from (4.26) and these three assumptions, is assumed to be homogeneous of degree 1 in *P* and *Yn*. So, the function,

$$M^d = M^d(Yn, P, rb, re, \dot{p}^e, h, t) \tag{4.27}$$

is homogeneous of degree 1 in *Yn* and *P* implying

$$M^d(\lambda Yn, \lambda P, rb, re, \dot{p}^e, h, t)$$

$$= \lambda M^d(Yn, P, rb, re, \dot{p}^e, h, t) \quad (4.28)$$

Putting $\lambda = \frac{1}{P}$, (4.28) can be rewritten as

$$M^d\left(\frac{Yn}{P}, 1, rb, re, \dot{p}^e, h, t\right) = \frac{M^d}{P} \quad (4.29)$$

$$\frac{M^d}{P} = M^d(Y, rb, re, \dot{p}^e, h, t) \quad (4.30)$$

Putting $\lambda = \frac{1}{Yn}$, (4.28) can also be written as

$$\frac{M^d}{Yn} = M^d\left(\frac{P}{Yn}, rb, re, \dot{p}^e, h, t\right) \quad (4.31)$$

These alternative forms are important for the purpose of the quantity theory which is based on the concept of a *velocity function*. Recall that the income velocity:

$$V^Y = \frac{P \times Y}{M^s} \quad \Rightarrow \quad \frac{1}{V^Y} = \frac{M^s}{Yn} = \frac{M^s}{P}\frac{1}{Y} \quad (4.32)$$

From (4.29), $\frac{M^d}{P}$ is a function of *rb, re,* etc. Assuming the money market in equilibrium, $\frac{M^s}{P}$ would depend on the same set of variables and, therefore, the velocity function in turn, can be written as

$$V^Y = V^Y\left(\frac{Yn}{P}, rb, re, \dot{p}^e, h, t\right) \quad (4.33)$$

combining (4.32) and (4.33), one can derive the more popular quantity theory equation:

$$Yn = V^Y\left(\frac{Yn}{P}, rb, re, \dot{p}^e, h, t\right) \cdot M \quad (4.34)$$

The equations (4.26)–(4.34) are derived for the economy as a whole by ignoring the problems of aggregation. All wealth-owning units are assumed to have similar expectations about the rate of inflation, same ratio of human and non-human wealth to income, etc.

It is evident once again that unlike the Keynesian demand for money functions, the quantity theory equations (4.26)–(4.34) do not distinguish between transaction and speculative balances. In this restatement of the quantity theory the real demand for money is stable not in the sense of a constant velocity of circulation but in the sense of a stable functional relation between this demand and the influencing variables. It is this contention of stability of the demand for money consistent with a variable velocity of circulation is what constitutes a major point of difference between the Keynesians and the monetarists. For, this stability extends the role of monetary policy in affecting a number of important macro variables in the economy, whereas in the Keynesian system, the only role of the demand and supply of money is to determine or affect the rate of interest — a role which would fail in the presence of a liquidity trap.

### 4.1.2 **A Monetarist Model**

Since the late 1960's, the Keynesian macroeconomic thought came under attack. The high rates of inflation coexisting with high unemployment questioned the validity of the Keynesian prescription of interventionist policy. The leading critic of Keynesian economics was Professor Friedman and, much of his work being in the area of monetary economics, this anti-Keynesian school of thought came to be branded as monetarism. Above everything else, this new line of thinking emphasised the role of money and the importance of monetary policy in influencing the output and the price level. Keynes was attacked also for minimising the role of wealth in his consumption and demand for money functions.

Friedman in his *A Theoretical Framework for Monetary Analysis*[12] offered a monetary theory of nominal income, *Yn*. Starting with "a simple common model"[13] of closed economy without any government sector, he showed the difference between the Keynesian and the former quantity theorists. This is similar in looks to the Keynesian IS-LM model rewritten in terms of nominal variables — denoted here by a small *n* after the respective real magnitudes:

12. Friedman, M., 1971.
13. Friedman (1971), pp. 29-38.

*Friedman's "Common Model"*

$$\frac{Cn}{P} = C\left(\frac{Yn}{P}, r\right) \tag{4.35i}$$

$$\frac{In}{P} = I(r) \tag{4.35ii}$$

$$\frac{Yn}{P} = \frac{Cn}{P} + \frac{In}{P} \tag{4.35iii}$$

$$M^d = P \cdot L\left(\frac{Yn}{P}, rn\right) \tag{4.35iv}$$

$$M^s = M^s(rn) \tag{4.35v}$$

$$M^d = M^s \tag{4.35vi}$$

The consumption function includes both real income and real interest rate as influencing variables. This is a blend of Keynesian and classical ideas and it reinforces the link between the real and monetary sectors and, therefore, plays an important role in the transmission mechanism in the monetarist model. The model in (4.35) ignores the government and foreign trade sectors. Staying within the IS-LM framework, one can derive the two reduced form equations (4.36) and (4.38). Using (4.35i)–(4.35iii),

$$\frac{Yn}{P} = C(\frac{Yn}{P}, r) + I(r) \tag{4.36}$$

and using (4.35v) and (4.35vi),

$$PL\left(\frac{Yn}{P}, rn\right) = M^s(rn) \tag{4.37}$$

In the model condensed in (4.36) and (4.37), there are four endogenous variables — *Yn, P, rn* and *r* but only two equations. Keynes and quantity theorists (or, monetarists for that matter) differ in how they supply the "missing equations". The assumption of price rigidity branded as "Keynesian" by Friedman can solve the problem of identification very easily. With $P = \overline{P}$, and $r = rn$ one has to solve for just *Yn* and *r* (or *rn*) from (4.36) and (4.37). The quantity theorists on the other hand reduced the number of endogenous variables by importing the assumption of full-employment, i.e. $Y = \overline{Y}$ or that the real output is determined from outside the model. However with professor Phillips's (1958) celebrated research into the relation between inflation and unemployment, the reliance on full-employment or on a fixed-price IS-LM model was very much on the wane. Friedman, in deriving his monetarist model, borrowed from both Keynes and the father of quantity theorists, Irving Fisher. As already pointed out in section 4.1.1 Friedman reinterpreted the Keynesian theory of the speculative demand as implying a long-term rate of interest; and this, he picked up as the idea of an expected or anticipated rate. Secondly following the quantity theory or monetarist tradition, the distinction between real and respective nominal magnitude was highlighted.

*The Monetarist Model of Nominal Income*[14]

This is derived from (4.35iv)–(4.35vi) by emphasising the distinction between: (a) the actual, i.e. observed or "measured" and the expected, i.e. unobserved or "permanent" and (b) the real and monetary or "nominal" components of interest rate, real income, etc. Friedman makes a series of assumptions to derive this model: first,

$$rn = r + \dot{p} \quad \text{and} \quad (rn)^e = r^e + \dot{p}^e \tag{4.41}$$

Second, assuming $rn = (rn)^e$ and using the relation between real and nominal income[15] he obtains

$$rn = r^e + \left\{ \frac{d(Yn)^e}{dt} / (Yn)^e \right\} - \left( \frac{\dot{Y}^e}{Y^e} \right)$$

$$\Rightarrow \quad rn = r^e - g^e + \left[ \frac{d(Yn)^e}{dt} / (Yn)^e \right] \tag{4.42}$$

Next, it is assumed that the difference

$$r^e - g^e = k, \quad \text{a constant} \tag{4.43}$$

Using (4.43), (4.42) yields

$$rn = \bar{k} + (\dot{Y}n)^e / (Yn)^e \tag{4.44}$$

The assumption (4.43) is justified on the following grounds:

---

14. This model was called a "theory of nominal income" first by Meltzer (1965).

15. $YN = P \times Y \;\Rightarrow\; \frac{dYn}{dt} = Y\dot{P} + \dot{Y}P \;\Rightarrow\; \left(\frac{dYn}{dt}\right) / Yn$

$= (\dot{P}Y + \dot{Y}P)/(PY) \;\Rightarrow\; \left(\frac{dYn}{dt}\right) / (Yn) = \dot{p} + \frac{\dot{Y}}{Y}$

(a) it agrees with the quantity theorists' assumption, $Y = \overline{Y}$ and Keynes's assumption, $P = \overline{P}$

(b) $r^e$ and $g^e$ do not vary in the short-run, and

(c) when $r^e$ and $g^e$ vary together the difference would be less than either.

Finally, the demand for money function (4.35iv) is assumed homogeneous of degree one in nominal income and the supply of money $M^s$ assumed exogenous like in the previous IS-LM models. Incorporating all these assumptions, the monetarist model of nominal income can be summarised as follows:

$$M^d = Yn\ L(rn, 1) = Yn\ M^d(rn) \qquad (4.45i)$$

$$M^d = M^s = M_t \qquad (4.45ii)$$

$$rn = \overline{k} + (\dot{Y}n)^e/(Yn)^e \qquad (4.44)$$

Obviously the assumption (4.44) imposes important dynamic elements into the model and, therefore, the solutions of the two endogenous variables, *Yn* and *rn* are obtained as functions of time, *t*:

$$Yn(t) = \frac{M(t)}{M^d(rn)} \qquad (4.46i)$$

$$\Rightarrow \quad Yn(t) = V^Y(rn) \cdot M(t) \qquad (4.46ii)$$

Where $V^Y$ is the velocity function and $M(t)$ (or as later called $M_t$) is the exogenously determined money supply at time $t$. The expected income $(Yn)^e$ is unobserved and Friedman (1957) implied an estimation procedure using a weighted average of past actual incomes with exponentially declining weights. Expected or "permanent" income at time *t* is measured as

$$(Yn)_t^e = \frac{1}{\Sigma\gamma^i} \sum_{i=0}^{\infty} \gamma^i (Yn)_{t-i}, \quad 0 < \gamma < 1 \qquad (4.47)$$

$$\Rightarrow \quad (Yn)_t^e = (1-\gamma)\,[Yn_t + \gamma Yn_{t-1} + \gamma^2 Yn_{t-2} + \cdots] \qquad (4.48)$$

This moving average method establishes an important link between observed and unobserved variables and is also obtainable from an adaptive expectation mechanism. Friedman (1957) however, applied Koyck transformation to (4.47): Lagging (4.47) by 1 period and multiplying the lagged series for $Yn^e_{t-1}$ by $\gamma$ derive

$$Yn^e_{t-1} = (1-\gamma)\,[\gamma Yn_{t-1} + \gamma^2 Yn_{t-2} + \cdots]$$

and then subtract this from (4.47) which yields

$$Yn^e_t - \gamma Yn^e_{t-1} = (1-\gamma)Yn_t \tag{4.48}$$

A relation like (4.48) can also follow from an adaptive expectation rule where expectations are adjusted on the basis of the forecast error made in the previous period:

$$Yn^e_t = Yn^e_{t-1} + \theta(Yn_t - Yn^e_{t-1}), \quad 0 < \theta < 1$$

$$\Rightarrow \quad Yn^e_t = \theta Yn_t + (1-\theta)Yn^e_{t-1} \tag{4.49}$$

The similarity between (4.49) and (4.47) or (4.48) can be seen by setting $\theta = 1 - \gamma$. Alternatively, one can derive $Yn^e_t$ as a weighted average of past incomes $Yn$ working from (4.49) and following the iterative method. Using (4.47), Friedman (1971) rewrites (4.46ii) as a dynamic equation:

$$Yn(t) = V^Y[Yn(t-i)]\; M(t), \quad 0 < i < t-1 \tag{4.50}$$

In (4.50), $V^Y$ is a function of "past history of income" which, in turn, is a function of "past history of money". So,

$$Yn(t) = F[M(t-i)] \cdot M(t), \quad 0 < i < t-1 \tag{4.51}$$

(4.51) depicts the dynamic behaviour out of nominal income and its long-term trend is determined by $\bar{k}, r^e$ and $g^e$. For rates of growth expressions, derivatives of logarithms w.r.t. time are used. So from the time derivatives of logarithms of (4.46ii), (4.44) etc., Friedman derives

$$\frac{Yn}{Yn} = \frac{\dot{V}^Y}{V^Y} + \frac{\dot{M}}{M} = \frac{\dot{r}n}{V^Y}\frac{dV^Y}{dr} + \frac{\dot{M}}{M} \tag{4.52}$$

$$\Rightarrow \quad \frac{\dot{Y}n}{Yn} = s\,\frac{dg^e}{dt} + \frac{\dot{M}}{M} \tag{4.53}$$

Where $s = \frac{d \log V^Y}{drn}$

Next it is assumed that the expected rate of growth of income is determined by an adaptive expectations scheme:

$$\frac{dg^e}{dt} = \gamma_2\left[\frac{\dot{Y}n}{Yn} - g^e\right], \quad 0 < \gamma_2 < 1 \tag{4.54}$$[16]

Substituting (4.54) in (4.53),

$$\frac{\dot{Y}n}{Yn} = g^e + \frac{1}{1-\gamma_2 s}\left[\frac{\dot{M}}{M} - g^e\right] \tag{4.55}$$

From (4.52),

$$\frac{\dot{Y}n}{Yn} - \frac{\dot{M}}{M} = \frac{\dot{V}^Y}{V^Y}$$

$$\Rightarrow \quad \frac{\dot{V}^Y}{V^Y} = g^e + \frac{1}{1-\alpha_2 s}\left[\frac{\dot{M}}{M} - g^e\right] - \frac{\dot{M}}{M} \qquad \text{from (4.55)}$$

$$\frac{\dot{V}^Y}{V^Y} = \frac{-\gamma_2 s g^e}{1-\gamma_2 s} + \frac{\gamma_2 s}{1-\gamma_2 s}\frac{\dot{M}}{M} = \frac{\gamma_2 s}{1-\gamma_2 s}\left(\frac{\dot{M}}{M} - g^e\right) \tag{4.56}$$

For $0 < \gamma_2 s < 1$, the equations (4.55) and (4.56) give a very important result of the quantity theory. If the rate of change of money equals the expected rate of change of nominal income, then nominal income changes at the same rate as money (or as expected nominal income) and the velocity remains constant. If $\left(\frac{\dot{M}}{M}\right) > g^e$, then $\left(\frac{\dot{Y}n^e}{yn^e}\right) > \left(\frac{\dot{M}}{M}\right)$ and $V^Y$ increases; this happens in a "boom". In a recession,

$$\left(\frac{\dot{M}}{M}\right) < g^e \quad \Rightarrow \quad \left(\frac{\dot{Y}n^e}{Yn^e}\right) < \frac{\dot{M}}{M}$$

$$\Rightarrow \quad \left(\frac{\dot{V}^Y}{V^Y}\right) < 0$$

or, that the velocity falls. So both Keynesians and the monetarists believe that $V$ is not a constant but changes with $M$, but as already pointed out, in the Keynesian System $V^Y$ and $M$ change in the opposite direction and, in the monetarist model, change in $V^Y$ reinforces the change in $M$.

Friedman has been criticised for some of the assumptions he has made to derive his model of nominal income.

---

16. This is the continuous analogue of the discrete formulation (4.49) above in terms of rates of growth.

(a) The assumption of homogeneity of degree one of nominal demand (i.e. homogeneity of degree zero of real demand) for money w.r.t. real income lacks sufficient theoretical justification. But this assumption has been an attractive one to many researchers. For example, Hacche (1974) tested the stability of the demand for money function for the U.K. on this assumption — for which, again, he was heavily criticised by Courakis (1978).

(b) Friedman assumed $rn = rn^e$ which can be true only in equilibrium.

(c) The original assumption of an endogenous money supply $M^s = M^s(rn)$ would have been worth pursuing but it was dropped from his final model.

(d) Most importantly, dumping the assumption of a simple price rigidity on Keynes does less than justice to Keynesian economics. Friedman's division of a change in nominal income between prices and output will be dealt with later.

### 4.1.3 Empirical Evidence on the Stability of the Demand for Money in the U.K.

A stable demand for money function is vital for the effectiveness of monetary policy in any country. Stability in its simplest interpretation means whether the demand for money continues to depend on the same variables with constant parameters over a long period of time. So, if the demand for money in the U.K. can be considered a stable function of, say, the real income, the real rate of interest, the rate of inflation etc., then, movements in these variables along with other structural changes that may have taken place should be able to explain why there has been a five fold increase in the demand for money in the U.K. during 1965-1982.[17] Structural changes or changes in variables other than those included in the function can lead to shifts of the demand function and thereby explain part of the variation. In the U.K. such structural changes are believed to have taken place as the government was strengthening monetary control to curb the rate of inflation. The various tools of monetary policy and the degree of control on them over time will be discussed in 4.2. For now we note that the methods of monetary control were more stringent in the

---

17. According to Begg *et al.* [1984, p. 521] the amount of money in the U.K. went up from £7.6 bn. in 1965 to £3.8 bn. in 1982.

period before the 1970s than in the period 1971-80 and the financial strategy in the 1980s again should be distinguished from that in the 1970s. In the empirical work on the demand for money in the U.K. this has been taken into account.

To name only a few, Laidler and Parkin (1970), Artis and Lewis (1976), Coghlan (1978), Laumas (1978), Rowan and Miller (1979) have considered the questions of stability of the demand for money in the U.K. For the ease of deriving various elasticities of demand the function has been estimated in the log-linear form in all these studies[18] and the quarterly data on $M1$ separated from that on $M3$.

In Laidler and Parkin's (1976) model desired/real cash balances depend on expected or permanent real income and the real rate of interest and actual cash balances adjust to the desired demand with a lag. These imply the following model:

$$\log M_t^* = a + b \log Y_t^e + d \log r_t \qquad \text{(i)}$$

$$\log Y_t^e = \log Y_{t-1}^e + \lambda(\log Y_t - \log Y_{t-1}^e)$$

$$\Rightarrow \quad \log Y_t^e = \lambda \log Y_t + (1-\lambda)\log Y_{t-1}^e \quad 0 < \lambda \leqq 1 \qquad \text{(ii)} \qquad (4.57)$$

$$\log M_t = \log M_{t-1} + \theta(\log M_t^* - \log M_{t-1})$$

$$\Rightarrow \quad \log M_t = \theta \log M_t^* + (1-\theta)\log M_{t-1}, \quad 0 < \theta \leqq 1 \qquad \text{(iii)}$$

The difference between (ii) and (iii) is that in (ii) expectations are adjusted (partially if $\lambda < 1$) on the basis of the discrepancy between actual and expected income in the previous period and in (iii), actual demand for money is adjusted to the desired demand for money. In long-run equilibrium the desired and actual demands are equal. The reduced form equation of the Laidler-Parkin model is obtained in the following way. The expected income and the desired demands for money are unobserved

---

18. Note that: in the continuous form elasticity of any variable, say, $y$, w.r.t. another variable, say, $x$, is $\frac{dy}{dx} \cdot \frac{x}{y}$ and that $d \log y = \frac{1}{y} dy$ and $d \log x = \frac{1}{x} dx$

$\Rightarrow \frac{d \log y}{d \log x} = \frac{dy}{dx} \cdot \frac{x}{y}$ = elasticity of $y$ w.r.t. $x$.

variables and, therefore, the equation to be estimated should be rewritten in terms of the observed variables. First lagging 4.57(i) and (iii), one obtains

$$\log M_{t-1} = \theta(a + b\log Y^e_{t-1} + d\log r_{t-1}) + (1-\theta)\log M_{t-2}$$

$$\Rightarrow \quad \log Y^e_{t-1} = \frac{1}{\theta b}\left(\log M_{t-1} - \theta a - \theta d \log r_{t-1} - (1-\theta)\log M_{t-2}\right)$$

Substituting for $\log Y^e_t$ and $\log Y^e_{t-1}$ in 4.57(ii), one obtains

$$\frac{1}{\theta b}(\log M_t - \theta a - \theta d\log r_{t-1}(1-\theta)\log M_{t-1}) = \lambda\log Y_t +$$

$$\frac{1-\lambda}{\theta b}(\log M_{t-1} - \theta a - \theta d\log r_{t-1} - (1-\theta)\log M_{t-2})$$

$$\Rightarrow \quad \log M_t = \theta a(1 - 1 + \lambda) + \theta b\lambda\log y_t + \theta d\log r_t - (1-\lambda)\theta d\log r_{t-1}$$

$$+ (1 - \theta + 1 - \lambda)\log M_{t-1} - (1-\theta)(1-\lambda)\log M_{t-2}$$

$$\Rightarrow \quad \log M_t = \theta a\lambda + \theta b\lambda\log Y_t + \theta d\log r_t - \theta(1-\lambda)d\log r_{t-1}$$

$$+ (2 - \theta - \lambda)\log M_{t-1} - (1-\theta)(1-\lambda)\log M_{t-2} \quad (4.58)$$

(4.58) is the equation estimated from the quarterly data for the U.K. for 1956-1967. A problem of over identification of this model can be easily noted from (4.58). The equation has got only five parameters *a, b, d,* $\lambda$ and $\theta$ but six coefficients estimated from the data.[19] An additional constraint was needed to tackle this problem. Equation (4.58) is a general from of the demand for money function which includes a number of special cases obtained by setting $\lambda = 1, \theta = 1$ etc. The results obtained by Laidler and Parkin were not all consistent — either with economic theory or with economic reality[20] but they generally favoured the forms with lagged values of the explanatory variables pointing to the importance of the role of expectation in behavioural equations.

Artis and Lewis had their quarterly data extended to 1973 and found evidence of instability in the 1970s. Their estimating form was:

---

19. Note that (4.58) can be rewritten as

$$\log M_t = b_0 + b_1\log Y_t + b_2\log r_t + b_3\log r_{t-1} + b_4\log M_{t-1} + b_5\log M_{t-2} + u_t$$

where $u_t$ is the random error term.

20. See Laidler and Parkin [1970] pp. 205-8.

$$\log M_t = b_0 + b_1 \log Y_t + b_2(\log r_t - \log r_t^m)$$

$$+ b_3 \log q_t + b_4 \log M_{t-1} + u_t \tag{4.59}$$

obtained from the assumptions that the desired demand for money depends, log-linearly, on real income, on the ratio of other rates of interest to the own rate on money, on an index of the quality of bonds $qt$ and that the actual demand adjusts to the desired demand with a *lag*, $\theta$. The equation (4.59) was tested for separate data periods 1963-1970, 1963-1971 and for 1963-1973. The instability evident after 1971 supports the view that the *Competition and Credit Control* (CCC) introduced by the Bank of England in 1971 produced important shifts of the demand for money function. Hacche too agreed with this view and concentrated on the appropriate structure of lags in the demand for money whereas Artis and Lewis preferred to include a number of important supply factors. In their opinion, the supply of money, $M1$ may be "demand-determined" but the supply including all interest bearing deposits, $M3$ should best be considered exogenous particularly in the post 1970s. The commonly held notion that money supply is demand-determined is based on a few well known facts. For example, the bank of England fixes the prices of gilt-edged securities and therefore the interest rate. A fixed interest rate, in turn, implies an infinitely elastic money supply at the rate set and, therefore, the data on $M$ reveal $M^d$ rather than $M^s$. This would also be the result under a fixed exchange rate regime. With the introduction of CCC in 1971 the exchange rate assumed some flexibility and the "pegging" policy in the gilt-edged market also underwent some changes. These were important enough to cast doubt on the assumption of a demand-determined money supply in the 1970s. Among the factors affecting money supply and which are independent of demand conditions, changes in high-powered money, the domestic borrowing requirement and various advances were found to be important during the 1970s. With an exogenous money supply, the responsibility of clearing the money market (i.e. making $M^d = M^s$) has to rest on the interest rate (like in the liquidity preference theory) and income. Artis and Lewis found evidence supporting the view that income and interest rates, i.e. the variables affecting money demand, are adjusting to money supply rather than the other way round and that "the changes in the money supply have been interacting with a relatively stable demand function".[21]

Laumas (1978) also tested the stability of the demand for money in the U.K. over the period 1964-1976. To capture the effect of CCC and other changes the data were split into the period 1964-1971 and 1971-76. He started with the measured income version of Laidler and Parkin's model which can be derived by setting $\lambda = 1$ in the final estimating equation (4.58) of Laidler and Parkin. So, Laumas's estimating equation is

$$\log M_t = \theta a + \theta b \log Y_t + \theta d \log r_t + (1-\theta)\log M_{t-1} \qquad (4.60)$$

where 0 is the speed with which actual demand adjusts to the desired demand for cash balances. Instead of using the common technique of the *F*-test[22] or dummy[23] variables, Laumas used the varying parameter approach to test the stability of the parameters of (3.60) over time. Writing equation (4.60) in a form similar to (4.59)

$$\log M_t = b_0 + b_1 \log Y_t + b_2 \log r_t + b_3 \log M_{t-1} \qquad (4.61)$$

where each $b_i$ follows the restrictions implied by (4.60), Lauma's technique is to assume that the parameters $b_{it}$ follows an adaptive structure:

$$\left.\begin{aligned} b_{it} &= b^*_{it} + u_t \\ b^*_{it} &= b^*_{it-1} + u_t \end{aligned}\right\} \quad \begin{aligned} i &= 0-3, \\ t &= 1, \cdots n \end{aligned} \qquad (4.62)$$

where $b^*_{it}$ is the permanent value of the *i*th parameter at time *t* and $u_t$ are stochastic variations in the actual and permanent values respectively.

The estimates for the period 1964-1971 indicated that the money demand equations based on *M*1 were stable when the interest rate used was that on long-term bonds. The results for the later period 1971-1976 indicated a major shift in these demand equations caused possibly by higher rates of inflation and rising rates of interest. The results for the broader money stock *M*3 were different as expected from those for *M*1 with a much slower adjustment between actual and desired values.

---

21. Artis and Lewis (1976) p. 176.
22. See Mayes (1981) p. 108.
23. See Mayes (1981) p. 181 on the use of dummy variables.

Grice and Bennett (1984) consider the role of wealth in influencing the demand for the wider aggregate £ *M*3 for the period 1953-1978. Ignoring the problems of aggregation, the demand for money for the non-bank private sector as a whole is written as

$$\log M_t = b_0 + b_1 \log V_t + b_2 \log Y_t + b_3 rm_t + b_4 rg_t$$

$$+ \sum_{i=1}^{3} b_{5i} D_i + b_6 \log M_{t-1} \qquad (4.63)$$

Quite a few amendments were made to this basic equation on various grounds. First, gross wealth can change because of revaluation of existing asset prices. So, $\log V_t$ was changed to $\log V_t + \log\left(1 + \frac{REV}{V}\right)$ where *REV* stands for cumulative revaluation of asset prices. $Y_t$ was proxied by deflated total final expenditure as in many other empirical studies. $rm_t$ is the own rate on money and $rg_t$ is the total return on gilts expressed as excess to the own rate on money, i.e., $rg = rm - \sum_i ri$ where *ri* is the return on the *i*th gilt. Three seasonal dummy variables were added on top of the one to capture the impact of CCC. So, $D_{4t} = 0$ before the 1971 first quarter and each $D_{4t} = 1$ thereafter. Finally to distinguish between the long and short-run elasticities, a five quarter lag was introduced on all variables other than the dummies. So, the final estimating form was

$$\log M_t = b_0 + \sum_{i=0}^{5} b_{1i} \log V_{t-i} + \sum_{i=0}^{5} b_{2i} \log Y_{t-i} + \sum_{i=0}^{5} b_{3i} rm_{t-i} + \sum_{i=0}^{5} b_{1i} \log\left(1 + \frac{REV}{V}\right)_{t-i}$$

$$+ \sum_{i=0}^{5} b_{4i} rg_{t-i} + \sum_{i=1}^{3} b_{5i} D_i + b_{54} D_4 + \sum_{i=0}^{5} b_{6i} \log M_{t-i} \qquad (4.64)$$

A new feature of this equation is the absence of a permanent or expected income approach and the direct inclusion of the wealth variable. In the previous studies, permanent income has been used as a proxy for wealth.[24] Because of this, the actual income $Y_t$ can capture the transactions demand effects alone. The more important results of Grice and Bennett's study can be summarised as follows. The long-run income elasticity (0.32) was not much different from the short-run (0.37) one but there was evidence of cyclical changes in this elasticity. The short and long-run

---

24. See Friedman, M. (1957).

estimates of $b_{54}$ indicated that the impact of CCC was significant and it raised £ $M3$ by 1.83 per cent in the short and by over 13 per cent in the long-run. The Chow-test[25] indicated no serious structural instability in the parameter values. The seasonal dummies also proved to be significant. All these results were based on the assumption of perfect foresight, implying that one can replace expected returns etc. by their ex-post values. The model was extended to include the case of imperfect foresight and measurement error and the results, although not all conclusive, indicated a very important role of financial wealth in determining £ $M3$ and that CCC had had a permanent upward effect on £ $M3$.

## 4.2 THE SUPPLY OF MONEY

### 4.2.1 **Definition of Money Supply**

In the simple Keynesian IS-LM models discussed so far, money supply has been assumed to be exogenous or fixed by the monetary authorities. In this section the determinants of money supply and how they are affected by the various instruments of monetary control are explained briefly. The previous chapters have also implied a uniquely defined aggregate as the supply of money. But in reality there are many definitions of money supply of which the following three are regarded as the most important ones: (a) $M1$ is the narrowest definition of money supply including only the notes and coins in circulation and the *demand deposits*[26] held by the U.K. residents. Demand deposits are those against which cheques can be drawn and no prior notice is required for withdrawal. (b) £ $M3$ contains $M1$ and all time deposits held in sterling by the U.K. private and the public sectors. All time deposits yield interest and require prior notice for withdrawal with no loss of interest. (c) $M3$ is the widest measure of money supply and comprises all sterling $M3$ (£ $M3$) and U.K. residents' deposits in foreign currencies. Since the late 1970's, £ $M3$ replaced $M3$ as the official target of monetary policy in the U.K. To these three, two other measures of private sector liquidity can be added: $PSL1$ defined to include private

---

25. It is similar to the $F$-test. See Mayes (1981) p. 108.
26. Begg et al. calls these "sight" deposits [1984, p. 508].

sector holding of £ *M*3, of short-term securities and certificates of tax deposits, and *PSL*2 defined to include *PSL*1, private sector's savings and deposits with non-clearing banks and building societies.

### 4.2.2 The Instruments of Monetary Control in the U.K.

Like fiscal policy, monetary policy too has a number of important macroeconomic goals, such as price stability, full employment, balance of payments equilibrium, a steady growth of real income, etc. The most basic objective of monetary control however is thought to be the attainment of price stability or a low rate of inflation. As long as money supply grows at the same rate as the productive potential of the economy, the price level remains stable. However, very few economies can ever achieve this ideal state. So controlling the money supply from time to time becomes important.

In the U.K. instruments of monetary control were changed from time to time. Before 1971, the Bank Rate (called the Minimum Lending Rate since 1972), Reserve Ratios, Special Deposits, ceilings on interest rates and bank lending were the main instruments of control imposed on the clearing banks. This system of control was not very effective since the merchant banks were able to continue expanding their lending business rapidly. In 1972, the Bank of England changed its policy to what is known as Competition and Credit Control (CCC). This system allowed the clearing banks to compete for deposits and advances since they were no longer subjected to the interest rate ceilings. Reserve Ratios were modified to require all banks to hold at least 121/2 per cent of their liabilities in the form of liquid assets. *MLR* was retained as well. Since the clearing banks were not controlled as severely as before, the quantity of £ *M*3 grew very rapidly during 1971-1973. The Bank of England was forced to introduce a much more severe form of control viz, the Supplementary Special Deposit known as the Corset. The Corset introduced a tax on deposit-financed lending by the banks. The Corset was abolished in 1980. Since 1980, the banks are allowed a great deal more freedom and relieved off the *MLR* and reserve requirements. Money markets have developed very rapidly since the 1970s and this, by offering easy convertibility, has, to some extent, reduced the importance of maintaining a high ratio of liquid assets to total liabilities.[27] In addition to these methods of control, open market operations meaning sale and purchase of government securities are generally used in every country to alter the monetary base.

### 4.2.3 *Money Creation*

Any method of controlling the money supply affects the process of money creation. The main causes of money creation are:

(i) The PSBR,
(ii) a fall in non-bank private sector lending to the public sector,
(iii) a rise in bank lending to the non-bank private sector,
(iv) a public sector purchase of foreign currency assets with sterling and,
(v) a rise in banking sector net claims on foreigners.[28],

In the next chapter, it will be discussed how government spending if not financed by taxation or bond sales must cause an equal increase in the money supply. This is a direct effect of the PSBR. Government spending also produces an indirect effect on money supply by raising the banks' claims on the public sector and thereby inducing the banks to lend more to the private sector.

It has already been pointed out that money supply must not grow any faster than the productive capacity of the economy. This link between the growth of money supply and the rate of inflation follows from the monetarist assumption that the growth of nominal money income, $Yn\ (= P \times Y)$, and the money supply are equal in the long run. On this assumption, Congdon (1982) shows how one can derive the following long-run relation between money supply, prices and the PSBR. This is done in a period analysis or a discrete form. First, it is assumed that

$$\frac{\Delta(PY)}{PY} = \frac{\Delta M}{M} = m, \quad \text{say} \qquad (4.65\text{i})^{29}$$

29

Next, excluding foreign complications,

27. The reader is referred to Begg et al. (1984) chs. 23 and 27 for details.
28. See Gowland [1982] for a detailed discussion of these causes.
29. This is the discrete analogue of Friedman's continuous formulation.

$$\Delta M = D - \Delta B + \Delta Ad \tag{4.65ii}$$

Where $D$ is the PSBR, $B$ is the stock of government debt held by the non-bank private sector and $Ad$ is the outstanding total of bank advances to the private sector, $B$ and $Ad$ are related to nominal income as:

$$B = a_1(PY) \quad 0 < a_1 < 1 \tag{4.66i}$$

and $$Ad = a_2(PY) \quad 0 < a_2 < 1 \tag{4.66ii}$$

implying $$\Delta B = a_1 \Delta(PY) \tag{4.67i}$$

and $$\Delta Ad = a_2 \Delta(PY) \tag{4.67ii}$$

implying in turn

$$\Delta M = D - a_1 \Delta(PY) + a_2 \Delta(PY)$$

$$\Rightarrow \quad \frac{\Delta M}{PY} = \frac{D}{PY} - a_1 \frac{\Delta(PY)}{PY} + a_2 \frac{\Delta PY}{PY}$$

$$\Rightarrow \quad \frac{\Delta M}{PY} = \frac{D}{PY} - (a_1 - a_2)m \quad \text{from} \qquad (4.65\text{i})$$

Now, $\frac{\Delta M}{PY}$ can be written as $\frac{\Delta M}{M} \cdot \frac{M}{PY}$

$$m \cdot \frac{M}{PY} = \frac{D}{PY} - (a_1 - a_2)m$$

$$\frac{D}{PY} = m\left(\frac{M}{PY} + a_1 - a_2\right)$$

$$m = \frac{\frac{D}{(PY)}}{\frac{M}{PY} + a_1 - a_2} \tag{4.68}$$

(4.68) shows that the rate of growth of money supply varies positively with the ratio of PSBR to GDP if

$$\frac{M}{PY}+a_1-a_2>0$$

i.e., if $$\frac{M}{PY}+a_1>a_2$$

i.e., if $$\frac{M}{PY}+\frac{B}{PY}>\frac{Ad}{PY}$$

ie, if $$M+B>Ad \tag{4.69}$$

which is certainly true. From the monetarist assumption (4.65i), the link between the rate of inflation and the rate of growth of money supply follows immediately. Expanding the L.H.S. of (4.65i), one obtains

$$\frac{Y\Delta P+P\Delta Y}{PY}=m$$

$$\Rightarrow \quad \frac{\Delta P}{P}+\frac{\Delta Y}{Y}=m$$

$$\Rightarrow \quad \frac{\Delta P}{P}=0 \quad \text{if } m\left(=\frac{\Delta M}{M}\right)=\frac{\Delta Y}{Y}$$

Inflation occurs only when money supply grows faster than real output.

### 4.2.4 **The Endogeneity of Money Supply**

Our only brief encounter with this has been with reference to Friedman's model in Section 4.1. In equation (4.35v), money supply was assumed to be a function of nominal rate of interest. Friedman (1971) also suggested an alternative formulation:

$$M^s=Hm\,M(rn) \tag{4.70}$$

where *Hm* is high-powered money and $M(rn)$ is the money multiplier. However, for the purpose of his model as described in 4.1, the idea of an endogenous money supply was not pursued much further.

Because of the difficulties of controlling money supply directly and as suggested in 4.2.1, it is more realistic to assume that money supply is endogenous.

Teigen (1964) developed a model of bank credit multiplier as follows: the public are assumed to hold currency in a proportion, say, $c_0$, to their bank deposits, *Bd*. That is,

$$\dot{c}u^P = c_0 Bd, \quad 0 < c_0 < 1 \tag{4.70i}$$

where $cu^P$ is the currency held by the Public. High-powered money *Hm*, or the monetary base is assumed to be the sum of bank reserves, *BR* and the currency held by the public:

$$Hm = cu^P + BR \tag{4.70ii}$$

Now money supply as already seen is

$$M = cu^P + Bd \tag{4.70iii}$$

From (4.70i) and (4.70ii)

$$\frac{M}{Hm} = \frac{cu^P + Bd}{cu^P + BR} = \frac{(c_0 + 1)Bd}{c_0 Bd + BR} \tag{4.70iv}$$

Let the reserve ratio be $cr_0 \Rightarrow$

$$BR = cr_0 Bd \quad \Rightarrow \quad \text{from (4.70iv)}$$

$$\frac{M}{Hm} = \frac{c_0 + 1}{(c_0 + \dot{c}r_0)} \quad \Rightarrow \quad M = \frac{c_0 + 1}{c_0 + cr_0} Hm \tag{4.71}$$

(4.71) is an oft-quoted relation defining the bank credit multiplier:

$$cm = \frac{c_0 + 1}{c_0 + cr_0} \tag{4.72}$$

A slightly different version of credit multiplier is obtained by separating bank reserves into a part which banks are legally required to hold and the part voluntarily held by banks in excess of legal requirements.

$$BR = BRL + BRE \tag{4.73i}$$

where *BRL* is legal and *BRE* is excess reserves; accordingly the reserve ratio can be split into a legally maintained ratio *crl* and a ratio of excess to total reserves, *cre*:

$$cr_0 = crl + cre \tag{4.73ii}$$

$$\text{where} \quad crl = \frac{BRL}{BD} \quad \text{and} \quad cre = \frac{BRE}{BD} \tag{4.73iii}$$

On this extension the money multiplier would be rewritten as:

$$\frac{M}{Hm} = \frac{c_0 + 1}{c_0 + crl + cre} \tag{4.74}$$

In this model, *crl* is a policy determined variable and whether money supply is controllable by altering high powered money depends on the stability of *crl* and $c_0$. Empirical studies suggest that in the U.K. *crl* has varied considerably over different time periods. As Sheppard (1971) found, between 1881-1962, cash ratio varied between 6 per cent and 17 per cent exhibiting greatest instability during the inter-war period. Prior to the introduction of competition and credit control cash ratio was 8 per cent and the liquid assets ratio was 28 per cent. The CCC changed the latter to 121/2 per cent and in the 1980's with easy marketability of all types of liquid assets *crl* is around 11/2 per cent — 1/2 per cent. The ratio $c_0$ is governed by portfolio decisions of the non-bank public. Like the demand for consumer goods, the demand for currency of non-bank public can be assumed to depend on real income, relative prices, etc. As interest rates on various types of time deposits increase the demand for currency falls. As consumers' real income increases, they tend to finance a larger part of their transactions by writing cheques implying that the demand for cash may fall. But there is no conclusive evidence as to how $c_0$ changes with real income. *cre* is the outcome of portfolio decisions of the banks. Sims and Takayama (1985) extend the money supply function to include securities, a whole range of relevant interest rates as well as *crl*.

Although there is doubt over the stability of the credit multiplier model, altering monetary base can control money supply in an indirect way. Given a certain quantity of base money over and above legal reserve requirement the banks and the non-bank public are in competition to obtain their voluntary excess reserves and currency holdings respectively. A change in the quantity of base money, therefore, can create discrepancies between actual and desired reserves of banks leading to changes in their acquisition of earning assets and; therefore, their deposits. From this idea a special case of the money base-money multiplier model has been developed (Artis and Lewis, 1990). This model is based on the "reserves available" approach and has found support for the United States. The reserves available to the banks are treated as an exogenous variable and it makes:

$$M = \left[\frac{1+c_0}{crl+cre}\right] \cdot BR \qquad (4.74i)$$

In the USA, short-run variations in the credit multiplier have been prominent. Disturbance to portfolio equilibrium can only be corrected over time implying a more stable multiplier in the long-run. Capie and Rodrik Bali (1986) have shown that this multiplier for the UK has fluctuated within a narrow range during 1871-1971 but, as a result of CCC, the money multiplier increased from around 4 to around 10 in the next decade 1971-81. The tremendous development of money and financial markets in the recent years means that the banks can buy in reserves anytime they need to and follow their own policy of liability management.

An alternative model follows from the Flow of Funds (FF) or the Credit Counterparts (CC) approach. This model also takes an explicit account of the foreign sector. The FF model separates the economy into four sectors: an official sector comprising the Central bank and the government, a private non-financial sector, a financial sector comprising only the banks and a foreign sector. It uses the basic national income accounting identity that total withdrawals equal total injection:

$$S + T + Im = I + G + X \tag{4.75i}$$

The banks are assumed to finance private investment through advances. An excess of exports over imports represents a borrowing requirement by the foreign sector and an excess of government spending over taxes or government revenue represents a borrowing requirement by the government sector. The total borrowing requirement has to be matched by the surplus of savings over investment in the non-financial private sector:

$$S - I = (X - Im) + (G - T) \tag{4.75ii}$$

Now, the excess of saving over investment represents an increase in net financial wealth of the non-bank public and it may take the forms of acquisition of foreign assets, additional holdings of bonds, cash, deposits or any other form of wealth. So, an excess of saving over investment in the real private sector will manifest into a capital outflow—*Ki*, an increase in the liability of the official sector, an increase in the deposit and non-deposit liabilities of the banks, *nBd*, and extra cash holding. This leads to the following equation for the banks' portfolio where the banks are assumed to have no net saving.

$$S - I = \Delta C + \Delta B + \Delta Bd + \Delta nBd - Ki - \Delta Ad \tag{4.75iii}$$

From (4.75ii) and (4.75iii) one can derive the increase in money supply:

$$\Delta C + \Delta Bd = \Delta M$$

Equating (4.75ii) with (4.75iii)

$$(X - Im) + (G - T) = \Delta M + \Delta B + \Delta nBd - Ki - \Delta Ad$$

$$\Rightarrow \quad \Delta M = (G - T) - \Delta B + (X - Im + Ki) + \Delta Ad - \Delta nBd \tag{4.76}$$

Artis and Lewis (1990) show how the money multiplier and credit counter parts approaches can be very closely linked together. Their relative applicability will depend on the institutional framework of a country. The advantage of the CC approach is that it identifies the components of the model with respective policies, viz., $(G-T)$ with fiscal, $\Delta B$ with debt management, $(\Delta Ad - \Delta nBd)$ with monetary and $(X - Im + Ki)$ with exchange rate policies. Until very recently the UK's emphasis was on the broader aggregate, the sterling $M_3$ and its relation to PSBR. In this framework, the CC approach is more applicable than the credit multiplier approach. In the USA, the narrower aggregates $M_1$, & $M_0$ have been accorded greater emphasis implying that the credit multiplier approach is more applicable. Of late, change are taking place in opposite direction in the two countries.[30]

## 4.3 EQUILIBRIUM IN THE MONEY MARKET

The above analysis shows that money can be treated as only one among many financial assets and therefore, the equality between the supply of and demand for money is but one component of overall equilibrium in the financial sector. If one applies Walras's law to the financial sector as a whole, then one need not discuss equilibrium in the money market separately since the latter will hold if the rest of the financial sector is in equilibrium. Then, the credit counterparts models merely show the breakdown of the total available quantity of money and the money multiplier model how the quantity of high powered money endogenously adjusts to demand.

The idea of an exogenous money supply accommodates a disequilibrium approach to the money market. Nominal money supply is determined by the authorities; the actual demand for real money balances is adjusted to the desired level via the price level; unwanted money balances will be spent on goods and services bidding up their prices and money balances will be released by spending less on goods and services bidding their prices down. Disequilibrium view is also the basis of the 'buffer-stock' theory. It holds that a disequilibrium in the financial sector can be met by varying the buffer-stock around its desired level. The

30. Artis and Lewis (1990) p. 11.

buffer-stock theory essentially is an extension of the quantity theory and can be separated from the former by the length of the time period over which money acts as a buffer. The buffer-stock models are based on a distinction between permanent and transitory money holdings. The buffer-stock role of money arises because the cost of transitory money holdings is less than costs of adjustment for other financial and real assets. Thus transitory money balances will be willingly held at unchanged given levels of income and interest rates. The implications of this disequilibrium model are:

(a) Unexpected changes in money supply will be willingly absorbed in transitory balances at constant income and interest rates.
(b) If such transitory balances are a significant volatile part of total money holdings then the demand functions ignoring such balances would exhibit instability over time.
(c) Prices will adjust to money supply with a lag.

## 4.4 BUFFER-STOCK MODELS

Research into BSM models was initiated by Darby's (1972) "shock absorber" hypothesis. This means that a large proportion of transitory savings will first reflect into transitory money balances and the latter will, only gradually, be adjusted to their permanent level as the surplus or deficit is eliminated by "transfers to or from financial assets or durable goods or transitory savings of opposite sign" (p. 930). So, Darby's model applies Friedman's income classification to money balances and assets — comprising non-monetary assets, consumer durables and human capital. In the discrete form the hypothesis is:

$$\Delta M_{Tt} = a_1 S_{Tt} + a_2 M_{Tt-1} \quad \Rightarrow \quad M_{Tt} = a_1 S_{Tt} + (1 + a_2) M_{Tt-1} \quad (4.76i)$$

where $a_1 > 0$ is the fraction of transitory savings, $S_{Tt}$, going directly into cash holding and $a_2 < 0$ gives the rate at which transitory money holdings, $M_{Tt}$ are adjusted. Non-monetary transitory savings, $S_{nTt}$, are defined as:

$$S_{nTt} \equiv S_{Tt} - \Delta M_{Tt} \quad (4.78)$$

Also transitory savings are assumed to equal transitory income, $Y_{Tt}$.

$$\Rightarrow \quad M_{Tt} = a_1 Y_{Tt} + (1 + a_2) M_{Tt-1} \quad (4.77ii)$$

Friedman's classification of income was applied to real money balances:

$$Y_t = Y_{pt} + Y_{Tt} \tag{4.79i}$$

$$M_t = M_{pt} + M_{Tt} \tag{4.79ii}$$

The adaptive expectation rule was assumed for the unobserved permanent income first estimated by a quadratic trend since the latter was well supported by the US quarterly data for 1947-66. Estimated permanent income is then last period's permanent income plus growth from a quadratic trend (4.80):

$$\log Y_t = b_1 + b_2 t + b_3 t^2 + e_{1t} \tag{4.80}$$

The growth rate$\left[\equiv \frac{dY}{dt} \cdot \frac{1}{Y} = \frac{d \log Y}{dt}\right]$ given by (4.80) is

$$\frac{d \log Y}{dt} = b_2 + 2b_3 \cdot t$$

$$\Rightarrow \quad Y^e_{pt} = Y_{pt-1} + (b_2 + 2b_3 t)\, Y_{pt-1}$$

$$\Rightarrow \quad Y^e_{pt} = (1 + b_2 + 2b_3 \cdot t) Y_{pt-1} \tag{4.81}$$

The estimate of permanent income $Y^e_{pt}$ was then put in the adaptive expectation framework such as (4.49) rewritten in the discrete form:

$$Y_{pt} = Y^e_{pt} + \lambda [Y_t - Y^e_{pt}] \tag{4.82i}$$

$$\Rightarrow \quad Y_{pt} = \lambda Y_t + (1 - \lambda)(1 + b_2 + 2b_3 \cdot t)\, Y_{pt-1} \tag{4.82ii}$$

where $0 < \lambda < 1$.

It should be noted that although the final equation (4.82ii) has the one-period lagged variable $Y_{pt-1}$ as found in adaptive expectation mechanism, the lag should have been present in the formation of expectation (4.82i) instead it results from the substitution of estimated permanent income from (4.81). This is to the mixing up of a continuous time trend with a discrete adaptive expectation formula.

For the US aggregate data the following estimates were obtained:

$$\hat{\lambda} = 0.1, \quad \hat{b}_2 = .0061, \quad \hat{b}_3 = .0000319$$

and $t$ was measured from 1947, first quarter.

The demand for permanent money balances was assumed, as usual, a function of permanent income, long and short-term interest rates and an estimated yield for money:

$$M_{pt} = a_3 + a_4 Y_{pt} + a_5 rl_t + a_6 rs_t + a_7 rm_t + e_{2t} \tag{4.83}$$

The long term interest rate *rl* is the quarterly average of US government long-term bond yield and *rs* is that of treasury 3 month bills' market yield. The yield on money was estimated from the rule (4.84).

$$rm_t = (1 - \frac{Hm}{M})rs_t \tag{4.84}$$

Real money balances comprised currency plus demand deposits deflated by consumer price index. In the above analysis, the price index has not been explicitly included for the sake of convenience. The final equation estimated by Darby follows from the shock absorber hypothesis (4.77ii) and the other assumptions described above. This is derived in the appendix. Because of the composite error term, estimates were obtained by generalised least squares method. The coefficients all had plausible signs and all but *rl* was statistically significant. The estimate for the coefficient of permanent income was rather low, only .2483 but this might have been due to linearity assumption (4.83) and a narrow definition of money. But the low estimate was enough to cast doubt on the assumption of unitary income elasticity of money demand. The estimated coefficient of transitory income was significant and equal to 0.5664. Despite the strong support from the data for the shock absorber hypothesis, Darby's results should be accepted with caution as he applied a number of simplifying assumptions in deriving his estimates.

Johnston (1983) estimates a similar demand for money equation to Darby's for the broader aggregate, £ $M_3$ and found that transitory income had a powerful effect on money holdings in the UK.[31] Cuthbertson (1988) has summarised a few other tests of the BSM model on the British and American data.[32] These will not be repeated here.

## 4.5 DEMAND FOR MONEY IN AN OPEN ECONOMY: CURRENCY SUBSTITUTION

In a developed open economy the public can hold money balances in both domestic and foreign currencies. This is a natural consequence of the increased integration of international markets and interdependency of asset holdings. By holding money in more than one currency the public can benefit from and safeguard against interest and exchange rates

---

31. Cuthbertson, K. (1988) p. 133.
32. Cuthbertson, K. (1988) p. 133-42.

fluctuations. The most important implication is that foreign as well as domestic monetary policies influence domestic money holdings and such influence is usually referred to as Currency Substitution (C.S.). The implications of C.S. will be more fully explored in Chapter 8. For now, it may be noted that the possibility of currency substitution can alter the stability of the demand function for money based on domestic currency alone. For example Brittain (1981) finds that foreign interest rates explain a considerable amount of the observed instability of velocity in the USA and Germany. However most empirical works in this field assume a perfect elasticity of substitution among different assets. The individuals money holdings in more than one currency are derived as part of an optimum portfolio choice.

Girton and Roper (1981) develop the following simple model and show how C.S. raises problems for determination of exchange rates. Money balances are assumed to be held in the domestic as well as in one foreign currency. Then, the exchange rate can be written as:

$$E = \frac{P_h}{P_f}$$

where $P_h$ and $P_f$ are the domestic and foreign price levels respectively. The demand for each currency holding is assumed to depend exponentially on domestic and foreign interest rates, the rate of return on assets other than money and wealth. The main focus of attention being C.S. and exchange rate, the wealth term is not being included in the following equations for demand for each currency.

$$\log(M_h/P_h) = a_h(r_h - r) + b_h(r_h - r_f) \tag{4.85}$$

$$\Rightarrow \quad \log M_h - \log P_h = a_h(r_h - r) + b_h(r_h - r_f) \tag{4.85$'$}$$

$$\log(M_f/P_f) = a_f(r_f - r) + b_f(r_f - r_h) \tag{4.86}$$

$$\Rightarrow \quad \log M_f - \log P_f = a_f(r_f - r) + b_f(r_f - r_h) \tag{4.86$'$}$$

(4.85) and (4.86) imply that the demand for each currency holding depends on the differential between the rates of return on substitutable competitive assets — foreign money and non-monetary assets. (4.85)′ and (4.86)′ can be rewritten in the following forms convenient to derive the exchange rate.

$$\log P_h = \log M_h - a_h(r_h - r) - b_h(r_h - r_f) \tag{4.87}$$

$$\log P_f = \log M_f - a_f(r_f - r) - b_f(r_f - r_h) \tag{4.88}$$

Subtracting (4.88) form (4.87) and assuming $a_h = a_f = a$ and $b_h = b_f = b$

$$\log(P_h/P_f) = \log(M_h/M_f) - a\,(r_h - r_f) - 2b\,(r_h - r_f)$$

$$\Rightarrow \quad \log E = \log(M_h/M_f) - (a + 2b)(r_h - r_f) \tag{4.89}$$

The symmetry condition $b_h = b_f = b$ identifies C.S. with the single parameter, $b$ and the condition $a_h = a_f = a$ makes the relative value of monies independent of the rate of return on non-monetary assets. The supply of each currency is assumed exogenous. The real rates of return $r_h$ and $r_f$ are expected rates of return and they are defined in the usual way as nominal return minus the expected rates of inflation in respective countries:

$$r_h - r_f = (nr_h - \dot{p}_h^e) - (nr_f - \dot{p}_f^e)$$

$$\Rightarrow \quad r_h - r_f = (nr_h - nr_f) - (\dot{p}_h^e - \dot{p}_f^e) \tag{4.90}$$

Now following Purchasing Power Parity (PPP) theory, the expected rate of changes in the exchange rate equals the difference between the rates of inflation in the two countries:

$$x = \dot{E}^e/E = \dot{p}_h^e - \dot{p}_f^e \tag{4.91}$$

Substituting this in (4.89)

$$\log E = \log(M_h/M_f) - (a + 2b)(nr_h - nr_f - x) \tag{4.92}$$

$M_h = \overline{M}_h$ and $M_f = \overline{M}_f$ because the supply of each currency is assumed exogenous and demand has to equal supply for equilibrium. Treating the nominal interest rates and $x$ as exogenous, the implications of C.S. can be easily derived from (4.92)

$$\frac{\delta \log E}{\delta x} = a + 2b \tag{4.93}$$

(4.93) shows that the greater the value of $b$ i.e., the greater the degree of C.S. the greater will be the fluctuations in the exchange rate needed to maintain monetary equilibrium for a given change in $x$. Under perfect C.S., i.e., when $b \to \infty$, the movement in the exchange rate required to satisfy equilibrium will be infinite. Even when $x$ is made endogenous by introducing rational and adaptive expectations the instability of exchange rate under currency substitution remains.[33]

These results are dependent on the assumptions that $M_h$ and $M_f$ and $nr_h$ and $nr_f$ are both fixed. But in reality the issuer of a currency can alter both $M$ and interest rates to eliminate or at least dampen the exchange rate fluctuations. The impact of a change in interest rate increases with the degree of currency substitution. In the presence of C.S. the issuers of various currencies face a "market pressure" to make their "money" more attractive. Under C.S., $rn - \dot{p}^e$ becomes a more powerful instrument.

33. See Girton and Roper (1981) pp. 27-29.

# APPENDIX TO CHAPTER 4

## 4.A.1 Derivation of Money Demand on the Shock Absorber Hypothesis

Substitution of (4.79ii) into (4.83) yields:

$$M_t - M_{Tt} = a_3 + a_4 Y_{pt} + a_5 rl_t + a_6 rs_t + a_7 rm_t + e_{2t}$$

$$\Rightarrow \quad M_t = a_1 Y_{Tt} + (1 + a_2) M_{Tt-1} + a_3 + a_4 Y_{pt} + a_5 rl_t + a_6 rs_t + a_7 rm_t + e_{2t}$$

$$\Rightarrow \quad M_t = (1 + a_2)(M_{t-1} - M_{pt-1}) + a_1 Y_{Tt} + a_3 + rm_t + e_{2t} \text{ from (4.77ii)}$$

Substitution of (4.83) lagged one period and rearranging terms yields:

$$M_t = a_3(1 - 1 - a_2) + (1 + a_2) M_{t-1} + a_1 Y_{Tt} + a_4 [Y_{pt} - (1 + a_2) Y_{pt-1}]$$

$$+ a_5 [rl_t - (1 + a_2) rl_{t-1}] + a_6 [rs_t - (1 + a_2) rs_{t-1}]$$

$$+ a_7 [rm_t - (1 + a_2) rm_{t-1}] + e_{2t} - (1 + a_2) e_{2t-1} \qquad (4.A.1)$$

Assuming $(1 + a_2)$ to range from .5 to .9, the explanatory variables were transformed in the way required for estimating (4.A.1).

$$\Rightarrow \quad M_t = -a_2 a_3 + (1 + a_2) M_{t-1} + a_1 Y_{Tt} + a_4 Y^*_{pt} + a_5 rl^*_t$$

$$+ a_6 rs^*_t + a_7 rm^*_t + e_{2t} - (1 + a_2) e_{2t-1} \qquad (4.A.2)$$

Where $\quad Y^*_{pt} = Y_{pt} - (1 + a_2) Y_{pt-1} \qquad (4.A.3i)$

and so on.

Generalised Least Squares method was applied for estimating (4.A.2) because of the composite error term.

It can be noted that instead of assuming a certain range of values for $(1 + a_2)$, Darby could have estimated (4.A.2) by a 2- step procedure. For example, $M_t$ could have been regressed on $M_{t-1}, Y_{pt}, Y_{pt-1}, rl_t, rl_{t-1} \cdots$ and the coefficient of $M_{t-1}$ could have been used as an estimate of $(1 + a_2)$ and then, in the second stage, this estimate could have been used to transform the explanatory variables.

# 5

# FINANCING OF BUDGET DEFICITS : THE DYNAMICS OF GOVERNMENT BUDGET CONSTRAINT

So far fiscal policy has been discussed in complete separation from monetary policy as if they are independent of each other. In reality however, the tools of fiscal and monetary policy are interlinked. This linkage is established through the method of financing government budget. Like a household budget, government budget is a relation between its outflow of expenditure and its inflow of revenue. The budget is in deficit if expenditure, $G$, outweighs tax revenue, $T$ (and is in surplus if tax revenue exceeds spending). The public sector borrowing requirement (PSBR) in the U.K. is the sum of the budget deficits of central and local governments and the deficit of the nationalised industries.

The government can finance its budget deficit in any of the following ways:

(a) By raising $G$ and $T$ to an equal extent, i.e., by maintaining a balanced budget without affecting the money supply or debt issue.
(b) By borrowing from the public i.e., by selling government bonds to the public. This is known as open market operations.
(c) By raising the nominal money supply.
(d) By combining policies (b) and (c).

## 5.1 THE BALANCED BUDGET MULTIPLIER IN THE STATIC CASE

Policy option (a) above is recommended by the Keynesians, who believe in the built-in stabilising effect of taxation. In the model where tax is treated as exogenous, the effect of raising $G$ and $T$ by the same amount is to raise real income by the same amount. In other words, the balanced budget multiplier is 1. This is easily proved by taking the first difference of the IS equation (2.29) and then assuming $\Delta G = \Delta T$. However, when the money market is included the balanced budget multiplier lies between 0 and 1. This is shown below.

$$\Delta Y(1-C') + \Delta TC' - I'\Delta r = \Delta G \tag{5.1}$$

$$L_1\Delta Y + L_2\Delta r = 0 \tag{5.2}$$

substituting from (5.2) into (5.1)

$$\Delta Y(1-C') + I'\frac{L_1}{L_2}\Delta Y = \Delta G - C'\Delta T$$

$$\Rightarrow \quad \Delta Y\left[(1-C') + I'\frac{L_1}{L_2}\right] = (1-C')\Delta G$$

$$\Rightarrow \quad \Delta Y = \frac{(1-C')\Delta G}{1-C'+I'\frac{L_1}{L_2}} \tag{5.3}$$

So, the highest value of the balanced budget multiplier $\Delta Y/\Delta G$ is 1 and this results when either $I' = 0$ or $L_2 = -\infty$. Barring these extreme cases, the balanced budget multiplier is positive but less than 1.

So far, the role of various policies has been discussed by considering all policy variables as exogenous. For instance, in Chapter 3, the relevant multipliers derived from the Keynesian model have already demonstrated that monetary policy does affect real output and employment. But in those models, such policy was confined to a change in the nominal money supply by the Central Bank. In the present Chapter, the government budget constraint. viz., that the gap between its expenditure and tax revenue has to be met by some combination of policies (a)–(c) is introduced specifically into the simple IS-LM model of Chapter 2. The effects of inflation and budget constraint would be considered separately in Chapter 7. For the present, prices are assumed fixed and, therefore, $P$ omitted from the LM equation.

## 5.2 THE GOVERNMENT BUDGET CONSTRAINT IN THE IS-LM MODEL WITH FIXED PRICES: THE DYNAMICS OF GOVERNMENT BUDGET

$$Y(1-b(1-t_1))-dr-A_2=G \tag{5.4}$$

$$\alpha Y+\beta r+L_0=M \tag{5.5}$$

$$G-t_0-t_1 Y=\Delta M+\Delta B \tag{5.6}$$

The IS equation in the simple linear form (2.7) has been modified to include all the autonomous consumption, tax and investment components together in $A_2$, i.e.,

$$A_2=a-bt_0+A$$

It is important to note that the government budget constraint (5.6) has dynamic components since

$$\Delta M \equiv M_t-M_{t-1} \quad \text{(i.e.,} \equiv \text{current } M - \text{previous } M\text{) and}$$

$$\Delta B \equiv B_t-B_{t-1} \quad \text{(i.e.,} \equiv \text{current } B - \text{previous } B\text{)}$$

Where the subscript, $t$, denotes the current time point and $t-1$ the previous time point. The variables $Y$, $r$, $G$, $M$, etc. without a time subscript all refer to the current values of the respective variables in the equation (5.4) – (5.6). The time-subscript, $t$, may now be attached to them whenever required.

### *Tax-Financed Government Spending*

Such a fiscal policy to keep the budget in equilibrium would mean that all government spending on goods and services, $G$, is exactly matched by taxes so that the government deficit is nil and the government has no need to issue new bonds ($\Delta B=0$) or to create new money ($\Delta M=0$). The tax equation (2.9) is assumed to include all transfer payments as negative taxes. Then with the government budget constraint the IS-LM model with fixed prices becomes:

$$Y[1-b(1-t_1)]-dr=G+A_2 \tag{5.7i}$$

$$\alpha Y+\beta r=M-L_0 \tag{5.7ii}$$

$$G-t_0-t_1 Y=0 \tag{5.7iii}$$

The multiplier effect in the above 2-sector Keynesian model with government budget can be observed by introducing an exogenous rightward shift in the IS curve. say, through a rise in $A_2$. In the simple static IS-LM analysis, an outward shift of the IS curve with no change in the money supply or the price level generates a positive multiplier effect on real output, $Y$. But with the budget constraint in the government sector, this multiplier effect will be larger than in the IS-LM model without the constraint. This can be proved easily by deriving the multipliers from the model comprising equations (5.7i) – (5.7iii). Following an exogenous increase in investment spending due to, say, a change in expectations implying an increase in the parameter, $A_2$, equilibrium income increases by more than that in the simple IS-LM model. In the present model, $G$ will have to be treated as an endogenous variable because of the need to maintain equilibrium in the government sector. Differentiating the system of equations (5.7) w.r.t. $A_2$, one has:

$$\begin{vmatrix} 1-b(1-t_1) & -d & -1 \\ \alpha & \beta & 0 \\ -t_1 & 0 & 1 \end{vmatrix} \times \begin{vmatrix} \delta y/\delta A_2 \\ \delta r/\delta A_2 \\ \delta G/\delta A_2 \end{vmatrix} = \begin{vmatrix} 1 \\ 0 \\ 0 \end{vmatrix} \tag{5.8}$$

Solving for $\frac{\delta Y}{\delta A_2}$ by Cramer's rule:

$$\frac{\delta Y}{\delta A_2} = \frac{\beta}{\beta(1-b+Bt_1)+d\alpha-bt_1} = \frac{1}{(1-b)(1-t_1)+d\frac{\alpha}{\beta}} \tag{5.9}$$

But in the simple IS-LM model, consisting of (i) and (ii) of (5.7), the multiplier would be

$$\frac{\delta Y}{\delta A_2} = \frac{\beta}{\beta(1-b+bt_1)+d\alpha} = \frac{1}{1-b+bt_1+d\frac{\alpha}{\beta}} \tag{5.10}$$

The multiplier in the solution (5.9) is greater than that in (5.10) because the denominator in (5.9) has an extra term $-t_1 < 0$. This is because in the short-run multiplier (5.10), there is just one right and upward shift of the IS curve which raises equilibrium income to a smaller extent. But when taxes rise with income, a budget surplus is created. Under a balanced budget constraint the government would have to either cut taxes or raise

$G$ to restore balance.[1] such a tax cut or an increase in government spending will create further stimulating effects on real output — the latter leading to a further upward shift of the IS curve in the second round. So, when the government budget constraint is included, the multiplier effect on income of an increase in an exogenous component is larger under a tax-financed fiscal policy with a constant marginal rate of tax, $0 < t_1 < 1$. However, the rise in the interest rate will reduce private investment spending. So, such tax-financed fiscal policy under a balanced budget constraint has expansionary effects on real output but it redistributes real output to the government sector and away from the private business sector. It is extremely important to note that these conclusions are subject to the limitations of the above model comprising (5.7i) to (5.7iii). In particular, this model ignores the wealth effects on consumption and money demands. Considering the general form of the model (5.4)–(5.6), a budget surplus may lead to: (a) a reduction in money supply or, (b) a retirement of government debt or, (c) a combination of both. Such policy options will have to be undertaken continuously until the budget is in balance again. If policy option (a) is chosen, the LM curve will shift inward continuously till the original equilibrium income is regained where the budget is in balance once again. So, the long-run multiplier is zero. If policy option (b) is undertaken, retirement of government debt would mean a reduction of the wealth of the private sector and, therefore, a shift of the IS curve to the left in the second round. So, the inclusion of the government budget destroys the independence of the IS and the LM functions because the emergence of a budget deficit or a surplus has important repercussions on the money and bond markets. The long-run effects of budget deficits/surpluses cannot but be examined in a dynamic model with the wealth effects and interest payments on bonds. The implication of government budget will be explained in several stages — first by including only the wealth effects on consumption and money demands and then introducing interest payments on government bonds and finally by including the effect of a changing capital stock on investment. The multipliers obtained from the simple IS-LM equations are the *short-run* or the *impact* multipliers.

---

1. Note that

$$\frac{\delta G}{\delta A_2} = \frac{t_1}{(1-b)(1-t_1)\frac{d\alpha}{\beta}} > 0$$

## 5.3 THE DYNAMICS OF GOVERNMENT BUDGET WHEN THE WEALTH EFFECTS ARE INCLUDED

As revealed by (5.6) the incorporation of the government budget equation introduces important dynamic elements[2] in the Static IS-LM model. Ott and Ott (1965) developed an IS-LM model with the government budget constraint and analysed the effects on income of fiscal and monetary policies and of shifts in consumption and investment functions. Their model is different from the one in (5.4)–(5.6) in that it includes the wealth effects in the consumption and demand for money functions. Government budget has important bearing on the net assets of the private sector: a deficit in the budget increases the net assets of the private sector which now holds more money or interest-bearing government bonds; and a surplus in the budget reduces the claims of the private sector on government.

*Ott and Ott's Model (00 Model)*

$$C_t = C(Y_t - T_t, V_t) \tag{5.11i}$$

$$T_t = T(Y_t) \tag{5.11ii}$$

$$I_t = I(r_t) \tag{5.11iii}$$

$$M_t^d = L(Y_t, r_t, V_t) \tag{5.11iv}$$

$$M_t^s = M_{t-1}^s \theta (G_{t-1} - T_{t-1}) + \Delta MA_t \tag{5.11v}$$

$$M_t^d = M_t^s = M_t \tag{5.11vi}$$

$$Y_t = C_t + I_t + G_t \tag{5.11vii}$$

$$V_t = M_t + B_t \tag{5.11viii}$$

$$G_{t-1} - T_{t-1} = \Delta V_t \tag{5.11ix}$$

2. An equation is called dynamic when it includes values of variables at different time points — current and past or current and future.

where $V_t$ is the net financial assets of the public, $\theta$ is a proportion of the budget deficit financed by new money creation,[3] $MA_t$ is an autonomous component of money supply. Equations (5.11vi) and (5.11vii) denote the conditions for equilibrium in the money and output markets respectively. $\Delta$ as before denotes the first difference of the variable it precedes. The other equations have been explained in previous models. The model does not consider the effects of a changing capital stock on investment demand. The reduced form equations of the above model are:

$$Y_t - C_t[Y_t - T(Y_t), V_t] - I(r_t) = G_t \tag{5.12}$$

$$L(Y_t, r_t, V_t) = M_t \tag{5.13}$$

$$\Delta M_t = \theta \Delta V_t + \Delta MA_t \tag{5.14}$$

and

$$\Delta V_t = G_{t-1} - T_{t-1} \tag{5.15}$$

To focus on the effects of various policies on income. $\Delta M_t$, $\Delta r_t$, $\Delta V_t$ are eliminated from (5.12)–(5.15) and this can be achieved in the following manner:

Taking the first difference of the IS equation (5.12), one obtains

$$\Delta Y_t\{1 - C_1(1 - T')\} - I'\Delta r_t = \Delta G_t + C_2 \Delta V_t \tag{5.16}$$

Taking the first difference of the LM equation (5.13), one obtains

$$L_1 \Delta Y_t + L_2 \Delta r_t + L_3 \Delta V_t = \Delta M_t$$

Now substitution from (5.14) and (5.15) yields

$$\Rightarrow \quad \Delta r_t = \frac{1}{L_2}\{(G_{t-1} - T_{t-1})(\theta - L_3) + \Delta MA_t - L_1 \Delta Y_t\}$$

Substituting for $\Delta r_t$ in (5.16), one obtains

$$\Delta Y_t\left\{1 - C_1(1 - T') + \frac{I'L_1}{L_2}\right\} = \Delta G_t + (G_{t-1} - T_{t-1})\left\{C_2 + \frac{I'(\theta - L_3)}{L_2}\right\} + \frac{I'}{L_2}\Delta MA_t \tag{5.17}$$

3. It would be a reduction in money supply if $G_{t-1} < T_{t-1}$, i.e., if there is a surplus.

The time-path of $Y_t$ is obtained from (5.17) by assuming a simple linear and proportional tax function $T(Y_t)$ implying $T(Y_t) = T'Y_t$ and $T_{t-1} = T'Y_{t-1}$ where one prime over a functional symbol indicates the first-order derivative of a function of a single variable only as throughout this book. Also, the policy implications are derived for $t > 1$ assuming the system in equilibrium at $t = 0$. The specific policy assumption is a sustained increase in government spending at $t = 1$ implying $G_t = G_1$ for all $t > 1$. $\Delta MA_t$ is assumed = 0. Then for $Y_t$ for $t > 1$ $G_t = G_{t-1}$ and $\Delta MA_{t-1} = 0$. (5.17) implies

$$\Delta Y_t \left\{1 - C_1(1-T') + \frac{I'L_1}{L_2}\right\} = \left\{C_2 + I'\frac{(\theta - L_3)}{L_2}\right\}(G_t - T'Y_{t-1})$$

$$\Rightarrow \quad Y_t = \frac{Z - T'X}{Z} Y_{t-1} + \frac{X}{Z} G_t \tag{5.20}$$

where $$Z = 1 - C_1(1-T') + \frac{I'L_1}{L_2} \tag{5.19a}$$

and $$X = C_2 + \frac{I'}{L_2}(\theta - L_3) \tag{5.19b}$$

The equilibrium value of $Y_t$ (as understood in dynamic equations[4]) is obtained by substituting

$Y_t = Y_{t-1} = Y^*$ in (5.20) and

$$Y^* = \frac{1}{T'} G_t \tag{5.21}$$

To study the behaviour of $Y_t$ away from this equilibrium value, the difference equation (5.20) is rewritten in terms of $DY_t$ where $DY_t$ stands for the deviation $Y_t - Y^*$ subject to (5.21). Assuming $Y_0$ to be known, the final solution is obtained in 5.A.1. as

$$Y_t = \left(Y_0 - \frac{G_t}{T'}\right)\left[1 - \frac{L_2C_2 + I'(\theta - L_3)}{L_2\{1 - C_1(1-T')\} + I'L_1}\right]^t + \frac{G_t}{T'} \tag{5.24}$$

---

4. The equilibrium value is the one which, once attained, will be repeated for ever.

The stability of the time path would depend on whether or not $\left(1-\frac{XT'}{Z}\right) \to 0$ as $t \to \infty$. The system would be stable only if

$$0<\left(1-\frac{XT'}{Z}\right)<1 \tag{5.25}$$

Rather than examining the stability properties Ott and Ott assume (5.25) to be the case and concentrate on the equilibrium value $\frac{G_t}{T'}$ which gives rise to the interesting and important result of the above mentioned policy:

$$\underset{t \to \infty}{Lt} \frac{\delta Y_t}{\delta G_1} = \frac{1}{T'} \tag{5.26}$$

(5.26) demonstrates that nothing matters but the fiscal parameters $G$ and $T'$. "Monetary policy cannot permanently affect income"[5] by altering $\theta$ or $M$. Changes in $\theta$ or $M$ affect only the time path of movement to equilibrium after a disturbance and the investment — consumption combination through changing the equilibrium rate of interest.

The result (5.26) was also obtained by Christ (1968). He also considered the case of variable marginal tax rate, $\Delta t_1 \neq 0$ where $t_1$ is $T'(Y)$ of the OO model. The wealth effects on consumption and money demands were not considered by Christ. In this model with fewer complications, it is easy to explain why the long-run multiplier of a change in $G$ must be the reciprocal of the constant tax rate. Starting from an initially balanced budget, (at period 0), let there be an once for all rise in $G$ in period 1, i.e., $\Delta G_1 > 0$ and $G_t = G_1$ for all $t \geq 1$. The first period effect of this rise is a rightward shift of the IS curve which leads to a rise in income[6] leading to a rise in tax receipts: $\Delta T_1 < \Delta G_1$ implying a budget deficit. In the second period this deficit is financed by the issue of high powered money shifting the LM curve to the right leading to a further rise in real income. This process will be repeated i.e., more money will be printed until the rise in real income raises enough tax revenue to balance the budget once again; this happens when the level of real income rises to $\frac{1}{t_1} \cdot G_1$ or, $\frac{1}{T'(Y)} \cdot G_1$

5. Ott and Ott (1965) p. 75.

6. This rise in income is $\frac{1}{1-C'(1-t_1)} \cdot \Delta G$ and the rise in tax receipts is $\Delta T_1 = \frac{t_1}{1-C'(1-t_1)} \Delta G$.

when the tax rate, $t_1$ or $T'$ is constant. This is explained in the following diagrams. In part (a) we reproduce the goods and money market equilibrium situations and part (b) portrays the government sector. The straight line $T(Y)$ has a negative vertical intercept because transfer payments are treated as negative taxes independent of income and because of the exemption limit already explained in Chapter 2. At the level of income, $Y_0$, the government budget is in balance and the goods and money markets are in equilibrium. In period 1, government spending is increased to $G_1$ and therefore, the IS curve shifts to $IS_1$ in part (a) leading to a rise in income to $Y_t$; but the tax revenue induced by $Y_1$ leads to a budget deficit measured by the distance, $d$, in part (b). If this is financed by issuing more money the LM curve keeps on shifting to the right period after period until it reaches $LM_t$, the consequent rise in real income being $Y_t$ which is enough to raise the tax revenue required to balance the budget at the new level of government spending $G_1$. In Christ's analysis, there is no bond financing or wealth effects so no shifting the IS curve after $IS_1$.

It is important to note the government spending multiplier depending only on the marginal rate of income tax, $T'$ and being independent of the other parameters of the system and to recall that in the original Keynesian case without the wealth effects and the government budget constraint the government spending multiplier depends on the MPC, $C'$ or $C_1$.

An important consequence of the dynamics of the government budget and of the wealth effects is that the long-run and the short-run effects of a rise in government spending on income are different and ought to be distinguished. The short-run effects are given by the multipliers $\frac{\delta Y_1}{\delta G_1}, \frac{\delta Y_2}{\delta G_2}$, etc as worked out from the equation (5.24) for $t = 1, t = 2$, etc. The long-run or the steady state effects are given by the multiplier $\underset{t \to \infty}{Lt} \frac{\delta Y_t}{\delta G_t}$ worked out from the time path (which may be convergent or divergent depending on the parameter values) of $Y_t$ given in (5.24). The long-run equilibrium is reached through various rounds of short-run effects; each round is caused by not only the rise in government spending but also the consequent wealth effects on consumption and money demands.

In the simple Keynesian IS-LM analysis there are no second-round effects of a rise in government spending. A rise in government spending means an outward shift of the IS curves and, therefore, a rise in income, with the LM curve unchanged, from $Y_0$ to $Y_1$ as in Fig. 5.1. In the present IS-LM analysis with government budget and wealth effects, the LM curve shifts too and there are various rounds of shifts in both IS and LM curves until the government budget is in balance again. Changes in government budget lead to shifts of both the IS and the LM curves by changing the stock and/or the composition of wealth. The IS and LM curves become interdependent.

## 5.4 THE DYNAMICS OF GOVERNMENT BUDGET WITH WEALTH EFFECTS AND INTEREST PAYMENTS ON GOVERNMENT BONDS

In this section, the effect of interest payments on bonds and their implication for the role of fiscal and monetary policies will be examined. For this purpose, we have chosen a number of models developed by Blinder and Solow (1973) and by Miller (1980) to reinstate the role of fiscal policy against the monetarists' claim that fiscal policy is ineffective. The Blinder-Solow models (BS) are more general than the Ott and Ott (OO) model. The latter ignored the effects of changes in the capital stock on net investment—and of interest payments on bonds. In the BS models the personal disposable income of the households is redefined as:

$$Y_d \equiv (1 - t_1)(Y + B) \tag{5.27a}$$

where $B$ is the interest income on government bonds: $r \times \frac{B}{r}$ and $\frac{B}{r}$ is the market value of bonds assumed to be perpetuities. The intercept of the tax function is assumed to be zero as in the OO model. Also, equation (5.11viii) of OO model is replaced by

$$V = K + M + \frac{B}{r} \tag{5.27b}$$

The government budget constraint is modified on account of the interest payments on bonds. The dynamics of the BS model is examined in the continuous form meaning that the discrete difference equations are replaced by differential equations. So,

$$\Delta M_t (\equiv M_t - M_{t-1}), \quad \Delta B_t (\equiv B_t - B_{t-1})$$

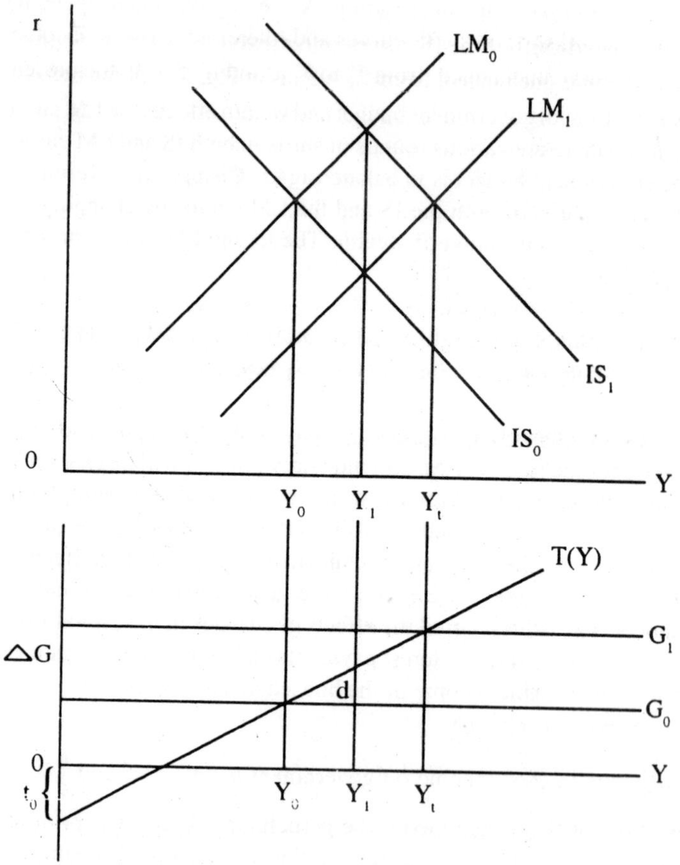


FIG. 5.1:

etc. of the discrete analysis are replaced by their continuous analogue $\frac{dM}{dt}, \frac{dB}{dt}$, etc., respectively. These time-derivatives are conveniently denoted by (.) over the respective variables. In the first BS IS-LM model with the budget constraint investment is made a function of *r* alone as in the previous models:

**BS Model – I**

$$Y = C\left[(1-t_1)(Y+B), M+\frac{B}{r}+K\right]+I(r)+G \quad (5.28)$$

$$M = L\left(Y, r, M+\frac{B}{r}+K\right) \quad (5.29)$$

$$G - t_1 Y + (1-t_1)B = \dot{M} + \frac{\dot{B}}{r} \quad (5.30)$$

(5.28) – (5.30) are respectively the IS, the LM and the government budget equations. This model is also a fixed price model and the time-subscript has been omitted for the sake of convenience. The term $B(1-t_1)$ is the net government spending on account of interest payments on outstanding debt.

Now if one assumes that the system is initially in long-run equilibrium with a balanced budget, then substituting $\dot{M} + \frac{\dot{B}}{r} = 0$ in equation (5.30), one obtains

$$G - t_1 Y + (1-t_1)B = 0$$

$$\Rightarrow \quad t_1 Y = G + (1-t_1)B$$

$$\Rightarrow \quad \frac{dY}{dG} = \frac{1+(1-t_1)\frac{dB}{dG}}{t_1} \quad (5.31)$$

This result implies that if government spending is raised from an initial situation of long-run equilibrium with a balanced budget, and if the deficit is financed by new money creation, the long-run multiplier is the same as in the OO model. [This is obtained by simply putting $\frac{dB}{dG} = 0$ in (5.31), which yields $\frac{dy}{dG} = \frac{1}{t_1}$]. If the deficit is met by bond financing implying

$$\frac{dB}{dG} > 0, \frac{dY}{dG} > \frac{1}{t_1} \quad (5.32)$$

(5.31) implies that bond-financing of budget deficit is even more expansionary than money-financing. The first round effect of money financing is more expansionary than that of bond financing. This is indicated by a rightward shift in the IS and LM curves each and a rise in income from $Y_0$ to $Y_2$ in Fig. 5.2. The rise in income leads to a rise in the tax revenue and tends to reduce the deficit. But under bond financing, the subsequent tax receipts would be lower and interest payments on a larger outstanding debt would be larger. The wealth effects lead to a second round of shifts of the IS curve to the right and of the LM curve to the left. [Since $C_2 > 0$ and $L_3 > 0$, greater wealth means higher consumption and a higher demand for money.] The IS and the LM curves continue to shift because of changes in the stock of wealth until the budget is in balance again. Provided that the net impact of the wealth effects is expansionary the rise in income will be greater under bond than under money-financing of government debt. But such discussion of long-run multipliers ignores the important question of stability of the dynamic behaviour of the endogenous variables under different modes of financing. The net impact of money or bond financing on income must be judged on the basis of the stability of the model.

Differentiating the IS equation (5.28) w.r.t. $t$, one obtains

$$\dot{Y}\{1-C_1(1-t_1)\} - \dot{r}\left\{I' - \frac{C_2 B}{r^2}\right\} = C_2\dot{M}$$

$$+\left\{C_1(1-t_1) + \frac{C_2}{r}\right\}\dot{B} + C_2\dot{K} + \dot{G} \tag{5.33}$$

Differentiating the LM equation, (5.29) w.r.t. $t$ and rearranging,

$$L_1\dot{Y} + \left(L_2 - \frac{L_3 B}{r^2}\right)\dot{r} = (1-L_3)\dot{M} - \frac{L_3\dot{B}}{r} - L_3\dot{K} \tag{5.34}$$

Solving for $\dot{Y}$ and $\dot{r}$ by Cramer's rule,

$$\dot{Y} = \frac{1}{J}\left[\left(L_2 - \frac{L_3 B}{r^2}\right)\left\{C_2\dot{M} + \left(C_1(1-t_1) + \frac{C_2}{r}\right)\dot{B} + C_2\dot{K} + \dot{G}\right\}\right.$$

$$\left. + \left(I' - \frac{C_2 B}{r^2}\right)\left\{(1-L_3)\dot{M} - \frac{L_3\dot{B}}{r} - L_3\dot{K}\right\}\right] \tag{5.34}$$

$$\dot{r} = \frac{1}{J}\left[\{1-C_1(1-t_1)\}\left\{(1-L_3)\dot{M} - \frac{L_3\dot{B}}{r} - L_3\dot{K}\right\}\right.$$

$$\left. - L_1\left\{C_2\dot{M} + \left(C_1(1-t_1) + \frac{C_2}{r}\right)\dot{B} + C_2\dot{K} + \dot{G}\right\}\right] \tag{5.35}$$

where $J = \{(1-C_1(1-t_1)\}\left(L_2 - \frac{L_3 B}{r^2}\right) + L_1\left(I' - \frac{C_2 B}{r^2}\right)$ (5.36)

(5.36) $\Rightarrow$ $J < 0$

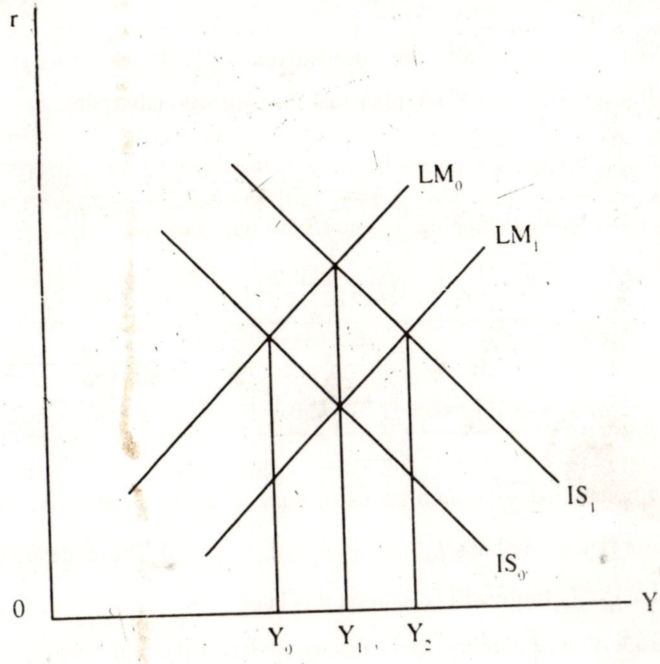


FIG. 5.2

The solutions for $Y$ and $r$ can be obtained from (5.34) and (5.35). Let these solutions be called

$$Y(t) = H(M, B, K, G) \tag{5.37}$$

and $$r(t) = Q(M, B, K, G) \tag{5.38}$$

from (5.34) above, it is clear that

$$\frac{\delta Y(t)}{\delta M} = \frac{C_2\left(L_2 - \frac{L_3 B}{r^2}\right) + (1 - L_3)\left(I' - \frac{BC_2}{r^2}\right)}{J}$$

$$\Rightarrow \quad \frac{\delta Y}{\delta M} = \frac{C_2 L_2 + I'(1 - L_3) - \frac{BC_2}{r^2}}{J}$$

$$\Rightarrow \quad \frac{\delta Y}{\delta M} = \frac{C_2\left(L_2 - \frac{B}{r^2}\right) + I'(1 - L_3)}{J} \tag{5.39}$$

Recalling the signs of the derivatives: $C_2 > 0, 0 < C_1(1 - t_1) < 1$, $I' < 0, 0 < L_3 < 1$ etc., (5.39) implies that the short-run multiplier

$$\frac{\delta Y}{\delta M} > 0$$

On the other hand, evaluating $\frac{\delta Y}{\delta B}$ from (5.34) one obtains

$$\frac{\delta Y}{\delta B} = \frac{\left\{C_1(1 - t_1) + \frac{c_2}{r}\right\}\left(L_2 - \frac{L_3 B}{r^2}\right) - \frac{L_3}{r}\left(I' - \frac{c_1 B}{r^2}\right)}{J}$$

$$\Rightarrow \quad \frac{\delta Y}{\delta B} = \frac{L_2\left\{C_1(1 - t_1) + \frac{c_2}{r}\right\} - \frac{L_3}{r}\left(I' + \frac{c_1 B}{r}\right)}{J} \tag{5.40}$$

(5.40) implies that $\frac{\delta Y}{\delta B}$ is ambiguous in sign. The first product on the numerator is negative but $-L_3 I' > 0$ and $-L_3 c_1(1 - t_1) < 0$. The monetarists claim that $\frac{\delta Y}{\delta B} < 0$. More will be said on this later.

The question of stability can be discussed in two alternative ways: (a) By eliminating $\dot{M}$ from (5.28) and (5.29) on substitution from the budget constraint (under money financing, $\frac{\dot{B}}{r} = 0$, i.e., $B = \overline{B}$) and under bond-financing $\dot{M}$ is assumed 0 , i.e., $M = \overline{M}$); (b) By substituting for $Y$ and $r$ in the budget constraint. Option (b) is much easier than the option (a). This is illustrated below:

Substituting for $\dot{Y}$ from (5.37) and assuming $\frac{\dot{B}}{r} = 0$, one obtains, under money-financing

$$\dot{M} = G + \overline{B} - t_1[H(M, \overline{B}, K, G) + \overline{B}] \tag{5.41}$$

Since $K$ is exogenous in the BS model (5.28)–(5.30), $K = \overline{K}$ can be assumed as well. (5.41) is a non-homogeneous differential equation in $M$ the solution of which is discussed in the Appendix 5.A.2. The condition for stability as given in (5.A.2.6) is that

$$-\frac{t_1}{J}\left[C_2\left(L_2 - \frac{B}{r^2}\right) + I'(1 - L_3)\right] < 0 \tag{5.42}$$

The condition (5.42) is clearly seen to be satisfied.

Under bond-financing the analogue of equation (5.41) is

$$\frac{\dot{B}}{r} = G + B - t_1 [H(\overline{M}, B, K, G) + B]$$

$$\Rightarrow \quad \dot{B} = Q[G + B(1 - t_1) - t_1 H] \tag{5.43}$$

An inspection of equations (5.37) and (5.38) for the detailed forms of $Q$ and $H$ reveals that (5.43) is a non-linear differential equation in $B$. Writing (5.43) as

$$\dot{B} = g_0 + g_1 B(t) \tag{5.44}$$

the condition for stability can be obtained, as before, as $g_1 < 0$. A much easier way than looking at the details of $Q[G + B(1 - t_1) - t_1 H]$ is adopted by Blinder and Solow. This is to look at $g_1(B)$ as

$$g_1(B) = \frac{\delta \dot{B}}{\delta B} = \frac{\delta Q}{\delta B}\{G + B(1 - t_1) - t_1 H\} + Q\left\{(1 - t_1) - t_1 \frac{\delta H}{\delta B}\right\}$$

$\therefore$ the condition for stability under bond financing implies $\frac{\delta \dot{B}}{\delta B} < 0$

$$\Rightarrow \quad Q\left\{1 - t_1\left(1 + \frac{\delta H}{\delta B}\right)\right\} < 0 \tag{5.45}$$

Since, in equilibrium, the government budget balances implying

$$G + B(1 - t_1) - t_1 Y = 0$$

From (5.38) and (5.45), the condition for stability under bond financing

$$1 - t_1\left(1 + \frac{\delta Y}{\delta B}\right) < 0, \quad \text{since } r \text{ cannot be} < 0$$

$$\Rightarrow \quad \frac{1 - t_1}{t_1} < \frac{\delta Y}{\delta B} \tag{5.46}$$

$$\Rightarrow \quad \frac{\delta Y}{\delta B} > \left(\frac{1}{t_1}\right) - 1 \quad \Rightarrow \quad \frac{\delta Y}{\delta B} > 0 \tag{5.47}$$

So, if the monetarists claim is valid, i.e., if $\frac{\delta Y}{\delta B} < 0$, fiscal policy does not work and the system is unstable. If $\frac{\delta Y}{\delta B} > 0$ but $< \frac{1 - t_1}{t_1}$, fiscal policy works as advocated by the Keynesians but the rise in income is insufficient to raise enough tax revenue to meet the net interest payments on outstanding government debt and close the budget deficit in the long-run. Only if condition (5.46) or (5.47) is satisfied would fiscal policy be expansionary and the system reach its long-run steady state equilibrium.

Blinder and Solow have also examined the comparative performance of fiscal and monetary policies in the context of a long-run model where the changing capital stock has a depressing effect on net investment. That is, the investment function is modified to

$$I = I(r, K), \quad I_1 < 0, I_2 < 0 \tag{5.48}$$

But the implication of a changing capital stock on the supply of output has not been examined. The supply of output is assumed to be given as before. The new investment function (5.48) necessitates the inclusion of another dynamic (definitional) equation in the previous BS model. viz., of

$$\dot{K} = I(r, K) \tag{5.49}$$

However, the dynamics of the model when $K$ is a variable would be considered in later chapters of the book. For now, only the conclusions of this model are given. The conditions for stability under bond-financing and for fiscal policy to be expansionary, i.e., for $\frac{\delta Y}{\delta B} > 0$, now become

$$\frac{\delta Y}{\delta B} > \frac{1 - t_1}{t_1} \tag{5.46}$$

and $$I_2 + C_2 < 0 \tag{5.50}$$

Condition (5.50) requires that the depressing effects of a higher capital stock on investment must be strong enough to outweigh the positive wealth effects on consumption. (5.46) and (5.50) are the sufficient but not necessary conditions for the effectiveness or stability of fiscal policy. The conditions for stability under pure money finance are certain to be satisfied. Blinder and Solow argue that although it is an empirical issue whether or not (5.46) and (5.50) would be satisfied in reality but given plausible values of the relevant parameters viz., the marginal rate of income tax, $t_1$, marginal propensity to spend out of income and wealth, $C_1$, $C_2$, etc., the sufficient conditions for fiscal policy to work and for the IS-LM model with budget constraint to be stable at the same time are likely to be satisfied.

Blinder and Solow later (1974) amended their models to include $Y$ as a separate variable in the investment function:

$$I \equiv \dot{K} = I(r, K, Y), \quad I_1 < 0, I_2 < 0, I_3 > 0 \tag{5.51}$$

Tobin and Buiter (1976) have shown that with the new investment function (5.51), the conditions (5.46), (5.50) and $\frac{\delta Y}{\delta K} < 0$ are no longer sufficient to ensure stability of the model. More importantly, stability of the model can no longer guarantee $\frac{dB}{dG} > 0$. If $\frac{dB}{dG} \leq 0$, it follows from (5.31) above, the long-run multiplier for bond-financed deficit spending no longer exceeds that for money-financed deficit spending; it is possible for $\frac{dB}{dG} < 0$ to be so large numerically that $\frac{dY}{dG}$ given in (5.31) becomes negative for bond-financing of government budget deficits. Tobin and Buiter (TB) have considered the implications for Keynesians and monetarists debate in terms of a long-run IS-LM model which will be considered later.

Scarth (1976) has shown that the stability condition in the BS model is satisfied only when "money accounts for no more than 13 per cent of wealth"[7] Assuming parameter values like $C_1 = 0.8$, $T' = 0.5$, $C_2 = 0.04$, $r = 0.08$ and unitary wealth and income elasticities of the demand for money, Scarth has shown that the case for fiscal policy as made out by Blinder and Solow is based on a rather weak empirical foundation. Apart from treating only the two polar cases of either pure bond financing or pure money financing, another deficiency of the BS models[8] has been pointed out by Thornton (1984), namely, that of treating money supply as exogenous. In reality it is hard to find pure money-financed government deficits since open market operations often imply the simultaneous issuance of new debt by the Treasury; also monetary policy often has interest rates as its operating target in which case there would be no pure bond-financed deficits either. So, a realistic case to consider is one of mixed money/bond financing.

Stephen Miller (1980) has developed a model of mixed money/bond financing of government deficits differing from Blinder and Solow's in a number of respects. This model is considered in the present section while the cases of endogenous money supply and variable capital stock and price levels would be the subjects of Chapter 7.

---

7. Scarth, W. [1976, p. 387]
8. Note that this criticism can also be directed against the OO and Christ's models.

Unlike Blinder and Solow, Stephen Miller's (1980) model considers the policy of combined bond and money financing and derives the stability conditions of which the Blinder-Solow conditions are special cases. Like the BS model, this model assumes the supply side of the real sector as given and a fixed price level. The main pursuit of the model is long-run equilibrium and, because of this, the demand for money is assumed to depend on interest rate and wealth, rather than interest rate and income with a wealth elasticity of demand equal to unity. So, the condition

$$M = M^d(r) \cdot V \tag{5.52}$$

describes the equilibrium in the money market. Unlike in the previous models, a similar demand function for bonds is introduced and the equilibrium condition in the bond market is:

$$\frac{B}{r} = B^d(r) \cdot V \tag{5.53}$$

Obviously $M^{d\prime} < 0$ and $B^{d\prime} > 0$ apply as before. The wealth constraint is much the same as in OO model:

$$V = M + \frac{B}{r} \tag{5.54}$$

(5.52), (5.53) and (5.54) imply that

$$M^{d\prime} + B^{d\prime} = 0 \tag{5.55a}$$

and $$M^d + B^d = 1 \tag{5.55b}$$

To these three equations (5.52)–(5.54) are added the IS and the government budget equations (5.56) and (5.59) respectively.

$$Y = C[(1 - t_1)(Y + B), V] + I(r) + G \tag{5.56}$$

First $Y(t)$ and $r(t)$ are solved out from only the IS[9] and the LM equations ignoring the bond market clearing equation. So, the solutions are derived in very much the same way as the BS model above with a constant capital stock:[10]

---

9. Miller combines consumption and investment spending into a single private expenditure function: $E[(1-t_1)(Y+B), V, r]$ with $0 < E_1 < 1, 0 < E_2 < 1$ and $E_3 < 0$. $E_3$ is our $I'$.

10. The details of $H$ and $Q$ are given in the Appendix 5.A.3.

$$Y(t) = H(M, B, G) \tag{5.57}$$

and $$r(t) = Q(M, B) \tag{5.58}$$

The long-run equilibrium condition for the asset markets is taken to be the constancy of the interest rate. Then, the model looks for the required rates of growth in the asset stocks, *M, B* and *V* which are compatible with a constant interest rate. So, the model permits long-run equilibrium growth. Now: from the wealth constraint and the budget equation for the government sector, it follows that the budget deficit:

$$D\,[\equiv G + B - t_1(Y + B)] = \dot{M} + \frac{\dot{B}}{r} = \dot{V} \tag{5.59}$$

if the interest rate is constant. Also the required compatible rates of growth in *M, B* and *V* are obtained by substituting $\dot{r}$ equal to zero in the expressions for $\dot{M}$ and $\dot{B}$ respectively obtained from (5.52) and (5.53).

Differentiating (5.52) w.r.t. *t*,

$$\dot{M} = M^{d'}\dot{r}V + M^{d}\dot{V}$$

$$\Rightarrow \quad \dot{M} = M^{d}(r)\dot{V} \tag{5.60a}$$

$$\Rightarrow \quad \frac{\dot{M}}{M}(\equiv m) = \frac{\dot{V}}{V}(\equiv v) \tag{5.60b}$$

Differentiating (5.53) w.r.t. *t*, and setting $\dot{r} = 0$,

$$\frac{\dot{B}}{r} = B^{d}\dot{V} \tag{5.61a}$$

$$\Rightarrow \quad (b \equiv)\frac{\dot{B}/r}{B/r} = \frac{\dot{V}}{V} \tag{5.61b}$$

So, the condition for long-run equilibrium in Miller's model, as revealed by (5.60b) and (5.61b) is that money, bonds and wealth all grow at the same rate. Assuming this long-run equilibrium growth rate to be $\psi$, the important result follows from (5.60b), (5.61b) and (5.59)

$$\psi = \frac{\dot{V}}{V} = \frac{D}{V} \quad \Rightarrow D = \psi V \quad \Rightarrow \frac{\dot{D}}{D} = \frac{\dot{V}}{V} = \psi \tag{5.62}$$

This solution for $\psi$ in terms of the parameters of the model and *r* (which is constant once long-run equilibrium is achieved) is given in the Appendix 5.A.3.

For a mixed money and bond financing, let the policy rule be that a proportion $\theta$ of the budget deficit, *D*, be financed by issuing money and the rest by issuing bonds. Then,

$$\dot{M} = \theta D \tag{5.63a}$$

and $$\frac{\dot{B}}{r} = (1 - \theta) D \tag{5.63b}$$

Using (5.52), (5.63a) can be rewritten as

$$\frac{\dot{M}}{M} = \frac{\theta}{M^d(r)} \cdot \frac{D}{V} \tag{5.64a}$$

Using the long-run equilibrium condition:

$$\frac{\dot{M}}{M} = \frac{V}{V} = \frac{D}{V}, \quad \text{one also obtains} \quad \frac{\theta}{M^d(r)} = 1 \tag{5.65a}$$

$$\Rightarrow \quad \theta = M^d(r) = \frac{M}{V} \quad \text{(from 5.52)} \tag{5.65b}$$

(5.65) imply that in long-run equilibrium the proportion of the deficit financed by issuing money must equal the ratio of the money stock to wealth. Thus, a government policy to lower $\theta$ would imply a fall in $\frac{M}{V}$ which must be accomplished by a rise in $r$. On the other hand, a decrease in $\theta$ means a rise in $1 - \theta$ and, therefore, a rise in $1 - M^d(r)$ in long-run equilibrium which, in turn, implies a rise in both $\psi$ and $\frac{Y}{V}$. Therefore:

$$\frac{d\psi}{d\theta} < 0 \tag{5.66a}$$

and $$\frac{d}{d\theta}(Y/V) < 0 \tag{5.66b}$$

The derivatives (5.66) imply that raising the proportion of bond financing would be expansionary in the long-run equilibrium since a fall in $\theta$ raises the growth rates of all assets and the ratio of wealth to income. This result is similar in spirit to the BS observation that bond financing is more expansionary in the long-run provided the stability conditions are satisfied.

For long-run stability of Miller's model, condition (5.62) already arrived at, implies that for stability

$$\frac{d}{dt}(D/V) \quad \text{must be} \quad = 0 \tag{5.67a}$$

The BS condition for long-run equilibrium, $D = 0$ is obviously, a trivial solution to (5.67a). A non-trivial solution of (5.67a) can be obtained as follows:

$$\frac{d}{dt}(D/V) = \frac{V\dot{D} - D\dot{V}}{V^2} = \frac{D}{V}\left(\frac{\dot{D}}{D} - \frac{\dot{V}}{V}\right) \quad (5.67b)$$

From (5.54)

$$V = \dot{M} + \frac{\dot{B}}{r} - \dot{r}\frac{B}{r^2} = D - \left(\frac{B}{r^2}\right)\dot{r}$$

$$\Rightarrow \quad \dot{V} = D - \frac{B}{r^2}\frac{dQ}{dt} \quad \text{from (5.58)}$$

$$\Rightarrow \quad \dot{V} = D - \frac{B}{r^2}(Q_1\dot{M} + Q_2\dot{B}) \quad (5.68)$$

differentiating the government deficit (5.59) w.r.t. $t$,

$$\frac{dD}{dt} = -t_1\frac{dH}{dt} + (1 - t_1)\dot{B}$$

$$\Rightarrow \quad \dot{D} = (1 - t_1)\dot{B} - t_1(H_1\dot{M} + H_2\dot{B})$$

$$\Rightarrow \quad \dot{D} = [1 - t_1(1 + H_2)]\,\dot{B} - t_1H_1\dot{M} \quad (5.69)$$

Using (5.68) and (5.69), (5.67b) can be rewritten as (5.70). The steps are: first from (5.67b),

$$\frac{d}{dt}[D/V] = \frac{\dot{D}}{V} - \frac{D}{V}\cdot\frac{\dot{V}}{V}$$

$$\Rightarrow \quad \frac{d}{dt}[D/V] = [1 - t_1(1 - H_2)]\frac{\dot{B}}{V} - t_1H_1\frac{\dot{M}}{V} - \frac{D}{V}\cdot\frac{\dot{V}}{V} \quad \text{from (5.69)}$$

$$\Rightarrow \quad \frac{d}{dt}[D/V] = [1 - t_1(1 + H_2)]\frac{\dot{B}}{V} - t_1H_1\frac{\dot{M}}{V} - \frac{D^2}{V^2} + \frac{D}{V}\left[Q_1\frac{\dot{M}}{V}\cdot + Q_2\frac{\dot{B}}{V}\right]\frac{B}{r^2} \quad \text{from (5.68)}$$

Using the policy rules (5.63),

$$\frac{d}{dt}[D/V] = [1 - t_1(1 + H_2)]\,r(1 - \theta) - t_1H_1\theta\frac{D}{V}$$

$$-\frac{D^2}{V^2}\left[1 - \frac{B}{r^2}\{Q_1\theta + Q_2r(1 - \theta)\}\right] \quad (5.70)$$

In the neighbourhood of equilibrium,

$$\dot{r} = Q_1\dot{M} + Q_2\dot{B} = \{Q_1\theta + Q_2r\,(1 - \theta)\}\,D = 0$$

$$\Rightarrow \quad Q_1\theta + Q_2r\,(1 - \theta) = 0$$

since $D \neq 0$ unlike in BS model.

$$\frac{d}{dt}(D/V) = [1 - t_1(1 + H_2)r(1-\theta) - t_1H_1\theta]\frac{D}{V} - \frac{D^2}{V^2}$$

$\therefore$, For $\frac{d}{dt}(D/V) = 0$, one requires

$$\{1 - t_1(1 + H_2)\}\, r(1-\theta) - t_1H_1\theta = \frac{D}{V} \quad (5.71)$$

So, Miller's results show that bond-financing of government deficits is expansionary because it raises the interest payments on government bonds $\left(r \times \frac{B}{r}\right)$ which, in turn, raises the ratio $\frac{B}{V}$. Obviously, this conclusion is based on the assumption of a constant interest rate in the long-run equilibrium. If the interest rates had to go up to make the bonds sufficiently attractive to the buyers, then there would always be the danger of crowding private investment out and thereby reducing the expansionary effects of bond-financing.

## 5.5 A GLIMPSE OF THE KEYNESIANS AND THE MONETARISTS DEBATE

So far we have noted the following features of a Keynesian macroeconomic system:

(a) The economy can be approximated by an IS-LM type model.
(b) Wages and prices are relatively stable but output and employment are unstable.
(c) Autonomous changes in expenditure have large multiplier effects on real output and employment.
(d) Unemployment is caused by insufficient aggregate demand and it can be reduced by a stimulative fiscal policy.
(e) The success of monetary policy to affect real output or employment is limited by the interest inelasticity of investment demand and high interest elasticity of the demand for money. Keynesians generally believe in steep IS and flat LM curves. Whereas the monetarists believe in flat IS and steep LM curves.

In general the Keynesians believe in the effectiveness of fiscal policy to change real output, employment and the rate of inflation.[11] The effectiveness of fiscal (and monetary) policy has been considered, up till now, in the contexts of a static IS-LM model, static three sector models and of IS-LM models made dynamic with the government budget constraint. In the third group of models, the effectiveness of fiscal policy has additionally had to consider the question of stability of the macro dynamics imposed by the government budget.

The *monetarists* led by Professor Milton Friedman disagree with the Keynesian features mentioned in (a)–(e) above. They believe in the inherent stability of the "free" enterprise system — i.e., the economic system free from fiscal intervention. In the opinion of the monetarists, the fiscal interventionist policies recommended by the Keynesians have negative and/or destabilising effects in the forms of recession, inflation or both; the multiplier effects of fiscal changes are important only in the short-run and at best, exert only a minor influence on real aggregate demand, nominal income and the price level. While the three different schools of thought known as *Keynesian, Monetarist* and *New Classical*, will be discussed in more detail in Chapter 8, it is relevant to note what the monetarists regard as negative consequences of fiscal policy in the context of the present Chapter. The monetarist proposition here is that pure fiscal policy — i.e., fiscal policy purged of any monetary changes — incidental or extrinsic — cannot affect real output (or the price level when production is supply-constrained). Aggregate real demand is changed very little through fiscal changes because a rise in government spending raises the real rate of interest which pulls private investment expenditure down. The negative consequences of expansionary fiscal policy are described as the "crowding out" effects of government spending. The monetarists believe that: it is the quantity of money which influences the course of aggregate nominal demand; and that the monetary financing of the same government programme would be more expansionary and longer lasting than the issue of interest-bearing debt. The OO model demonstrates that the long-run fiscal multiplier does not depend on any tool of monetary policy whatsoever but only on the fiscal parameter or the reciprocal of the marginal tax rate and the proportion of budget deficit financed by money merely effects the speed of adjustment of actual

11. The Keynesian hypothesis on inflation will be considered in Ch. 6.

income to its long-run equilibrium level. The BS models demonstrate that: fiscal policy is effective (that is, it over compensates for the crowding-out effects) and is more expansionary than monetary policy whenever the model is stable; and that "if the monetarists are right, the system must be unstable".[12]

Miller's model demonstrates that fiscal policy is more expansionary when all assets grow at the same rate such that the rate of interest is constant in the long-run equilibrium. But the nature of crowding-out considered in BS or Miller models is indirect crowding out or what results via changes in interest rates etc. For a stronger vindication of the effectiveness of fiscal (or monetary) policy a further look at the crowding out debate is necessary.

## 5.6 THE CROWDING-OUT CONTROVERSY

Crowding-out in simple words means a rise in government spending leading to a fall in private spending — consumption, investment or both. The degree of crowding out determines the effectiveness of fiscal policy. Also, one has to look at both short-run and long-run effects of crowding-out. In the simple IS-LM model, only the short-run effect is considered. For example a rise in $G$ implies a rightward shift of the IS curve which, given a downward sloping IS and an upward sloping LM curve, implies a rise in both $Y$ and $r$. The rise in $r$ reduces private investment spending and, as a result, real income increases but the multiplier is smaller than in the model without the money market:

$$\frac{1}{1-C'+I'\frac{L_1}{L_2}} < \frac{1}{1-C'}$$

In the more realistic models with government budget constraints considered in the present Chapter, both short-run and long-run effects of crowding-out have been analysed. The short-run means the first round and long-run the final effect when all the successive rounds of movements of the IS curves have been considered. The short-run multiplier is often called the *impact multiplier*. It has already been indicated that when some private spending has been replaced by public or government spending in such a way that the long-run multiplier $\frac{\delta Y}{\delta G}$ is still positive, the crowding-out

12. Blinder and Solow (*op. cit.*, p. 336).

is *partial*. In the case of complete crowding-out, $\frac{\delta Y}{\delta G}=0$ implying the ineffectiveness of fiscal policy. It has already been noted that there is complete crowding out in the classical full-employment model for a closed economy — without the government budget constraint [Chapter 3].

Also, crowding-out can be *direct* or *indirect*. Direct crowding-out occurs when a rise in real government spending leads to a fall in real private spending. This can happen when the government provision is a substitute for a private provision or when, full-employment prevails, raising government spending implies withdrawing resources which have hitherto been employed in the private sector. Indirect crowding-out occurs due to the feedbacks and various side-effects from within the entire macroeconomic model-effects which tend to negate the effects of the initial rise in government spending.

Models incorporating direct crowding-out effects introduce public goods in the households utility function and the firms' production (e.g., Grossman and Lucas, Possen and Slutsky, Groenewold etc.) or separate consumption and investment spending into a private and a public or government component (e.g., Buiter). In this chapter, we have chosen a few models of direct crowding out retaining the assumptions of a fixed price level and a fixed capital stock.

Grossman and Lucas (1974) (GL) developed two simple 2-equation models of the real sector comprising the labour and the output markets — one examined in the market-clearing and the other in an excess supply demand-constrained situation. Supply of labour is considered exogenous in both models. The short-run production function in the GL models is:

$$Y = Y(N, G) \tag{5.72a}$$

where diminishing marginal product rule applies to $N$ and $G$ implying $Y_1 > 0, Y_2 > 0$ but $Y_{11} < 0, Y_{22} < 0$. But $Y_{12}$ or $Y_{21} \geq 0$. Government's objective function is to maximise aggregate consumption:[13]

$$C = Y - G \tag{5.72b}$$

Subject to (5.72a). The necessary condition for this constrained maximisation is easily obtained as:

$$\frac{\delta Y}{\delta G} - 1 = 0 \quad \Rightarrow \quad Y_2 = 1 \tag{5.72c}$$

13. Consumption is the only component of private demand in the GL models.

(5.72c) reveals that the optimum consumption rule is such that government spending increases at the expense of private consumption until the point where the marginal product of public goods equals unity. Because of the diminishing marginal productivity assumption $Y_2 < 1$ would imply that the level of government spending should be brought down (in which case $Y_2$ rises towards 1) and $Y_2 > 1$ would imply that the level of government provision is lower than the level required to maximise consumption.

On the other hand the private firms maximise profits by varying the level of employment — considering $G$ as exogenous. Assuming perfectly competitive markets the necessary condition for profit maximisation is:

$$Y_1(N, G) = w \tag{5.72d}$$

From this a demand function for labour results as:

$$N^d = N^d(w, G) \tag{5.72e}$$

$N_1^d < 0$ as before but $N_2^d$ is ambiguous in sign.

The GL model is somewhat too simple for our purpose since real money balances is the only form of wealth and only an entirely tax financed government spending is considered. So, the model is not pursued any further.

Possen and Slutsky (1980) analyse the effects of temporary increases in government spending:

$$\Delta G_1 > 0, \Delta G_t = 0 \quad \text{for} \quad t > 1 \quad \Rightarrow \quad G_t = G_1 \quad \text{for} \quad t \geq 1,$$

of pre-announced permanent future increases in government spending:

$$\Delta G_t > 0 \quad \text{for all} \quad t > 1$$

and of counter cyclical changes in government spending

$$\Delta G_t > 0 \quad \text{for} \quad t = i \quad \text{and} \quad \Delta G_t < 0 \quad \text{for} \quad t = j, i \neq j$$

on private consumption. The consumers are assumed to have multi-period utility functions depending on private and public goods. The consumption function for each consumer is then derived from a budget-constrained maximisation of utility over his finite life-time. This paper mainly analyses the short-run effects of the above mentioned policies and the expansionary potential of temporary and counter cyclical changes in government spending are shown to be higher than that of the permanent changes. But since the analysis is not in the framework of a complete macroeconomic model, it will not be considered in detail in the present sections.

Groenewold (1984) in his two-period macro model with direct crowding-out has followed up from Grossman-Lucas' idea that government spending can enhance the productive potential and, therefore, be entered as an argument in the production function of the private sector. Also, like Possen and Slutsky, part of government spending is used as an argument in the consumption function of the private sector. Unlike in Possen and Slutsky, the consumers maximise the present value of discounted future utilities not over their finite life-time but over just a two-period horizon. Groenewold's analysis is summarised below.

Government spending, $G$, is split into two components — spending on consumption, $g^c$ and spending on factors, $g^f$. The representative household's utility function is written as:

$$U(C_t^*, M_t, B_t, N_t^s) \tag{5.73a}$$

where $C_t^* \equiv C_t + C(g_t^c)$ (5.73b)

is "useful consumption" with $C' > 0, C'' < 0, U_1, U_2, U_3 > 0, U_{11}, U_{22}, U_{33} < 0$ and households are assumed to derive positive marginal utility from employment only when there is unemployment. The utility function in (5.73a) is assumed additively separable in employment and, therefore, can be rewritten as

$$U(C_t^*, M_t, B_t) + f(N_t^s) \tag{5.73c}$$

$t = 1$ represents the short-run and $t = 2$ represents the long-run in this 2-period model. In the long-run prices are assumed flexible and this flexibility is assumed to ensure full-employment but in the short-run prices are assumed rigid.

Assuming lump-sum taxes and a rate of interest $r^m$ for money, the budget constraint for the household is written as:

$$Y_t + M_{t-1} + B_{t-1}, + (r_t^m - \dot{p}_t)M_t + (r_t - \dot{p}_t)B_t$$

$$= C_t + T_t + M_t + B_t$$

$$\Rightarrow \quad C_t^* - Y_t + T_t + M_t(1 - r_t^m + \dot{P}_t) + B_t(1 - r_t + \dot{p}_t)$$

$$- C(g_t^c) - M_{t-1} - B_{t-1} = 0 \tag{5.74a}$$

The useful consumption for each period is derived by maximising the discounted present value of utility:

$$PVU = U(C_1^*, M_1, B_1) + f(N_1^s) + \rho\,[U(C_2^*, M_2, B_2) + f(N_2^s)] \tag{5.74b}$$

Subject to the two budget constraints given in (5.74a) for $t = 1, 2$ where $\rho > 0$ is the constant, exogenous discount factor.

Similarly demand for labour in each period follows from an analysis of profit maximisation subject to the production constraint:

$$Y_t = Y(N_t, g_t^f) \tag{5.75a}$$

Along an isoquant, the change in output is zero. So, taking the total differential of (5.75a)

$$dY_t = \frac{\delta Y_t}{\delta N_t} dN_t + \frac{\delta Y_t}{\delta g_t^f} dg_t^f = 0 \;\Rightarrow \frac{dN}{dg} = -\frac{Y_2}{Y_1} \tag{5.75b}$$

So, the labour demand in period 1 is given by

$$N_t^d = N^d(Y_t, g_t^f)$$

Such that $\dfrac{\delta N_t^d}{\delta Y_t} = \dfrac{1}{\frac{\delta Y_t}{\delta N_t}}$ and $\dfrac{\delta N_t^d}{\delta g_t^f} = -\dfrac{Y_2}{Y_1}$ for $t = 1$.

In the long-run, assumption of full employment implies that the firms supply an output

$$Y_2^s = Y^s(\overline{N}, g_2^f)$$

Because of the assumption of excess supply, output is demand determined in period 1 so that

$$Y_1 = C_1 + g_1^c + g_1^f$$

$$\Rightarrow \quad Y_1 = c_1^* - C(g_1^c) + g_1^c + g_1^f$$

$$\Rightarrow \quad Y_1 + c(g_1^c) - g_1^c - g_1^f \equiv (Y_1^*) = C_1^* \tag{5.76a}$$

In period 2, price flexibility is assumed to ensure

$$Y_2^* = C_2^*$$

$$\Rightarrow \quad Y_2 + c(g_2^c) - g_2^c - g_2^f = Y_2^* = C_2^* \tag{5.76b}$$

where $Y_t^*$ is labeled "useful output" and

$$Y_2 = Y_2^s = Y^s(\overline{N}, g_2^f) \tag{5.76c}$$

The government budget constraints are

$$M_t(1 - r_t^m + \dot{p}_t) - M_{t-1} + B_t(1 - r_t + \dot{p}_t) - B_{t-1}$$

$$= g_t^c + g_t^f - T_t, \quad t = 1, 2 \tag{5.77a}$$

Unlike in the previous models, real stocks of bonds are assumed to be $B_t$ and not $\frac{B_t}{r}$.

Assuming $\dot{p}_1 = 0$ and $\dot{p}_t = r_t^m$ for $t = 1, 2$, (5.77a) can be rewritten as:

$$M_t - M_{t-1} + B_t(1 - r_t + \dot{p}_t) - B_{t-1}$$

$$= g_t^c + g_t^f - T_t \quad t = 1, 2 \tag{5.78}$$

The equations (5.76a)–(5.76c) and the pair in (5.78) summarise Groenewold's model with government budget. It is evident that the model does not explain the equilibrium conditions in either the money or the bond markets. Money and bonds enter the utility functions of the representative household[14] because they offer "liquidity services" to the households.

The impacts of a balanced budget and a bond financed government spending on $Y_t$, $C_t$, etc. for $t = 1, 2$ can now be examined.

First the balanced-budget policy implies that only the lump sum taxes are varied and the real asset stocks are unchanged:

$$M_2(1 + \dot{p}_2) = M_1 = M_0 \tag{5.79a}$$

$$B_2(1 + \dot{p}_2) = B_1 = B_o \tag{5.79b}$$

From (5.79a) and (5.79b), the balanced-budget policy implies

$$B_2 = (M_2/M_0)\, B_o \tag{5.80}$$

Working out the long-run multipliers first from (5.76b) and (5.76c)

$$\frac{dy_2}{dg_2^c} = 0 \tag{5.81a}$$

and

$$\frac{dY_2^*}{dg_2^c} = \frac{dC_2^*}{dg_2^c} = c'(g_2^c)c'(g_2^c) - 1 \gtreqless 0 \quad \text{as} \quad c' \geq 1 \tag{5.81b}$$

So, in the long-run, useful output and useful consumption rise only if $[c'(g_2^c) - 1] > 0$. The bracketed expression $[c'(g_2^c) - 1]$ can be labelled "efficiency" of government expenditure. Because full-employment is

14. The assumptions of a representative household and a representative firm enable Groenewold to ignore the problems of aggregation.

assumed in the long-run, a rise in $g_2^c$, provided $g_2^f$ does not fall, means a reallocation of spending from the private to the public sector $\left(\therefore \frac{dC_2}{dg_2^c} = -1\right)$ but the households as free riders get a positive benefit if $c'(g_2^c) > 1$. These long-run multipliers are independent of the short-run spending $g_1^c$ or $g_1^f$.

Now from (5.76a) the short-run multipliers can be derived as:

$$dY_1 + c'(g_1^c)dg_1^c - dg_1^c - dg_1^f = dC_1^* = dY_1^*$$

Assuming $g_1^f$ does not change,

$$\frac{dY_1}{dg_1^c} = \frac{dC_1^*}{dg_1^c} + [1 - c'(g_1^c)] \tag{5.81c}$$

From (5.73b):

$$\frac{dC_1}{dg_1^c} = \frac{dC_1^*}{dg_1^c} - c'(g_1^c) \tag{5.81d}$$

It is shown in the Appendix 5.A.4. that $C_1^*$ depends on $g_2^c$ and that $\frac{dC_1^*}{dg_2^c}$ is ambiguous in sign implying that when both $g_1^c$ and $g_2^c$ change the multiplier $\frac{dY_1}{dg_1^c/dg_2^c}$ will be of ambiguous sign. If only $g_1^c$ changes, then $\frac{dY_1}{dg_1^c} > 0$ only if $1 - c'(g_1^c) > 0$, i.e., only if government spending is inefficient in period 1 or in the short-run.

In the bond-financed case, the real money stock satisfies condition (5.79a) which can be rewritten as

$$1 + \dot{p}_2 = \frac{M_0}{M_2} \tag{5.82a}$$

and to satisfy the budget constraint in the first period[15]

$$(B_1 - B_0) = g_1^c + g_1^f - T_1 + (r_1)B_1 \tag{5.82b}$$

15. Groenewold makes a simplifying assumption here and includes all interest payments in lump-sum taxes.

In the long-run, however, the condition for equilibrium is that the budget be balanced: From (5.79b) and (5.82a) and (5.82b), one gets

$$B_2 = \frac{B_1}{1+\dot{p}_2} = \frac{M_2}{M_0}(g_1^c + g_1^f - T_1 + B_1 r_1 + B_0)$$

The long-run multipliers for bond-financed change in $g_2^c$ with $g_2^f$ constant, $\frac{dY_2}{dg_2^c}$ and $\frac{dC_2}{dg_2^c}$ and $\frac{dC_2^*}{dg_2^c}$ are the same as in the tax financed case implying that these multipliers depend only on the efficiency of government spending and are independent of the method of financing the budget.

The short-run multipliers derived in the appendix show that they are greater than those in the tax-financed case under a number of simplifying assumptions.

## 5.7 SUMMARY AND CONCLUSIONS

This chapter has shown the effects of extending the basic Keynesian IS-LM model to include the government budget constraint. The government budget constraint makes the hitherto static IS-LM model dynamic and thereby raises the question of the stability of the model. This extension has been shown in several stages in an ascending order of complications first including the wealth effects and then the interest payments on government bonds.

The main purpose of this chapter was to show the efficacy of fiscal as against the monetary policy to finance the government budget. An important result obtained is that the long-run government expenditure multiplier is equal to the reciprocal of the tax-rate and, therefore, independent of any tool of monetary policy. The proportion of the deficit financed by money merely adjusts the speed of response. In the models including wealth effects as well as interest payments on bonds, the question of stability is shown to be more complicated. The important conclusion following from these models is that the system is always stable under pure money financing and pure bond-financing of government deficits can be more expansionary than pure money financing only if the conditions of stability are satisfied. So the monetarists claiming the ineffectiveness of fiscal policy must believe that the system is unstable. In the model with mixed money-bond financing the system is shown to be locally stable even when asset stock are allowed to grow at a constant rate such that the rate of interest is constant in the long-run. In this case a rise in the fraction of the deficit financed by money is shown to be contractionary in the sense that the income-wealth ratio falls and the economy grows at a slower rate. So this holds some more support for the Keynesians.

Since the Keynesians-Monetarists debate centres around the crowding out controversy, an attempt has also been made to incorporate direct crowding out in a model of the real sector with the government budget constraint. But the impacts of a rise in government spending both short-run and long-run are seen to be ambiguous in most cases depending on the efficiency of such spending.

## *APPENDIX TO CHAPTER 5*

### 5.A.1 **The Derivation of (5.24)**

In terms of deviation from its equilibrium, $Y^*$, the difference equation (5.20) can be written in the deviation form:

$$DY_t = \frac{Z - XT'}{Z} DY_{t-1} \tag{5.22}$$

where $DY_t = Y_t - Y^*$ and $DY_{t-1} = Y_{t-1} - Y^*$

The general solution to the first order homogeneous difference equation is given by $A\lambda^t$ where $A$ is to be evaluated from the initial value of $Y_0$. Putting $DY_t = A\lambda^t$ in (5.22), one gets

$$\lambda^t = \frac{Z - XT'}{Z} \lambda^{t-1}$$

Dividing through by $\lambda^{t-1} (\neq 0)$, $\lambda = \frac{Z - XT'}{Z}$

At $t = 0$,

$$DY_0 = \left(\frac{Z - XT'}{Z}\right)^0 A$$

$$\Rightarrow \quad A = DY_0 = Y_0 - Y^* = Y_0 - \frac{G_t}{T'} \tag{5.23}$$

So, the complete solution of $DY_t = \left(Y_0 - \frac{G_t}{T'}\right)\left(\frac{Z - XT'}{Z}\right)^t$ and, therefore, the solution of $Y_t$ is

$$Y^* + \left(Y_0 - \frac{G_t}{T'}\right)\left(1 - \frac{T'X}{Z}\right)^t$$

Substituting for $Y^*$, $Z$ and $X$,

$$Y_t = \left(Y_0 - \frac{G_t}{T'}\right)\left(1 - \frac{L_2 C_2 + I'(\theta - L_3)}{L_2\{1 - C_1(1 - T')\} + I'L_1}\right)^t + \frac{G_t}{T'} \tag{5.24}$$

### 5.A.2 **The Solution and the Stability of (5.41) and (5.43)**

Equation (5.41) is of the form

$$\dot{M} = h_0 + h_1 M(t) \tag{5.A.2.1}$$

where $h_0$ is all the terms containing $G, \overline{B}, \overline{K}$ and the parameters in (5.41) and

$$h_1 = -\frac{t_1}{J}\left[C_2\left(L_2 - \frac{B}{r^2}\right) + I'(1 - L_3)\right] \tag{5.A.2.2}$$

where $J$ is given in (5.36). As before, one has to find the equilibrium value of $M, \overline{M}$, which is such that $\dot{M} = 0$.

Substituting $\dot{M} = 0$ in (5.A.2.1), the equilibrium $\overline{M}$ is obtained as

$$-\frac{h_0}{h_1} \tag{5.A.2.3}$$

Let $DM(t)$ be the deviation of $M(t)$ from its equilibrium $\overline{M}$. Then the differential equation (5.A.2.1) in $M_t$ can be rewritten as

$$\frac{dDM}{dt} = h_1 DM \tag{5.A.2.4}$$

(5.A.2.4) is a homogeneous equation the general solution of which is given by $A_0 e^{\lambda t}$ where $A_0$ is the constant of integration to be evaluated from the initial given value $M_0$ at time $t = 0$.

Substituting $M(t) = A_0 e^{\lambda t}$ in (5.A.2.4), one gets

$$A_0 e^{\lambda t} = A_0 h_1 e^{\lambda t} \quad \Rightarrow \quad \lambda = h_1$$

At $t = 0, M(t) = M_0$ assumed to be known and one gets

$$M_0 = A_o e^0 = A_0$$

The general solution of (5.A.2.4) is then

$$DM(t) = M_o e^{h_1 t} \tag{5.A.2.5}$$

$\Rightarrow$ The general solution for $M(t)$ is $M(t) = \overline{M} + M_0 e^{h_1 t}$

$$\Rightarrow \quad M(t) = -\frac{h_0}{h_1} + M_0 e^{h_1 t} \tag{5.A.2.6}$$

The solution for $M(t)$ is stable only if $M(t)$ tends to its equilibrium value $-\frac{h_0}{h_1}$ as $t \to \infty$. In other words, the condition for stability is that as $t \to \infty, e^{h_1 t} \to 0$. This will be satisfied only when $h_1 < 0$. The condition for stability under money finance is, therefore,

$$-\frac{t_1}{J}\left[C_2\left(L_2-\frac{B}{r^2}\right)+I'(1-L_3)\right]<0 \tag{5.42}$$

The solution for (5.43) can be obtained in an identical manner. This is left as an exercise.

### 5.A.3 The Derivation of the Detailed Forms (5.57), (5.58) and the Stability Condition in Miller's Model

Differentiating the IS and the LM equations (5.56) and (5.52) respectively w.r.t. $t$ and using (5.54) one obtains

$$\dot{Y}[1-C_1(1-t_1)]-(I'-C_2B/r^2)\dot{r}=\dot{G}$$

$$+\{C_1(1-t_1)+C_2/r\}\dot{B}+C_2\dot{M} \tag{5.A.3.1}$$

and $$(VM^{d\prime}-M^d B/r^2)\dot{r}=\dot{M}(1-M^d)-M^d\dot{B}/r \tag{5.A.3.2}$$

Solving (5.A.3.1) and (5.A.3.2) for $\dot{Y}$ and $\dot{r}$ by Cramer's rule,

$$\dot{Y}=\frac{(VM^{d\prime}M^dB/r^2)[\dot{G}+\{C_1(1-t_1)+c_2/r\}\dot{B}+C_2\dot{M}]+(I'-C_2B/r^2)\{\dot{M}(1-M^d)-M^d\dot{B}/r\}}{\{1-C_1(1-t_1)\}\{VM^{d\prime}-M^dB/r^2\}} \tag{5.3.A.3}$$

and $$\dot{r}=\frac{\{1-C_1(1-t_1)\}\{\dot{M}(1-M^d)-M^d\dot{B}/r\}}{(VM^{d\prime}-M^dB/r^2)(1-C_1(1-t_1))}$$

$$\Rightarrow\quad \dot{r}=\frac{\dot{M}(1-M^d)-M^d\dot{B}/r}{VM^{d\prime}-M^dB/r^2} \tag{5.3.A.4}$$

(5.A.3.3) and (5.A.3.4) indicate the details of (5.57) and (5.58) respectively. It can be noted in particular that $\dot{r}$ does not contain $\dot{G}$ and therefore $Q$ does not contain $G$ and this is because the long-run LM curve depends on wealth and not on income.

For the details of the solution for $\psi$ of equation (5.62), we proceed as follows:

Differentiating the L.H.S. of the budget constraint and assuming $\dot{G}=0$ one gets

$$\dot{D}=\dot{B}(1-t_1)-t_1\dot{Y} \tag{5.A.3.5}$$

From the first part of (5.62), $D=\dot{V}$ substituting in (5.A.3.5)

$$\frac{\dot{D}}{D}=\left[\frac{\dot{B}}{B}(1-t_1)\frac{B}{V}-t_1\frac{\dot{Y}}{Y}\cdot\frac{Y}{V}\right]\frac{V}{\dot{V}} \tag{5.A.3.6}$$

Proceeding in the same way as in the case of BS model, $\dot{Y} = H_1\dot{M} + H_2\dot{B}$ when $G$ is constant and when

$$H_1 = \frac{C_2(VM^{d\prime} - M^d B/r^2) + (I' - C_2 B/r^2)(1 - M^d)}{\{1 - C_1(1 - t_1)\}\{VM^{d\prime} - M^d B/r^2)} \tag{5.A.3.7}$$

and

$$H_2 = \frac{\{C_1(1 - t_1) + C_2/r\}(VM^{d\prime} - M^d B/r^2) - M^d/r(I' - C_2 B/r^2)}{\{1 - C_1(1 - t_1)\}(VM^{d\prime} - M^d B/r^2)} \tag{5.A.3.8}$$

Using (5.A.3.7) and (5.A.3.8) in (5.A.3.6),

$$\frac{\dot{D}}{D} = [1 - t_1(1 + H_2)]\frac{B}{V} - t_1 H_1 \frac{M}{V} = \psi \tag{5.A.3.9}$$

where $H_1$ and $H_2$ are given in (5.A.3.7) and (5.A.3.8) respectively.

## 5.A.4 The Derivation of $\frac{dC_1^*}{dg_2^c}$ in (5.82a)

In Groenewold's model, the consumer maximises the Lagrangian

$$L = U(C_1^*, M_1, B_1) + f(N_1^s) + \rho[U(C_2^*, M_2, B_2) + f(N_2^s)]$$
$$- \lambda_1[C_1^* - Y_1 + T_1 + M_1(1 - r_1^m + \dot{p}_1) + B_1(1 - r_1 + \dot{p}_1) - c(g_1^c) - M_0 - B_0]$$
$$- \lambda_2[C_2^* - Y_2 + T_2 + M_2(1 - r_2^m + \dot{p}_2) + B_2(1 - r_2 + \dot{p}_2) - c(g_2^c) - M_1 - B_1] \tag{5.A.4.1}$$

The variables the representative household chooses are $C_1^*$, $M_1$, $B_1$ and $C_1^*$, $M_2$, $B_2$. $L$ is maximised w.r.t. these and $\lambda_1$ and $\lambda_2$. Writing only the former 6 first-order conditions:

$$\frac{\delta U}{\delta C_1^*} - \lambda_1 = 0 \tag{i}$$

$$\frac{\delta U}{\delta M_1} - \lambda_1 (1 - r_1^m + \dot{p}_1) + \lambda_2 = 0 \tag{ii}$$

$$\frac{\delta U}{\delta B_1} - \lambda_1 (1 - r_1 + \dot{p}_1) + \lambda_2 = 0 \tag{iii}$$

$$\rho \frac{\delta U}{\delta C_2^*} - \lambda_2 = 0 \tag{iv}$$

$$\rho \frac{\delta U}{\delta M_2} - \lambda_2 (1 - r_2^m + \dot{p}_2) = 0 \tag{v}$$

and

$$\rho \frac{\delta U}{\delta B_2} - \lambda_2 (1 - r_2 + \dot{p}_2) = 0 \tag{vi}$$

Eliminating $\lambda_1$ and $\lambda_2$ from (i), (ii) and (iv) one obtains

$$\frac{\delta U}{\delta M_1} = \frac{\delta U}{\delta C_1^*}(1 - r_1^m + \dot{p}_1) - \rho \frac{\delta U}{\delta C_2^*} \tag{5.A.4.2}$$

Eliminating $\rho$ and $\lambda_2$ from (iv) and (v),

$$\frac{\delta U}{\delta M_2} = \frac{\delta U}{\delta C_2^*}(1 - r_2^m + \dot{p}_2) \tag{5.A.4.3}$$

Eliminating $\lambda_1$ and $\lambda_2$ from (i), (iii) and (iv)

$$\frac{\delta U}{\delta B_1} = \frac{\delta U}{\delta C_1^*}(1 - r_1 + \dot{p}_1) - \rho \frac{\delta U}{\delta C_2^*} \tag{5.A.4.4}$$

and eliminating $\rho$ and $\lambda_2$ from (iv) and (vi)

$$\frac{\delta U}{\delta B_2} = \frac{\delta U}{\delta C_2^*}(1 - r_2 + \dot{p}_2) \tag{5.A.4.5}$$

The consumption levels $C_1$, $C_2$ and $C_1^*$, $C_2^*$ can be solved from (5.A.4.2) through to (5.A.4.6) which are a lot simpler when one uses Groenewold's assumptions:

$$\dot{p}_1 = 0 \quad \text{and} \quad r_t^m = \dot{p}_t \quad \text{for} \quad t = 1, 2$$

Taking the total differential of (5.A.4.2) and assuming $M_1 = M_0$ and $B_1 = B_0$ for the tax-financed balanced budget policy, one obtains

$$\left(\frac{\delta_2 U}{\delta M_1 \delta C_1^*} - \frac{\delta_2 U}{\delta C_1^{*2}}\right) dC_1^* = -\rho \left[\frac{\delta^2 U}{\delta C_2^{*2}} dC_2^* + \frac{\delta^2 U}{\delta C_2^* \delta M_2} dM_2 + \frac{\delta^2 U}{\delta C_2^* \delta B_2} dB_2\right] \tag{5.A.4.6}$$

⇒ $dC_1^*$ is independent of $dg_1^c$ since $dC_2^*$, $dM_2$ and $dB_2$ are all independent of $g_1^c$, i.e., $dC_1^*$ is independent of short-run fiscal policy.

For the bond-financed fiscal policy $dM_1 = 0$ but

$$B_1 - B_0 = g_1^c + g_1^f - T_1 + (rB_1) \tag{5.A.4.7}$$

Groenewold makes a simplifying assumption that all interest payments on bonds are included in lump-sum taxes. Then, for the short-run multiplier $\frac{dC_1^*}{dg_1^c}$, he uses the relation

$$dC_1^* = \frac{1}{\frac{\delta^2 U}{\delta M_1 \delta C_1} - \frac{\delta^2 U}{\delta C_1^{*2}}} \left[-\rho \left\{\frac{\delta^2 U}{\delta C_2^{*2}} dC_2^* + \frac{\delta^2 U}{\delta C_2^* \delta M_2} dM_2 + \frac{\delta^2 U}{\delta C_2^* \delta B_2} dB_2\right\} + \left\{\frac{\delta^2 U}{\delta C_1 \delta B_1} - \frac{\delta^2 U}{\delta M_1 \delta B_1}\right\} dg_1^c\right] \tag{5.A.4.7}$$

# 6

# INFLATION AND UNEMPLOYMENT IN MACRO MODELS: THE WAGE-PRICE SECTOR

## INTRODUCTION

Inflation is a persistent rise in the general price level. In the UK and other developed market economies of the world, it became a major problem of the 1970's. Keynes was more concerned with the problem of recession and unemployment perpetuated by wage-price inflexibility than with that of inflation. It is only when full-employment has already been achieved that a rise in aggregate demand would lead to a rise in the general price level in the Keynesian system. In other words, inflation is of the "demand-pull" type. Since the equilibrium price level is determined by the intersection of aggregate demand and aggregate supply, a rise in the price level can also be caused by a shift of the supply curve to the left caused by, say, a rise in the costs of production. This is "cost-push" inflation. Labour or wage costs take up a major share in the total costs of production and therefore cost-push implies a wage-push. A direct relation between the rate of inflation as measured by the rate of change of the price level and the rate of change of money wages follows from the "mark-up" pricing of final output in an oligopolistic market structure. The employer adds a mark-up on the total labour costs per unit of the product to take care of his overheads. So, the price,

$$P = mr \times \text{unit labour costs} \qquad (6.1a)$$

where $mr > 1$ is the mark-up factor.[1] Substituting for labour costs per unit of output, (6.1a) can be rewritten as

$$P = mr\frac{WN}{Y} \tag{6.1b}$$

Taking the time derivative of (6.1b)

$$\dot{P} = mr\left[\frac{Y(W\dot{N} + N\dot{W}) - WN\dot{Y}}{Y^2}\right] \tag{6.1c}$$

Dividing (6.1c) through by (6.1b)

$$\frac{\dot{P}}{P}(\equiv \dot{P}) = \frac{Y}{WN}\left[\frac{W\dot{N} + N\dot{W}}{Y} - \frac{WN\dot{Y}}{Y^2}\right]$$

$$\Rightarrow \quad \dot{p} = \frac{\dot{N}}{N} + \frac{\dot{W}}{W} - \frac{\dot{Y}}{Y} \tag{6.2}$$

Noting that $\frac{Y}{N}$ is a measure of output/head or average productivity of labour, the difference $\left(\frac{\dot{Y}}{Y} - \frac{\dot{N}}{N}\right)$ is the rate of change of average productivity over time, $\dot{q}$. Then (6.2) can be written as

$$\dot{p} = \dot{w} - \dot{q} \tag{6.3}$$

(6.3) shows that the rate of inflation is positively related to the rate of change of money wage and negatively to the rate of change of productivity. So as long as wage rises are less than productivity rises, rate of inflation is negative.

Other sources of cost-push inflation are increased raw material prices such as the OPEC price hike of 1973-74 and profit push. The latter occurs when product prices are administered upwards in an attempt to widen profit margins.[2]

## 6.1 THEORIES OF INFLATION

Although it is not a theory but an empirical regularity observed by Phillips between the rate of change of money wage and the rate of unemployment in the UK, the Phillips Curve relation is usually at the centre of any

1. If $mr = 1.4$, say, then the employer adds 40 per cent of labour costs as fixed costs in pricing his product.

2. See Greenaway and Shaw for details (p. 259).

discussion on inflation. Phillips (1958) observed a non-linear inverse relationship between the percentage rate of change of money wages and the rate of unemployment in the UK during 1861-1913. The equation to the Phillips Curve is

$$\frac{\dot{W}}{W} = -a + bu^c, \quad a > 0, b > 0, c < 0 \tag{6.4}$$

Measuring $u$ along the horizontal and $\frac{\dot{W}}{W}$ along the vertical axes, it is clear from (6.4) that as $u \to \infty, \frac{\dot{W}}{W} \to -a$ implying that the latter is the lower asymptote of $\frac{\dot{W}}{W}$ and the horizontal intercept is $u = \left(\frac{a}{b}\right)^{\frac{1}{c}}$ (obtained by setting $\frac{\dot{W}}{W} = 0$ and solving for $u$).

The Phillips Curve is shown in Fig. 6.1. On this diagram, the length OA measure $-a$ and OB measures $\left(\frac{a}{b}\right)^{\frac{1}{c}}$.

OB is the rate of unemployment where the demand for labour is equal to its supply and the rate of change of wages is zero. This corresponds to the equilibrium wage rate, $OW^*$ of Fig. 6.2(a). At this rate, there will be some people unemployed but their number will be matched by an equal number of unfilled vacancies and there will be jobs available for all those who wish to work at the equilibrium wage $OW^*$. The Phillips Curve is a dynamic hypothesis relating the rate of wage change to the rate of unemployment.

Lipsey (1961) developed the interrelations between this dynamic hypothesis and the static analysis of wage changes in response to excess demand in the labour market. The theoretical foundation provided by Lipsey was developed in a number of steps. First the static part — wages rise (fall) when demand for labour exceeds (falls short of) the supply of labour. This is static because it does not refer to the speed of adjustment. The next step is to relate the (percentage) rate of excess demand to the rate of wage change in a linear form:

$$\frac{\dot{W}}{W} = \alpha\left(\frac{N^d - N^s}{N^s}\right) \times 100, \quad \alpha > 0 \tag{6.5a}$$

Wages rise (implying $\frac{\dot{W}}{W} > 0$) whenever there is excess demand $N^d > N^s$ and wages fall (implying $\frac{\dot{W}}{W} < 0$) whenever there is excess supply $N^d < N^s$. The third step is to relate the rate of excess demand for labour to the more easily observed variable, $u$, the rate of unemployment:

$$\frac{N^d - N^s}{N^s} = f(u), \quad f' < 0 \tag{6.5b}$$

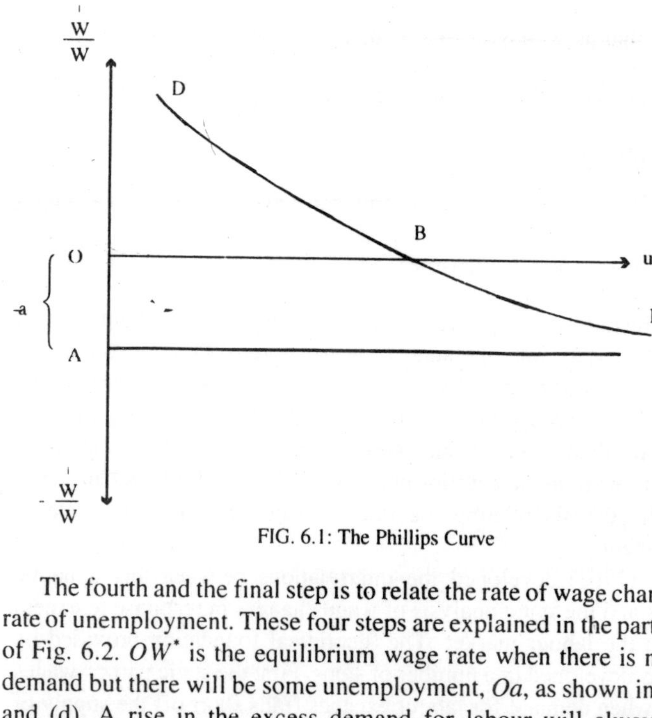


FIG. 6.1: The Phillips Curve

The fourth and the final step is to relate the rate of wage change to the rate of unemployment. These four steps are explained in the parts (a)–(d) of Fig. 6.2. $OW^*$ is the equilibrium wage rate when there is no excess demand but there will be some unemployment, $Oa$, as shown in parts (c) and (d). A rise in the excess demand for labour will always reduce unemployment but the latter can never be negative; as excess demand approaches infinity, unemployment approaches zero. Although equation (6.5a) emphasises only a linear relation, wages rise faster for a further fall in unemployment when unemployment is already low; so, to the left of point a in part (d) the relation is non-linear.[3] Phillips also paid attention both to the dynamics and non-linearity of money wage changes and unemployment. When unemployment is falling, the rate of increase in money wages would be higher than that predicted by (6.4) and when unemployment is rising the rate of fall in money wages, due to downward rigidity, would be lower than that predicted by (6.4). So, the rate of change of unemployment is an additional determinant of money wage inflation. Lipsey's reproduction of the Phillips Curve is a cross between the classical and Keynesian assumptions. With some manipulation of (6.5b) it can be shown why the rate of unemployment can be used as a proxy for the level of aggregate excess demand.[4] Using the short-run macro production function (3.2) and expanding around the full-employment level using Maclaurin's Series,

$$F(N) \cong F(\overline{N}) + (N-\overline{N})F'(\overline{N}) + \frac{(N-\overline{N})^2}{2.1}F''(\overline{N}) + \frac{(N-\overline{N})^3}{3.2.1}F'''(\overline{N}) + \cdots \tag{6.6a}$$

Approximating the series up to the second term, output, $Y$, is approximately equal to

$$Y \cong \overline{Y} + (N-\overline{N})F'(\overline{N})$$

$$\Rightarrow \quad Y - \overline{Y} \cong F'(\overline{N})(N-\overline{N}) \tag{6.6b}$$

The difference $Y-\overline{Y}$ can be viewed as the level of excess demand and the difference $N-\overline{N}$ is the negative of the level of unemployment. So (6.6b) shows an inverse relation between excess demand in the output market and the rate of unemployment.

$$-\overline{N}ua = Y - \overline{Y}$$

$$\Rightarrow \quad u = -\frac{Y-\overline{Y}}{a\overline{N}}, \quad a > 0 \tag{6.7}$$

3. For further detail, see Surrey (1976, pp. 310-11).
4. See Turnovsky, S.J. (1979) p. 107.

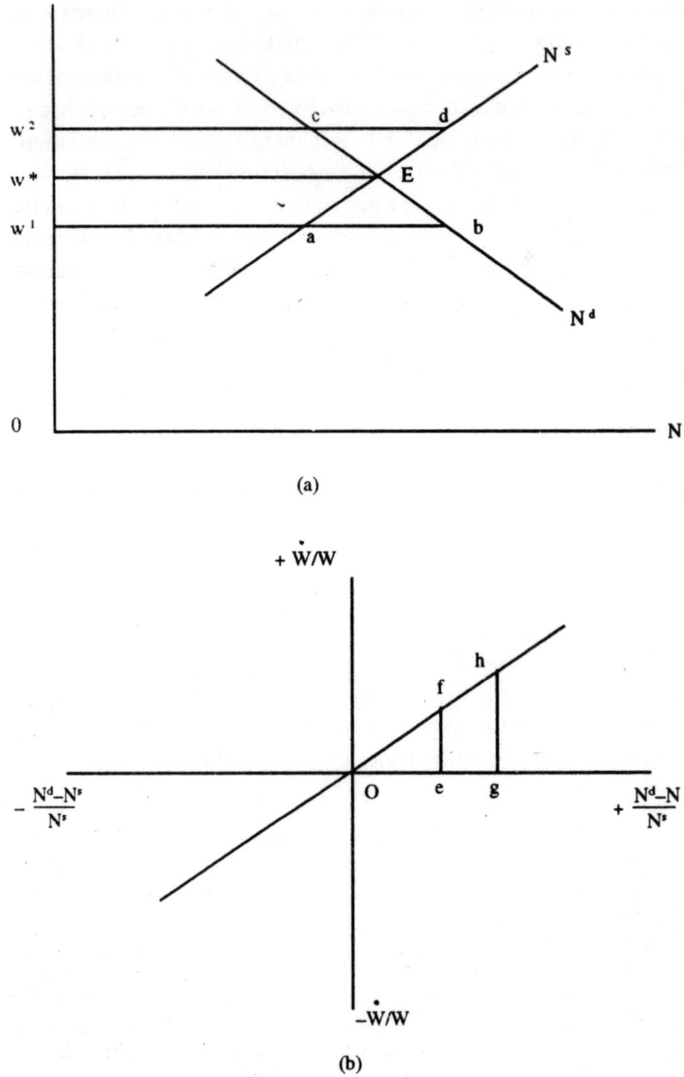


FIG. 6.2: Lipsey's Reproduction of the Phillips Curve

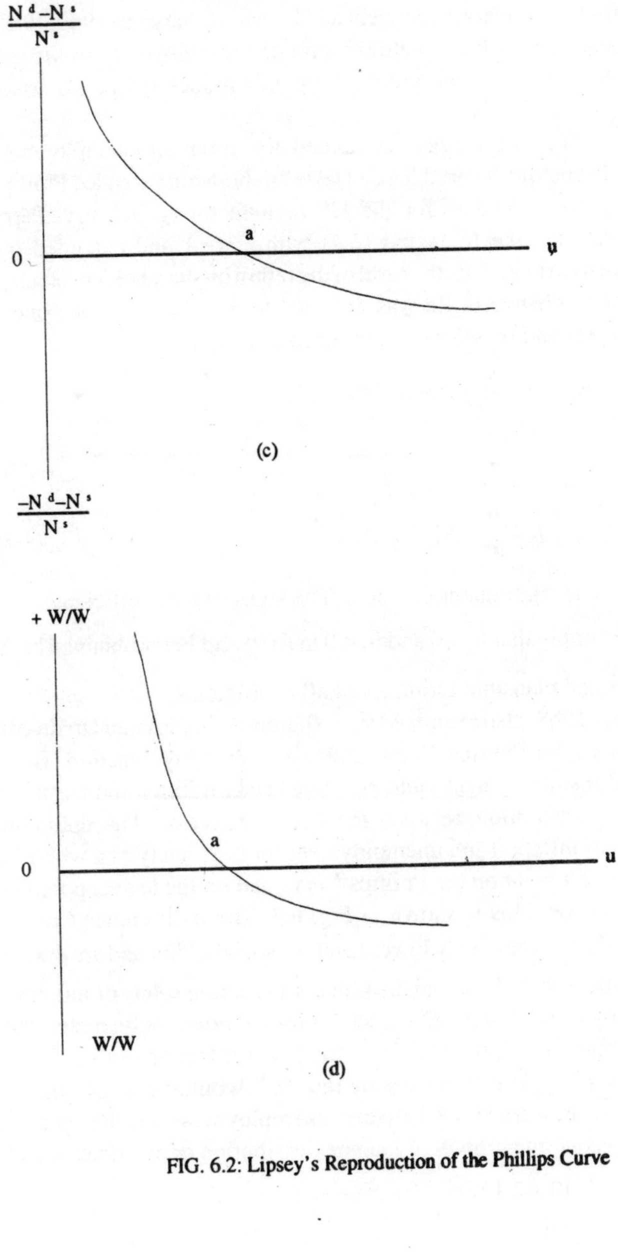


FIG. 6.2: Lipsey's Reproduction of the Phillips Curve

This excess demand explanation adds considerable Keynesian flavour to the Phillips Curve analysis. Sargent and Lucas and Sargent (1969, 1981) used a similar approach to relate the rate of unemployment to the gap between actual and 'normal' output. Sargent's model will be discussed later on.

Perry (1966), like Lipsey, combined the inflation-unemployment trade-off with cost-push variables and tested a short-run extended Phillips Curve using post-war data for the US manufacturing industry. Perry assumed relations like (6.3) and (6.4) with $c = -1$ and extended the resulting equation to include the level of the return on shareholders' equity, Re. The rate of change in Re was assumed to be zero. The component equations (6.8a) and (6.8b) were combined into equation (6.9):

$$\dot{w} = a_0 + \frac{a_1}{U} + a_2\dot{p} + a_3 Re \tag{6.8a}$$

$$\dot{p} = \dot{w} - \dot{q} \tag{6.8b}$$

$$\Rightarrow \quad \dot{p} = b_0 + \frac{b_1}{U} + b_2\dot{q} + b_3 Re \tag{6.9}$$

where $U$ is the level of unemployment. The signs of the coefficients of $\dot{q}$ and $\frac{1}{U}$ in (6.8) imply that $b_1 > 0$ and $b_2 < 0$ in (6.9) and Perry obtained both correct signs and plausible estimates of all coefficients.

Brechling (1968) also examined the inflation-unemployment trade-off with a Lipsey-type Phillips Curve and a social utility function. Both inflation and unemployment yield negative social utilities and the marginal rate of substitution between the two is negative. The optimum combination of inflation and unemployment for the society as a whole is then $(p^*, U^*)$ — a point on the Phillips Curve and on the lowest possible indifference curve. This is shown in Fig. 6.3. The indifference Curves $I_0$, $I_1$ and $I_2$ reflect successively lower levels of social utility and are drawn on the assumption that the social disutility is a function solely of inflation and unemployment. Point '$E$' is an optimum point only under the assumption that the resulting trade-off does not affect any other social objective adversely. Brechling asserts that '$E^*$' would be a suboptimal choice if there is a trade-off between unemployment and balance of payments or economic growth or income distribution or any other social objective.

For a given aggregate level of excess demand, and, therefore, of the rate of unemployment, various structural or cost-push variables change the rate of inflation and, therefore, lead to shifts of the Phillips Curve. The aim of the incomes policies, e.g., is to shift the Phillips Curve to the left, i.e., to lower the rate of inflation for any given level of excess demand. So whenever such structural variables are more important the trade-off between inflation and unemployment is not so meaningful. On the other hand, the rightward shifts of the Phillips Curve caused by changing expectations do not necessarily make the trade-off concept meaningless as alleged by Friedman and Phillips (1968). Brechling found some empirical evidence on slopes of the Phillips Curve: (a) that it is fairly flat in the short-run and (b) that it is much steeper in the long-run.

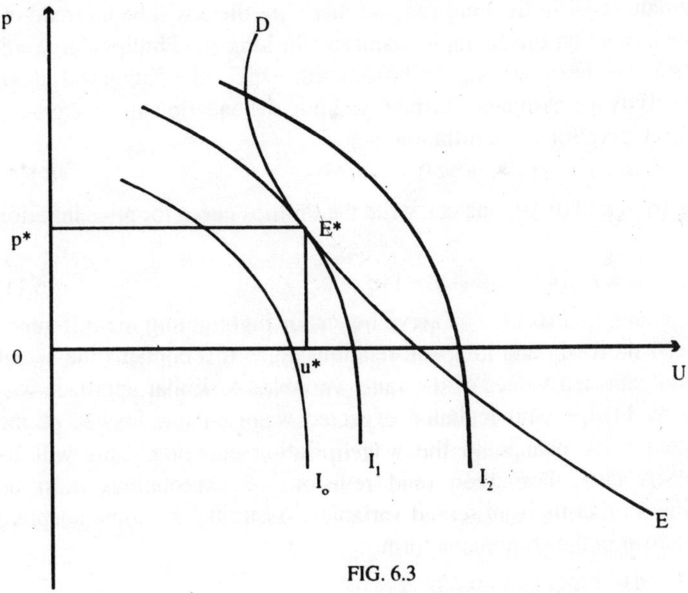


FIG. 6.3

## 6.2 EXPECTATIONS-AUGMENTED PHILLIPS CURVE

The simple Phillips Curve equation (6.4) and the discussion thereof does not take into account the feedback from current wages and current prices on to expected wages and expected prices. Friedman (1968) and Phelps

(1968) point to this as a "basic defect" of the Phillips Curve analysis and hold that the influence of such expectations is important in determining the nature of the long-run trade-off between unemployment and inflation. The difference between the short-run and the long-run trade-off can be demonstrated in the following way.[5]

Combining (6.3) and (6.4) and adding expected rate of price change, one can write

$$\dot{w} = Ph(u) + \alpha\dot{p}^e + \beta\dot{q} \tag{6.10a}$$

where the function $Ph(u)$ is the general form of the unemployment-wage change trade-off replacing the simple form in (6.4). $Ph(u)$ is non-linear in $u$ and $Ph'(u) < 0$. $\dot{q}$ is the rate of change of labour productivity as in (6.3) and $0 < \beta < 1$ is the fraction of productivity rises that are rewarded by money-wage increases. The magnitude of the coefficient of the expected rate of inflation is the centre of controversy. According to Friedman, $\alpha = 1$ in the long-run and therefore there will be no trade-off between inflation and unemployment and the long-run Phillips Curve will be vertical in the $(u, \dot{w})$ axes. In the short-run expected inflation and labour productivity are assumed constant, yielding the equation to the short-run Phillips Curve for wage inflation as

$$\dot{w} = Ph(u), \quad Ph' < 0 \tag{6.10b}$$

Using (6.3) and (6.10) one can write the Phillips curve for price inflation as

$$\dot{p} = Ph(u) + \alpha\dot{p}^e + (\beta - 1)\,\dot{q} \tag{6.11}$$

The equation (6.11) can serve better for highlighting the difference between short-run and long-run relations since this contains the actual and the expected values of the same variable. A similar approach was taken by Phelps who included expected wage change instead of the expected price change in the wage-inflation equation. This will be discussed later. Formation (and revision) of expectations must be explained in terms of observed variables. Assuming a simple adaptive mechanism in the continuous form

$$\frac{d\dot{p}^e}{dt} = \lambda(\dot{p} - \dot{p}^e), \quad 0 < \lambda < 1 \tag{6.12}$$

---

5. This is adapted from Tobin (1975) pp. 11-17.

Expectations are adapted to actual changes at a speed, $\lambda$. (6.12) is the continuous time analogue of the discrete form used in the equations (4.47)–(4.49). Expected rate of inflation is a weighted average of actual rates with exponentially declining weights $\lambda^i$ attached to $\dot{p}_{t-i}$, $i = 0, 1, 2, \cdots$. The equilibrium rate is such that once attained it will be repeated for ever implying $\frac{d\dot{p}^e}{dt} = 0$ in equilibrium. On substitution in (6.12a), the equilibrium expected rate of inflation is equal to the actual rate: In equilibrium,

$$\dot{p}^e = \dot{p} = \dot{p}^* = \dot{p}^{e*} \tag{6.13}$$

The equilibrium condition (6.13) is a general one. Whenever expectational variables are included, the condition for equilibrium is an equality between the expected and the actual values of the respective variables. Including the adaptive expectations mechanism, the Phillips Curve equation (6.11) becomes

$$\frac{1}{\lambda}\frac{d\dot{p}^e}{dt} = Ph(u) - (1-\beta)\dot{q} - (1-\alpha)\dot{p}^e \tag{6.14}$$

Using the equilibrium condition, $\dot{p}^{e*}$ is given by

$$0 = Ph(u) - (1-\beta)\dot{q} - (1-\alpha)\dot{p}^{e*} \quad \text{for } 0 < \alpha < 1$$

$$\Rightarrow \quad \dot{p}^{e*} = \frac{Ph(u) - (1-\beta)\dot{q}}{1-\alpha} \quad \text{for } 0 < \alpha < 1 \tag{6.15a}$$

Using the relation between price and wage change (6.3),

$$\dot{w}^{e*} = \dot{p}^{e*} + \dot{q} = \frac{Ph(u) + (\beta-\alpha)\dot{q}}{1-\alpha} \quad \text{for } 0 < \alpha < 1 \tag{6.15b}$$

(6.15a) and (6.15b) are the equations to the long-run Phillips Curves and the long-run trade-off between inflation and unemployment is shown by the term $\frac{Ph(u)}{(1-\alpha)}$. An increase in the value of $\alpha$ raises the long-run equilibrium rate of inflation. Increases in productivity can reduce the rate of inflation only if $\beta < \alpha$. This is readily visible from the long-run equilibrium wage inflation equation (6.15b).

It is important to use the concept of the equilibrium rate of inflation in the dynamic equation (6.14). On the assumption that $\alpha < 1$, and using (6.15a), (6.14) yields

$$\frac{1}{\lambda}\frac{d\dot{p}^e}{dt} = (1-\alpha)(\dot{p}^{e*} - \dot{p}^e) \tag{6.16a}$$

which shows that expected inflation accelerates (decelerates) when it is below (above its equilibrium rate at a given rate of unemployment and a given rate of productivity growth. Similarly for the actual rate of inflation a dynamic equation can be derived by using (6.16a) and (6.12a). From (6.12a)

$$\dot{p} = \dot{p}^e + \frac{1}{\lambda}\frac{d\dot{p}^e}{dt} = \dot{p}^e + (1-\alpha)(\dot{p}^{e*} - \dot{p}^e)$$

$$\Rightarrow \quad \dot{p} = \dot{p}^{e*} + \alpha(\dot{p}^e - \dot{p}^{e*}) \qquad (16.6b)$$

$$\Rightarrow \quad \frac{d\dot{p}}{dt} = (1-\alpha)\frac{d\dot{p}^{e*}}{dt} + \alpha\frac{d\dot{p}^e}{dt}$$

$$\Rightarrow \quad \frac{d\dot{p}}{dt} = (1-\alpha)\frac{d\dot{p}^{e*}}{dt} + \alpha\lambda(1-\alpha)(\dot{p}^{e*} - \dot{p}^e) \quad \text{from (6.16a)}$$

$$\Rightarrow \quad \frac{d\dot{p}}{dt} = (1-\alpha)\frac{d\dot{p}^{e*}}{dt} + \lambda(1-\alpha)(\dot{p}^{e*} - \dot{p}) \quad \text{from (6.16b)}$$

$$\Rightarrow \quad \frac{1}{\lambda}\frac{d\dot{p}}{dt} = \frac{(1-\alpha)}{\lambda}\frac{d\dot{p}^{e*}}{dt} + (1-\alpha)(\dot{p}^{e*} - \dot{p}) \qquad (6.16c)$$

(6.16a) and (6.16c) imply that for a given $u$ and a given $\dot{q}$, the speed of adjustment to equilibrium is the same for actual and expected inflation. for $\alpha = 1$, yields[6] simply

$$\frac{1}{\lambda}\frac{d\dot{p}^e}{dt} = Ph(u) - (1-\beta)\dot{q} \qquad (6.17a)$$

and (6.11b) and (6.12a) yield

$$\frac{1}{\lambda}\frac{d\dot{p}}{dt} = Ph'(u)\dot{u} - (1-\beta)\frac{d\dot{q}}{dt} + \frac{d\dot{p}^e}{dt}$$

$$\Rightarrow \quad \frac{d\dot{p}}{dt}\frac{1}{\lambda} = [Ph(u) - (1-\beta)\dot{q}] + Ph'(u)\frac{du}{dt} - (1-\beta)\frac{d\dot{q}}{dt}$$

$$(6.17b)$$

6. This is Friedman's assumption discussed later.

Once again the acceleration of actual is the same as that of expected inflation for given $u$ and $\dot{q}$. (6.17) also define a unique equilibrium rate of unemployment, $u^*$ such that the inflation rate is constant. This $u^*$ may be defined as the non-accelerating inflation rate of unemployment (NAIRU). The rate is obviously the one where $\frac{d\dot{p}^e}{dt} = \frac{d\dot{p}}{dt} = 0$ implying

$$Ph(u^*) = (1 - \beta)\dot{q} \tag{6.18}$$

So, the NAIRU is determined from outside the labour market. Among its determinants, the monetarists emphasise the rate of growth of the quantity of money but structural changes, factors affecting the rates of growth of aggregate demand and supply are popular among suggestions made by other economists.[7]

Friedman's (1968) expectation-augmented Phillips Curve and the natural rate of unemployment (NRU) hypothesis follow a similar analysis as above and assume $\alpha = 1$.

**Friedman**

Friedman (1968) adapts Wicksell's analysis of a "natural" rate of interest to the labour market. The "natural" rate of unemployment is the rate of unemployment consistent with equilibrium in the labour market and with equilibrium in the structure of real wages. At the corresponding level of unemployment real wage rates are rising at a "normal" secular rate consistent with long-run trends of investment, technical progress etc. This concept of the natural rate of unemployment (NRU) is broad enough to accommodate market imperfections, 'search costs', vacancies and other structural characteristics of the labour and commodity markets. Any change in such structural characteristics can raise or lower the natural rate. For example, an easier access to information about job vacancies would lower the natural rate. Wicksell improved his analysis by employing Irving Fisher's distinction between money and real rates of interest. Friedman modified Phillips's analysis by distinguishing between money and real wages. In a world of rising nominal prices and changing expectation this distinction is important. When all economic agents expect prices to rise

7. See Brechling (1968).

at some rate, $\dot{p}_0^e$, money wages rising at a rate lower than $\dot{p}_0^e$ (i.e., $\frac{\dot{w}}{w} < \dot{p}_0^e$) would lead to an excess supply of labour and an unemployment higher than NRU.

At the natural rate of unemployment, there is no change in the real wage rate and in equilibrium, expected rate of price change equals the actual rate of price change. The NRU is then obtained by substituting

$$\frac{d\left(\frac{w}{p}\right)}{dt}\frac{p}{w} = 0 \quad \Rightarrow \quad \frac{\dot{w}}{w} - \dot{p} = 0 \quad \text{and} \quad \dot{p} = \dot{p}^e$$

into (6.10a) and maintaining $\alpha = 1$. The latter implies that there is no long-run trade-off between inflation and unemployment.[8] The trade-off exists only in the short-run. For, any attempt by the policy makers to reduce unemployment below NRU would succeed only temporarily until expectations are revised. Let expansionary monetary policies be undertaken in an attempt to lower unemployment below the natural rate. This raises nominal cash balances above the desired level and, therefore, stimulates income and the nominal demand for output. The producers respond by increasing output and employment but only initially. Unemployment falls because the workers have been used to a stable price level so far and therefore the rise in nominal income is taken as a rise in real income; selling prices of products are revised upwards much faster than wages resulting in a fall in real wages to the employers. Once the workers notice the fall in their real wages due to rising product prices, they revise their price expectation and ask for wage rises; more work efforts are offered only at a higher real wage. So gradually the economy returns to the NRU but at a higher rate of inflation. In Fig. 6.4 the economy is in equilibrium with stable wages, stable expectation and unemployment at the natural rate, $\bar{u}$, i.e., at $\bar{u}$ on the short-run Phillips Curve AB, one has $\dot{w} = 0, \dot{p}^e = 0$. If Phillip's analysis was correct, the expansionary monetary policy to reduce unemployment would move the economy to a point like $E_1$ on the same Phillips Curve AB implying that the cost of a lower unemployment, $u_1$ is a positive wage inflation $\dot{w}_1$. But Friedman says that this wage inflation causes people to revise their expectation upwards

8. Note that, in this case, $\dot{w} = \dot{p} = \frac{Ph(u)}{1-\alpha}$ ignoring changes in productivity so, $\frac{d\dot{w}}{du} = \infty$ for $\alpha = 1$.

resulting in a rightward shift of the short-run Phillips Curve to A′B′ implying the same unemployment $\bar{u}$ at a positive inflation rate. In the long-run, the Phillips Curve is $L\bar{u}$ showing that the economy stabilises only around the natural rate.

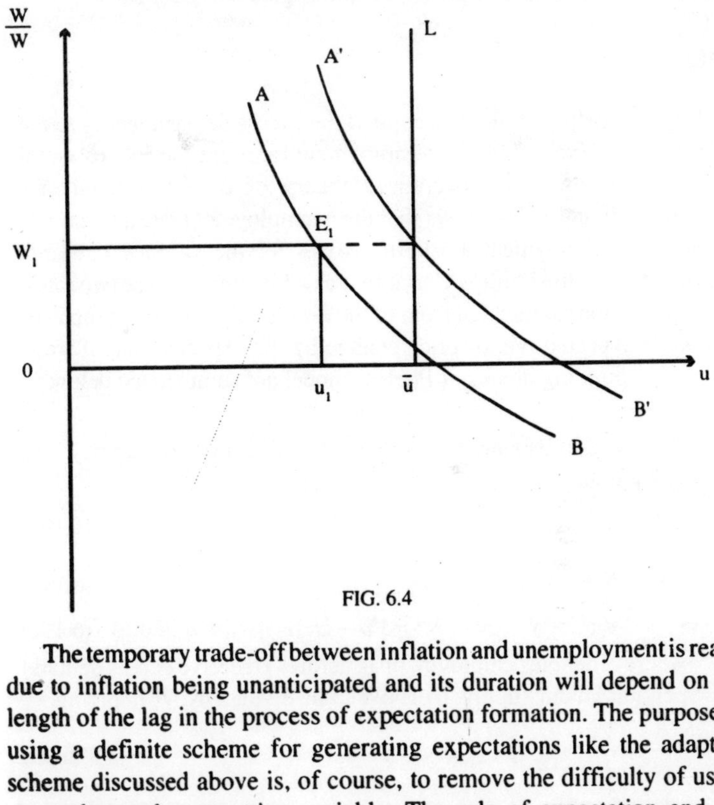


FIG. 6.4

The temporary trade-off between inflation and unemployment is really due to inflation being unanticipated and its duration will depend on the length of the lag in the process of expectation formation. The purpose of using a definite scheme for generating expectations like the adaptive scheme discussed above is, of course, to remove the difficulty of using an unobserved expectation variable. The role of expectation and the natural rate hypothesis of unemployment have been tested also by using extrapolative and generalised finite distributed lags, e.g., by Turnovsky (1972) for Canada and by using rational expectation formation by Sargent and others. On the extrapolative scheme, agents extrapolate from the past trends of actual inflation:

$$\dot{p}^e_t = \dot{p}_t + a\,(\dot{p}_t - \dot{p}_{t-1})$$

where '$a$' is the coefficient of extrapolation. A positive sign of '$a$' would imply that past trends are expected to continue and a negative sign that the past trends are likely to be reversed. The finite distributed large scheme is very similar to the adaptive mechanism already discussed. Turnovsky's data for Canada for 1949-69 did not offer much support to Friedman's hypothesis: $\alpha = 1$ on any of the expectations generating schemes.

**Phelps**

Like Lipsey, Phelps (1968) also applied the excess demand theory to the labour market. Vacancy and unemployment rates are the two essential ingredients of Phelps's "generalised theory of excess demand" for money-wage changes. He shows that the unemployment rate and the rate of change of employment are both proxies for the vacancy rate and, therefore, derives the Phillips Curve first as a function of these two rates. In the expectation-augmented from of the Phillips Curve, Phelps replaces Friedman's expected rate of price change by the expected rate of wage change. The building blocks of Phelps' model are summarised below.[9]

(a) The excess-demand for labour, $N^x$, is related to yacancy and unemployment, $Va$ and $U$ respectively:

$$N^s = N + U \tag{6.19a}$$

and

$$N^d = N + Va \tag{6.19b}$$

$$\Rightarrow \quad N^x \equiv N^d - N^s \quad \Rightarrow \quad N^x = Va - U \tag{6.19c}$$

where $N$ denotes employment as before. To derive excess demand per unit labour supply, (6.19c) can be divided by $N^s$ implying

$$\frac{N^x}{N^s} = \frac{Va}{N^s} - \frac{U}{N^s} \quad \Rightarrow \quad n^x = va - u \tag{6.20}$$

where vacancy and unemployment rates are denoted by the respective small letters.

9. Reader may skip points (a)–(b) without much loss of continuity.

(b) The *i*th firm's desired differential between the wage it wishes to pay, $W_i^*$ and the average wage paid elsewhere, $W$, is assumed to depend upon the number of vacancies in the firm, $Va_i$, the number of workers employed elsewhere , $N - N_i$, the sizes of the labour force and unemployment pool. That is;

$$D_i^* \equiv \frac{W_i^* - W}{W} = D_i^*(u, va, Va_i, N - N_i, U, N^s) \tag{6.21a}$$

The inclusion of $u$ and $va$ (6.21a) reflects the modified role of unemployment in Phelps's theory. The new role of unemployment is not to lower money wage through unemployed workers underbidding for jobs but is assumed to affect the quit rates and thereby affect the costs to the firm of its "turnover rate"[10] — costs in terms of reduced output and profits, of new recruitment and training etc. At a given differential between the firm's wage rate and the wage rates paid by other firms a fall of the unemployment rate tends to increase the quit rate experienced by the firm. So it will be in the firm's interest to raise the wage differential in response to a high quit rate corresponding to a low unemployment rate. Without including expectations and assuming all firms attempt to raise this differential the general wage index rises. The quit rate, in turn, depends on the unemployment and vacancy rates. The wage-differential function $D_1^*$ is assumed homogeneous of degree zero in the four variables mentioned above. So dividing through by $N^s$

$$D_i^* = D_i^*\left(u, va, \frac{Va_i}{N^s}, \frac{N - N_i}{N^s}, u, 1\right)$$

approximating $\frac{N-N_i}{N^s}$ by $\frac{N}{N^s} = 1 - u$, one can rewrite:

$$D_i^* = D_i^{**}(u, va, va_i) \tag{6.21b}$$

Assuming all firms to be alike, a macro form of the average desired wage-differential equation for the economy as a whole is derived as

10. Phelps (1979), p. 686.

$$D^* = D^*(u, va) \tag{6.22}$$

where $Va = \sum_i Va_i$ and $va = \sum_i va_i$. The average desired wage differential rises as $u$ falls (i.e., $\frac{\partial D^*}{\partial u} < 0$) and changes in the same way as the vacancy rate (i.e., $\frac{\partial D^*}{\partial va} > 0$).

The rate of change of average wage is assumed to be a simple proportional function of $D^*$:

$$\frac{\dot{W}}{W} = \alpha D^*, \quad \alpha > 0 \tag{6.23}$$

(d) The employment dynamics is also explained with the help of the same variables, $u$ and $v$ as follows. The increase of employment per unit time $\frac{dN}{dt}$ is made up of hiring from the unemployment pool less the number retired or dead among the employed persons and the number in search of new jobs per unit of time. Retirement is assumed to be a proportion of total employment per unit time and the other two are assumed to depend on the same aggregate variables $U$, $Va$ and $N^s$. Then

$$\frac{dN}{dt} = \dot{N}(U, Va, N^s) \tag{6.24}$$

and the rate of change of employment is obtained by assuming (6.24) to be homogeneous of degree 1.

$$\frac{\dot{N}}{N} = \dot{n} = \dot{n}(u, va) \tag{6.25a}$$

$$\dot{n}_1 \equiv \frac{\partial \dot{n}}{\partial u} > 0, \dot{n}_2 \equiv \frac{\partial \dot{n}}{\partial va} > 0 \tag{6.25b}$$

The Phillips Curve is finally obtained by combining (6.22), (6.23) and (6.25). Since reliable data on vacancy rates are not available for most countries, $va$ is substituted in terms of $u$ and $\dot{n}$

$$va = va(u, \dot{n}) \tag{6.26}$$

and then the Phillips Curve becomes

$$\dot{w} \equiv \frac{\dot{w}}{w} = \alpha D^*(u, va(u, \dot{n})) = \dot{w}(u, \dot{n}) \tag{6.27}$$

The signs of the derivatives of the $\dot{w}$ function in (6.27) are dependent on those of the $va$ function in (6.26). For the usual Phillips Curve in the $(u, \dot{w})$ axes, one needs the sign of the partial derivative $\frac{\partial \dot{w}}{\partial u}$. Differentiating (6.27) partially w.r.t. $u$,

$$\frac{\partial \dot{w}}{\partial u}(\equiv \dot{w}_1) = \alpha\left[D_1^* + D_2^* \frac{\partial va}{\partial u}\right]$$

$$\Rightarrow \quad \frac{\partial \dot{w}}{\partial u} = \alpha\,[D_1^* + D_2^*\, va_1] \tag{6.28}$$

From (6.25) and (6.26), $va_1$ can be derived as

$$va_1 = \frac{\partial va\,(u, \dot{n})}{\partial u} = \frac{\partial va}{\partial u}[u, \dot{n}\,(u, va)]$$

$$\Rightarrow \quad va_1 = \left[va_1 + va_2\left(\dot{n}_1 + \dot{n}_2 \frac{\partial va}{\partial u}\right)\right]$$

$$\Rightarrow \quad va_1 = [va_1 + \dot{n}_2 va_2 va_1 + \dot{n}_1 va_2]$$

$$\Rightarrow \quad va_1(1 - 1 - \dot{n}_2 va_2) = va_2 \dot{n}_1$$

$$\Rightarrow \quad va_1 = \frac{-\dot{n}_1}{\dot{n}_2} = \frac{-\frac{\partial \dot{n}}{\partial u}(u, va)}{\frac{\partial \dot{n}}{\partial va}(u, va)} < 0 \tag{6.29}$$

Substituting (6.29) back in (6.28)

$$\frac{\partial \dot{w}}{\partial u} = \alpha\left[D_1^* - D_2^* \frac{\dot{n}_1}{\dot{n}_2}\right] < 0 \tag{6.30}$$

(6.30) implies that with every constant rate of change of employment, the Phillips Curve is negatively sloped in the $(u, \dot{w})$ axes. Phelps's theory provides firmer ground to the negative slope of the Phillips Curve. With the inclusion of the vacancy rate as another variable into the analysis a fall in unemployment not only directly leads to a rise in wage differentials but also reinforces this upward pressure by a concomitant increase of vacancies resulting from a constant $\dot{n}$ and a decreased unemployment. The convexity of the Phillips Curve in (6.27) depends on the signs of the second-order derivatives of the component functions and is less certain in some cases.[11]

(e) The role of expectations is added to the above theory of generalised excess demand in terms of expected wage change rather than expected price change. The equation of the expectation-augmented Phillips Curve is, then

$$\frac{\dot{W}}{W}=\alpha d^{*}+\frac{\dot{W}^{e}}{W}=\dot{W}(u,\dot{n})+\frac{\dot{W}^{e}}{W} \qquad (6.31)$$

In equilibrium,

$$\frac{\dot{W}}{W}=\frac{\dot{W}^{e}}{W} \text{ implying } D^{*}(u,v)=0 \qquad (6.32)$$

The condition (6.32) does not require a constant average money wage or a market clearing for labour-market equilibrium.

Expected rate of wage change rather than that of price change is justified on the ground that an employer grants a wage increase only when he expects other firms to do the same. A rise in the expected rate of inflation does not alter an employer's behaviour if he expects other employers to stick to their same wage rates as before. Also a worker is unlikely to quit and search for a new job if it is expected that wage rates everywhere else are unchanged even after the rise in expected inflation. The condition for steady-state equilibrium is

$$\dot{u}=0 \qquad (6.33)$$

and the required rate of unemployment, $\bar{u}$ is to satisfy both the condition (6.32) and $\dot{\bar{u}}=0$. At this unique unemployment rate $\bar{u}$, the equilibrium steady-state Phillips Curve is shown to be vertical under certain simplifying assumptions. Once the assumption of money illusion in the sense of workers' resistance to accept a cut in money wages is included, the wage-inflation-unemployment trade-off is reinforced due to downward rigidity of money wages. To sum up: without money-illusion, the equilibrium steady-state Phillips Curve is vertical at a unique unemployment rate but with money-illusion the equilibrium steady-state curve is downward

11. For derivation, see Phelps (1979), p.694.

sloping below and is vertical above a sufficiently high $\dot{w}$. In Fig. 6.5, $\dot{w}^*$ is sufficiently high to circumvent the money-illusion problem. The curve AB portrays the Phillips Curve resulting from the theory of generalised excess demand as summarised by equation (6.27); CD is the equilibrium steady-state locus obtained from (6.31), (6.32) and (6.33); and the curve consisting of a vertical and a negatively sloped region, CEF, is the equilibrium steady-state Phillips Curve under money-illusion.

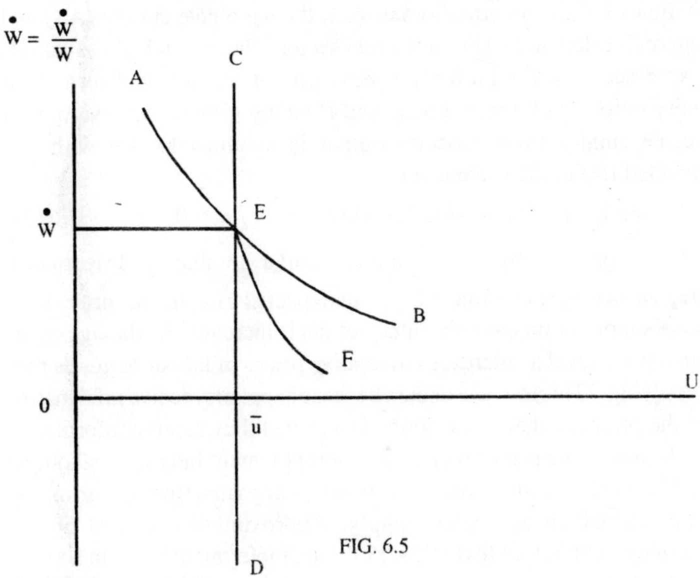


FIG. 6.5

## Sargent

Sargent like Friedman tested Fisher's theory of interest rate and NRU hypothesis on the assumption of rational expectation and in the context of an IS-LM Phillips Curve model. It is shown that

(a) systematic change in monetary and fiscal policy variables do not influence the real rates of interest, output or the rate of unemployment.

(b) a systematic or predictable change in the price level does not alter the rate of unemployment and

(c) systematic changes in monetary policy can alter the nominal rate of interest only through their effect on the expected rate of inflation. Unsystematic or unpredictable changes are reflected through random variables.

## 6.3 THE IS-LM PHILLIPS CURVE MODEL UNDER RATIONAL EXPECTATION

Sargent uses linear functions in the logarithms of all relevant variables except the nominal rate of interest. The IS equation is, as already explained many times before, an equality between the aggregate supply (AS) and the aggregate demand (AD) in the real sector. The AS and AD equations are expressed in deviation form — deviation of actual from "normal" or capacity output. Following Lucas and Rapping (1969) the deviation of aggregate supply from capacity output is assumed to rise with any unexpected rise in the price level:

$$\log Y_t - \log \overline{Y}_t = a_1 (\log P_t - \log P_t^e) + er_t^1, \ a_1 > 0 \tag{6.34}$$

$a_1 > 0$ is supported by an argument similar to that of Friedman's. Aggregate supply rises due to any unexpected rise in the price level because suppliers mistakenly interpret such increases in the aggregate nominal price level as increases in relative prices of labour or goods they are supplying. "This mistake occurs because suppliers receive information about the prices of their own goods faster than they receive information about the aggregate price level".[12] So unemployment falls and real output rises. The random error term $er^1$ represents any unsystematic or unpredictable change in aggregate supply. Approximating normal by the full-employment output level, $\overline{Y} \equiv Y(\overline{N})$, unemployment rate can be used as an inverse index of $Y_t - \overline{Y}$ as shown in (6.7), which can be rewritten as

$$u = b\,(Y - \overline{Y}), \quad b < 0 \tag{6.35}$$

(6.35) implies that the aggregate supply function (6.34) is an alternative presentation of the inflation-unemployment trade-off.[13] The aggregate supply is boosted by any unexpected rise in the aggregate price level because suppliers (of labour and goods) mistakenly interpret this rise as increases in the relative price (respectively of labour and goods).

---

12. Lucas, R. and Sargent, T. (1981, p. 163).
13. Lucas, R. and Sargent, T. (1969).

To the AS Curve (6.34) is added the aggregate demand curve in deviation form. The excess demand depends inversely on the gap between the real interest rate and the expected rate of inflation. The IS curve in the log-linear form is written as

$$\log Y_t = \log \overline{Y}_t + a_2[rn_t - (\log P^e_{t+1} - \log P_t)]$$

$$+ d(\log G_t - \log \overline{G}_t) + er^2_t \qquad (6.36)$$

$a_2 < 0$ because the investment demand over and above its "normal" level, $I_t - \overline{I}$ falls as the real rate of interest rises and because consumption demand over and above its "normal" level falls as the actual price level rises above the expected level. The government demand — actual and normal — are both treated as exogenous. The error term $er^2_t$ is added in the multiplicative form. The demand for money equation in the log-linear form assumes a unitary income elasticity and is written as

$$\log\left(\frac{M}{P}\right)_t = \log Y_t + a_3 rn_t + er^3_t$$

$$\Rightarrow \quad \log M_t = \log P_t + \log Y_t + a_3 rn_t + er^3_t \qquad (6.37)$$

Some arguments concerning income elasticity of the demand for money have already been considered in Chapter 4. $a_3 < 0$ follows from the inverse relation between speculative demand and interest rate. The values of $b$ (or, the slope of the Phillips Curve) in (6.34), of $a_3$ in (6.37) (or, the slope of the LM curve) and the slope of the investment demand (or, the slope of the IS curve) have rather important implications for the effects of an exogenous rise in expected inflation on the nominal interest rate and real output. As long as $b < 0, a_1 > 0$ and $a_3 < 0$, an exogenous rise in $(P^e_{t+1} - P_t)$ leads to an upward shift of the IS curve and a rise in both $rn$ and $Y_t - \overline{Y}$. The steepness of the short run Phillips Curve, the interest-sensitivity of investment demand or, the flatness of the IS curve and the steepness of the LM curve will determine the effects of an exogenous rise in expected inflation on the nominal rate of interest and real output. Finally, Sargent tests his model by making expectations rational. The main argument given in favour of rationality is that people use information other than past prices in forming their forecasts of the price level. On rational expectation, Sargent shows that the real interest rate is statistically independent of the systematic part of the money supply such that predictable changes in the money supply affect the nominal rate only via the expected rate of inflation.

**Rational Expectation**

On the assumption of rationality the subjective or psychological expectation of (the logarithm of) the price level is made equal to the objective or mathematical conditional probabilistic expectation using all the relevant information obtained from the model at hand about the endogenous and exogenous variables including random components, if any, up to the time when expectations are being formed. In Sargent's model, this amounts to,

$$\log P^e_{t+1} = E\left(\frac{\log P^e_{t+1}}{If_t}\right) = \frac{E_t}{If_t} \qquad (6.38a)$$

where $If_t$ stands for all the information available as of time $t$. The next step is to detail the information obtained from the model at hand which is included in $If_t$. The model consists of the AS equation (6.34), the AD equation (6.36), the demand for money equation (6.37) and the rationality assumption (6.38a). Eliminating $rn_t$ from (6.36) by using (6.37), one gets (6.37a) and (6.36a).

The solution for real output subject to a linear feedback rule for money supply is given in the Appendix 6.A.1. Sargent assumed an infinite linear feedback mechanism for money supply:

$$\log M_t = \sum_{i=1}^{\infty} a_i \log M_{t-i} + \sum_{i=1}^{\infty} b_i X_{t-i} + er^4_t, \qquad (6.39)$$

where $X_t$ is a function of all the exogenous, target and random variables of the system. As target variables, we have taken the unemployment rate (since this can be an important policy goal). One could also include price level as price stability could be another important policy objective. For exogenous variables only government expenditure has been included. The equation is given in the appendix as (6.A.3). As the solution for real output shows, only the unanticipated components of monetary policy appear in the R.H.S. of (6.A.9) implying that the expected value of output is independent of monetary policy anticipated or unanticipated but the latter can affect the variance of output around its normal or expected level as shown in (6.A.10). The policy parameters can be chosen so as to minimise this variance i.e., fluctuations of output around its normal level.

Before Sargent (1977), the policy ineffectiveness proposition was also stated by Lucas (1972) and then reinforced by Sargent and Wallace (1975). Since then a lot of empirical research has been directed at the Lucas-Sargent-Wallace (LSW) (which has been dubbed also as macro rational expectation (MRE) models.[14] Mishkin (1982), Hillier (1985), Chen and Steindl (1987) to name a few. Some of these tests have been conducted by adding the government budget constraint explicitly into the MRE model. Mishkin's tests of MRE hypothesis have used seasonally adjusted quarterly data on $M_1$ growth in the U.S. over the period 1954-76. His results show that anticipated monetary policy does matter and unanticipated movements in monetary policy do not have a larger impact on output and unemployment than anticipated movements. So the two main contentions of the MRE model are rejected by Mishkin. However, the data offer support to the rational expectation assumption.

Brian Hillier (1985) had added government budget constraint to the LSW model and provided a theoretical proof that the government should allow exogenous shocks to affect at least one of its policy variables — either money supply or the stock of bonds. He has included the wealth effect and interest payments on bonds in the ways discussed in Chapter 5 and added a Lucas type AS function (6.34) and rational expectations to the model. The government budget deficit/surplus is then derived from the model as a function of the exogenous shocks to the system and the options available to the government are:

(a) either allow money supply to adjust in response to unavoidable exogenous shocks; or
(b) allow bond stocks to adjust holding money supply constant.

Hillier[15] shows that option (a) would be better as a counter cyclical policy than option (b). Chen and Steindl (1987) have tested the LSW model with two different monetary policy rules:

---

14. Ef Mishkin, F. (1982), p. 23.
15. Hillier (1985), p. 49.

(a) one derived from a government budget constraint similar to a logarithmic version of (5.11) or (5.30) and
(b) a linear feedback rule similar to Barro's (1977) reaction function.

Inclusion of government budget reflects the interdependence of monetary and fiscal policies. The solution of the LSW model subject to policy rule (b) is very similar to that of Sargent's model as described above. The government budget constraint in the logarithmic form and the endogenous tax equations modify and/or extend the previously described Sargent's model in the following way.

## 6.4 THE LSW MODEL INCLUDING GOVERNMENT BUDGET

$$\log Y_t = b_0 + b_1 \log Gn_t + a_2[\log rn_t - (\log P^e_{t+1} - \log P_t)]$$

$$- b_3 \log Tn_t - (b_1 - b_3)\log P_t + e^2_t \qquad (6.36)'$$

where $a_2 < 0$ and $b_1, b_3 > 0$

$$\log Gn_t = b_4 + b_5(\log Gn_{t-1} - \log P_{t-1}) + b_6 \log Y_{t-1}$$

$$+ \log P_t + e^4_t \qquad (6.40)$$

$$\log Y_t = c_0 + a_1(\log P_t - \log P^e_t) + c_1 \log Y_{t-1} + e^1_t \qquad (6.41)$$

$$\log Gn_t = \log Tn_t + \Delta \log Hm_t + \Delta \log B_t \qquad (6.42)$$

$$\log M^s_t = a_4 + a_5 \log Gn_t + a_6 \log Tn_t + a_7 \log B_t$$

$$a_8 \log B_{t-1} + a_9 \log Hm_{t-1} + e^3_t \qquad (6.43)$$

where $a_5, a_8, a_9 > 0$ and $a_6, a_7 < 0$

$$\log M^d_t = \log P_t + \log Y_t + a_3 \log rn_t + e^5_t \qquad (6.37)'$$

$$\log Tn_t = d_0 + d_1 \log Y_t + d_2 \log Y_{t-1} + \log P_t + e^6_t \qquad (6.44)$$

where $d_1, d_2 > 0$

$$\log P^e_t = \underset{t-1}{E}(\log P_t / If_{t-1}) \qquad (6.38a)'$$

Noting that the real government spending and tax are, respectively, $\log G = (\log Gn - \log P)$ and $\log T = (\log Tn - \log P)$ and assuming $b_0 = \log \bar{Y} - d \log \bar{G}$, the IS equation (6.36)′ is only a simple modification of (6.36) to include the government budget explicitly. The government demand (6.40) and aggregate supply of output (6.41) are autoregressive to the first order as they depend, (positively) on their own previous values. Still, the aggregate supply equation is of the Lucas type as in (6.34). That government spending depends positively on previous year's real output is justified on the ground of an observed upward trend over time. As already pointed out, the government budget constraint (6.42) is similar in spirit to (5.11)/(5.30). The money supply rule (6.43) is derived from (6.42) and the credit multiplier rule (4.72). The money demand equation is almost identical to Sargent's (6.37). The tax equation including previous year's income reflects the view that "tax law permits carry-back to adjust losses in previous yers".[16] It is an extended version of (2.9) as it includes previous year's real income as well. All the disturbance terms, $e_t^1 - e_t^6$ are assumed to have zero expectation, zero autocorrelation, and independent between equations. The reduced form equations for real output and price level from the model (6.36)′–(6.44) can be derived in exactly the same way as in Sargent's model above. This is why it is not pursued here.

Chen and Steindl have tested the policy ineffectiveness hypothesis for the U.S. for the period 1954-1983 applying three stage least squares to the reduced form equations. The estimates of $a_4 - a_9$ and of $b_4 - b_6$ yielding, respectively, estimates of $\log M_t$ and $\log G_t$ for all $t$ are treated as the "anticipated" and the residuals (or the differences between actual and estimated values) are treated as "unanticipated" policy variables. The results of the tests support the policy ineffectiveness proposition. Anticipated monetary and fiscal variables were not significant in Chen and Steindl's tests whereas unanticipated monetary policy did have a significant effect on output and, therefore on employment.

**Fischer**

Fischer contradicts Sargent and shows that even under rational expectations, activist monetary policy can affect employment and real output if wage contracts are made in nominal terms and for longer than one period. In Sargent's model as discussed above, all relevant expectations are made only one period earlier. Fischer constructs a model where labour contracts

16. Chen and Steindl, (p. 257).

are made for more than one period and this means expectations of $P_t$ made in periods earlier than $t-1$ are also relevant. The use of longer-term nominal contracts leads to a rigidity in nominal wage which, in turn, assigns a role to even a completely anticipated monetary policy. Even on Fischer's model if labour contracts are made for just one period Sargent's result of complete irrelevance of monetary policy as regards real output prevails. But on longer-term labour contracts in nominal terms the only way in which monetary policy can lose its effectiveness is when such contracts index the wage so as to produce the same effects as one-period contracts.

Nominal wage is assumed predetermined in Fischer's model and two-period contracts are drawn up to maintain constancy of the real wage:

$$W_{t+1} = E_t P^e_{t+i} \quad i = 1, 2 \tag{6.45}$$

where the L.H.S. of (6.45) shows the wage to be paid in period $t+1$ and $t+2$ as specified in contracts drawn up in the current period, $t$ and the R.H.S. shows the expected price level, expectations being formed rationally in period, $t$. In period $t+2$, half the firms are assumed to be operating in the first year of a contract drawn up at $t+1$ and the other half in the second year of a similar contract drawn up at the end of $t$. It amounts to an AS equation of the form (6.34) rewritten as:

$$\log Y_{t+2} = \frac{1}{2}\sum_{i=1}^{2}[\log P_{t+i} - \log_t W_{t+i}] + e^1_t$$

Substituting from (6.45)

$$\Rightarrow \quad \log Y_{t+2} = \frac{1}{2}\sum_{i=1}^{2}[\log P_{t+i} - \log P^e_{t+i}] + e^1_{t+2} \tag{6.34$'$}$$

where $e^1_{t+2}$ is the random disturbance term. Although the AS equation is similar to Sargent's, the proxy for the LM equation is much simpler than (6.37) — viz.,

$$\log (M/P)_t = \log Y_t + e^2_t$$

$$\Rightarrow \quad \log Y_t = \log M_t - \log P_t - e^2_t \tag{6.46}$$

$e^2_t$ being the error term.

Each error term is assumed to follow a first order auto-regressive structure:

$$e_t^1 = \rho e_{t-1}^1 + \varepsilon_t \tag{6.47i}$$

$$e_t^2 = \rho_2 e_{t-1}^2 + \eta_t \tag{6.47ii}$$

where $\varepsilon_t$ and $\eta_t$ are serially independent and $|\rho_i| < 1, i = 1, 2$. In the same way as in Sargent's model, the single price level is obtained from the IS and LM equations (6.34)′ and (6.46) applying the RE assumption. So, $P_t$ is obtained as a linear function of $M_t, e_t^1, e_t^2$ and their conditional expectations given information up to two periods earlier. Money supply, $M_t$ is determined by the disturbances which have occurred up to and including the period $t - 1$:

$$\log M_t = \sum_{i=1}^{\infty} a_i e_{t-1}^1 + \sum_{i=1}^{\infty} b_i e_{t-i}^2 \tag{6.48}$$

This money supply rule implies, in turn, that the difference between actual money stock and the predicted at $t$ given all the information available up to $t$ depends on the reactions of the monetary authority to the random and serially independent disturbances occurring in the interim period:

$$\log M_{t+2} - \log M_{t+2}^e \mid If_t = a_1 \varepsilon_{t+1} + b_1 \eta_{t+1} \tag{6.49}$$

Finally, real output is derived as:

$$\log Y_{t+2} = \frac{1}{2}[\varepsilon_{t+2} - \eta_{t+2}] + \frac{1}{3}[\varepsilon_{t+1}(a_1 + 2\rho_1)$$

$$\eta_{t+1}(b_1 - \rho_2)] + \rho_1^2 e_t^1 \tag{6.50}$$

(6.50) shows that the parameters of money supply rule affect real output implying a role for monetary policy. Even if $a_1$ and $b_1$ were completely known, monetary policy would still affect the behaviour of real output because monetary authority can react to new information obtained in the interim period; such reaction can change the price level but nominal wage cannot change before the contract expires; so real wage changes and employment and real output change with it. The parameters $a$ and $b$ are chosen such that the asymptotic variance of real output is minimised.

**Phelps and Taylor**

Another application of RE by Phelps and Taylor (1977) restores the old faith that even systematic changes in monetary policy matter for the fluctuation of output and employment. Although the principal theme of their paper is the same as Fischer's the structural forms of their models are different. Firms choose to set their prices and wages at which they want to sell and hire one period in advance. They adopt this strategy to save their customers and employees the cost of acquiring information on the firms' offer. So wages and prices are predetermined when monetary authorities decide on the money supply. The information set available to the authorities is later and larger than the set available to the price and wage setters. Prices and wages being set before monetary rule is set in motion imply that the effectiveness of monetary policy in Phelps and Taylor's model relies on wage-price rigidity — same as we found in Keynes's models. Because such effectiveness is shown in a framework of rational expectations, Phelps and Taylor claim to have produced "an old wine in a new and more secure bottle".[17] A monetary policy, to be effective must take into account the system effects of expectations of future price levels that the policy itself creates or permits. A policy based on current data only — current output, nominal interest and price levels fails to attain its own objectives. Phelps and Taylor also choose as IS-LM — Phillips curve framework to establish the result that even perfectly anticipated monetary policy can affect the variance of output and employment.

The output determining equation is different from Lucas's in that it includes the price variable via the interest rates. The quantities that firms decide to produce are positively related to the difference between the expected natural rate of interest and their expected real rate of interest $\bar{r}^e - r^e$. The natural rate is defined as the marginal efficiency of inventory investment and is approximated by a linear decreasing function of the expected end of period inventory level. Intended inventory investment is, therefore, a decreasing function of expected real rate of interest and of expected end-of-period inventory stocks. Marginal propensities to consume out of actual and expected incomes are assumed to be different and the combined prosperity to satisfy Samuelson's correspondence principle. In addition, expected real rate of interest is assumed to affect consumption negatively. Transactions demand for money also is assumed to depend on actual and expected real income separately — the speculative part depending inversely on nominal interest; real demand and real supply of money are brought into equilibrium through the nominal interest rate,

17. Phelps and Taylor (1977) p. 166.

The stock of inventory at the end of period $t$ is the given inventory at the beginning (i.e., at the end of period $t-1$) plus any surplus of actual output over consumption. Next, the rational expectations mechanism is applied to the price and output equations. The model resulting from these considerations is used to solve for output and inventory. The reduced-form equations for output and inventory will obviously depend on money supply and expected price. The money supply rule chosen will determine the policy effectiveness. Phelps and Taylor show that if the authorities choose and "unconditional full-employment policy" output and employment will remain unaffected by monetary policy. If money supply rule is chosen, on the other hand, to depend on the predetermined variables of the model, i.e., the given stock of inventory $In_{t-1}$ and price level, $P_{t-1}$ at the beginning of period $t$, then assuming white noise in all the equations money supply can be shown to affect output, employment, the rate of inflation and interest rates.

Phelps and Taylor's IS-LM model including RE follows from the above considerations as given below.

$$Y_t = \overline{Y} + a_1(\overline{r}_t^e - r_t^e) + e_t^1 \tag{6.51}$$

$$r_t^e = rn_t - \underset{t-1}{E}(\log P_t - \log P_{t-1}) \tag{6.52i}$$

$$\overline{r}_t^e = b_1 - b_2 \underset{t-1}{E} \; In_t \tag{6.52ii}$$

$$rn_t = a_2(\log P_{t-1} - \log M_t) + a_3 Y_t + a_4 \underset{t-1}{E} \; Y_t + e_t^2 \tag{6.53}$$

$$C_t = a_5 r_t^e + a_6 Y_t + a_7 \underset{t-1}{E} \; Y_t + e_t^3 \tag{6.54}$$

$$a_5 < 0, 0 < a_6 < 1, 0 < a_7 < 1, 0 < (a_6 + a_7) < 1$$

$$In_t = In_{t-1} + Y_t - C_t \tag{6.55}$$

$$\log P_t = \underset{t-1}{E} \log P_t + e_t^4 \tag{6.56}$$

$$\underset{t-1}{E} Y_{t+s} = \overline{Y}, \tag{6.57}$$

$$\log M_{t+s} = a_8 + a_9 \log P_{t-1+s} + a_{10} In_{t-1+s} \tag{6.58}$$

$$s = 0, 1, 2$$

In the above formulation $\underset{t-1}{E}$ is, as already noted, the mathematical conditional expectation of the variable it precedes given the information set $If_t$. Here $If_t$ consists of $\log P_{t-1}, In_{t-1}, In_{t-1}$ and $\log M_t$. The reduced form equations for real output and inventory are derived in the appendix:

$$Y_t = \overline{Y} + a_1 b_1 - a_1(1+a_2)\log P_{t-1} - a_1 b_2 \underset{t-1}{E} In_t + a_1 \underset{t-1}{E} \log P_t a_1$$

$$a_2 \log M_t - a_1 a_3 Y_t - a_1 a_4 \underset{t-1}{E} Y_t - a_1 e_t^2 + e_t^1 \quad (6.A.11)$$

Taking expectation of $Y_t$ yields

$$\underset{t-1}{E} Y_t = A_0 + A_1 \underset{t-1}{E} \log M_t + A_2 \underset{t-1}{E} \log P_t$$

$$+ A_3 \underset{t-1}{E} In_t + A_4 \log P_{t-1} + A_5 \overline{Y} \quad (6.A.13)$$

Where $A_0 - A_5$ are functions of the coefficients $a_0 - a_4$ and $b_1, b_2$ as given in (6.A.14). Expectation of real output $s$ periods ahead of time is equated to full employment output as a future equilibrium condition as shown in (6.57). Inflationary expectations are summarised in (6.56). Finally the money supply rule as given in (6.58) is passive if the coefficients $a_9$ and $a_{10}$ are equated to zero. But such passive policy is ineffective. An active monetary policy depending on the predetermined state of the economy (i.e., $a_9$, $a_{10}$ being non-zero) can be effective.

Phelps and Taylor show that the variance of real output around the full employment level can be affected by the choice of the coefficients $a_9$ and $a_{10}$. If, on the other hand, an unconditional full employment policy is chosen, i.e., if nominal interest rates are raised to lower expected output to the full employment level, firms will feel free to raise prices they are setting for the next period by enough to completely negate the effect on the expected real rate of interest. Such full employment monetary policy will be completely ineffective in altering output or employment.

## 6.5 INTERACTIONS BETWEEN TAX-STRUCTURE AND INFLATIONARY EXPECTATIONS: EFFECTIVENESS OF MONETARY POLICY

**Turnovsky**

The foregoing discussion shows that effectiveness of monetary policy relies on some form of wage-price rigidity either through long period contracts made in nominal terms or through predetermined wages and prices corresponding to a money supply rule. In the Keynesian model such rigidity did not accommodate the role of rational expectations. Assumption of rational expectation however is not sufficient to negate the impact of monetary policy. On the other hand, if inflationary expectations are an exogenous variable, then monetary policy retains its effectiveness but, as Turnovsky shows, the short-run monetary policy multiplier has a smaller value than in the fixed price model.[18] This is because the price adjustment equation introduces a negative feedback. Turnovsky (1979) derives the policy multipliers from IS-LM models including inflationary expectations. His models differ from Sargent, Fischer and Phelps-Taylor's in that:

(a) expected rate of inflation is treated as an exogenous variable implying no rational expectation;
(b) government budget is explicitly included;
(c) fiscal parameters are given prominence in the wage-bargaining equation. This is partly due to the emphasis on government budget and on an endogenous income tax structure depending on nominal income;
(d) he derives an expectation—augmented Phillips curve from a wage bargaining scheme which assumes that workers and/or Trade Unions try to protect their real income in the face of rising inflation and tax rates over each period.

Turnovsky's models are very similar in structure to the models discussed in Chapter 3. Below we summarise the model including the wage bargaining scheme.

Assuming a progressive income tax system depending on nominal income the tax equation is rewritten as:

$$Tn = t_0 + t_1 Yn \tag{6.59}$$

$$\Rightarrow \quad Yn - Tn = -t_0 + (1 - t_1)\, Yn$$

$$\Rightarrow \quad Y - T = \frac{Yn - Tn}{P} = \frac{(-t_0 + Yn\,(1 - t_1))}{P} \tag{6.60}$$

18. Turnovsky (1979) p. 113.

is the real disposable income. As already mentioned a progressive tax system implies $t_0 < 0$ and $0 < t_1 < 1$.

Inflationary expectations enter all the demand functions through the relevant variables as well as the Phillips curve equation. In addition, the Phillips curve equation accommodates the wage-bargaining scheme. The effect of wage-bargaining is split into:

(a) an "income claims" effect, and
(b) an "expectations progressivity", effect.[19]

On the additional considerations, the IS-LM Phillips curve and the government budget equations are rewritten, respectively, as (6.61), (6.62), (6.63) and (6.64).

$$\left[\frac{Yn}{P}\right] - C\left[\frac{Yn\,(1-t_1)-t_0}{P}\right] - I\,(rn - \dot{p}^e) - G = 0 \tag{6.61}$$

$$L\left[\frac{Yn}{P}, rn, \dot{p}^e\right] - \frac{M}{P} = 0 \tag{6.62}$$

$$a_0 + a_1\left[\frac{Yn}{P} - \overline{Y}\right] + a_2\left[1 - \frac{t_0}{\lambda Yn\,(1-t_1)}\right]\dot{p}^e$$

$$+ a_3\left[\frac{\Delta t_0}{\lambda(1-t_1)Yn} + \frac{\Delta t_1}{(1-t_1)}\right]\dot{p}^e - \dot{p} = 0 \tag{6.63}$$

$$\Delta M - \theta\,(PG - t_0 - t_1 Yn) - MA = 0 \tag{6.64}$$

While the other equations are easy to explain, the equation to the Phillips curve is substantially changed due to the introduction of the wage-bargaining such that there is no change in the workers' real standard of living ⇒ there is no change in $(Y - T)$ as defined in (6.60), as tax rates and the price level change. The derivation of the equation (6.63) and of the monetary policy multiplier is given in the appendix as (6.A.32) and (6.A.36) respectively. The coefficient $a_2$ is restricted to $0 \le a_2 \le 1$. Due to a progressive income tax structure the workers have to be compensated by more than the expected rate of inflation so that they can enjoy the same standard of living as before. If they are entirely successful $a_2 = 1$. Under

19. Turnovsky, S. (1979) p. 119.

partial compensation, $a_2 < 1$. This is called expectations progressivity effect because the magnitude of this effect (of inflationary expectations) depends on the progressiveness of the tax structure; if the latter is made more progressive raising the marginal rate, $t_1$, the effect increases and, if on the other hand the tax threshold increases, the effect weakens. The income claims effect is shown in the fourth group of terms in (6.13) and it disappears if tax rates stay constant. This effect is added on to the Phillips curve in order to protect workers' real income against rising tax rates. If full compensation can be obtained, then $a_3 = 1$ but for partial compensation, $0 \leq a_3 < 1$. The endogenous variables of the model are $Yn, rn, M, P$ and $\dot{p}$ and the exogenous variables now include $t_0$ and $t_1$ as additional policy parameters. However the number of endogenous variables can be further reduced by one by adding a simple definitional price adjustment equation: The current year's price is previous year's price plus inflation. Dropping the '$t$' subscript for convenience, the price adjustment equation added to the model (6.61)–(6.64) is:

$$P = P_{-1}(1 + \dot{p}) \tag{6.65}$$

$P_{-1}$ is a predetermined variable like $M_{-1}$. The monetary policy multiplier has to be derived with respect to the exogenous component of money supply $\frac{\partial Y}{\partial MA}$. As shown in (6.A.2) in the appendix the value of the multiplier is less than in the models without inflation. This is because of an additional negative feedback entering through a higher rate of inflation. The initial effects of a higher money supply are as noted in previous chapters as: a lower interest rate leading to a higher investment demand leading, in turn, to a higher income; the higher income now not only raises the demand for money leading to an offsetting rise (fall) in interest rate (real income) but also raises the rate of inflation reducing real money balances and leading, in turn, to a further offsetting rise [fall in interest rate (real income)].

The expectations-augmented Phillips curve (6.63) uses excess demand as a proxy for unemployment as already explained in (6.7) implying that $a_1$ should be positive. The expectations progressivity and income-claims effects are derived from a wage bargaining equation:

$$\Delta\left[\frac{\lambda Yn\,(1-t_1)-t_0}{p^e}\right] = 0 \tag{6.66}$$

where $0 < \lambda < 1$ is the proportion of wage in aggregate income.

The equation (6.66) implies that the workers or Trade Unions bargain in the face of changeable tax rates and price levels in a way to protect their real standard of living (or such that there is no change in real disposable income over the period $t$).

**Fackler**

Interactions among inflationary expectations, monetary policy and a realistic tax structure have also been examined by Fackler (1982). Unlike Turnovsky, Fackler includes a labour supply function depending on expected after-tax real wage, assumes rational expectation but excludes the government budget constraint.

The demand and supply functions are of the constant elasticity form. The aggregate production function (6.67) follows constant returns to scale. Fackler excludes interest rate from his model and, assigns no role to government spending so, the IS equation includes virtually the same variables as the aggregate supply equation.

The demand for labour is derived following the simple profit maximising rule. This is given in (6.68). Supply of labour is assumed to depend on expected real disposable wage income as in (6.69). As real tax liabilities increase, workers are assumed to substitute leisure for work (since the price of leisure falls as tax liabilities increase). The income effect of a tax rise (which implies supply of labour should go up in order to protect real income) is assumed weaker than the substitution effect $\Rightarrow a_3 < 0$ in (6.69). Labour supply depends on expected rather than actual prices because unlike their employers, the workers do not have full information about the prices of≠output and to gather such information may be costly. Fackler includes (6.70) as a tax equation which is not only progressive but also income — elastic in real terms. The demand for money function is simpler and it is as in Fischer's -- (6.46) whereas the money rule (6.71) includes an autonomous growth, previous year's money supply and real income. To behave counter cyclically, money supply as to fall as past income increases $\Rightarrow a_8 < 0$ in (6.71). These structural equations in Fackler's model are given below.

$$\log Y_t = a_1 \log K_t + a_2 \log N_t + e_t^1 \quad \text{where} \quad a_1 + a_2 = 1 \tag{6.67}$$

$$\log N_t^d = 1/a_1 [\log_2 + (1 - a_2)\log K - \log W$$
$$+ \log P + e_t^1] \tag{6.68}$$

$$\log N_t^s = a_3 \log T + a_4(\log W_t - \log P_t^e), \quad a_3 < 0, a_4 > 0 \tag{6.69}$$

$$\log T_t = t_0 + t_1 \log Y_t + (t_1 - 1)\log P_t, \quad t_0 < 0, t_1 > 1 \tag{6.70}$$

$$\log M_t^d = a_5 + a_6 \log Y_t + e_t^3 \tag{6.46)'}$$

$$\Rightarrow \quad \log Mn_t^d = \log P + a_5 + a_6 \log Y_t + e_t^3 \tag{6.46)'}$$

$$\log M_t^s = a_7 + a_8 \log Y_{t-1} + a_9 \log M_{t-1},$$
$$0 < a_9 < 1, a_8 < 0 \tag{6.71}$$

and $\log P_t^e = \underset{t-1}{E} (\log P_t / If_{t-1})$ (6.38a)′

The aggregate supply equation is derived from the production function and labour market equilibrium condition as (6.72) (explained in the appendix). Although the aggregate supply function retains the unexpected price rise as its main explanatory variable as in the LSW model, it is carried over from the labour supply function $\Rightarrow b_1 > 0$ and $b_2 < 0$ in (6.72).

$$\log Y_t = b_0 + b_1\left(\log P_t - \underset{t-1}{E} \log P_t\right) + b_2 \log T_t + e_t^5 \tag{6.72}$$

where $b_0$, $b_1 > 0$ and $b_2 < 0$ depend on $a_1 - a_4$ and $\log K$ as given in (6.A.41).

Fackler shows that in the deterministic version of the output equation [i.e. equation (6.A.44) excluding the random error term], monetary policy parameters $a_7$, $a_8$, and $a_9$ influence the real output. This role of monetary policy can be ascribed to the progressive and elastic tax structure $\Rightarrow t_1 > 1$. If the tax structure is elastic as well as progressive, an increase in money supply increases the price level and real tax liabilities; now if the income effect of the latter is stronger on labour supply than the substitution effect $\Rightarrow a_3 > 0$, employment will rise in response to a rise in tax liabilities raising real output in turn. So, monetary policy has an expansionary effect on real output as long as $t_1 > 1$ and $a_3 > 0$ even if expectations are formed rationally. If real tax liabilities do not rise with the price level $\Rightarrow t_1 = 1$, monetary policy will be ineffective. If, on the other hand, the substitution effect of tax liabilities dominates in the labour supply decisions $\Rightarrow a_3 < 0$, a rise in money supply will lead to a fall in employment and output.

Coming to the variance of output around the full employment level, it is evident from equation (6.A.47) that such variance is independent of the policy parameters $-a_7 - a_9$. If, on the other hand, a counter cyclical monetary policy is followed $\Rightarrow a_8 < 0$ then fluctuations of output will be accentuated under a dominating substitution effect of tax changes on labour supply. These results are evident from the reduced form equation for output (6.A.44) which has been derived in the appendix.

**The Dynamics of IS-LM Model with Government Budget Under Adaptive Expectations**

The dynamics of IS-LM model including a government budget constraint have been considered in the context of full employment and a fixed price level in Chapter 5. This was shown to have important implications for fiscal and monetary policies and the closely related question of crowding out in the economy. With the exception of Fackler's the models in the previous sections of the present Chapter consider implications for monetary and fiscal policies under employment and inflation. In the present section the stability of the economy under full employment and inflation will be considered.

**Tobin and Buiter (TB)**

Tobin and Buiter (1976) have considered a number of models very similar to those of Blinder and Solow's discussed in 5.4 with constant and variable capital stocks, with fixed and flexible prices and with unemployment and full-employment. In this section their model with a variable capital stock, full-employment and a changing price level will be considered. Because the other variants of macro models have already been discussed in the book. As already noted in Chapter 5 the dynamic models in the continuous time form highlight the difference between the short-run or the impact effects and the long-run or steady-state effects of fiscal or monetary policies.

The TB model considered here differs from Turnovsky's in that it makes inflationary expectations endogenous formed by an adaptive mechanism. The TB model (1976) includes wealth effects, interest payments on government debt as in the BS model of Chapter 5. The main component equations of TB model are discussed below: The long-run production function includes both labour and capital as variable inputs and it obeys constant returns to scale; assuming labour supply as infinitely elastic and employment as a numeraire, it can be written solely as a function of $K$:

$$Y = Y(K, N) \Rightarrow Y/N = Y(K/N, 1) \Rightarrow Y = f(K),$$

$$f' > 0, f'' < 0 \tag{6.73}$$

The real rate of return on capital is equated to its marginal product, $f'$. Investment is made an increasing function of the difference between the rate of return on investing in the new capital goods and that on existing assets; the nominal rate of return on money is as already explained in Chapter 3 is zero and the real rate is, then $-\dot{p}^e$; capital and bonds are regarded as perfect substitutes; that is why Tobin and Buiter do not add a separate demand function for bonds; finally the net investment is nothing but the rate of change of capital stock:

$$\dot{K} = I\,[f'(K) - (rn - \dot{p}^e)]$$

$$\Rightarrow \quad \dot{K} = I\,[f'(K) - rn + \dot{p}^e], \quad I' > 0 \tag{6.74}$$

Saving is assumed to take place to adjust actual wealth to its desired level and to exactly compensate for erosion of its real value due to inflation; desired level of wealth is assumed to be a proportion of real income and actual wealth consists of real capital money and bonds as in (5.27b):

$$S = s\,(V^* - V) + \dot{p}\,(M + Bn)/P, \quad 0 < s < 1 \quad \text{where}$$

$$V^* = \mu Y \quad \text{and} \quad V + (M + Bn)/P + K$$

$$\Rightarrow \quad s\,[\mu f(K) - (M + Bn)/P - K] + \dot{p}\,(M + Bn)/P \tag{6.75}$$

The government budget constraint modifies (5.30) only to the extent that the real value of government debt falls with inflation:

$$G + \frac{Bn \cdot rn}{P} - t_1\left(Y + \frac{Bn \cdot rn}{P}\right) - \dot{p}\,(M + Bn)/P = (\dot{M} + \dot{B}n)/P$$

$$\Rightarrow \quad G + \frac{Bn \cdot rn}{P}(1 - t_1) - t_1 f(K) - \dot{p}\,(M + Bn)/P = (\dot{M} + \dot{B}n)/P$$

(6.76)

In (6.76) $Bn/P$ replaces $B$ of Chapter 5 $(Bn \cdot rn)/P$ stands for real interest payment on debt. In Chapter 5 $(B/r)$ was used to denote the market value of bonds for which Tobin and Buiter use nominal value $Bn$ in our terminology. The real interest payments are assumed to be taxed at the same rate $-t_1$. The third term on the L.H.S. of (6.76) is the fall in the real value of money supply and debt due to inflation. Since money supply is the liability of the government $(M/P)$ can be interpreted as "monetary debt" and $Bn/P$ non-monetary debt in real terms.[20]

The demand for money is assumed proportional to real wealth and depends on real after-tax income differential on various assets.

Turnovsky (1979) has ignored the role of tax in affecting the demand for money. If tax parameters are allowed to vary, it makes a difference to the multipliers. However, it cannot solve the problem of ambiguity of signs of these multipliers.[21]

The demand for money takes into account the three assets — money, capital and bonds. The nominal rate of return on money is zero as before and capital and bonds are perfect substitutes. So the real after-tax rate of return differential is

$$(0-\dot{p}^e)(1-t_1)-(rn-\dot{p}^e)(1-t_t)$$

$$= -rn(1-t_t) \quad \Rightarrow$$

Demand for money depends inversely on $rn(1-t_t)$:

$$L\,[rn\,(1-t_1),\, Y/V]\,[V] = M^d/P \qquad (6.77)$$

For TB model written in this way, $L_1 < 0$.

The equation to the IS curve is taken in the form:

$$I+G=S+T$$

Substituting for investment, government spending, saving and taxes from (6.74)–(6.76) above, the IS equation can be rewritten as:

$$I\,[f'(K)-rn+\dot{p}^e]+G+(1-t_1)\left[\frac{Bn \cdot rn}{P}\right]$$

$$=t_1 f(K)+s\,[\mu f(K)-(M+Bn)/p-K]+\dot{p}^e(M+Bn)/P \qquad (6.78)$$

Tobin and Buiter redefine government spending to include net of tax interest payment on government debt:

$$G' = G+(1-t_1)Bn \cdot rn/P \qquad (6.79)$$

20. See Smith (1987).

21. See Tobin and Buiter (1976, p. 304).

and treats $G'$ as the main parameter of fiscal policy. Equating money demand to money supply, the LM curve equation is written as:

$$L\,[rn\,(1-t_1),\, pf(k)/(M+Bn+PK)]\left[\frac{M+Bn}{P}+K\right]=\frac{M}{P} \qquad (6.80)$$

To close the model, an adaptive expectations rule such as (6.12) is added: expectations are adjusted at a speed $0<\lambda<1$:

$$(d\dot{p}^e/dt)=\lambda[\dot{p}-\dot{p}^e] \qquad (6.81)$$

In a stationary long-run equilibrium, expectations are realised $\Rightarrow \dot{p}=\dot{p}^e \Rightarrow d\dot{p}^e/dt=0$ and $Bn=Bn^*, K=K^* \Rightarrow \dot{B}N=\dot{K}=0$. Tobin and Buiter considered the effects of a fiscal policy with a constant nominal quantity of money $\Rightarrow \dot{M}=0$; also actual and desired stocks of wealth are equal $\Rightarrow V-V^*=0$. With these considerations the LM and government budget equation change to (6.84), (6.82) respectively and the IS curve equation leads to an equation (6.83) for $K$. First, the government budget constraint reduces to:

$$G'=t_1 f(K) \qquad (6.82)$$

(6.82) and the long-run equilibrium conditions reduce the IS equation to:

$$I\,[f'(K)-rn]=0 \Rightarrow \dot{K}\,[f'(K)-rn]=0 \Rightarrow K \text{ can be solved from}$$

$$f'(K)=rn, \text{ say } K=K(rn) \qquad (6.83)$$

where $K'=\frac{1}{f''(K)}<0$

The LM equation can be rewritten as

$$L\,[rn\,(1-t_1),\, Y/V^*]\cdot V^*=\frac{M}{P}$$

$$\Rightarrow \quad L\,[rn\,(1-t_1),\, 1/\mu]\cdot \mu f(K)=\frac{M}{P} \qquad (6.84)$$

From the two long-run equilibrium equations (6.82) and (6.84), $rn$ and $P$ can be solved. The slope of the long-run LM curve in the $(rn, P)$ axes is obtained by differentiating (6.84) w.r.t. $P$.

$$L_1(1-t_1)\frac{drn}{dP}\mu f(k)+L\cdot\mu\left[f'\frac{dk}{drn}\cdot\frac{drn}{dP}\right]=-\frac{M}{P^2}$$

$$\Rightarrow \quad \frac{drn}{dP}[L_1(1-t_1)\mu f(k)+L\cdot\mu\cdot f'/f'']=-\frac{M}{P^2}$$

$$\Rightarrow \quad \left[\frac{drn}{dP}\right]_{LLM}=\frac{-M/P^2f''}{L_1(1-t_1)\mu f''f(K)+L\mu f'} \tag{6.85}$$

$$\Rightarrow \quad \left[\frac{drn}{dP}\right]_{LLM}>0$$

since the numerator and the denominator are both positive.

The slopes of the long-run government budget is zero as (6.82) does not contain any *rn*. This is, therefore, shown by a horizontal line GB in the $(P, rn)$ axes in diagram 6.5 from the partial derivatives of (6.82) and (6.84) w.r.t. $G'$, one gets:

$$t_1 f'\cdot K'\frac{drn}{\partial G'}=1 \tag{6.86}$$

$$L_1(1-t_1)\,\mu f(K)\frac{\partial rn}{\partial G'}L\mu f'(K')\frac{\partial rn}{\partial G'}+\frac{M}{P^2}\frac{\partial P}{\partial G'}=0$$

$$\Rightarrow \quad \frac{\partial rn}{\partial G'}[L_1(1-t_1)\,\mu f(K)+L\mu f'K']+\frac{M}{P^2}\frac{\partial P}{\partial G'}=0 \tag{6.87}$$

The long-run multipliers are:

$$\frac{\partial rn}{\partial G'}=[\,[M/P^2]/J] \tag{6.88}$$

and $$\frac{\partial P}{\partial G'}=[-\{L_1(1-t_1)\,\mu f(K)+L\mu f'K'\}/J] \tag{6.89}$$

where $J$ is the $2\times 2$ jacobian of (6.86) and (6.87)

$$J=\begin{vmatrix} t_1 f'K' & 0 \\ L_1(1-t_1)\,\mu f(K)+L\mu f'K' & M/P^2 \end{vmatrix}$$

$$\Rightarrow \quad J=t_1 f'K'M/P^2=(t_1 f'/f'')(M/P^2) \tag{6.90}$$

$$\Rightarrow \quad J \text{ in } (6.90)<0$$

Substituting (6.90) in (6.89)

$$\frac{\partial rn}{\partial G'} < 0 \text{ and } \frac{\partial P}{\partial G'} < 0$$

⇒ The crowding out effects of fiscal policy are removed in the long-run in the model with variable capital stock and variable price level. An increase in $G'$ shift the government budget line downward and its intersection with the long-run LM curve occurs below and to the left of the point prior to the change. So, the increase in $G'$ lowers both $rn$ and $P$ implying $\left(\frac{\partial Y}{\partial G'}\right) > 0$ even in the full-employment model. Tobin and Buiter point out (p. 299) that this rise in output is due to capital deepening and not elimination of unemployment. The long-run stationary state fiscal policy multiplier is obtained following the chain rule:

$$\frac{\partial Y}{\partial G'} = \frac{\partial}{\partial G'}[f(K)] = \frac{\partial}{\partial G'}[f\{K(rn)\}]$$

$$\Rightarrow \quad \frac{\partial Y}{\partial G'} = f'K'\frac{\partial rn}{\partial G'} = \left(\frac{f'}{f''}\right)\frac{\partial rn}{\partial G'}$$

$$\Rightarrow \quad \frac{\partial Y}{\partial G'} > 0 \tag{6.90}$$

This is shown in the Fig. 6.6 as a movement of equilibrium point from $E_1$ to $E_2$. As $G'$ increases, GB line shifts from $GB_1$ to $GB_2$ along the long-run curve LLM. The reasoning behind (6.90) is that with a fixed tax rate, an increase in $G'$ requires a higher income; With a fixed labour force and full employment a higher income requires a larger capital stock which, in turn, requires a lower interest rate and a higher $V = V^*$. The long-run LM shows that both these effects increase the demand for real money balances; with nominal quantity of money fixed, it requires a lower price level. Because the impact multipliers have opposite signs (shown later), the long-run equilibrium will be stable only if these impact effects are reversed. The impact multipliers have opposite signs because an increase in $G'$ shifts the IS curve to the right which increases both $rn$ and $P$. The slope of the IS curve (6.78) subject to (6.79) is:

$$\left[\frac{drn}{dP}\right]_{IS} = \frac{(M + Bn)(s - \dot{p}^e)}{P^2(-I')} \tag{6.91}$$

If this IS curve has to cut the LLM, then $\dot{p}^e = 0 \Rightarrow$

$$\left[\frac{drn}{dP}\right]_{IS} = \frac{-s\,(M+Bn)}{I'\cdot P^2} < 0 \tag{6.91)'$$

$$\left[\frac{\partial rn}{\partial G'}\right]_{IS} = \frac{-1}{-I'} = \frac{1}{I'} > 0 \tag{6.92}$$

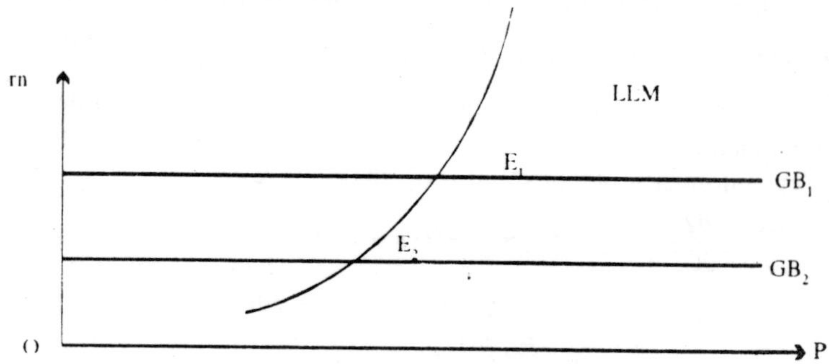


FIG. 6.6

Even in TB's model the long-run government spending multiplier is the reciprocal of the tax rate since it is obtained by using the relation $G' = t_1 f(K)$. Fischer (1976) not only points this out but also comments on TB's assumption of long-run price inflexibility as "extraordinary" (p. 327) and argues that the signs of the long-run multipliers $\left(\frac{\partial rn}{\partial G'}\right) < 0$ and $\left(\frac{\partial P}{\partial G'}\right) < 0$ are due to the strength of the budget constraint in TB's model. The dynamics of the TB model is discussed in the Appendix 6.A.5.

Smith (1982) checks stability of TB's model under active and passive monetary and fiscal policies. His model differs from TB's in that a separate Phillips curve equation has been added to the adaptive expectations frame. The form of the expectations augmented Phillips curve used by Smith is simple and one which has been discussed on many occasions in this Chapter. It uses excess demand measured by the difference between actual and full-employment output as a proxy for unemployment. The equation used by Smith is:

$$\dot{p} = a\,[Y - f(K)] + b\dot{p}^e, \quad a > 0, 0 \le b \le 1 \tag{6.93}$$

$f(K)$ is taken to be the full-employment level of output consistent with a zero steady state rate of inflation. (6.93) also includes Friedman's natural rate hypothesis $\Rightarrow b = 1$ and $f(K)$ the natural rate of output. With $b < 1$ there is a long as well as a short-run trade off between output (or unemployment) and inflation. Equation (6.93) is a special case of Turnovsky's equation (6.63) with a constant tax rate, $T_1 \Rightarrow T = t_1 Y$ and no wage bargaining. Smith also applies a simplifying assumption that desired capital stock is:

$$K^* = \alpha Y / r \tag{6.94}$$

In the model consisting of (6.73)–(6.81) and (6.93) and (6.94), a passive policy is identified as pegging $G'$ and $M$ and letting bond supply residually adjust to finance budget imbalances. Such a policy is shown to be unstable. The weakness of passive policies is that a higher rate of inflation reduces that real rate of interest and thereby reduces the demand for money. If an active monetary stance is adopted by pegging the real interest rate, then an increase in $G'$ merely raises $\dot{p}$ without affecting $Y$ or $K$. An expansionary monetary policy with both $r$ and $G'$ pegged is stable in the long-run.

To be realistic however, the pegging of nominal and not real interest rate should be considered but the model loses stability in the long-run under such policy. Expansionary fiscal policies (on their own) are not successful or stable in the long-run since they lead to higher rates leading to less capital to higher prices to less output to less tax revenue to more bond sales and back to higher interest rates. If joint monetary and fiscal policies such as pegging real output and real interest rate are undertaken, then an increase in $G'$ and $\left(\frac{M}{P}\right)$ from an initial steady state equilibrium can raise $Y$ to a higher level without altering $r$. This leads to a higher budget deficit, more investment and higher saving. Monetary and fiscal policies are then employed to offset these pressures on the IS and LM curves so to maintain real output and real interest rate constant. This is shown to be the most stable policy. The proof of stability (or the lack of it) is run in a similar manner as shown in 6.A.5. for TB's model. The addition of the NRU hypothesis does not affect the results.

As Fischer (1976) points out, adaptive expectations mechanism is consistent with an ever-accelerating rate of inflation to produce a rate of unemployment below the natural rate. So the short-run trade-off continues under adaptive expectations.

## 6.6 SUMMARY AND CONCLUSION

This chapter has concentrated on IS-LM models under inflationary conditions with and without explicit inclusion of the government budget. The inflation unemployment trade-off and how the nature of such trade off changes when expectations are taken into account have been discussed in some detail. Two main schemes of generating expectations considered are rational expectations and adaptive expectations.

Inclusion of flexible prices and expectations significantly alter the roles of monetary and fiscal policies in influencing the real and nominal variables in the economy. RE distinguishes between the anticipated and unanticipated parts of a policy and include the latter in random stochastic disturbances. Sargent's model of RE shows that anticipated or systematic changes in monetary (or fiscal) variables cannot affect the real rate of interest, output or employment. Later on, Fischer and Phelps and Taylor show that monetary policy can be effective even under RE provided there exists some form of wage-price rigidity. In Fischer's RE model such (wage) rigidity enters through long period wage contracts which are non-indexed and are made in nominal terms.

In Phelps-Taylor's model prices and wages are predetermined as they are set before the authorities choose the money supply rule; they show that monetary policy even when it is perfectly anticipated can affect real output and employment except under an unconditional full-employment policy.

The introduction of government budget constraint in the flexible price IS-LM models leads to ambiguity in the signs of some important derivatives and therefore the effects of policies cannot always be judged with precision. When tax rates are regarded as separate policy parameters in such IS-LM government budget models with inflationary expectations wage bargaining and labour supply decisions are seen to be important in determining the effectiveness of various policies. If the rate of inflation is treated as an exogenous variable then monetary policy retains its effectiveness but the value of the short-run monetary policy multiplier is less than that in the case of fixed pice IS-LM models with government budget.

Finally the debate between Keynesians and Monetarists concerning roles of fiscal and monetary policies for financing budget deficits (the debate discussed in much detail in the previous chapter) has been resumed under flexible prices, variable capital stock and full-employment. Tobin-Buiter show that bond financing of government budget deficit will be stable in the long-run if the impact effect of a rise in inflationary expectations is to increase the price level — expectations being generated by the adaptive rule. Smith, however seems to go along with the monetarists and shows, on the basis of TB's model, that joint monetary and fiscal policies will be the most stable in the long-run. Also in TB-Smith model, the natural rate hypothesis does not make much difference to the results. This is not surprising. As Fischer points out the adaptive expectations mechanism is required to produce an ever accelerating rate of inflation to maintain unemployment below the natural rate. It is only the assumption of RE which can destroy the trade-off between inflation and unemployment. As Fischer put it the assumption of RE is vital to consider the optimality of the natural rate hypothesis.

# APPENDIX TO CHAPTER 6

## 6.A.1 Derivation of the Reduced Form for Real Output in Sargent's Model

From (6.37)

$$rn_t = \frac{1}{a_3}[\log M_t - \log P_t - \log Y_t - er_t^3] \tag{6.A.1}$$

Substituting this into the IS equation (6.36)

$$\log Y = \log \overline{Y} + a_2/a_3 [\log M_t - \log P_t - \log Y_t - er_t^3]$$

$$- a_2(\log P_{t+1}^e - \log P_t) + d(\log G_t - \log \overline{G}) + er_t^2 \tag{6.A.2}$$

Assuming a simple two period version of linear feedback rule for money supply:

$$\log M_t = a_4 \log M_{t-1} + a_5 \log M_{t-2} + a_6 er_{t-1}^3 + a_7 er_{t-2}^3$$

$$+ a_8 er_{t-1}^2 + a_9 er_{t-2}^2 + a_{10} U_{t-1} + a_{11} U_{t-2}$$

$$+ a_{12} \log G_{t-1} + a_{13} \log G_{t-2} + er_t^4 \tag{6.A.3}$$

Substituting (6.A.3) into (6.A.2)

$$\log Y_t = \log \overline{Y} - a_2(\log P_t^e - \log P_t) - (a_2/a_3) \log P_t$$

$$- (a_2/a_3) \log Y_t + d(\log G_t - \log \overline{G}) + er_t^2 + (a_2/a_3)$$

$$[\text{R.H.S. of (6.A.3)}] \tag{6.A.4a}$$

$$\Rightarrow \quad \log Y_t = B_0 + B_1(\log P_t^e - \log P_t) - B_2 \log P_t + B_3 \log G_t$$

$$+ B_4 \ [\text{R.H.S. of (6.A.3)}] + B_5 er_t^2 \tag{6.A.4b}$$

where $B_0 = (\log \overline{Y} - d \log \overline{G})/B^*$

$$B_1 = -a_2/B^*, B_2 = [-a_2/a_3]/B^*$$

$$B_3 = \frac{d}{B^*}, B_4 = [a_2/a_3]/B^*$$

and $B_5 = \frac{1}{B^*}$ where $B^* = \frac{1}{1+(a_2/a_3)}$

Substitution of (6.A.4b) into the AS equation (6.34), a solution for the price level can be obtained in a few steps as follows:

$$a_1 [\log P_t - \log P_t^e] + \log \overline{Y} + er_t^1 = B_0 + B_1 [\log P_t^e - \log P_t]$$

$$- B_2 \log P_t + B_3 \log G_t + B_4 [\text{R.H.S. of (6.A.3)}] + B_5 er_t^2$$

$$\Rightarrow \quad B_2 \log P_t = (B_0 - \log \overline{Y}) - (a_1 + B_1) [\log P_t - \log P_t^e]$$

$$+ B_3 \log G_t + B_4[\text{R.H.S. of (6.A.3)}] + B_5 er_t^2 \qquad (6.A.5)$$

Taking expectation of (6.A.5)

$$B_2 \log P_t^e = (B_0 - \log \overline{Y}) + B_3 \log G_t + B_4(a_4 \log M_{t-1} + a_5 \log M_{t-2}$$

$$+ a_{10} U_{t-1} + a_{11} U_{t-2} + a_{12} \log G_{t-1} + a_{13} \log G_{t-2}) \qquad (6.A.6)$$

Since all the random disturbance terms of the model have zero expectation (and constant variance and zero autocorrelation) subtracting (6.A.6) from (6.A.5) the unexpected change in the price level is obtained as

$$(B_2 + a_1 + B_1) [\log P_t - \log P_t^e] = er_t^4 + B_5 er_t^2 + B_4[a_8 er_{t-1}^2$$

$$+ a_9 er_{t-2}^2 + a_6 er_{t-1}^3 + a_7 er_{t-2}^3] \qquad (6.A.7)$$

$$\Rightarrow \quad \log P_t - \log P_t^e = \left[\frac{1}{a_1 + B_1 + B_2}\right] [\text{R.H.S. of (6.A.7)}] \qquad (6.A.8)$$

Finally substitution of (6.A.8) into the AS equation (6.34) yields the real output:

$$\log Y_t = \log \overline{Y} + \frac{a_1}{a_1 + B_1 + B_2} [\text{R.H.S. of (6.A.7)}] + er_t^1 \qquad (6.A.9)$$

Taking expectation of (6.A.9)

$$\log Y_t^e = \log \overline{Y}$$

Taking variance of (6.A.9)

$$Var(\log Y_t) = \left[\frac{a_1}{a_1 + B_1 + B_2}\right]^2 [var\, er_t^4 + \{B_5^2 + B_4^2(a_8^2 + a_9^2)\, var\, er_t^2\}$$

$$+ B_4^2(a_6^2 + a_7^2)\, var\, er_t^3] + var\, er_t^1 \tag{6.A.10}$$

## 6.A.2 Derivation of the Reduced Form Equations of Output and Inventory in Phelps-Taylor Model

Substitution of (6.52) into (6.51) yields:

$$Y_t = \overline{Y} + a_1\left[b_1 - b_2 \underset{t-1}{E} In_t - rn_t + \underset{t-1}{E} \log P_t - \log P_{t-1}\right] + e_t^1 \tag{6.A.11}$$

Substitution of (6.41) yields

$$Y_t = \overline{Y} + a_1\left[b_1 - b_2 \underset{t-1}{E} In_t - \{a_2(\log P_{t-1} - \log M_t) + a_3 Y_t\right.$$

$$\left. + a_4 \underset{t-1}{E} Y_t + e_t^2\} + \underset{t-1}{E} \log P_t - \log P_{t-1}\right] + e_t^1$$

$$\Rightarrow \quad Y_t = \overline{Y} + a_1 b_1 - a_1(1 + a_2)\log P_{t-1} - a_1 b_2 \underset{t-1}{E} In_t + a_1 a_2 \log M_t$$

$$- a_1 a_3 Y_t - a_1 a_4 \underset{t-1}{E} Y_t + a_1 \underset{t-1}{E} \log P_t - a_1 e_t^2 + e_t^1 \tag{6.A.12}$$

Taking expectation of (6.A.12) and noting that the expectations of predetermined variables are equal to their given values and that the error terms have zero expectation, the following equation is obtained:

$$\{1 + a_1(a_3 + a_4)\} \underset{t-1}{E} Y_t = a_1 a_2 \underset{t-1}{E} \log M_t + a_1 \underset{t-1}{E} \log P_t$$

$$- a_1 b_2 \underset{t-1}{E} In_t - a_1(1 + a_2)\log P_{t-1} + \overline{Y} + a_1 b_1 \tag{6.A.13}$$

$$\Rightarrow \quad \underset{t-1}{E} Y_t = A_0 + A_1 \underset{t-1}{E} \log M_t + A_2 \underset{t-1}{E} \log P_t$$

$$+ A_3 \underset{t-1}{E} In_t + A_4 \log P_{t-1} + A_5 \overline{Y} \tag{6.A.14}$$

where $A_0 = (a_1b_1)/A^*$

$$A_1 = (a_1a_2)/A^*$$

$$A_2 = a_1/A^*$$

$$A_3 = (-a_1b_2)/A^* \tag{6.A.15}$$

$$A_4 = (-a_1(1+a_2)/A^*$$

$$A_5 = 1/A^*$$

and $A^* = 1 + a_1(a_3 + a_4)$

Equation (6.57) can be interpreted as the long-run equilibrium condition where expectations formed at $t-1$ about real output $s$ periods ahead of the current period is to be equated to the full employment level of output. To accommodate the future equilibrium condition (6.57) all the expectational variables in (6.A.12) refer to the respective conditional expectation formed at $t-1$ for $s$ periods ahead of $t$. Noting this and substituting for monetary policy rule (6.58), the reduced form equation can be rewritten as

$$\underset{t-1}{E}\, Y_{t+s} = \overline{Y} = A_0 + A_5\overline{Y} + A_1 \underset{t-1}{E}\,[a_8 + a_9 \log P_{t-1+s} + a_{10} In_{t-1+s}]$$

$$+ A_2 \underset{t-1}{E}\, \log P_{t+3} + A_3 \underset{t-1}{E}\, In_{t+s} + A_4 \underset{t-1}{E}\, \log P_{t-1+s} \tag{6.A.16}$$

For the sake of convenience asterisks can be used to denote the conditional expectations and the $t$ subscript can be dropped. Then (6.A.16) can be rewritten as

$$Y_s^* = \overline{Y} = A_0 + A_5\overline{Y} + A_2 \log P_s^* + A_3 In_s^*$$

$$+ (A_4 + A_1a_9) \log P_{s-1}^* + A_1a_{10} In_{s-1}^*$$

$$Y_s^* = \overline{Y} = A_5\overline{Y} + A_0 + A_1a_8 + A_2 \log P_2^* + A_3 In_s^*$$

$$+ A_1a_{10} In_{s-1}^* + (A_4 + A_1a_9) \log P_{s-1}^* \tag{6.A.17}$$

To derive the reduced form equation for inventory, first the equation for real consumption is obtained in terms of price and money supply variables.

Substitution of (6.53) and (6.52i) into (6.54) yields

$$C_t = a_5\Big[(a_2+1)\log P_{t-1} - \underset{t-1}{E}\log P_t - a_2 \log M_t + a_3 Y_t$$

$$+ a_4 \underset{t-1}{E} Y_t + e_t^2\Big] + a_6 Y_t + a_7 \underset{t-1}{E} Y_t + e_t^3 \qquad (6.A.18)$$

Taking expectations for $s$ periods ahead of (6.A.18) yields

$$C_s^* = a_5(1+a_2)\log P_{s-1}^* - a_5 \log P_s^* - a_5 a_2 \log M_s^*$$

$$+ (a_5 a_3 + a_5 a_4 + a_6 + a_7)Y^* \qquad (6.A.19)$$

Substitution of money supply rule into (6.A.19) yields

$$C_s^* = a_5(1+a_2)\log P_{s-1}^* - a_5 \log P_s^* - a_5 a_2 [a_8 + a_9 \log P_{s-1}^*$$

$$+ a_{10} In_{s-1}^* + a_{10} In_{s-1}^*] + [a_5 a_3 + a_5 a_4 + a_6 + a_7]\, Y^*$$

$$\Rightarrow \quad C_s^* = [a_5(1+a_2) - a_5 a_2 a_9]\log P_{s-1}^* - a_5 \log P_s^* - a_5 a_2 a_{10} In_{s-1}^*$$

$$+ (a_5 a_3 + a_5 a_4 + a_6 + a_7)Y^* - a_5 a_2 a_8 \qquad (6.A.20)$$

Taking expectation of (6.55) $s$ periods ahead yields

$$In_s^* = In_{s-1}^* + Y_s^* - C_s^* \qquad (6.A.21)$$

Finally (6.A.17) and (6.A.19) can be substituted to yield the equation for intended inventory:

$$In_s^* = B_0 + B_1 In_{s-1}^* + B_2 \log P_{s-1}^*$$

$$+ B_3 \log P_{s-1}^* + B_4 Y_s^* + B_5 \overline{Y} \qquad (6.A.22)$$

where

$$B_0 = (A_0 + A_1 a_8 + a_5 a_2 a_8)/B^*$$

$$B_1 = (1 + a_5 a_2 a_{10})/B^*$$

$$B_2 = (A_2 + a_5)/B^*$$

$$B_3 = (A_1 a_9 + A_4 - a_5(1+a_2) + a_5 a_2 a_9)/B^*$$

$$B_4 = (a_5 a_3 + a_5 a_4 + a_6 + a_7)/B^*$$

$$B_5 = A_5/B^* \text{ and } B^* = 1 - A_1 a_{10} - A_3$$

The above set of six definitions will be referred to as (6.A.23).

The equation (6.A.17) subject to (6.A.15) and the equation (6.A.22) subject to (6.A.23) summarise the Phelps-Taylor model. The parameters of money supply rule $a_9$ and $a_{10}$ are present in both equations.

The equations (6.A.17) and (6.A.22) are two stochastic difference equations which have to be consistent with each other or solved simultaneously. Substitution of (6.A.22) into (6.A.17) yields a stochastic difference equation in $\log P_s^*$ or $E_{t-1} \log P_{t+s}$ as follows:

$$Y_s^* = (A_5 + A_3B_5)\overline{Y} + (A_0 + A_1a_0 + A_3B_0)$$

$$+ (A_2 + A_3B_2)\log P_s^* + (A_4 + a_1a_9 + A_3B_3)\log P_{s-1}^*$$

$$+ (A_1a_{10} + A_3B_1)In_{s-1}^* + B_4Y_s^* \quad (6.A.24)$$

Applying the future equilibrium condition for real output

$$Y_s^* = \overline{Y} \quad (6.A.24)$$

can be rewritten as

$$\overline{Y}[1 - B_4 - (A_5 + A_3B_5)] = (A_0 + A_1a_8 + A_3B_0) + (A_2 + A_3B_2)\log P_s^*$$

$$+ (A_4 + a_1a_9 + A_3B_3)\log P_{s-1}^* + (A_1a_{10} + A_3B_1)In_{s-1}^*$$

$$\Rightarrow \quad \log P_s^* = C_0 + C_1\overline{Y} + C_2P_{s-1}^* + C_3In_{s-1}^* \quad (6.A.25)$$

Where $C_0 = -(A_0 + A_1a_8 + A_3B_0)/C^*$

$$C_1 = [1 - B_4 - (A_5 + A_3B_5)]/C^*$$

$$C_2 = -[A_4 + a_1a_9 + A_3B_3]/C^* \quad (6.A.26)$$

$$C_3 = -(A_1a_{10} + A_3B_1)/C^*$$

and $C^* = A_2 + A_3B_2$

Phelps and Taylor rewrite equation (6.A.25) as

$$\log P_{s-1}^* = c'_0 + c'_1\overline{Y} + c'_2 \log P_s^* + c'_3 In_{s-1}^* \quad (6.A.25)'$$

and derives the solution through forward substitution. For stability $c'_2 < 1$ is to be satisfied. Since solution to difference equations has already been considered in the previous chapters this is not pursued any further. We concentrate instead on the point that even the fully anticipated monetary policy can affect the variance of output and employment. In other words the coefficients $a_9$ and $a_{10}$ are important determinants of the variance of output.

$$Var(Y_t) \equiv E(Y_t - EY_t)^2 \Rightarrow Var(Y_t) = E(Y_t - \overline{Y})^2 \qquad (6.A.27)$$

It is evident from equation (6.A.12) and from substitution of (6.55) into (6.A.12) that

$$Y_t = \overline{Y} + a_1b_1 - a_1(1+a_2)\log P_{t-1} - a_1b_2[In_{t-1} + \underset{t-1}{E}Y_t - \underset{t-1}{E}C_t] + a_1a_2\log M_t - a_1a_3Y_t - a_1a_4\underset{t-1}{E}Y_t + a_1\underset{t-1}{E}\log P_t - a_1e_t^2 + e_t^1 \qquad (6.A.28i)$$

$\underset{t-1}{E}C_t$ can be obtained after taking expectation of (6.A.18) and substitution of $\underset{t-1}{E}C_t$ will then yield

$$Y_t(1+a_3) = \overline{Y} + a_1b_1 - a_1(1+a_2)\log P_{t-1} - a_1b_2In_{t-1} - a_1b_2\Big[\underset{t-1}{E}Y_t - a_5(a_2+1)\log P_{t-1} + a_5\underset{t-1}{E}\log P_t + a_5a_2\underset{t-1}{E}\log M_t - (a_5a_3 + a_5a_4 + a_6 + a_7)\underset{t-1}{E}Y_t\Big] + a_1a_2\log M_t - a_1a_4\underset{t-1}{E}Y_t + a_1\underset{t-1}{E}\log P_t - a_1e_t^2 + e_t^1$$

$$\Rightarrow \quad Y_t = \frac{1}{1+a_3}\Big[\overline{Y} + a_1b_1 - (a_2+1)(a_1 - a_5a_1b_2)\log P_{t-1} - a_1b_2In_{t-1} + (a_1a_2 - a_1b_2a_5a_2)\underset{t-1}{E}\log M_t + (a_1 - a_1b_2a_5)\underset{t-1}{E}\log P_t - a_1e_t^2 + e_t^1 - a_1b_2(1 - a_5a_3 - a_5a_4 - a_6 - a_7)\underset{t-1}{E}Y_t a_1a_4\underset{t-1}{E}Y_t\Big] \qquad (6.A.28ii)$$

Substituting from (6.56) and (6.57) (6.A.28ii) can be rewritten as

$$Y_t = \frac{1}{1+a_3}[\overline{Y}\{1-a_1a_4-a_1b_2(1-a_5a_3-a_5a_4-a_6-a_7)\}$$

$$+a_1b_1+(a_1-a_1b_2a_5)(\log P_t - e_t^4)-a_1b_2In_{t-1}$$

$$-(1+a_2)(a_1-a_1b_2a_5)\log P_{t-1}+(a_1a_2-a_1b_2a_5)\underset{t-1}{E}\log M_t$$

$$-a_1e_t^2+e_t^1] \quad (6.A.28iii)$$

Taking variance of $Y_t$ from (6.A.28iii), one can derive

$$Var(Y_t) = \frac{1}{(1+a_3)^2}[(Var\ e_t^1 + a^2 Var\ e_t^2)+(a_1-a_1b_2a_5)^2$$

$$\{Var\,(\log P_t - (1+a_2)\log P_{t-1} + Var\ e_t^4\} + (a_1b_2)^2$$

$$Var\ In_{t-1} + a_9^2(a_1a_2-a_1b_2a_5)^2\{Var\,(\log P_{t-1})\}$$

$$-2a_1b_2(a_1-a_1b_2a_5)\{Cov(\log P_t, In_{t-1}) - Cov$$

$$(\log P_{t-1}, In_{t-1})(1+a_2)\} + 2(a_1a_2-a_1b_2a_5)a_9a_{10}$$

$$Cov(\log P_{t-1}, In_{t-1}) + 2a_{10}(a_1-a_1b_2a_5)$$

$$Cov(\log P_t, In_{t-1}) + 2a_9(a_1-a_1-a_1b_2a_5)$$

$$Cov(\log P_t, \log P_{t-1}) - 2a_{10}a_1b_2\,Cov(In_t, In_{t-1})$$

$$(a_1a_2-a_1b_2a_5)] \quad (6.A.29)$$

assuming covariances of all error terms between themselves and with other variables of the system to be zero.

Rewriting equation (6.A.25) for $s=0$, one can obtain the covariance between $\underset{t-1}{E}\log P_t$ [which is the difference, $\log P_t - e_t^4$] and $In_{t-1}$ and between $\underset{t-1}{E}\log P_t$ and $\log P_{t-1}$:

$$\underset{t-1}{E}\log P_t = c_0 + c_1\overline{Y} + c_2\log P_{t-1} + c_3 In_{t-1} \quad (6.A.25)^{11}$$

$\Rightarrow$ *Cov* $(\log P_t, \log P_{t-1})$ and *Cov* $(\log P_t, In_{t-1})$ will have $C_2$ and $C_3$ which is turn depend on $a_9$, $a_{10}$ as given in (6.A.26). In this light (6.A.29) does show that *Var* $(Y_t)$ depends on the crucial monetary policy rule parameter,

$a_9$. Phelps and Taylor provide a proof on certain additional assumptions that if the variance of the price level is held to a minimum, then the variance of output can be reduced by raising $a_9$. If $a_9$ is increased to its maximum value,[1] then output will be reduced to its minimum value.

### 6.A.3 Derivation of the Expectations — Augmented Phillips Curve in Turnovsky's Model including Wage-bargaining: Effectiveness of Monetary Policy

From equation (6.60), real income after tax is $\frac{Yn(1-t_1)-t_0}{P^e}$. Assuming that wage income is a certain proportion $0<\lambda<1$ of aggregate nominal income, one can write

$$(H-\ell)W=\lambda Yn$$

where $(H-\ell)$ is the total number of hours worked.

Then, total real wage income after tax is

$$\frac{\lambda Yn(1-t_1)-t_0}{P^e} \tag{6.A.30}$$

The workers are assumed to negotiate such that the change in (6.A.30) is zero when $t_0$, $t_1$ and $P^e$ change. Taking the first difference of (6.A.30) and equating that to zero, one gets

$$\frac{1}{(P^e)^2}[P^e\{\lambda Yn(-\Delta t_1)-\Delta t_0+(1-t_1)\Delta(\lambda Yn)\}$$

$$-\{\lambda Yn(1-t_1)-t_0\}\Delta P^e]=0\Rightarrow$$

$$\frac{\Delta(\lambda Yn)(1-t_1)-\Delta t_0-\Delta t_1\lambda Yn}{P^e}=\frac{1}{P^e}\cdot\frac{\Delta P^e}{P^e}(\lambda Yn(1-t_1)-t_o) \tag{6.A.31}$$

Now $\frac{\Delta P^e}{P^e}$ can be replaced by the expected rate of inflation $\dot{p}^e$ and the first difference of $(\lambda Yn)$ is actually the change in nominal wage income $(H-\ell)\Delta W$ assuming no change in the number of hours worked. Taking this into account and rewriting $\lambda Yn$ in terms of money wage (6.A.31) yields

$$(1-t_1)[(H-\ell)(\Delta W-\dot{p}^e W)]+t_0\dot{p}^e-\Delta t_0=\Delta t_1(H-\ell)W \qquad (6.A.32)$$

Dividing (6.A.32) through by $(1-t_1)(H-\ell)W$:

$$\frac{\Delta W}{W}-\dot{p}^e+\frac{t_0\dot{p}^e-\Delta t_0}{(1-t_1)(H-\ell)W}=\frac{\Delta t_1}{1-t_1}$$

Replacing $\frac{\Delta W}{W}$ by the rate of change of money wage symbol, $\dot{w}$, this can be rewritten as

$$\dot{w}=\dot{p}^e+\frac{\Delta t_1}{1-t_1}+\frac{\Delta t_0-t_0\dot{p}^e}{(H-\ell)\,W\,(1-t_1)} \qquad (6.A.32)$$

substituting $\lambda Yn$ back for $(H-\ell)\,W$:

$$\dot{w}=\dot{p}^e\left[1-\frac{t_0}{\lambda Yn(1-t_1)}\right]+\left[\frac{\Delta t_1}{1-t_1}+\frac{\Delta t_0}{\lambda Yn(1-t_1)}\right] \qquad (6.A.32)$$

The equation (6.A.32) gives the additional terms to go into the equation to the Phillips curve (6.63) on account of the assumed scheme for wage bargaining. The first term on the RHS of (6.A.32) is the expectations progressivity effect and the second term is the income-claims effect. With the cost of living and tax rates all rising, the workers have to be compensated by more than the expected rate of inflation, due to a progressive tax structure, if they are to maintain their real standard of living.

The Jacobian of the model containing (6.61)–(6.64) can be derived in the same way as before.

$$\begin{vmatrix} \{1-C'(1-t_1)\}/P & -I' & 0 & \dfrac{-Yn(1-C')+C't_0}{P_{-1}(1+\dot{p})^2} \\ L'_{Yn}/P & L'_{rn} & -\dfrac{1}{P_{-1}(+\dot{p})} & \dfrac{M-L_{Yn}Yn}{P_{-1}(1+\dot{p})^2} \\ \dfrac{a_1}{P}-\left[\dfrac{\Delta t_0 a_3-a_2 t_0\dot{p}^e}{\lambda Yn^2(1-t_1)}\right] & 0 & 0 & -\dfrac{a_1 Yn}{P_{-1}(1+\dot{p})^2}-1 \\ \theta t_1 & 0 & 1 & -\theta P_{-1}G \end{vmatrix}$$

$$\Rightarrow \quad J = \frac{1 - C'(1-t_1)}{P}\left[L'_{rn}\left(\frac{a_1 Yn}{P_{-1}(1+\dot{p})^2}+1\right)\right] + I'\left[\frac{L'_{Yn}}{P}\left(1+\frac{a_1 Yn}{P_{-1}(1+\dot{p})^2}\right)\right.$$

$$+\left(\frac{I'}{P_{-1}(1+\dot{p})}\right)\left\{\frac{-a_1}{P}+\left(\frac{a_3\Delta t_0 - a_2 t_0 \dot{p}^e}{\lambda(1-t_1)Yn^2}\right)\right\}\theta P_{-1}G$$

$$\left.+\theta t_1\left\{1+\frac{a_1 Yn}{P_{-1}(1+\dot{p})^2}\right\}\right] + \frac{I'(M - L_1 Yn)}{P_{-1}(1+\dot{p})^2}$$

$$\left[\frac{a_1}{P} - \left\{\frac{a_3\Delta t_0 - a_2 t_0 \dot{p}^e}{\lambda(1-t_1)Yn^2}\right\}\right] - \left\{\frac{Yn(1-C') - C' t_0}{P_{-1}(1+\dot{p})^2}\right\}$$

$$L'_{rn}\left\{\frac{a_1}{P} - \left(\frac{a_3\Delta t_0 - a_2 t_0 \dot{p}^e}{\lambda(1-t_1)Yn^2}\right)\right\}$$

$$\Rightarrow \quad J = \left(1+\frac{a_1 Yn}{P_{-1}(1+\dot{p}^2)}\right)\left[\frac{\{1 - C'(1-t_1)\}L'_{rn} + I'L'_{Yn} + I'\theta t_1}{P}\right]$$

$$+\left[\frac{a_1}{P} - \left(\frac{a_3\Delta t_0 - a_2 t_0 \dot{p}^e}{\lambda(1-t_1)Yn^2}\right)\right]\left[\frac{I'}{P_{-1}(1+\dot{p})^2}(M - \theta PG - L_{Yn} Yn)\right]$$

$$\Rightarrow \quad J = \left(1+\frac{a_1 Yn}{P(1+\dot{p})}\right)\left[\left\{\frac{1 - C'(1-t_1)\}\, L'_{rn} + I'\theta t_1}{P}\right] + \left(\frac{I'L'_{Yn}}{P}\right)$$

$$+\left[\frac{a_1}{P} - \left(\frac{a_3\Delta t_0 - a_2 t_0 \dot{p}^e}{\lambda Yn^2(1-t_1)}\right)\right]\left[\frac{I'}{P(1+\dot{p})}\right](M - \theta PG)$$

$$-L'_{rn}\,[Yn(1-C') - C' t_0] + \left(\frac{a_3\Delta t_0 - a_2 t_0 \dot{p}^e}{\lambda Yn^2(1-t_1)}\right)\frac{I' L_{Yn} Yn}{P(1+\dot{P})}$$

(6.A.33)

The first group of terms is unambiguously negative; $I'L'_{Yn} < 0$; the third group of terms $< 0$ assuming $|\Delta t_0| < |t_0|$ (recall $t_0 < 0$ and $M - \theta PG > 0$); the last group of terms $< 0$ as well since $I' < 0$. (6.A.33) implies $J < 0$.

To derive the monetary policy multiplier, $\frac{\partial Yn}{\partial MA}$, we can apply Cramer's rule as before. Since MA is present only in the LM equation the multiplier is obtained very easily by replacing column 1 of $|J|$ by $(0\,0\,0\,1)'$ and dividing this by $|J| \Rightarrow$

$$\frac{\partial Yn}{\partial MA} = \frac{I'}{PJ}\left[1 + \frac{a_1 Yn}{P_{-1}(1+\dot{p})^2}\right] \tag{6.A.34}$$

Since $J < 0 \Rightarrow \frac{\partial Yn}{\partial MA} > 0$

$\Rightarrow$ A rise in the exogenous component of money supply leads to a rise in the nominal output. For the effect on real output, one can rewrite $\frac{\partial Yn}{\partial MA}$ as

$$\frac{\partial Yn}{\partial MA} = \frac{\partial}{\partial MA}(PY) = P\left(\frac{\partial Y}{\partial MA}\right) + Y\frac{\partial P}{\partial MA}$$

$$\Rightarrow \quad P\frac{\partial Y}{\partial MA} = \frac{\partial Yn}{\partial MA} - YP_{-1}\frac{\partial \dot{p}}{\partial MA}$$

$$\Rightarrow \quad \frac{\partial Y}{\partial MA} = \frac{1}{P}\frac{\partial Yn}{\partial MA} - \frac{Y}{(1+\dot{p})}\frac{\partial \dot{p}}{\partial MA} \tag{6.A.35}$$

Applying Cramer's rule again

$$\frac{\partial \dot{p}}{\partial MA} = \frac{I'}{PJ}\left[\frac{a_1}{P} + \frac{a_2 t_0 \dot{p}^e - a_3 \Delta t_0}{\lambda Yn^2(1-t_1)}\right] \tag{6.A.36}$$

(6.A.36) consists of two parts one of which is positive but if the other part is sufficiently negative, which we have already assumed then monetary policy will be effective in raising real as well as nominal output. Also if $t_0$ is constant then it is more likely that

$$\frac{\partial \dot{p}}{\partial MA} < 0 \quad \Rightarrow \frac{\partial Y}{\partial MA} > 0.$$

Under inflationary conditions and a progressive tax structure, therefore, inclusion of the government budget constraint renders policy effects ambiguous.

### 6.A.4 Derivation of Reduced Form for Output in Fackler's Model: Effectiveness of Monetary Policy Under RE

Since the IS curve equation is only implicit, the aggregate supply equation is to be used. To derive the latter, first the logarithm of labour demand is obtained by using the profit maximising rule of employment in neoclassical economics — marginal productivity of labour equals real wage.

Differentiating the Cobb-Douglass production function — $Y = \left(\frac{e^1}{e}\right) K^{a_1} N^{a_2}$ — underlying (6.67) with respect to $N$ and equating it to real wage:

$$(a_2 Y/N) = \frac{W}{P} \quad \Rightarrow \quad \text{labour demand,}$$

$$N^d = a_2 Y P/W \Rightarrow \log N^d = \log a_2 - \log W + \log Y + \log P$$

$$\Rightarrow \quad \log N^d = \log a_2 - \log W + \log P + a_1 \log K + a_2 \log N^d + e_t^1$$

$$\Rightarrow \quad \log N^d = \frac{1}{1-a_2}[\log a_2 - \log W + \log P + a_1 \log K + e_t^1]$$

(6.A.37)

(6.A.37) is identical to (6.68) since $a_1 + a_2 = 1$.

Equating the logarithm of labour demand with that of labour supply, one ensures the equilibrium in the labour market. From (6.A.37) and (6.69)

$$[\log a_2^1 - \log W + \log P + a_1 \log K + e_t^1]$$

$$= a_1[a_3 \log T + a_4(\log W - \log P_t^e)].$$

$$\log a_2 + a_1 \log K - \log\left(\frac{W}{P}\right) + e^1$$

$$= a_1 a_3 \log T + a_1 a_4 \log\left(\frac{W}{P}\right) + a_1 a_4 \log P - a_1 a_4 \log P_t^e$$

$$\Rightarrow \quad (1 + a_1 a_4) \log\left(\frac{W}{P}\right) = \log a_2 + a_1 \log K - a_1 a_4(\log P - \log P^e)$$

$$- a_1 a_3 \log T + e^1$$

$$\Rightarrow \quad \log\left(\frac{W}{P}\right) = \left(\frac{1}{1 + a_1 a_4}\right)[\log a_2 + a_1 \log K - a_1 a_4(\log P - \log P^e)$$

$$- a_1 a_3 \log T + e^1] \qquad (6.A.38)$$

Resubstitution of (6.A.38) into (6.A.37) gives equilibrium employment which then needs substituting in the production function (6.67) to yield aggregate supply of output.

$$\log N = \frac{1}{a_1}[\log a_2 + a_1 \log K - (\text{R.H.S. of (6.A.38)}) + e^1] \tag{6.A.39}$$

$$\Rightarrow \quad \log Y = a_1 \log K + a_2[\text{R.H.S. of (6.A.39)}] + e^1$$

$$\Rightarrow \quad \log Y = a_2 a_4 \log a_2 + a_1 \log K\left[\frac{1+a_4}{1+a_1a_4}\right] + \frac{a_2a_4}{1+a_1a_4}$$

$$(\log P - \log P^e) + \left[\frac{a_2a_3}{1+a_1a_4}\right]\log T + \left[\frac{a_2a_4}{1+a_1a_4}\right]e^1 \tag{6.A.40}$$

Equation (6.A.40) gives the aggregate supply of output as in (6.A.72). Assuming the stock of capital to be fixed in the short-run, $\log K$ can be included in the constant term $\Rightarrow$.

$$b_0 = a_2a_4 \log a_2 + \left[\frac{a_1(1+a_4)}{1+a_1a_4}\right]\log K;$$

$$b_1 = \left[\frac{a_2a_4}{1+a_1a_4}\right]; \qquad b_2 = \left[\frac{a_2a_3}{1+a_1a_4}\right] \tag{6.A.41}$$

and $$e^5 = \left[\frac{a_2a_4}{1+a_1a_4}\right]e^1$$

It is clear from the set of equations (6.A.41) that $b_1 > 0$ and $b_2 < 0$, because $a_3 < 0$. The reduced form equation for real output can be derived in the following steps:

From the demand for money equation in nominal terms (6.46)″ and the money supply rule (6.71)

$$\log P_t = \log M_t - a_5 - a_6 \log Y_t + e_t^3 \cdots$$

$$\Rightarrow \quad \log P_t = a_7 + a_8 \log Y_{t-1} + a_9 \log M_{t-1}$$

$$- a_5 - a_6 \log Y_t + e_t^3 \tag{6.A.42}$$

Taking expectation of (6.A.42) given $M_{t-1}$ and $Y_{t-1}$

$$\underset{t-1}{E} \log p_t = a_7 + a_8 \log Y_{t-1} + a_9 \log M_{t-1} - a_5 - a_6 \underset{t-1}{E} \log Y_t$$

$$\Rightarrow \quad \log P_t - \underset{t-1}{E} \log P_t = -a_6\left(\log Y_t - \underset{t-1}{E} \log Y_t\right) + e_t^3 \tag{6.A.43}$$

Substituting (6.A.43) and the tax equation (6.70) into (6.72)

$$\log Y_t = b_0 - b_1 a_6 \log Y_t + b_1 a_6 \underset{t-1}{E} \log Y_t$$

$$+ b_2[t_0 + t_1 \log Y_t + (t_1 - 1) \log P_t] + e_t^5$$

Substituting for $\log P_t$ again

$$\log Y_t = b_0 - b_1 a_6 \log Y_t + b_1 a_6 \underset{t-1}{E} \log Y_t + b_2[t_0 + t_1 \log Y_t + (t_1 - 1)$$

$$(a_7 + a_8 \log Y_{t-1} + a_9 \log M_{t-1} - a_5 - a_6 \log Y_t + e_t^3)] + e_t^5$$

$$\Rightarrow \quad \log Y_t[1 + a_6(b_1 + b_2) - b_2 t_1]$$

$$= [b_0 + b_2 t_0 + b_2 a_7(t_1 - 1) - b_2 a_5(t_1 - 1)]$$

$$+ b_1 a_6 \underset{t-1}{E} \log Y_t + b_2 a_8(t_1 - 1) \log Y_{t-1}$$

$$+ b_2 a_9(t_1 - 1) \log M_{t-1} + b_2(t_1 - 1)e_t^3 + e_t^5 \tag{6.A.44}$$

The equation (6.A.44) shows that real output depends on the monetary policy parameters $a_7 - a_9$. Taking expectation of (6.A.44)

$$\underset{t-1}{E} \log Y_t = d_0 + d_1 \log Y_{t-1} + d_2 \log M_{t-1} \tag{6.A.45}$$

where $d_0 = [b_0 + b_2 t_0 + b_2(t_1 - 1)(a_7 - a_5)]/d^*$

$$d_1 = b_2 a_8(t_1 - 1)/d^*$$

$$d_2 = b_2 a_9(t_1 - 1)/d^* \tag{6.A.46}$$

and $d^* = 1 + b_2 a_6 - b_2 t_1$

From (6.A.44) and (6.A.46) it follows that the variance of output

$$\left[\equiv E\left(\log Y_t - \underset{t-1}{E} \log Y_t\right)^2\right]$$

does not include the policy parameters $a_7 - a_9$. Assuming white noise in all the equations and independence of $e^i$ and $e^j$ for $i \neq j$ and $i, j = 1 \cdots 6$.

$$var\ (\log Y_t) = \left(\frac{a_2 a_4}{1 + a_6(b_1 + b_2) - b_2 t_1}\right)^2 [\{b_2(t-1)\}^2 var\ e_t^3 + var\ e_t^5]$$

(6.A.47)

If $t_1 = 1$, then

$$\Rightarrow \quad var\ (\log Y_t) = \left[\frac{a_2 a_4}{(1 + a_1 a_4)\{1 + a_6 b_1 - b_2(1 - a_6)\}}\right]^2 var\ e_t^1 \qquad (6.A.48)$$

from (6.A.41)

Since $e^1$ is the stochastic part of the aggregate supply of output the variance of real output is completely independent of monetary policy parameters — anticipated and unanticipated — if tax liabilities do not increase with inflation.

### 6.A.5 The Dynamics of Tobin-Buiter Model

Since all the equations except (6.81) are given in the general form, the reduced form equations for *rn* and *P* are derived in the general form only as in the BS model of Chapter 5.

$$rn = Q^1(B, K, \dot{p}^e, M, G', t_1) \qquad (6.A.49)$$

and $$P = Q^2(B, K, \dot{p}^e, \quad M, G', t_1) \qquad (6.A.50)$$

The dynamic equations can be derived for either $\dot{B}, \dot{K}$ and $\dot{p}$ or for $\dot{M}, \dot{K}$ and $\dot{p}$. Since Tobin and Buiter were interested in the Keynesian-Monetarist debate centering around the efficacy of fiscal versus monetary policies, equations for $\dot{B}, \dot{K}$ and $\dot{p}^e$ were derived from (6.76), (6.74) and (6.81) respectively.

$$\dot{B}n = P[G' - t_1 f(K)] = Q^2[G' - t_1 f(K)] \qquad (6.A.51)$$

$$\dot{K} = I\,[f'(K) - rn + \dot{p}^e]$$

$$\Rightarrow \quad \dot{K} = I\,[f'(K) - Q^1 + \dot{p}^e] \qquad (6.A.52)$$

and $$\left[\frac{d\dot{p}^e}{dt}\right] = \lambda\left[\frac{\dot{Q}^2}{Q^2} - \dot{p}^e\right] \qquad (6.A.53)$$

Considering $M, G'$ and $t_1$ as given, the solutions to *rn* and *P* become functions of *Bn*, *K* and $\dot{p}^e$. For convenience the functions are still called $Q^1$ and $Q^2$:

$$rn = Q^1[Bn, K, \dot{p}^e] \tag{6.A.51}$$

and $$P = Q^2[Bn, K, \dot{p}^e] \tag{6.A.52}$$

With these the dynamic equations for $\dot{B}n, \dot{K}$ and $(d\dot{p}^e)/dt$ are expanded around the long-run equilibrium values:

$Bn = Bn^*, K = K^*$ and $\dot{p}^e = 0$. Note that $G' - t_1 f(K) = 0$ at such equilibrium values.

A linear approximation of $\dot{B}n, \dot{K}$ and $(d\dot{p}^e/dt)$ can be obtained around $(Bn^*, K^*, O)$ using a Taylor's Series. Expanding (6.A.51) $\dot{B}n$ can be approximated by

$$Q^2(Bn^*, K^*, O)(O) + \left[\left(\frac{\partial Q^2}{\partial Bn}\right)(Bn - Bn^*) + \frac{\partial Q^2}{\partial K}(K - K^*)\right.$$

$$\left. + \frac{\partial Q^2}{\partial \dot{p}^e}(\dot{p}^e - O)\right](G'_1 - t_1 f(K)) + Q^2[-t_1 f'(K - K^*)] \tag{6.A.54}$$

Simplifying (6.A.54) and writing $Q^{2*}$ for the value of $Q^2$ in long-run equilibrium, one gets

$$B\dot{n} = -t_1 f'(K^*) Q^2 (K - K^*) \tag{6.A.55}$$

Similarly $\dot{K}$ can be approximated by expanding (6.A.52) up to the first order:

$$\dot{K} \simeq \left(-I'\frac{\partial Q^2}{\partial Bn}\right)(Bn - Bn^*) + \left[I'\left(f'' - \frac{\partial Q^1}{\partial K}\right)\right](K - K^*)$$

$$+ I'\left(1 - \frac{\partial Q^1}{\partial \dot{p}^e}\right)(\dot{p}^e - O) \tag{6.A.56}$$

Note that $I^* = 0$ since $K = K^* \Rightarrow \dot{K} = 0$ in long-run equilibrium.

Finally expansion of (6.A.53) requires double substitution and so it is slightly more complicated.

$$[\frac{d\dot{p}^e}{dt} = \lambda\left[\left\{\left(Q_1^2 B\dot{n} + Q_2^2 \dot{K} + Q_3^2 \frac{d\dot{p}^e}{dt}\right)/Q^2\right\} - \dot{p}^e\right]$$

$$\Rightarrow \quad \left(1 - \frac{\lambda}{P} Q_3^2\right)\frac{d\dot{p}e}{dt} = \lambda[\{(Q_1^2 B\dot{n} + Q_2^2 \dot{K})/Q^2\} - \dot{p}^e]$$

Put $A_0 = 1 - \frac{\lambda}{P} Q_3^2 = (p - \lambda Q_3^2)/p$

$$\Rightarrow \quad \frac{d\dot{p}^e}{dt} = \frac{\lambda}{(A_0P^2)}[Q_1^2\{-t_1f'Q^2(K-K^*)\} + Q_2^2\{-I'Q_1^1(Bn-Bn^*)$$

$$+I'(f''-Q_2^1)(K-K^*)+I'(1-Q_3^1)(\dot{p}^e)\}Q^2$$

$$-\left\{\left(Q_1^2B\dot{n}+Q_2^2\dot{K}+Q^2\frac{d\dot{p}^e}{dt}\right)\{Q_3^2(Bn-Bn^*)\right.$$

$$+Q_2^2(K-K^*)+Q_3^2(\dot{p}^e)\}] - \frac{\lambda}{A_0}(\dot{p}^e) \tag{6.A.57}$$

Since $B\dot{n} = \dot{K} = \frac{d\dot{p}^e}{dt} = 0$ in equilibrium and $Q^2 = P$, (6.A.57) simplifies to

$$\frac{d\dot{p}^e}{dt} = \frac{\lambda}{A_0P}[-I'Q_1^1Q_2^2(Bn-Bn^*)+(K-K^*)\{Q_2^2I'(f''-Q_2^1\}$$

$$-t_1f'Q_1^2P] + \dot{p}^e\left[\frac{\lambda}{A_0}\{I'(1-Q_3^1)/P-1\}\right]$$

Substituting for $A_0$

$$\frac{d\dot{p}^e}{dt} = \left[\frac{\lambda}{P-\lambda Q_3^2}\right][I'Q_1^1\,Q_2^2(Bn-Bn^*)+(K-K^*)Q_2^2I'(f''-Q_2^1)-tf'Q_1^2P)]$$

$$+\left[\frac{\lambda P}{(P-\lambda Q_3^2)}\right][I'(1-Q_3^1/P-1)]\;\cdots \tag{6.A.58}$$

The system of equation (6.A.55)–(6.A.56) and (6.A.58) can be written in the matrix form as:

$$\begin{vmatrix} B\dot{n} \\ \dot{K} \\ \dfrac{d\dot{p}^e}{dt} \end{vmatrix} = J_E \begin{vmatrix} Bn-Bn^* \\ K-K^* \\ \dot{p}^e-0 \end{vmatrix} \tag{6.A.59}$$

where $J_E$ is the Jacobian evaluated at equilibrium values $Bn = Bn^*, K = K^*$ and $\dot{p}^e = 0$

$$J_E = \begin{vmatrix} 0 & -t_1 f' Q^2 & 0 \\ -I' Q_1^1 & I'(f'' - Q_2^1) & I'(1 - Q_3^1) \\ (-\lambda I' Q_1^1 Q_2^2)/(P - \lambda Q_3^2) & \dfrac{\lambda(Q_2^2 I'(f'' - Q_2^1) - t_1 f' P Q_1^2}{P - \lambda Q_2^3} & \{I'(1 - Q_1^3)/P \\ & & -1\}\lambda P / P - \lambda Q_3^2) \end{vmatrix} \tag{6.A.60}$$

From (6.A.59)

$$\begin{vmatrix} B\dot{n} \\ \dot{K} \\ \dfrac{d\dot{p}^e}{dt} \end{vmatrix} = J_E \begin{vmatrix} Bn \\ K \\ \dot{p}^e \end{vmatrix} - J_E \begin{vmatrix} Bn^* \\ K^* \\ 0 \end{vmatrix} \tag{6.A.61}$$

Since all the partial derivatives are evaluated at equilibrium points, the second term on the RHS of (6.A.61) is zero because all the functions $B\dot{n}(Bn, K, \dot{p}^e), \dot{K}(Bn, K, \dot{p}^e)$ and $\frac{d\dot{p}^e}{dt}(Bn, K, \dot{p}^e)$ are zero at $(Bn^*, K^*, 0) \Rightarrow$

(6.A.61) can be rewritten as

$$\begin{vmatrix} B\dot{n} \\ \dot{K} \\ \dfrac{d\dot{p}^e}{dt} \end{vmatrix} = J_E \begin{vmatrix} Bn \\ K \\ \dot{p}^e \end{vmatrix} \tag{6.A.62}$$

(6.A.62) is the reduced linearisa on of the dynamic system. Obviously local stability i.e., stability aroun.. $(Bn^*, K^*, O)$ will depend on the make up of $J_E$. To find the complementary functions of the system of differential equations, one can try $Bn = a_1 e^{\gamma t}$, $K = a_2 e^{\gamma t}$ and $\dot{p}^e = a_3 e^{\gamma t}$ as solutions to (6.A.62).

Then substitution in (6.A.62) yields

$$\begin{vmatrix} a_1 \\ a_2 \\ a_3 \end{vmatrix} \gamma e^{\gamma t} = J_E \begin{vmatrix} a_1 \\ a_2 \\ a_3 \end{vmatrix} e^{\gamma t}$$

$$|\gamma j - J_E| \begin{vmatrix} a_1 \\ a_2 \\ a_3 \end{vmatrix} = 0 \tag{6.A.63}$$

where $j = \begin{vmatrix} 1 & 0 & 0 \\ 0 & 1 & 0 \\ 0 & 0 & 1 \end{vmatrix}$

For non-trivial solutions $(a_1\, a_2\, a_3)' \neq 0 \;\Rightarrow |\gamma j - J_E| = 0$ (6.A.64)

(6.A.64) gives the characteristic equation of the dynamic system. Obviously this will be cubic. Substituting from (6.A.60) into (6.A.64), the characteristic equation is obtained as

$$\begin{vmatrix} \gamma & t_1 f'P & 0 \\ I'Q_1^1 & \gamma - I'(f'' - Q_2^1) & -I'(1-Q_3^1) \\ \dfrac{-\lambda I'Q_1^1 Q_2^2}{P - \lambda Q_3^2} & \dfrac{\lambda[Q_2^2 I'(f'' - Q_2^1) - t_1 f'PQ_1^2]}{P - \lambda Q_3^2} & \gamma - \dfrac{[I'(1-Q_3^1)/P - 1]\lambda P}{P - \lambda Q_3^2} \end{vmatrix} = 0$$

(6.A.65)

Expanding the determinant on the LHS of (6.A.65) by its first row the characteristic equation is:

$$\gamma \begin{vmatrix} \gamma - I'(f'' - Q_2^1) & -I'(1-Q_3^1) \\ \dfrac{\lambda[Q_2^2 I'(f'' - Q_2^1) - t_1 f'PQ_1^2]}{P - \lambda Q_3^2} & \gamma - \dfrac{\{I'(1-Q_3^1)/P - 1\}\lambda P}{P - \lambda Q_3^2} \end{vmatrix}$$

$$- t_1 f'P \begin{vmatrix} I'Q_1^1 & -I'(1-Q_3^1) \\ \dfrac{-\lambda I'Q_1^1 Q_2^2}{P - \lambda Q_3^2} & \gamma - \dfrac{\{I'(1-Q_3^1)/P - 1\}\lambda P}{P - \lambda Q_3^2} \end{vmatrix} = 0$$

The intercept term is

$$\frac{t_1 f'PI'(1-Q_3^1)\lambda I'Q_1^1 Q_2^2}{P - \lambda Q_3^2}$$

$$+ \frac{\{t_1 f'PI'(1-Q_3^1)/P - t_1 f'PIQ_1^1\}\lambda P}{P - \lambda Q_3^2} \qquad (6.A.66)$$

(6.A.66) must be positive for stability for stability requires the coefficient of $\gamma^3$ and the intercept to have the same sign. (6.A.66) can be positive only if

$$-\left(\frac{\lambda P}{P - \lambda Q_3^2}\right) > 0 \qquad (6.A.67)$$

i.e., only if $Q_3^2 > 0$. $\Rightarrow$ The necessary condition for stability boils down to

$$Q_3^2 > 0 \quad \Rightarrow \quad \frac{\partial P}{\partial \dot{p}^e} > 0 \tag{6.A.68}$$

i.e. that a rise in inflationary expectations raises the price level. It is also clear from (6.A.67) that the model will not be stable if the speed of adaptation, $\lambda = 0$.

# 7

# KEYNESIAN, MONETARIST, NEW CLASSICAL AND NEW KEYNESIAN MACROECONOMICS

## 7.1 INTRODUCTION

Previous discussion implies that aggregative analysis of a closed economy has remained within the confines of the IS-LM models for more than a generation. Patinkin (1965), Clower (1965), Tobin and Trevithick (1977) and others provided an alternative interpretation of Keynes (1936) in terms of the microfoundations of macroeconomics. Later extensions introduced government budget constraint, flexible prices, variable capital stock, etc. and separated the short-run (or impact) effects of various policies from the long-run (or steady state) and "intermediate" run effects. In Keynesian interpretations the short-run response to monetary and fiscal policy is transmitted mainly by interest rates and depends on interest elasticities of demand for money, for investment etc. A large interest elasticity of the demand for money (investment) increases the short-run response of real output to fiscal (monetary) policy.

A significant area of disagreement between the Keynesians and monetarists seems to be over the short and medium-run effects of fiscal policy on aggregate nominal income. Friedman challenged with his argument that the historical evidence shows changes in the money stock to have a dominating effect on nominal income; pure macro fiscal policy can have only a "temporary" and "minor" impact.

The Keynesian models assume, at least in the short-run, prices and expectations to be constant. Changes in government expenditure, at less than full employment, change real output but have no effect on prices because the price level is fixed. As a consequence, no distinction is made between real and market rates of interest. Debt and capital are regarded as perfect substitutes and wealth effects are relevant only in the long-run.

Although the previous discussion in the book has adopted the relative importance and effectiveness of fiscal and monetary policies as the main area of disagreement between neo-Keynesians and Monetarists there are other versions of what constitute the central issue in the debate between the two groups. Tobin, regards the proposition that "pure fiscal policy does not matter for aggregate real demand, nominal income and price level"[1] as typically monetarist.

On the other hand Stein (1976) defines monetarism as the following three propositions contradicting the Keynesians:

1. Fiscal instruments have to be supported by monetary instruments to exert a net effect on output or the price level. The former on their own can be effective in the short-run but only monetary policy and not fiscal policy, can be used to control the level of aggregate demand for a period longer than a year.
2. Lowering the rate of unemployment below the natural rate requires a continuous rise in the money stock but this leads to a continuous rise in the actual rate of inflation. Inflation is exclusively a monetary phenomenon.
3. There is a consistent though not precise relationship between the rate of growth of the quantity of money and the rate of growth of the nominal income.

## 7.2 STEIN'S MONETARIST MODEL

Stein (1976) developed a general macro model to provide an analytic foundation of monetarism and which "can produce the post keynesian model as a particular case and the monetarist and classical models as alternative cases" (p. 185). The model has seven equations the most important one for the monetarists — Keynesians controversy being the rate of inflation equation. The rate of inflation equation follows from a linear combination of the cost — push and demand pull effects and is gradually developed step by step though the main component equations of the model into the general form:

$$\dot{p} = \dot{p}\,(U, \dot{p}^e, M/P, G, B/M)$$

---

1. Stein, J. (1976), p. 150.

Although the above symbols have been used before, they are to be interpreted slightly differently in the context of Stein's model. Stein measures all demand and supply variables per unit of capital. For the sake of convenience the symbols have not been changed here. It is the algebraic sign of the policy derivative, $\partial \dot{p}/\partial B/M$ ($\equiv \dot{p}_5'$), that, Stein holds, is crucial to the monetarists versus fiscalists debate. The monetarists hold that $\dot{p}_5' \leq 0$ and in the non-monetarists' view $\dot{p}_5' > 0$ Stein also tested which group is irically inconsistent; however his results were not clear-cut in favour of any group.

Stein's monetarist model consists of the following seven equations each of which is derived from very detailed economic reasoning:

$$\dot{w} = h(U) + \alpha + (\dot{p}^e - \dot{p}) \tag{7.1}$$

$$U = F\,[w/A(t), G1] \tag{7.2}$$

$$rn = rn\,(U, \dot{p}^e, M/PK, B/M) \tag{7.3}$$

$$\dot{m} = \dot{n}m - n - \dot{p} \tag{7.4}$$

$$\dot{p} = \dot{p}\,(U, \dot{p}^e, M/PK, B/M) \tag{7.5}$$

$$(d\dot{p}^e/dt) = \lambda(\dot{p} - \dot{p}^e), \quad 0 < \lambda < 1 \tag{7.6}$$

$$G - T = (M/PK)\,[(\dot{B}/M) + \dot{n}m + \dot{n}m(B/M)] \tag{7.7}$$

The equation (7.1) means that the rate of change of real wage depends on the rate of unemployment, rate of change of labour productivity, $\alpha$, and the gap between actual and expected rates of inflation.

Equation (7.2) shows that the rate of unemployment depends on real wage rate, level of technology, $A(t)$, and government employment, $G1$. Stein splits total real government spending per unit of capital into two parts — real spending on labour services per unit of capital, $G1$, and real spending on goods and services per unit of capital, $G$ and assumes $G \geq G1$. The economic theory underlying these two real sector equations is explained in very much detail and monetarists assumptions introduced on the way. The rate of change of money wage is explained by a Walrasian labour market equation (7.8) which states that the rate of change of nominal wage is a linear combination of the expected long-run rate of labour — augmenting or Harrod — Neutral technical progress, $\alpha$, the expected rate of inflation and the rate of excess demand for labour. No difference is assumed between expectations of employers and employees so that $\dot{p}^e$ is both the expected rate of change in the price of output and of the goods purchased by the consumers.

$$(dW/dt)/W = b_1\alpha + b_2\dot{p}^e + b_3(N^d - N^s)/N^s \tag{7.8}$$

Typical monetarists' assumptions are imposed on (7.8) — viz., the coefficient of expected rate is unity and that there is no money illusion $\Rightarrow b_2 = 1$ and $b_1 = 1$ respectively. An alternative basis is provided for assuming $b_2 = 1$ as both employers and employees expect the prices of goods sold and bought to rise by one percentage point, there is no reluctance to raise the money wage by the same.

So, (7.8) is rewritten as:

$$\dot{W}/W = \alpha + \dot{p}^e + b_3(N^d - N^s)/N^s \tag{7.9a}$$

As noted in Chapter 6, excess demand for labour is unobserved but it is assumed to affect the rate of unemployment positively:

$$U = U\,[(N^d - N^s)/N^s], \quad U' < 0 \tag{7.10a}$$

Following the inverse-function rule, (7.10a) yields excess demand

$$(N^d - N^s)/N^s = h\,(U), \quad h' < 0 \tag{7.10b}$$

Substitution of (7.10b) into (7.9a) then yields

$$(\dot{W}/W) = \alpha + \dot{p}^e + h\,(U) \tag{7.9b}$$

where $h = b_3 \cdot U^{-1}$ and $h' < 0$

The rate of change of real wage is the rate of change of money wage minus the actual rate of inflation $\Rightarrow$

$$\dot{w} = (\dot{W}/W) - \dot{p} = \alpha + (\dot{p}^e - \dot{p}) + h\,(U) \tag{7.1}$$

Total employment consists of both private and government employment implying excess demand for labour is to be explained separately for the two sectors. In the private sector excess demand for labour per unit of capital depends inversely on the real wage rate deflated by the level of productivity which grows at the rate, $\alpha$. This is implied by the principles of profit maximisation and marginal productivity theory as already explained in Chapter 3.

The government sector is not assumed to be a profit maximiser. Combining the two sectors, total excess demand for labour is written as (7.11a).

$$[(N^d - N^s)/N^s] = X\,[(W/P)/A(t), GI] \tag{7.11a}$$

where $X'_1 < 0, X'_2 > 0$

Substitution of (7.11a) into (7.10a) yields the macroeconomic equation (7.2):

$$U = F\,[w/A(t), GI]$$

where $F = H[X()], F'_1 > 0$ and $F'_2 < 0$

Although $F'_2 \neq 0$, this does not imply that fiscal policy in the form of changes in $Gl$ can affect the unemployment rate for any sustained period of time. The effect of $Gl$ on $U$ is via real wage $w/A(t)$.

In equations (7.9b) and (7.1) the level of $U$ affects the growth of the nominal wage and the latter then reacts back upon the level of $U$.

In this case, the effect of fiscal policy is much less than in models which assume money wage as exogenous, e.g., the one in Chapter 3.

The nominal rate of interest equation (7.3) is a very general one and it includes real money stock per unit of capital, ratio of bond to money as well as unemployment and anticipated inflation rates as explanatory variables. The nominal rate of interest on bonds is to be such that the demand for bonds equals the supply of bonds. The demand for bonds depends positively on nominal interest rate, quantity of real capital and real money balances and inversely on rent per unit of capital $R$, and the rate of inflation:

$$B = B[rn, M/PK, R, \dot{p}^e] \tag{7.12a}$$

A new assumption is Stein's model is that the rent per unit of capital, $R$ is a function of the rate of unemployment, $R(U)$ which means (7.12a) can be rewritten as:

$$B = B[rn, M/PK, U, \dot{p}^e] \tag{7.12b}$$

It is important to explain the signs of the partial derivatives of (7.12b). A rise in the unemployment rate lowers the rent per unit of capital implying that bonds will be more attractive than real capital $\Rightarrow B'_3 > 0$. A rise in the expected rate of inflation increases the attractiveness of holding real capital relative to bonds (and money) $\Rightarrow B'_3 < 0$. If $rn$ and $\dot{p}^e$ change in the same direction and by the same amount, there will be no substitution effect between bonds and real capital but bonds will be substituted for money the real yield of which declines because of inflation. Stein assumes the net effect on demand for bonds to be positive even if $rn$ and $\dot{p}^e$ change by the same amount $\Rightarrow B'_1 + B'_4 > 0$. As real balances per unit of capital rise investors hold more bonds $\Rightarrow B'_2 > 0$. From (7.12b) one can solve for $rn$ in terms of $U, \dot{p}^e$, etc. and obtain (7.3). Also the signs of partial derivatives of the function, $rn$, can be explained by those of the function, $B: rn'_1 < 0$ from $B'_3 < 0$, $rn'_2 > 0$ from $B'_4 > 0, rn'_3 < 0$ from $B'_2 > 0$ and $rn'_4 > 0$. It is evident by now that the monetarists as opposed to the Keynesians, consider a wide range of assets. The role of investment demand in relation to rent per unit of capital will be explained soon.

The rate of change of real money stock as given in (7.4) is easy to explain and a simple extension of the definition — that growth rate of real stock is a growth of the nominal stock minus the rate of inflation — to include the rate of growth of labour which is equal to the rate of growth of capital in the long run equilibrium:

$$[(\dot{M}/P)/(M/P)] = (\dot{M}/M) - (\dot{K}/K) - (\dot{P}/P) \Rightarrow \dot{m} = \dot{n}m - n - \dot{p} \qquad (7.4)$$

The government budget equation (7.7) is a familiar one. The excess of government spending over taxes both being measured per unit of capital is to be financed by changing money and bonds per unit of capital.

$$G - T = (\dot{B} + \dot{M})/(PK)$$

$$\Rightarrow \quad G - T = \frac{d}{dt}[B + M]/PK$$

$$\Rightarrow \quad G - T = \frac{d}{dt}[(M \times B/M) + M]/PK$$

$$\Rightarrow \quad G - T = [M\,(\dot{B}/M) + (B/M)\dot{M} + \dot{M}]/(PK)$$

$$\Rightarrow \quad G - T = (M/PK)\,[(\dot{B}/M) + (\dot{M}/M)(B/M) + \dot{M}/M]$$

$$\Rightarrow \quad G - T = (M/PK)\,[(\dot{B}/M) + \dot{n}m\,(1 + B/M]$$

The rate of price change equation (7.5) is somewhat broader than what we have come across so far. It combines a cost-push effect with a demand — pull one. The degree of cost-push is the excess of wage rise over rise in labour — productivity measured by $(\dot{W}/W) - \alpha$. The demand pull effect (which we have so far measured by the gap between actual and full-employment output, $Y - \overline{Y}$) is measured by excess demand, i.e., by excess of the sum of consumption, investment and government demand over output per unit of capital:

$$E^d \equiv C + I + G - Y \qquad (7.13a)$$

Where the same symbols have been used to denote the respective items of spending redefined per unit of capital. Output per unit of capital, $Y$ is a declining function of the rate of unemployment and consumption is a positive function of wealth consisting of capitalised output, $Y/R$ and real balances per unit of capital and the ratio of government debt to the stock of money:

$$C = C(Y/R, M/PK, B/M)$$

$$\Rightarrow \quad C = C(U, M/PK, B/M) \qquad (7.13b)$$

where $C_1' < 0, C_2' > 0, C_3' > 0$

The consumption function (7.13b) can be rewritten in terms of government budget balance by solving for $M/PK$ from (7.7) and resubstituting the value in (7.13b) $\Rightarrow$

$$C = C[U, (G-T)/\{(\dot{B}/M) + (1 + B/M)\dot{n}m\}, B/M] \qquad (7.13c)$$

Whenever the budget is not in balance, consumption function can be written as (7.13c). If the debt-money ratio is constant, then consumption will be positively related to government spending

$$\partial C/\partial G = -\partial C/\partial T = (C_2')/(1 + B/M)\dot{n}m \qquad (7.13d)$$

(7.13d) gives the Keynesian fiscal policy multiplier which, in this context, shows that government spending (and government revenue) affects consumption through wealth. Christ (1976) in his comments on Stein's model regards this consumption function as "promonetarist". Because consumption, as in (7.13b) depends on unemployment rate, physical capital, money and bonds, fiscal policy can affect consumption only indirectly through its effect on any of those three variables. Most economists would simply allow for the direct effects of fiscal policy, at least of taxes and transfer payments on consumers' disposable income and thereby in turn, on consumption. Also even at given levels of wealth, changes in interest rates can affect consumption but Stein's model does not allow for that possibility.

The investment demand is derived from a general theory of investment as explained in Keynes (1930) and Tobin (1969). The desired rate of change of the ratio of physical capital to output, $(K/Y)$ depends positively on the ratio of market prices of existing capital and current output, say, $q \equiv \rho/P$ where $e$ is the price per unit of existing capital. If $\rho$ exceeds $P$ ($\Rightarrow q > 1$) it is more profitable to purchase a unit of current output and use it as a capital good. If $P$ exceeds $\rho$ ($\Rightarrow q < 1$), it makes sense to buy a unit of existing capital asset. So there is a demand for investment if $q > 1$ and investment is discouraged if $q < 1$. All durable goods which can produce a flow of goods and services constitute capital goods. The general theory can be formalised as:

$$[(\dot{K}/Y)/(K/Y)] = f(q-1), \quad f' > 0 \qquad (7.14a)$$

(7.14a) can be used to derive investment demand. The L.H.S. of (7.14a) can be rewritten as:

$$(\dot{K}/K) - \dot{Y}/Y = (I/K) - (\dot{Y}/Y) = f(q-1) \tag{7.14b}$$

$\dot{Y}/Y$ is the rate of growth of output which in the long-run equals the rate of growth of effective labour and all investment is with a view to keeping the existing stock of capital intact $\Rightarrow$ no new investment $\Rightarrow q = 1$ $\Rightarrow \dot{Y}/Y = n + d$ where "$d$" is the rate of depreciation $\Rightarrow$ investment demand in (7.14) can be rewritten as:

$$(I/K) = n + d + f(q-1) \tag{7.15a}$$

Finally the price ratio, $q$ is explained by the present value or the marginal efficiency of investment principle. In long run equilibrium marginal efficiency of investment, *MEI* equals the real rate of interest:

$$MEI = rn - \dot{p}^e \text{ in long-run} \Rightarrow R - d = rn - \dot{p}^e \tag{7.15b}$$

where $R$ is the rent per unit of capital. Stein assumes rent per unit of capital to be an inverse function of the rate of unemployment: $R = R(U), R' < 0$. Investment will take place as long as *MEI* exceeds the real rate of interest, i.e., as long as $q$ exceeds unity. In long-run equilibrium when (7.15b) holds, $q = 1$. With this, the investment demand can finally be obtained by replacing $f(q-1)$ in (7.15a) with the function $I$ to give investment per unit of capital as:

$$(I/K) = n + d + I\,[R(U) - d - (rn - \dot{p}^e)]$$

$$\Rightarrow \quad (I/K) = n + d + I\,[R(U) + \dot{p}^e - rn - d] \tag{7.16}$$

Investment increases as long as there is a positive difference between $R(U) - d$ and $rn - \dot{p}^e$

$$\Rightarrow \quad I'[R(U) + \dot{p}^e - rn - d] > 0 \tag{7.17}$$

Substituting for consumption and investment into the excess demand function in (7.13a) the demand pull effect on inflation becomes

$$E^d = C\,(U, M/PK, B/M) + n + d$$

$$+ I\,[R(U) + \dot{p}^e - rn - d] + G - Y(U) \tag{7.18a}$$

$$\Rightarrow \quad E^d = E(U), \dot{p}^e, M/PK, rn, G, B/M) \tag{7.18b}$$

Using a linear combination of the cost-push and the demand pull effects, the price change equation is written as:

$$\dot{p}^e = a_1 \cdot [(\dot{W}/W) - \alpha] + a_2 E^d.$$

Substituting for wage change from (7.9b), for $rn$ from (7.3) and $E^d$ from (7.18), and assuming $a_1 = 1$, the price inflation equation can be written as

$$\dot{p} = \dot{p}^e + h(U) + b_4 E\,[U, \dot{p}^e, M/P, rn(), G, B/M] \tag{7.19}$$

$$\Rightarrow \quad \dot{p} = \dot{p}\,(U, \dot{p}^e, M/P, G, B/M) \tag{7.20}$$

The equation (7.20) is used to highlight the difference between monetarists and Keynesians or fiscalists. Stein defines an important coefficient based on the partial derivative, $\dot{p}_5'$, the sign of which crucially indicates the difference between the two schools. This coefficient is the partial derivative of the price change function w.r.t. the ratio of government debt to money stock. This derivative has more than one component and more than one expression because the nominal rate of interest which figures in the investment demand function is determined in the bond market.

$$\left[\frac{\delta \dot{p}}{\delta(B/M)}\right] \equiv \dot{p}_5' = b_4\left[\left\{\left(\frac{\delta E}{\delta rn}\right) \cdot \frac{\delta rn}{\delta(B/M)}\right\} + \frac{\delta E}{\delta(B/M)}\right]$$

From (7.18a), $\dot{p}_5'$ can be evaluated as:

$$\Rightarrow \quad \dot{p}_5' = b_4\left[\left(\frac{\delta rn}{\delta(B/M)}\right]\frac{\delta I}{\delta rn} + \frac{\delta C}{\delta(B/M)}\right] \tag{7.21}$$

The signs of the derivatives can be explained as follows:

A rise in $B/M$ means as increase in the quantity of interest bearing bonds given real balances per unit of capital. For example a reduction in taxes financed by increasing bond sale will raise $B/M$. $\Rightarrow$ This will raise consumption $\frac{\delta C}{\delta(B/M)} > 0$ and there will be a rise in excess aggregate demand. The other part of the effect can be explained by portfolio balance. To induce people to hold a larger quantity of bonds, $rn$ must be raised $\Rightarrow \frac{\delta rn}{\delta(B/M)}$ is positive but a higher $rn$ discourages investment demand $\Rightarrow \frac{\delta I}{\delta rn} < 0 \Rightarrow \dot{p}_5'$ is the sum of two effects on excess aggregate demand — one of which is stimulating and the other depressing. Stein argues that the entire monetarist — neo-Keynesian controversy hinges on the sign of $\dot{p}_5'$. The price change equations (7.19) and (7.20) are consistent with the monetarist's (e.g., Friedman's) view of the transmission mechanism. A rise in the rate of monetary expansion raises the amount of cash balances relative to other assets; in response, people holding excess cash adjust their portfolios by buying other assets; prices of competitive assets (interest rates) tend to rise (fall); this, in turn, encourages spending to produce new assets and encourages spending on current services and discourages that on existing assets. So agent's attempt to adjust their portfolios finally gets reflected into an effect on income and spending. The difference between Keynesians and monetarists is that the former consider only a narrow range of assets and market interest rates whereas the latter consider a much wider range of assets including durable and semi-durable consumer goods and the entire spectrum of relevant interest rates (Friedman 1970).

Stein's proposition 2 given above has already been considered in the previous Chapter. Monetarists and neo-Keynesians, as already pointed out more than once, disagree on the path that the economy will follow in response to fiscal policy. The logical basis of this disagreement and the steady state characteristics can be discussed in the context of the Stein model.

The monetarist model contained in (7.1)–(7.7) uses the rate of expansion of nominal money stock, $\dot{n}m$, real government spending per unit of capital, $G$ and $G1$ and real taxes per unit of capital, $T$, as the exogenous instruments of control. The endogenous variables of the model are $U, \dot{p}, \dot{p}^e, w, M/P, rn$ and $B/M$. The model can be reduced to just the two equations which can be interpreted as the IS and LM equations in the steady state. Stein's conditions for steady state have been criticised as inadequate. He assumes that in steady state, $U, \dot{M}/M, G$ and $Gl/G$ are constant and that $\dot{p} = \dot{p}^e = 0$. These assumptions give rise to the following implications of the steady state. Using asterisks to denote steady state values, it follows from respective equations of the model

$$h(U^*) = 0 \tag{7.21a}$$

$$w^* = \alpha \tag{7.21b}$$

Since $\dot{P}^* = \dot{p}^{e*} = 0$ the goods market is cleared implying a zero excess demand for goods per unit of capital.

$$\Rightarrow \quad E^{d*} = E(U^*, \dot{P}^{e*}, M/PK, rn, G^*, B/M) = 0 \tag{7.21c}$$

Also the nominal rate of interest at steady state equilibrium.

$$rn^* = rn(U^*, \dot{p}^*, M/PK, B/M) \tag{7.21d}$$

(7.21c) and (7.21d) resemble the IS and LM equations respectively. The nominal interest equation equilibrates the bond market (and not the money market as in the conventional LM equation); so Stein calls (7.21d) the BB′ curve. Since these curves are derived at steady state equilibrium only, the IS-LM model is only a special case of the more general monetarist model. It is clear from (7.21c) and (7.21d) that the two endogenous variables are $rn$ and $M/PK$. The IS and BB′ curves, therefore, are to be drawn in the $(M/PK, rn)$ axes. A rise in real balances per unit of capital will raise excess aggregate demand; so the nominal interest rate must rise to restore equilibrium in the goods market. ⇒ The IS curve must be upward sloping in the $(M/PK, rn)$ axes. On the other hand, a rise in real balances per unit of capital induces a rise in the demand for bonds (as holders of excess cash adjust their portfolio buying other assets); a fall in interest rates is necessary for equilibrium in the bond market. ⇒ The BB′ curve is downward sloping in the $(M/PK, rn)$ axes. The IS and BB′ curves are shown in Fig. 7.1. The effects of policy can be explained in terms of shifts of both curves as before. Let the initial equilibrium be at $S_1$. If the government finances a tax reduction with bond sales both the IS and BB′ shift upward as a result of the rise in $(B/M)$. The reason for the upward shift in the IS curve is that the budget deficit (when $T$ is reduced) raises private wealth and, thereby, consumption demand for goods; only if $rn$ increases sufficiently to crowd out an equal amount of private investment will the goods market be cleared at the given $(M/PK)$ as shown by point $S_2$ in Fig. 7.1.

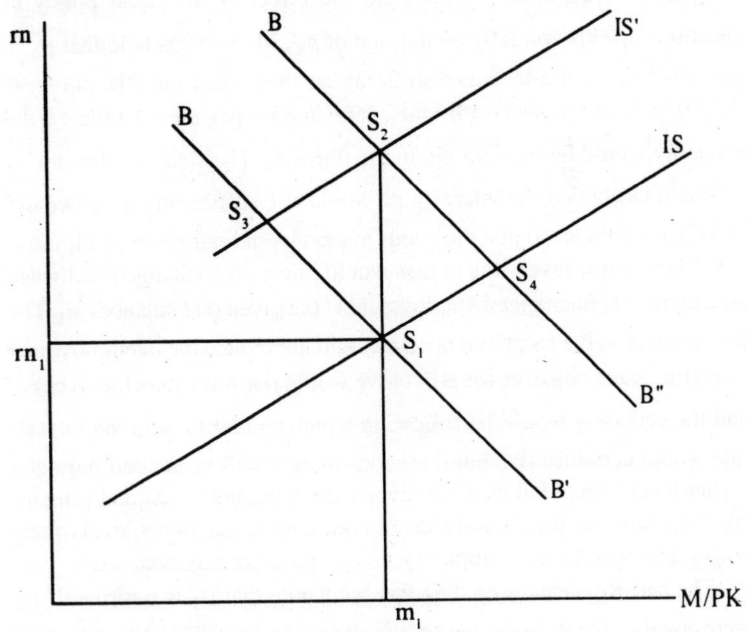


FIG. 7.1

⇒ The IS curve keeps on shifting until $S_2$ is reached. On the other hand the higher $B/M$ (as a result of the deficit) means the bond market can remain in equilibrium only if the nominal rate of interest rises sufficiently. ⇒ The BB′ curve keeps shifting upwards until $S_2$ is reached.

Now from (7.21c) and (7.21d) respectively $\left[\frac{drn}{d(B/M)}\right]$ can be obtained as:

$$\left[\frac{\delta rn}{\delta(B/M)}\right]_{IS} = \frac{E_6'}{(-E_4')} \tag{7.22a}$$

$$\left[\frac{\delta rn}{\delta(B/M)}\right]_{BB'} = rn_4' \tag{7.22b}$$

The difference between the vertical shifts of the IS and BB′ curves per unit of time can be worked out from (7.22) as

$$\left[\frac{E_6'}{-E_4'}\right] - rn_4' = \frac{E_6' + E_4' rn_4'}{-E_4'} = \frac{\dot{p}_5'}{-E_4'} \tag{7.23}$$

A rise in $rn$ lowers investment demand and, therefore, excess demand for goods ⇒ $E_{rn}' < 0 \Rightarrow -E_4' > 0$. So the effect of the fiscal policy in question depends crucially on the sign of $\dot{p}_5'$. Monetarists hold that $\dot{p}_5'$ is non-positive ⇒ the IS curve shifts by no more than the BB′ curve; if $\dot{p}_5' = 0 \Rightarrow$ both curves rise by the same amount per unit of time ⇒ the economy would be moving along the line $S_1S_2$. The final equilibrium at $S_2$ would imply that the interest rate would rise sufficiently to crowd out enough investment so that the goods market would remain in equilibrium at the same price level; this in turn would imply an unchanged real wage and, therefore, unchanged employment at the given real balances $m_1$. The fiscal policy in the form of a tax cut would not reduce the unemployment rate. If $\dot{p}_5'$ were negative the BB′ curve would rise more than the IS curve and the economy would be following a path similar to $S_1S_4$; the interest rate would certainly rise but the goods market will be cleared only at a higher level of real balances; if money stock per unit of capital remains constant the price level would have to fall implying a higher level of real wages and, therefore, a temporary rise in the unemployment rate.

The neo-Keynesians on the other hand hold that $\dot{p}_5'$ is positive. If $\dot{p}_5'$ were positive, the IS curve would move up relative to BB′ and the economy would be moving in the direction $S_1S_3$ implying that equilibrium in the goods market would hold only if real balances per unit of capital declined. At given money stock this would require a rise in the price level leading to a fall in the real wage and, therefore, unemployment. Fiscal policy would be effective in reducing unemployment.

The dynamic analysis of the monetarist and fiscalist positions has been conducted using a model consisting of three dynamic variables, $\dot{U}$, $\dot{p}$ and $\dot{p}^e$. The derivation of the dynamic equations will be discussed in the Appendix 7.A.1. For empirical testing the following dynamic equations were chosen by Stein:

$$\begin{bmatrix} \dot{U} \\ \dot{p} \end{bmatrix} = [a_{ij}] \begin{bmatrix} U \\ P \end{bmatrix} + [b_{ij}] \begin{bmatrix} \dot{G} \\ \dot{M}/M \\ (\dot{B}/M) \end{bmatrix} \tag{7.24}$$

where $[a_{ij}]$ is a $(2 \times 2)$ and $[b_{ij}]$ a $(2 \times 3)$ matrix of coefficients of respective variables. $a_{ij}$'s and $b_{ij}$'s are derived in (7.A.10).

The results of estimating (7.24) were in Stein's words "not clear cut" except when he integrated them over an arbitrary interval of time. Christ (1976) criticised the econometric specification (7.24) as being incapable of performing a number of important functions. For example, it cannot

(a) explain what determines the equilibrium price level itself;
(b) study the effect of a balanced budget step increase in both $G$ and $T$ at the same time;
(c) study the policy effect of changes in money and bond holdings brought about by an open market operation;
(d) study the effect of past interest rates upon unemployment or inflation or;
(e) study the role of expectations in the economy in shaping the latter's reaction to fiscal or monetary policies.

Some of the empirical results obtained by Stein lend muscles to the monetarist view. For example, increase in the rate of growth of money stock have large and statistically significant effects in reducing unemployment and raising inflation whereas increases in the rate of growth of the stock of bonds have small but statistically significant effects raising unemployment and reducing inflation.

Christ points out that the ratio of money to bonds should also have been regarded as constant under steady state.

### 7.3 NEW CLASSICAL MACROECONOMICS (NCM)

Keynesian economics was also attacked by the group known as new classical economists. The new classical school criticised Keynesian macroeconomics on a number of grounds [Pesaran, (1982)]:

(a) The behavioural relations in Keynesian macromodels cannot be derived from optimising behaviour of individual consumers and entrepreneurs and, therefore, it does not have any microfoundations.

Various attempts by the neo-Keynesians to provide such microfoundations have already been discussed in Chapter 3—e.g., by Clower, Leijonhufvud, Tobin and Trevithick, etc. But the new classical economists regard these foundations as "totally unsound".[2]

(b) It denies market clearing by price and wage movements and, therefore, cannot be a realistic description of capitalist market economics. Some retionalisation for sticky wages has been provided in terms of implicit contract theory. The contributions of Azariadis and Grossman will be discussed later on in the present Chapter.

(c) Expectations are formed on an ad hoc basis and in a non-rational way.

Consequently, the NCM chooses to analyse macroeconomic behaviour within a classical framework of market clearing and optimising behaviour of agents.

Lucas (1972) is generally regarded as the founder of the NCM. This system of thought generally adheres to the NRU hypothesis of Friedman (1967) and Phelps (1968) already discussed in Chapter 6 and the RE hypothesis due to Muth (1961).[3] Friedman and Phelps's emphasis on adjustment lags in expectation (e.g., in the adaptive expectation rule) was replaced by an emphasis on information lags in Lucas and Rapping (1969) and Phelps (1970) and incomplete information became a general feature

2. Levacic and Rebman (1982, p. 361).

3. As McMahon (1984) points out, RE idea was put forward by Knight (1921) long before Muth.

of the NCM models. Without lags either in the adjustment of or in the transmission of information about prices and wages, business cycles would never occur.[4] Barro (1981) provides an excellent review of the business cycle models based on the new classical ideas. In this review, he summarises the major characteristics of the NCM as:

(a) continuous market clearing;
(b) rational formation of expectation;
(c) imperfect information about some current aggregate variables;
(d) a Lucas-type supply function; and
(e) a natural rate hypothesis.

Because of its reliance on RE hypotheses, the NCM is sometimes referred to as rational expectations macroeconomics. Unlike in the Keynesian tradition, the NCM places at least equal, if not greater, emphasis on the aggregate supply which is thought to depend on a relative price to be explained in Lucas's sense; for this, NCM is occasionally referred to as supply side economics.

This class of models looks at business cycles as equilibrium phenomena — changes in relative prices leading to movements in output and employment. These relative prices are derived under imperfect information conditions — e.g., in Phelps "islands" models (1970). There exists a large number of localised markets or "islands" where individuals receive current information on local prices, $P_{it}$ for the $i$th market, $i = 1, 2, \cdots$ but only lagged information, if at all, on the general price level or on the other aggregate variables in the economy. In influencing individual workers' and employers' behaviour, local prices are far more important than the aggregate variables. The local prices are determined not only by various relevant local factors, e.g., technology, tastes, available skill specific to respective "islands" but also by completely unperceived or inadequately perceived nominal aggregate variables. Under imperfect information the agents attempt to purge the general price component from their observed price signals in making their decisions. So, the relevant price variable in the demand and supply functions in the $i$th market or 'island' is $(P_{it} - E_{it}P_{t+1})$ where $P_{it}$ is the currently observed

4. Nelson (1981), p. 1.

price in the $i$th market and $E_{it}P_{t+1}$ is the rational expectation formed in the $i$th market about the general price level in the next future period. Now such a comparison of current prices with future expected but undiscounted prices means that paper money which earns a zero nominal rate of return is the only available asset. To make the model wider and include a wider range of assets, this price variable ought to be modified to $P_{it}-(E_{it}P_{t+1}-rn_{it})\equiv RP_{it}$, say; where $rn_{it}$ is the current nominal interest rate in the $i$th market. The composite variable $RP_{it}$ is the expected one-period real rate of return in the $i$th market. Aggregate supply functions of relative price $(P_t-E_tP_{t+1})$ have been used in many applications of NCM models and some of these have already been discussed in Chapter 6.

Lucas (1972) in his seminal contribution to NCM constructed a model using Samuelson's (1958) over-lapping generations framework. Each period, $N$ identical individuals are born and they live for two periods, $t$ and $t+1$. In each period, therefore, there is a constant population of $2N$, $N$ of age $O$ and $N$ of age 1.

The individuals work and produce commodities only in the first period and each person supplies in units of labour yielding the same $n$ units of output. The latter cannot be stored; so the younger generation sell some of their output to the older generation for money and accumulate money balances as the only asset. Under such conditions, the economy will experience fluctuations in real output whenever $n$ varies.

The only function of the government is issuing money and injecting it in the economy at the beginning of each period to the older half of the population in proportion to the quantity already held. Any money left unspent by the older generation goes back to the issuer.

Lucas considers two cases:

(a) Trading takes place in two separate markets with a known monetary injection; and
(b) Trading takes place in one big market with an unknown money injection.

In case (a) markets are assumed to have no transfer between them during the period. Most importantly information is made incomplete or imperfect by making the model stochastic on two accounts:

(a) the younger traders are randomly allocated across markets and this introduces fluctuations in relative prices between the two markets; and

(b) there are random changes in the quantity of money.

Prices in the agents' own market cannot convey the above information on real and nominal disturbances or changes in the economy completely or perfectly. The agents are therefore unable to determine whether the change in price, if any, is done to local real shocks (i.e., changes in relative demand across local markets) or to global monetary shocks. This results into non-neutrality of money as an unknown monetary disturbance can fool agents into thinking that relative prices have moved in favour of raising labour-supply and producing more output. But such support for Phillips curve is bound to be short lived and in the long-run, i.e., in case (b) the classical results on neutrality of money or independence of real and nominal variables continue to hold. In addition, Lucas shows that in the "boom" periods all agents will be better off than in the average periods — older generation because they receive the monetary injection causing the boom and the younger generation will feel better off only until they realise that higher than expected prices for their output or services have been exactly compensated by a rise in the global price level. In the case of just one big market with an unknown monetary injection local relative price changes will be known to all agents and the absence of any real shocks will prevent agents from being misled into thinking that relative prices have risen as nominal shocks change only the nominal global price level.

Lucas offered extensions of this basic model in 1973 and 1975 by including, respectively, a multiple market framework and capital accumulation. In the 1973 paper he considered "some international evidence' on the Phillips curve including 18 countries and the time period 1953-67. It was basically a test of Lucas's own version of the aggregate supply function and not a straight forward test of Friedman's NRU hypothesis in terms of the coefficient of expected rate of inflation being equal to one in the equation (6.1). The log-linear form of the aggregate supply functions was a slightly extended version of (6.34):

$$\log Y_{it} = \log \overline{Y}_{it} + \log Y_{ict} \tag{7.22a}$$

$$\log \overline{Y}_{it} = a + bt \tag{7.22b}$$

$$\log Y_{ict} = a_0 [\log P_{it} - \log P_t^e] + a_1 \log Y_{ict-1} \tag{7.22c}$$

The first equation explains that the output in each market has a secular or 'normal' component and a cyclical component denoted with the subscript $c$. The equation (7.22b) explains the normal output level by a linear trend and the cyclical component of output is affected by any discrepancy between actual and expected price levels and its own logged value as shown in (7.22c). As already explained $P_t^e$ is the expectation of the global price level formed rationally in each market with full local and incomplete global information. The required restriction on $a_1$ is that it be less than one. The aggregate supply function is then derived from (7.22) on the basis of a "correct" distribution of the unobserved current price level, $P_t$. This distribution of the price variable is made dependant on current and past exogenous demand shifts and actual real output levels and the normal level of output which constitute the "relevant history" of the economy. Assuming the demand shifts to be independent and normally distributed variables the equilibrium values of the rate of inflation and real output are derived in terms of such mean and variance and lagged demand shifts and lagged supply. These equilibrium values are the intersection points of an aggregate demand schedule shifted by changes in exogenous shift variables and an aggregate supply schedule shifted by variables such as lagged prices which determine expectations. Lucas mentions the observed value of the logarithm of nominal GNP as a possible exogenous shift variable affecting aggregate demand. During the period under consideration Lucas's tests establish that in a stable price country like the U.S.A., policies which increase nominal income tend to have a large initial effect on real output together with a small but positive initial effect on the rate of inflation. On the other hand in a volatile price country of which Argentina is an example, nominal income changes are accompanied by price changes with no discernible effect on real output.

In his 1975 paper, Lucas extends the basic model of 1972 to include capital accumulation. It is shown that a neoclassical growth model including money is incapable of explaining the cyclical movements of real and nominal variables observed in reality. This is because in the neoclassical economy with perfect competition, there is full and complete information in the hands of all traders. As a direct result of this, no trader ever alters the real decision variables in response to a change in nominal variable. Going back to the islands model next, trading is assumed to take place in a continuum of markets with an incentive for capital accumulation. With serially correlated monetary injections in each market, Lucas shows that unsystematic monetary shocks and an accelerator effect interact and generate serially correlated cyclical movements in real output. In addition Lucas is able to show that a business cycle cannot occur if all trading takes place in one big market. In this extended model the accelerator effect varies inversely with the variance of nominal shocks impinging upon the economy and tends to dampen the price effects of monetary expansion. Extra capital generates extra future productive capacity and raises potential supply of future goods. Capital stock is eventually brought back to its normal level through disinvestment. So there is a period when investment and employment are below the normal level. Monetary effects will linger until the required disinvestment takes place to bring the capital stock back to its normal level.[5]

Barro in his review explains the mathematical formulation of this new classical group of equilibrium business cycle models in a relatively simple way. His approach is adapted here. As already pointed out such models typically incorporate a positive speculative response of supply to perceived excesses of observed prices over expected values the latter reflecting obviously higher than usual real rate of return opportunities. On the demand side, this "relative price" variable exerts a negative effect.

The existence of a speculative demand effect necessitates a symmetric treatment of the aggregate demand and supply functions in NCM models and this obviously is a new feature of this group of models. In the log-linear form these can be written as (7.23) and (7.24) for the *i*th market.

$$\log Y_{it}^{s} = a_1 \log RP_t + a_2(\log M_t - \log M_{it}^{e}) + e_{1t} \tag{7.23}$$

$$\log Y = a_3 \log RP_t + a_4(\log M_t - \log M_{it}^{e}) + e_{2t} \tag{7.24}$$

(7.23) and (7.24) are, respectively, the aggregate supply and the aggregate demand equations for the *i*th market implying that $a_1 > 0$, $a_3 < 0$, $a_2 < 0$ and $a_4 > 0$ and $e_1$ and $e_2$ are random shocks for the *i*th market and they

5. McMahon, M.R., (1984).

sum to zero in aggregation over markets. Assuming that goods do not travel across markets, and that local prices are completely flexible, the equilibrium condition for the $i$th market is:

$$\log Y_{it}^{s} = \log Y_{it}^{d} = \log Y_{it} \tag{7.25a}$$

(7.25a) implies that one can derive expressions for local output and expected real rate of return as follows:

Multiplying the supply equation by $a_3$ and demand equation by $a_1$ and subtracting the former from the latter one obtains (7.26)

$$(a_1 - a_3)\log Y_{it} = (a_4 a_1 - a_2 a_3)(\log M_t - \log M_{it}^{e})$$

$$+ a_1 e_{2t} - a_3 e_{it}$$

$$\Rightarrow \quad \log Y_{it} = 1/(a_1 - a_3)[(a_4 a_1 - a_2 a_3)(\log M_t - \log M_{it}^{e})$$

$$+ (a_1 e_4 - a_3 e_{it})] \tag{7.26}$$

An expression for $RP_{it}$ can be obtained by simply applying the equilibrium condition:

$$\log Y_{it}^{s} - \log Y_{it}^{d} = 0 \tag{7.25b}$$

Subtracting (7.24) from (7.23),

$$0 = (a_1 - a_3)\log RP_{it} + (a_2 - a_4)(\log M_t - \log M_t^{e})$$

$$+ (e_{1t} - e_{2t})$$

$$\Rightarrow \quad \log RP_{it} = 1/(a_1 - a_3)[(a_2 - a_4)(\log M_t - \log M_t^{e})$$

$$+ (e_{1t} - e_{2t})] \tag{7.27}$$

Final solutions are to be obtained from (7.26) and (7.27) by specifying the distribution of $P_{it}$'s, explaining $rn_{it}$ (which is included in the composite variable, $RP_{it}$) and the expectational variables. Before going on to the final solutions, it can be pointed out that the equations (7.26) and (7.27) are important because they specify a number of general properties attributable to this class of equilibrium business cycle models. For example they show that:

(i) it is only the unexpected part of money growth which affects real output and expected real rate of return. Sargent's contribution in this respect has already been discussed in Chapter 6.

(ii) this important role of unexpected component of money growth is a result of excess demand depending on money shocks, i.e., on $a_2$ and $a_4$ and it does not depend on the particular definition of $RP_{it}$.

(iii) Since money shocks affect excess demand positively, the relative price variable, $RP_{it}$ also increases with unperceived money growth for the sake of local market clearing.

(iv) The net effect of money shocks on output will depend on the relative magnitudes of elasticities, $a_2$ and $a_4$. For the net effect to be positive the demand elasticity $a_4$ ought to be greater than the supply elasticity $|a_2|$., and that

(v) This key role of money shocks in influencing real variables is due to incomplete information on nominal aggregates. The effects of money shocks on real variables would disappear if the quantity of money supply and the global price level were observed without a significant time lag or if they could be predicted accurately from the observed behaviour of local commodity prices and nominal rates of return. The model generalised above in (7.23)–(7.27) is a single period model and cannot, therefore, deal with persistence of the impact of unexpected shocks.

The model summarised in (7.23)–(7.27) can be solved (as shown in Chapter 6) by introducing a standard demand function for money, such as (6. ), a "correct" distribution for $P_{it}$, rational expectations rules for $P^e_{it}$ and $M^e_{it}$ (or their logarithms) and then deriving $RP_{it}$. The classical result of neutrality of money will hold if the traders have full information implying $M^e_{it} = M_t$ and, therefore, implying in turn that output and expected real rate of return are equal to respective natural values. Barro (1981) regards the reliance of these models on incomplete information as a shortcoming. The policy irrelevance result of macromodels has already been discussed in very much detail in Chapter 6.

Equilibrium business cycle models have also been criticised for their reliance on market clearing. Policy effectiveness or the lack of it has also been demonstrated to depend on a type of wage and price stickiness. The contributions of Fisher and Phelps and Taylor in this respect have already been discussed in the previous Chapter. Barro (1981) points out that the role of incomplete current information on nominal aggregates in NCM parallels that of adjustment costs in Keynesian macroeconomics. In the latter workers refuse to accept a cut in money wages (as this destroys the wage differentials) and sticky wages and prices lead to "inefficient determination" of quantities.

So the underpinning of both types of models is weak. However the NCM provides important econometric insights into the interplay between expectations and policy shifts and into the natural rate hypothesis. Pesaran (1982) closely examines the joint tests of natural rate (NR) and rational expectation hypothesis carried out in the literature with a view to judging the superiority of the new classical to the Keynesian approach to unemployment. This is regarded as important because the policy ineffectiveness proposition of the NCM stands or falls with NR/RE hypothesis. He uses the LSW framework and critically reviews the information availability assumption vital to RE hypothesis and Barro's "important and influential" tests of the NR/RE hypothesis. The main points of his paper are summarised here:

(i) The objections to the RE hypothesis do not arise because the individuals are assumed to use the available information "optimally" but because the amount of information the individuals are assumed to possess is "excessive and unacceptable".

(ii) There are some methodological ambiguities in Lucas (1972) and Sargent (1973)'s joint tests of the NR/RE.

(iii) Barro's joint tests (1977) suffer from a number of defects as well:

  (a) His empirical results cannot be given a satisfactory theoretical explanation;

  (b) A Keynesian type of unemployment equation fitted Barro's data (for testing NR/RE) equally well implying that the NR/RE hypothesis cannot be accepted against its rival explanation. Pesaran computed an $F$-statistic[6] to test the Keynesian against Barro's hypothesis and it showed that neither hypothesis was capable of rejecting the other.

---

6. Such an $F$-Statistic compares the residual sum of squares relative to the degree of freedom of each regression. For example:
$= [(RSS_K - RSS_N)/d]/(RSS_K)/d_K$ where $K$ and $N$ stand for Keynesian and NR hypothesis respectively and $d$ for differences in degrees of freedom in the Keynesian eq.

(iv) On the basis of the above findings, Pesaran concludes that Barro or Sargent's tests do not provide any empirical basis for rejecting the Keynesian explanations of unemployment.

## 7.4 NEW-KEYNESIAN ECONOMICS: MICRO FOUNDATIONS

Like Pesaran, Alan Blinder (1988) has put forward a strong defense for Keynesian economics. He admits that the main weakness of Keynesian economics is the lack of microeconomic foundations and because of this shortcoming, it could not explain the breakdown of the Phillips curve in the late sixties; but it is Keynesian theory which explains the events of the eighties in the USA and in Europe much better than the new Classical theory. According to the new Classical theory anticipated monetary policy should not have any effects. Yet severe recessions resulted in the USA and the UK following the adoption of tight money policies by the Bank of England and the Federal Reserve. According to old Keynesian theory, the contractionary effects of anti-inflationary monetary policies are anything but surprising. The Keynesian theory can also explain the deep depression in Europe in a pretty straight forward manner. It was the direct result of the highly restrictive monetary policies pursued by the British and German central banks strengthened by the European Monetary System.

Blinder compares Keynesian with monetary and new classical economics on the following points:

(a) The rift between Keynesians and the monetarists on the straight forward roles for fiscal and monetary policies seems to be narrowing down in the decade of the Eighties. Most modern Keynesians and monetarists now believe that both fiscal and monetary policies can affect aggregate demand. However, the possibility still exists that monetary policy might destroy the macroeffects of fiscal policy by controlling nominal GNP. The new classical doctrine of debt neutrality however contradicts the Keynesians on this tenet.

(b) Changes in demand lead to positive multiplier effects on real income. Whereas most monetarists accept the monetary counterpart of these Keynesian effects the new classicals hold that only the unanticipated changes in money affect the real output.

(c) Both the monetarists and the new classicals are in disagreement with the Keynesians on the sluggish response of the market forces. That markets clear is a distinctive feature of new classical economics but prices and wages move too slowly for market clearing in the Keynesian system.

(d) New classicals differ sharply from Keynesians on the latters' involuntary unemployment issue. Keynesian economics does not provide a strong theoretical justification for unemployment being both high and variable. The monetarists assume a somewhat intermediate position on this issue. Keynesians unlike the monetarists and new classicals advocate interventionist policies to reduce the amplitude of business cycles regarded as important disequilibrium phenomena. In new classical economics business cycles are consistent with equilibrium.

(e) In Keynesian economics, the discussion of and remedies to the problem of unemployment always received higher priority than that of inflation.

The previous discussion in the book makes it clear that the monetarists have debated with the Keynesians mainly on points (d) and (e) above whereas the new classicals have attacked the non-market-clearing aspect more vigorously. Also cyclical fluctuations are not only regarded as equilibrium phenomena but their importance is also open to question in NCM.

Blinder agrees with Fischer and Phelps and Taylor that the RE hypothesis does not constitute a real difference between keynesian and new classical economics as the former is consistent with the RE rule. Like Pesaran (1982) Blinder also holds that joint tests of NRU and RE are generally unfavourable to the NCM whereas the Phillips curve modified to include supply shocks and to be treated as part of keynesian economics can explain the events of the eighties in the USA and Europe.[7]

Blinder (1988), Gordon (1990) and Mankiw (1990) all agree that the main ingredients of a solid, firmer Keynesian economics to be called New Keynesian economics can be obtained from the following which therefore constitute the theoretical foundations of new Keynesian economics:

---

7. Blinder, A.S. (1988), p. 288.

(a) Price-setting behaviour of firms lies at the root of Keynesian non-market-clearing models. This calls for a monopolistic or an imperfectly competitive market structure as the agents are not price takers but price setters. In a monopolistic set-up, prices are higher than marginal costs implying that the firms would like to sell more at current prices. Output produced or sold always falls short of the socially optimum level as social welfare can be increased as long as total benefit exceeds total costs, i.e., till the point, *E* is reached in Fig. 7.2 Instead an output level like *OF* being sold under an imperfectly competitive market, output and, therefore, employment would be consistent with Keynesian less than full-employment level.

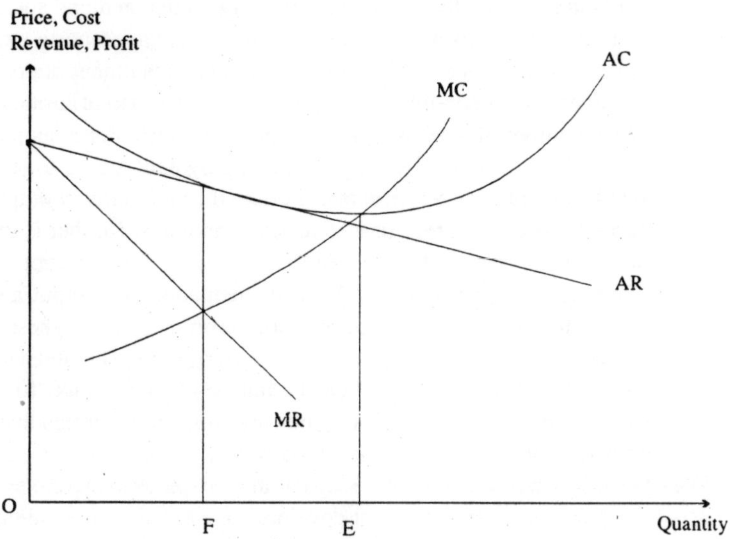


FIG. 7.2

A Fig. like 7.2 can be reproduced from any textbook of microeconomics. Under monopolistic competition the demand, i.e., the average revenue AR line is downward sloping and fairly though not infinitely elastic. Equilibrium output is obtained at the level where marginal cost, *MC* is equal to marginal revenue, *MR* and *MC* exceeds *MR* thereafter. Because of a large number of atomistic firms, the output sold can be where average cost, *AC* is just equal to average revenue, i.e., where *AC* curve is tangent to the AR line; but such tangency, given the negative slope of $AR$, is bound to occur to the left of the point, $E$, implying that social benefit is not being maximised.

However, the monopolistic market structure as summarised above is still based on theory of relative prices and not on nominal prices emphasised in Keynesian economics. This problem has been tackled by adding fixed costs of changing money prices. The fixed or menu costs of changing prices in response to, say, a small drop in money supply may discourage firms to actually cut the absolute prices although theoretically the latter should change equiproportionately with money supply. The result of nominal prices falling less than proportionately with money supply is a decline in real balances and, therefore, a decline in real demand and social welfare. The results will be reversed for a less than proportionate rise in absolute prices in response to a small rise in money supply. However, the monopolistic price theory is still not in total harmony with a number of aspects of Keynesian economics. For example, while it can explain why output and employment are below the socially desirable levels, it cannot explain the variability or output fluctuations as required for Keynesian economics. Neither is the monopolistic price theory comfortable with the concept of involuntary unemployment. Cyclical fluctuations of output and employment as already noted are quite prominent in Keynesian economics and such fluctuations can be eased by fiscal or monetary stabilisation policies; but given the nature of explanation for a socially sub-optimum level of output, the policy prescription from the monopolistic models is an output subsidy.

(b) The other ingredient of new Keynesian economics is involuntary unemployment. In the recent developments of micro and labour theories explanations have been provided for the occurrence of involuntary unemployment. For example efficiency wage models, implicit contract theory, etc., all explain how unemployment can arise even when markets are otherwise in equilibrium. These theories will be discussed in some detail in the following section.

(c) Keynesian economics assumes an hysteresis in the market system. Prices, wages, etc. are sluggish to respond to shocks. But a theoretical basis for such hysteresis has to be provided in the new and improved version of Keynesian economics. Labour market theories based on the conflict between trade union members called 'insiders' and workers not belonging to trade unions called 'outsiders' provide important examples of hysteresis models. The following section includes a brief discussion on union wage bargaining models.

### 7.4.1 *Microfoundations of New-Keynesian Economics* *Implicit Contract Theory*

The classical theory of competitive markets holds that both real wages and employment fall (rise) in response to a fall (rise) in the demand for output. Such price flexibility can be ensured only by a smooth and continuous operation of an auction market. This is why the classical/neo-classical wage price determination models are often referred to as complete auction models where Pareto optimality is obtained as a rule rather than as an exception. But this complete auction model cannot explain the frequently observed phenomenon that in a recession unneeded workers are made redundant whereas the rest of the workforce enjoy the same wages. Keynes and Keynesians like Patinkin, Clower and others chose to account for this deviation from Pareto optimality by adhering to the assumption of non-market clearing and quantity rather than price adjustment in response to changes in demand for output.

In the 1970's another line of research initiated by Bailey (1974) Azariadis (1975), Grossman (1979) put forward an alternative explanation of wage rigidity. Wages take time to change because of mutual understanding — an "implicit contract" — between firms and workers that there be some security of wages and employment for a reasonable and "more or less understood"[8] period of time. The auction model cannot be applied very successfully to labour for two main reasons:

(a) Relative immobility over markets due to occupational or geographical reasons; and
(b) Markets for exchanging claims on future labour services are virtually non-existent.

Under such circumstances workers indulge in risk shifting. The risk of an uncertain income stream of workers is transferred to that of the employers. The latter undertake a commitment either legal or verbal to

8. Gordon, D. (1974, p. 76).

guarantee their workers wages, hours of work, etc. even under conditions of falling demand for output. If there is a contraction in product demand and price unchanged wages will have to be paid out of profits. It goes without saying that the firms will not be willing to extend such generosity or informal agreement to their entire personnel. They have to investigate each worker's qualifications very carefully and likewise each worker has to check out a potential employer's offer. Employers are expected to favour workers with higher productivity, reliability, adaptability, etc. and those in whose training firms have already undertaken substantial investment. Also labour income will not be substantial at the cost of profit if there is any fear of bankruptcy. Risk shifting of labour income still remains a reasonable assumption because the firm's net worth far outweighs that of an average worker and because the entrepreneurs are assumed to be "risk neutral".

Implicit contract theory is based on the assumption that workers are risk-averse and employers are risk-neutral or at least the employers are less risk-averse than their workers.

The workers compare all available (implicit) contracts before the demand situation facing any industry is known. The range of contracts offered by each firm will depend on its attitude towards risk, the variety of skill in its workforce, administrative costs of striking, monitoring and enforcing each agreement, the duration of each agreement etc. The valuation of a contractual offer by workers is inversely related to the size of the labour force. The larger the number of people agreeing to a contract, the smaller will be the chance of everyone being included in the contract. The equilibrium condition in this respect is interpreted such that "no economic agent values the bargain he/she has actually agreed to less than any other feasible contract".[9] Such contracts are generally regarded as enforceable since otherwise the firm runs the risk of being labelled as a "cheater". Implicit contract theory assumes, implicitly, that there is a market in labour contracts rather than in labour itself.[10]

Nickell (1990) reviews theories of unemployment including implicit contract and efficiency wage models. Optimal labour contracts as explained above imply a "sticky" real wage for the risk averse workers whereas the risk neutral firms absorb the income fluctuations. The

---

9. Azariadis, (1975) p. 1185.
10. Hall and Taylor (1988), p. 446.

efficiency wage idea follows from the implicit contract model. Although it is difficult to observe productivity higher wages are likely to ensure efficiency and raise workers' efforts by raising the opportunity cost of unemployment. So in the efficiency wage model an individual workers' efforts are made an increasing function of wages paid by the firm in equation relative to wages paid elsewhere and unemployment:

$$e = e\left(\frac{W_i}{\overline{W}}, U\right), \quad e_1' > 0, e_2' > 0 \tag{7.28}$$

Firm's revenue then can be regarded as a function of total efforts, $e \cdot N_i$, and demand factors. With the help of such a revenue function the emergence of long-run unemployment from efficiency wage model can be shown as a consequence of "profit maximisation": The firm maximises the difference between revenue and total wage costs; unlike in the competitive market model of Chapter 3, both the wage paid by the firm and its employment $N_i$ are variables. The *i*th firm maximises the

$$A_i TR\left[e\left(\frac{W_i}{\overline{W}}, U_i\right)N_i\right] - W_i N_i \tag{7.29}$$

where $A_i$ stands for factors affecting the demand for the *i*th firm's output and *TR* the total revenue function. Necessary conditions for maximising (7.29) are (7.30a) and (7.30b):

$$A_i TR'\left(\frac{e_1'}{\overline{W}}\right)N_i - N_i = 0$$

$$\Rightarrow \quad \frac{A_i TR' e_1'}{\overline{W}} - 1 = 0$$

$$\Rightarrow \quad A_i TR' e_1' = \overline{W} \tag{7.30a}$$

and $\quad A_i TR' \cdot e - W_i = 0$

$$\Rightarrow \quad A_i TR' e = W_i \tag{7.30b}$$

Eliminating the common factors (7.30a) and (7.30b) can be combined as the single condition (7.31):

$$\left[\frac{(e_1')}{e}\right] = \frac{\overline{W}}{W_i}$$

$$\Rightarrow \quad e_1' \cdot \left(\frac{W_i}{\overline{W}}\right) = e\left(\frac{W_i}{\overline{W}}, U\right) \tag{7.31}$$

There are two important points to note about (7.31)

(i) It implies that the factors affecting the demand for the firm's output (as included in $A_i$) have no effect on the wage setting; and

(ii) If there are a large number of identical firms such that $W_i = \overline{W}$ in equilibrium, then (7.31) shows that equilibrium unemployment is given by (7.32):

Putting $W_i = \overline{W}$ in (7.31) yields

$$e_1' = e \Rightarrow e_1'(1, U) = e\,(1, U) \qquad (7.32)$$

This unemployment will differ from the competitive unemployment [Nickell (1990), p.409].

On an additional assumption, the efficiency wage model can generate unemployment even if $W_i \neq W_j$ for $i \neq j$, i.e; even if efficiency wages are not paid by all firms but are confined to only a small sector of the economy. The assumption is that it is easier to obtain a job in the efficiency wage sector from unemployment than from a job in the low wage competitive sector. This type of unemployment, therefore, can be regarded as 'wait' or 'queue' unemployment.

An objection to the efficiency wage idea was given by the "bonding critique" [Nickell (1990), p. 410]. Workers do not have to be paid efficiency wages to perform better. An alternative is that workers post a performance bond when they take up a job and that they forfeit this bond if they perform badly. The existence of rising wage profiles seems to support this idea of bond payment. On the bond payment idea payment of efficiency wages is ruled out and so the resulting unemployment disappears.

Overall however there is evidence in favour of the efficiency wage idea. As long as there are benefits accruing to a firm from higher wages. There will be an incentive for the firm to pay efficiency wages. Such benefits include the following:

(i) higher wages enable firms to attract better qualified job candidates;

(ii) higher wages reduce quitting rates;

(iii) higher wages lead to lower hiring/training costs [Nickell (1990), p. 412].

## 7.5 UNION WAGE BARGAINING

A simple model of union wage bargaining assumes that the union's utility is an increasing function of wage and employment:

$$V(W, N), V_1' > 0, V_2' > 0 \tag{7.33}$$

Firm's profit being the difference between revenue and wage costs is also a function of wage and employment:

$$\pi(W, N), \pi_1' < 0, \quad \pi_2' > 0 \tag{7.34}$$

If the union negotiates with the firm and wages are set bilaterally, then the outcome has to satisfy the conditions of maximising (7.33) and (7.34) simultaneously:

$$\frac{V_1'}{V_2'} = \frac{\pi_1'}{\pi_2'} \tag{7.35a}$$

If the firm sets employment unilaterally, then employment must lie on the labour demand curve or satisfy the conditions:

$$\frac{\delta \pi_i}{\delta N_i} = 0 \quad \text{or} \quad \pi_{i2}' = 0 \tag{7.35b}$$

The outcome (7.35a) can be consistent with (7.35b) only if the union is indifferent to employment, i.e., if $V_2' = 0$. Alogoskoufis and Manning (1989) have presented evidence why the wage employment data may not lie on a labour demand curve implying a conflict between (7.35a) and (7.35b). The idea of efficiency wages discussed above, for example, constitutes evidence against the notion of a standard labour demand curve to explain the observed wage employment data. Conditions (7.35a) and (7.35b) can be consistent if workers were laid off on, say, a "last in first out" basis.

There is no clear-cut evidence, as yet, whether the unions bargain over employment or not.

Assuming that unions bargain only over wages and firms set employment, a static model can be developed as follows to explain the emergence of unemployment from wage bargaining. The standard model in this context is that due to Nash (1983). First the utility function of the union takes explicit account of the membership and is written as:

$$V(W_i, N_i) = \begin{cases} N_i V(W_i) + (q_i - N_i) V^e \text{ for } q_i \geq N_i \\ q_i V(W_i) \text{ for } q_i < N_i \end{cases} \tag{7.36}$$

where $q$ is exogenous membership prior to the bargain, $V$ is the utility function of the representative member and $V^e$ is the expected utility of workers outside the union. $V^e$ is assumed a function of outside wage, unemployment benefit, $b$, and the proportion of the period for which the workers is unemployed, $t(U)$:

$$V^e = V(\overline{W})[1 - t(U)] + V(b) \cdot t(U) \tag{7.37}$$

Since the firm is assumed to set only the level of employment its profit function is rewritten solely in terms of $N_i$:

$$\pi_i(W_i, N_i) = A_i TR(N_i) - W_i N_i \tag{7.38}$$

If the workers in the $i$th firm go on strike, their expected utility is $V^e$ as they can work elsewhere but the firm gets nothing. This model which is based on the firms retaining the power to set the employment level is sometimes called the "right to manage" model.

The consequence of bargaining in the right to manage model is to generate unemployment as an increasing function of the benefit-wage or the replacement ratio and union bargaining power. This can be shown by assuming simple log-linear utility and firm-union bargaining functions. This is shown in the Appendix 7.A.2.

## 7.6 CONCLUSIONS

The present chapter repeats some of the main conclusions reached in the previous chapters, provides a more complete discussion of monetary and new classical macroeconomics, compares between Keynesian and non-Keynesian schools of thought and finally discusses the theoretical foundations of new Keynesian economics. It is noted that the nature of the debate between various schools has been changing over time. Although policy effectiveness is still an important part of the debate there are other equally and more important issues. For example, output and employment fluctuations, market clearing, price wage inertia. Both the monetarists and new classicals believe in market forces and disagree with the non-market clearing feature of Keynesian economics. The expectations issue has lost some of its importance in the debate between Keynesians and new classicals as Keynesian economics has been shown to retain its main conclusions even when expectations are rationally formed. The main weakness of old fashioned Keynesian economics is the lack of solid microeconomic underpinnings. In addition to Clower,

Barro-Grossman and Patinkin's earlier attempts to provide such underpinnings discussed in Chapter 3, implicit contract theory, efficiency wage models etc., also attempt to provide the theoretical foundations of new Keynesian economics.

## APPENDIX TO CHAPTER 7

### 7.A.1 Derivation of the Dynamic System in Stein's Model

First the dynamic equation is derived for $\dot{U}$, *i.e.*, $dU/dt$ from (7.2) and (7.1). Differentiation of (7.2) w.r.t. $t$ yields

$$\dot{U} = F_1'[\{(dw/dt)/A(t)\} - (w^{dA}/dt)/\{A(t)\}^2] + F_2'dGI/dt \tag{7.A.1}$$

(7.A.1) can be rewritten as

$$\dot{U} = F_1'w/A(t)[\{(dw/dt)/w\} - \{(dA/dt)/A(t)\}] + F_2'\dot{G}1 \tag{7.A.2}$$

Now $\{(dA/dt)/A(t)\}$ is the rate of change of labour productivity which is assumed equal to $\alpha$. Substituting for the rate of change of real wage from equation (7.1) (7.A.2) can be rewritten as

$$\dot{U} = F_1'w/A(t)(w - \alpha) + F_2'\dot{G}1$$

$$\Rightarrow \quad \dot{U} = F_1'w/A(t)\{h(u) + \dot{p}e - \dot{p}\} + F_2'\dot{G}1 \tag{7.A.3}$$

The second dynamic equation is for $\dot{p}$. This is derived by differentiating (7.20) w.r.t. $t$ and then substituting (7.A.3), (7.6) and (7.4). Differentiation of (7.20) yields

$$(d\dot{p}/dt) = \dot{p}_1\dot{U} + \dot{p}_2'd\dot{p}e/dt + \dot{p}_3'\{d(M/P)/dt\}$$
$$+ \dot{p}_4\dot{G} + \dot{p}_5'(\dot{B}/M) \tag{7.A.4}$$

Substitution of (7.A.3) (7.6) and (7.4) into (7.A.4) yields

$$(d\dot{p}/dt) = \dot{p}_1\{(F_1'w/A(t)\{h(U) + \dot{p}e - \dot{p}) + F_2'\dot{G}1\}$$
$$+ \dot{p}_2'\lambda(\dot{p} - \dot{p}e) + \dot{p}_3'(\dot{n}m - n - \dot{p}) + \dot{p}_4'\dot{G} + \dot{p}_5'(\dot{B}/M)$$

$$\Rightarrow \quad (d\dot{p}/dt) = \{\dot{p}_1'F_1'w/A(t)\}h(U) - \dot{p}\{\dot{p}_1'F_1'w/A(t) - \dot{p}_2\lambda' + \dot{p}_3'\}$$
$$+ \dot{p}e\{\dot{p}_1'F_1'w/A(t) - \dot{p}_2'\lambda\} + \dot{p}_1'F_2'\dot{G}1 + \dot{p}_4'\dot{G}$$
$$+ \dot{p}_5'(\dot{B}/M) + \dot{p}_3'(\dot{n}m - n) \tag{7.A.5}$$

The last term on the R.H.S. of (7.A.5) is a pure number.

The third dynamic equation of the model is the adaptive expectation rule (7.6). Stein makes a number of assumptions to analyse the differences between the monetarists and the Keynesians on the basis of the three equation dynamic model comprising (7.A.3), (7.A.5) and (7.6). These are: (i) that the government expenditure on employment is zero $\Rightarrow G1 = 0$; (ii) that only the real balance effect of price changes remains and the other effects of price changes cancel out. This rather complex assumption implies that only $\dot{p}_3'$ is non-zero and $\{\dot{p}_1' F_1' w/A(t)\} - \dot{p}_2'\lambda$ is close to zero; A rise in $\dot{p}$ raises $\dot{p}e$ by $\lambda$ units and this in turn raises $\dot{p}$ by $\dot{p}_2'\lambda$ units. On the other hand, a rise in $\dot{p}$ reduces the real wage adjusted for productivity, $\{w/A(t)\}$ by the same percentage point and, thereby, raises employment by $\{F_1' w/A(t)\}$ units. This raises both saving and investment and Stein assumes that the former increases by more than the latter as a result of which the rate of price change is reduced by $\dot{p}_1' F_1' w/A(t)$. The rise in $\dot{p}$ by $\dot{p}_2'\lambda$ units is assumed to cancel the fall in $\dot{p}$ by $\dot{p}_1' F_1' w/A(t)$ units $\Rightarrow |\dot{p}_2'\lambda| = |\dot{p}_1' F_1' w/A(t)|$. The net impact of a rise in the rate of price change is then only $\dot{p}_3' \neq 0. \Rightarrow$ (7.A.5) is simplified to (7.A.6):

$$(d\dot{p}/dt) = \{\dot{p}_1' F_1' w/A(t)\}\, h(U) - \dot{p}_3'\dot{p} + \dot{p}_4'\dot{G}$$

$$\dot{p}_5'(\dot{B}/M) + \dot{p}_3'(nm - n) \tag{7.A.6}$$

Another simplifying step is taken by linearising the function $h(U)$ around its equilibrium value, $U^*$. using Maclaurin's series $h(U)$ (7.A.3) and (7.A.6) can be approximated by

$h'(U^*)(U - U^*) \Rightarrow \dot{U}$ can be rewritten in terms of deviation $(U - U^*) = Ud$, say

$\dot{U}d = \dot{U} - \dot{U}^* = \dot{U} \Rightarrow$ can be rewritten respectively as

$$(\dot{U}d) = \{F_1' w/A(t)\}\, \{h'(U^*)Ud + \dot{p}e - \dot{p}\} \tag{7.A.7}$$

and

$$(d\dot{p}/dt) = \{\dot{p}_1' F_1' w/A(t)\}\, \{h'(U^*)\, Ud\} - \dot{p}_3'\dot{p}$$

$$\dot{p}_4'\dot{G} + \dot{p}_5'(\dot{B}/M) + \dot{p}_3'(\dot{n}m - n) \tag{7.A.8}$$

The dynamic model is further simplified by assuming the expected inflation rate as exogenous which implies that one can ignore the adaptive expectation equation (7.6). The resulting system can be rewritten in the vector matrix form as

$$\begin{bmatrix} (\dot{U}d) \\ (d\dot{p}/dt) \end{bmatrix} = \begin{bmatrix} a_{11} & a_{12} \\ a_{21} & a_{22} \end{bmatrix} \begin{bmatrix} Ud \\ \dot{p} \end{bmatrix} + \begin{bmatrix} b_{11} & b_{12} & b_{13} \\ b_{21} & b_{22} & b_{23} \end{bmatrix} \begin{bmatrix} \dot{G} \\ \dot{n}m \\ (\dot{B}/M) \end{bmatrix}$$

$$+ \begin{bmatrix} c_{11} & c_{12} \\ c_{21} & c_{22} \end{bmatrix} \begin{bmatrix} \dot{p}^e \\ n \end{bmatrix} \tag{7.A.9}$$

where

$$a_{11} = \{F_1'w/A(t)\}\, h'(U^*), \quad a_{12} = -F_1'w/A(t),$$

$$a_{21} = \dot{p}_1' F_1' w/A(t) h'(U^*), \quad a_{22} = -\dot{p}_3'$$

$$b_{11} = 0, \quad b_{12} = 0, \quad b_{13} = 0$$

$$b_{21} = \dot{p}_4', \quad b_{22} = \dot{p}_3' \quad \text{and} \quad b_{23} = \dot{p}_5'$$

$$c_{11} = F_1'w/A(t), \quad c_{12} = 0$$

$$c_{21} = 0, \quad c_{22} = -\dot{p}_3'$$

The above 15 equations will be regarded as (7.A.10).

It is easily noted that (7.A.10) $\Rightarrow$ that (7.A.9) reduces to

$$\begin{bmatrix} (\dot{U}d) \\ (d\dot{p}/dt) \end{bmatrix} - [a_{ij}] \begin{bmatrix} Ud \\ \dot{p} \end{bmatrix} = [c_{ij}] \begin{bmatrix} \dot{p}^e \\ n \end{bmatrix} \tag{7.A.11}$$

Since $[b_{ij}] = 0$ because each element in the first row of $B$ is zero. The coefficient matrix of $(\dot{U}d)$ and $(d\dot{p}/dt)$ can be substituted as follows to rewrite (7.A.11) as

$$\begin{bmatrix} 1 & 0 \\ 0 & 1 \end{bmatrix} \begin{bmatrix} (\dot{U}d) \\ (d\dot{p}/dt) \end{bmatrix} - [a_{ij}] \begin{bmatrix} Ud \\ \dot{p} \end{bmatrix}$$

$$= [c_{ij}] \begin{bmatrix} \dot{p}^e \\ n \end{bmatrix} \tag{7.A.12}$$

Following exactly the same method as in Chapter 6, the particular integral is obtained by using $Ud = \overline{U}\,\overline{d}$ and $\dot{p} = \overline{\dot{p}}$. Then (7.A.12) reduces to

$$\begin{bmatrix} \overline{U}\,\overline{d} \\ \overline{\dot{p}} \end{bmatrix} = -[a_{ij}]^{-1} [c_{ij}] \begin{bmatrix} \dot{p}^e \\ n \end{bmatrix}$$

For complementary functions $Ud = me^{\alpha t}$ and $\dot{p} = ne^{\alpha t}$ are tried in the equation:

$$I_2\begin{bmatrix}(\dot{U}d)\\ d\dot{p}/dt\end{bmatrix}-[a_{ij}]\begin{bmatrix}Ud\\ \dot{p}\end{bmatrix}=0$$

where $I_2$ is the identity matrix of order 2 $\Rightarrow$

$$\begin{bmatrix}1 & 0\\ 0 & 1\end{bmatrix}\begin{bmatrix}m\\ n\end{bmatrix}\alpha e^{\alpha t}=[a_{ij}]\begin{bmatrix}m\\ n\end{bmatrix}e^{\alpha t}$$

$$\Rightarrow \quad \alpha I_2-[a_{ij}]=0 \quad \text{since } m,n\neq 0$$

$$\Rightarrow \quad \begin{bmatrix}\alpha-a_{11} & -a_{12}\\ -a_{21} & \alpha-a_{22}\end{bmatrix}=0$$

$$\Rightarrow \quad (\alpha-a_{11})(\alpha-a_{22})-a_{12}a_{21}=0$$

$$\Rightarrow \quad \alpha^2-(a_{11}+a_{22})\alpha+a_{11}a_{22}-a_{12}a_{21}=0 \tag{7.A.13}$$

(7.A.13) is the characteristic equation. The quadratic can be solved to yield the roots

$$\alpha_1,\alpha_2=\frac{(a_{11}+a_{22})\pm\sqrt{(a_{11}+a_{22})^2-4(a_{11}a_{22}-a_{12}a_{21})}}{2} \tag{7.A.14}$$

The complete solution to the dynamic model (7.A.11) can then be written as

$$\begin{bmatrix}Ud\\ \dot{p}\end{bmatrix}=\begin{bmatrix}m_1e^{\alpha_1 t}+m_2e^{\alpha_2 t}\\ n_1e^{\alpha_1 t}+n_2e^{\alpha_2 t}\end{bmatrix}+\begin{bmatrix}\overline{Ud}\\ \bar{\dot{p}}\end{bmatrix} \tag{7.A.15}$$

Where $\overline{U}\,\overline{d}$ and $\bar{\dot{p}}$ are given in (7.A.12) and the constants $m_1, m_2$ and $n_1$ and $n_2$ are obtained from the initial conditions. For stability, $Ud$ and $\dot{p}$ must converge to $\overline{U}\,\overline{d}$ (which is zero if $U=U^*$) and $\bar{\dot{p}}$ as $t\rightarrow\infty$.

As usual the necessary condition for local stability can be obtained from the characteristic equation (7.A.12). The roots are real if $(a_{11}+a_{22})^2 - 4(a_{11}a_{22}-a_{12}a_{21})\geq 0$. In this case stability will be ensured if both roots are negative $\Rightarrow$ the sum of the roots is negative and the product positive. In the case of real roots, therefore, the necessary condition for stability is:

$$a_{11}+a_{22}<0$$

$$\Rightarrow \quad [F_1'w/A(t)h'(U^*)-\dot{p}_3']<0 \tag{7.A.16i}$$

and

$$\frac{1}{4}[(a_{11}+a_{22})^2-\{(a_{11}+a_{22})^2-4(a_{11}a_{22}-a_{12}a_{21})\}]>0$$

$$\Rightarrow \quad (a_{11}a_{22}-a_{12}a_{21})>0$$

$$\Rightarrow \quad -\dot{p}_3'F_1'w/A\,h'(U^*)+\dot{p}_1[F_1'w/A]^2h'(U^*)>0$$

$$\Rightarrow \quad F_1'w/A\,h'[\dot{p}_1'F_1'w/A-\dot{p}_3']>0 \qquad (7.A.16ii)$$

Since (7.A.16i) has to hold, (7.A.16ii) yields the necessary conditions for stability in the case of real roots as

$$[\dot{p}_1'F_1'w/A(t)-\dot{p}_3']<0 \qquad (7.A.16iii)$$

The roots of (7.A.12) will be complex when

$$(a_{11}+a_{22})^2<4(a_{11}a_{22}-a_{12}a_{21})$$

In this case the model will have cyclical fluctuations but it will be stable if (7.A.16) hold. It can be easily shown as follows. In the case of complex roots, the sum of the roots is still $(a_{11}+a_{22})$ and the product is

$$\frac{1}{4}[(a_{11}+a_{22})^2+4(a_{11}a_{22}-a_{12}a_{21})-(a_{11}+a_{22})^2]$$

$$=(a_{11}a_{22}-a_{12}a_{21})$$

$\Rightarrow$ The necessary condition for stability is the same as (7.A.16) even when the model has cyclical fluctuations.

### 7.A.2 The Consequence of Nash Bargaining in the Right to Manage Model

Simplifying the utility function (7.36) to depend on $N_i(V-V^e)$, the firm-union bargaining has the objective function, in the log-linear form, as

$$\{N_i[V(\dot{W}_i)-V^e]\}^{\beta}[A_iTR(N_i)-W_iN_i]^{1-\beta} \qquad (7.A.17)$$

where $\beta$ reflects the union power, $0<\beta<1$. For the utility function, again a constant elasticity form is assumed:

$$V(W_i)=W_i^{\alpha} \quad 0<\alpha\le 1 \qquad (7.A.18i)$$

$$\Rightarrow \quad V^e=V(\overline{W})[1-t(u)]+b^{\alpha}t(u) \qquad (7.A.18ii)$$

$$\Rightarrow \quad V^e=\overline{W}^{\alpha}[1-t(u)]+b^{\alpha}t(u) \qquad (7.A.18iii)$$

Substituting (7.A.18i) and (7.A.18ii) in (7.A.17) the objective function becomes

$$N_i^{\beta}\left\{W_i^{\alpha} - \overline{W}^{\alpha}(1-t(u))\, b^{\alpha}t(u)\right\}^{\beta}\{A_iTR - W_iN_i\}^{1-\beta}$$

$$\Rightarrow \quad N_i^{\beta}\overline{W}^{\alpha\beta}\left\{\left(\frac{W_i}{\overline{\overline{W}}}\right)^{\alpha} + t(u)\left[1-\left(\frac{b}{\overline{\overline{W}}}\right)^{\alpha}\right] - 1\right\}^{\beta}$$

$$\{A_iTR - W_iN_i\}^{1-\beta}$$

The unemployment benefit wage ratio $\left(\frac{b}{\overline{\overline{W}}}\right)$ can be called the replacement ratio, $Rr$ and the above objective function be rewritten as:

$$N_i^{\beta}\overline{W}^{\alpha\beta}\left\{\left(\frac{W_i}{\overline{\overline{W}}}\right)^{\alpha} + t(u)(1-Rr^{\alpha}) - 1\right\}^{\beta} \quad \{A_iTR - W_iN_i\}^{1-\beta} \tag{7.A.19}$$

For the sake of convenience, we write

$$z = \left(\frac{W_i}{\overline{\overline{W}}}\right)^{\alpha} + t(u)(1-Rr^{\alpha}) - 1$$

$\Rightarrow$ (7.A.19) can be rewritten as

$$N_i^{\beta}\overline{W}^{\alpha\beta}z^{\beta}\{A_iTR(N_i) - W_iN_i\}^{1-\beta} = F(W_iN_i) \tag{7.A.20}$$

The necessary conditions for maximising (7.A.20) are obtained by setting the partial derivatives of $F(W_i, N_i)$ w.r.t. $N_i$ and $W_i$ equal to zero:

$$\frac{\partial F}{\partial N_i} = \beta\frac{F}{N_i} + (1-\beta)\frac{F\,(A_iTR' - W_i)}{(A_iTR - W_iN_i)} \tag{7.A.21}$$

$$\frac{\partial F}{\partial W_i} = \beta\left(\frac{F}{z}\right)\frac{\partial z}{\partial W_i} - (1-\beta)\frac{N_iF}{(A_iTR - W_iN_i)} \tag{7.A.22}$$

Setting (7.A.21) and (7.A.22) to zero, we obtain respectively

$$\frac{\beta}{N_i} = -(1-\beta)\frac{(A_iTR' - W_i)}{(A_iTR - W_iN_i)} \tag{7.A.23}$$

and

$$\frac{\left(\beta\frac{\partial z}{\partial W_i}\right)}{z} = (1-\beta)\frac{N_i}{(A_iTR - W_iN_i)} \tag{7.A.24}$$

Differentiating $z$ w.r.t. $W_i$

$$\frac{\partial z}{\partial W_i} = \alpha\left(\frac{W_i}{\overline{\overline{W}}}\right)^{\alpha-1} \cdot \frac{1}{\overline{\overline{W}}} \tag{7.A.25}$$

From (7.A.23) one obtains

$$\frac{A_iTR - W_iN_i}{N_i} = -\left[\frac{1-\beta}{\beta}\right](A_iTR' - W_i)$$

$$\Rightarrow \quad W_i\left\{\left(\frac{1-\beta}{\beta}\right)+1\right\} = -A_i\frac{TR}{N_i} - \left(\frac{1-\beta}{\beta}\right)A_iTR' \qquad (7.A.26)$$

Defining labour share in total revenue as $sr = \frac{W_iN_i}{A_iTR} = \frac{A_iTR'N_i}{A_iTR}$ (7.A.26) can be written as (7.A.27)

$$\frac{W_i}{\beta} = -\frac{A_iTR}{N_i}\left\{\left(\frac{1-\beta}{\beta}\right)sr+1\right\} \qquad (7.A.27)$$

From (7.A.24) and (7.A.26) one obtains

$$\alpha\left(\frac{W_i}{\overline{W}}\right)^{\alpha-1}\frac{1}{\overline{W}} = -\frac{\left(\frac{W_i}{\overline{W}}\right)^{\alpha} + t(u)(1-Rr^{\alpha})-1}{A_iTR - W_iN_i}\left(\frac{1-\beta}{\beta}\right)N_i$$

$$\Rightarrow \quad \alpha\left(\frac{W_i}{\overline{W}}\right)^{\alpha-1}\frac{1}{\overline{W}} = -\left(\frac{1-\beta}{\beta}\right)\frac{N_i}{A_iTR}\left[\frac{\left(\frac{W_i}{\overline{W}}\right)^{\alpha} + t(u)(1-Rr^{\alpha})-1}{1-sr}\right]$$

(7.A.28)

Multiplying (7.A.27) and (7.A.28) one obtains

$$\left(\frac{W_i}{\overline{W}}\right)^{\alpha}\frac{\alpha}{\beta} = \left\{\left(\frac{1-\beta}{\beta}\right)sr+1\right\}\left(\frac{1-\beta}{\beta}\right)\left\{\frac{\left(\frac{W_i}{\overline{W}}\right)^{\alpha} + t(u)(1-Rr^{\alpha})-1}{1-sr}\right\}$$

$$\Rightarrow \quad \left(\frac{W_i}{\overline{W}}\right)^{\alpha}\left[\frac{\alpha}{\beta} - \left(\frac{1-\beta}{\beta}\right)\left\{\frac{1+\left(\frac{1-\beta}{\beta}\right)sr}{1-sr}\right\}\right]$$

$$= \left\{\left(\frac{1-\beta}{\beta}\right)sr+1\right\}\left(\frac{1-\beta}{\beta}\right)\left\{\frac{t(u)(1-Rr^{\alpha})-1}{1-sr}\right\} \qquad (7.A.29)$$

Taking logarithms of both sides of (7.A.29), a log-linear equation for $\left(\frac{W_i}{\overline{W}}\right)$ and, therefore, for $W_i$ can be obtained in terms of labour share, replacement ratio etc.

On the other hand, a log-linear equation for the rate of unemployment can also be obtained by taking logarithms of both sides of (7.A.29)′. From (7.A.29)

$$t(u) = \frac{(1 - sr)\,[\text{L.H.S. of (7.A.29)}] + \left\{\left(\frac{1-\beta}{\beta}\right) sr + 1\right\} \frac{1-\beta}{\beta}}{\left(\frac{1-\beta}{\beta}\right)(1 - Rr^{\alpha})}$$

(7.A.29)′

The logarithms of (7.A.29)′ will yield a log-linear equation for the rate of unemployment in terms of $\frac{W_i}{\overline{W}}$, $Rr$, $sr$ and union bargaining power $\beta$. In an economy which is fully unionised and which consists of a large number of nuclear firm-union pairs, $W_i$ can be assumed to tend to $\overline{W}$ in general equilibrium implying that the rate of unemployment in equilibrium would be increasing with replacement ratio and union bargaining power but decrease as $\alpha$ increases.

# 8

# OPEN-ECONOMY MODELS

## 8.1 INTRODUCTION

In this Chapter a number of open economy models will be discussed, many of them assuming a small economy. The attribute "small means that the changes in the domestic economy under consideration do not affect the world economy and, therefore, world income, interest rates, etc. can be treated as exogenous to the domestic economy. A few definitions and concepts will be explained first.

### The Balance of Payments (BOP)

The BOP accounts for a country are a record of all its international transactions over a period of time — usually a year. The *Current Account* (CU) records flows of goods and services and other income flows and transfers to and from abroad. Exports and Imports are classified as *visible trade* and *invisibles* include all services, transfers and income flows. The Capital Account (CA) records all transactions in external assets and liabilities. Credit items are a potential inflow or supply of and debit items an outflow or demand for foreign exchange.

Exports and Imports constitute the most important part of the CU of a country. Any excess of imports (Im) over exports (X) is counted as a balance of trade (BOT) deficit and a surplus of *X* over *Im* as a BOT surplus. An overall BOP deficit on the CU has to be financed by running down the country's overseas assets or by borrowing implying that there must be a surplus on the CA. On the other hand a surplus on the CU has to be matched by a CA deficit since the excess of foreign income over spending releases surplus to invest overseas or reduce external debt.

## 8.2 THEORIES OF BOP AND THE EXCHANGE RATE DETERMINATION

### 8.2.1 The Traditional Theory

*The Exchange Rate*

The exchange rate can be defined in two alternative ways:

1. As the price per unit of foreign currency in terms of domestic currency (E) or
2. as the price per unit of domestic currency in terms of any foreign currency (Er). *E* and *Er* are the reciprocals of each other.

In an open economy, Importers demand foreign currency and exporters supply foreign currency. In this sense a simple demand-supply model can be conceived to determine the equilibrium price of domestic currency in terms of a foreign currency. Assuming that the UK trades with the USA, then equilibrium price of sterling in terms of the US dollar is determined where the demand for and the supply of dollars are equal. Obviously, the demand for US $ is a derived demand — the ultimate demand being the demand for US commodities. As implied by the definitions of the exchange rate, supply and demand relationships in international currency can be expressed in either the domestic or the foreign currency.

In Fig. 8.1a, the exchange rate is measured in terms of US $ per unit of £. As the exchange rate falls, the sterling prices in British imports (i.e., of American exports) rise and therefore the quantity of dollars demanded (i.e., of pounds sold for $) will also fall and therefore the supply curve of pound is upward sloping. On the other hand the quantity demanded of pounds sterling rises as the exchange rate falls because the dollar price of British exports (i.e., of American imports) falls. Obviously this positive and the negative slopes of the supply of and demand for pounds are derived on the assumption that the British demand for American exports and that the American demand for British exports are not completely inelastic. The relation between elasticities and the effect of a fall in exchange rate on the BOT will be examined in the next section. To explain Fig. 8.1b, one needs to reverse the above arguments. The equilibrium exchange rate is given by the point of intersection *E* of the demand and supply curves. However, this equilibrium will be stable only if the supply curve is upward sloping. If the demand for American exports is inelastic the supply curve of pounds will be backward bending. In the case of a backward bending supply curve, the equilibrium may not be stable. For stability of equilibrium with backward bending supply curve the elasticity of supply has to be lower than that of the demand curve in absolute terms.

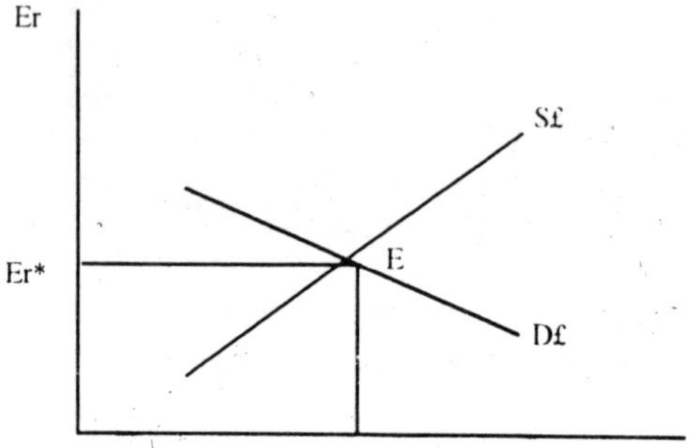


Figure (8.1a)

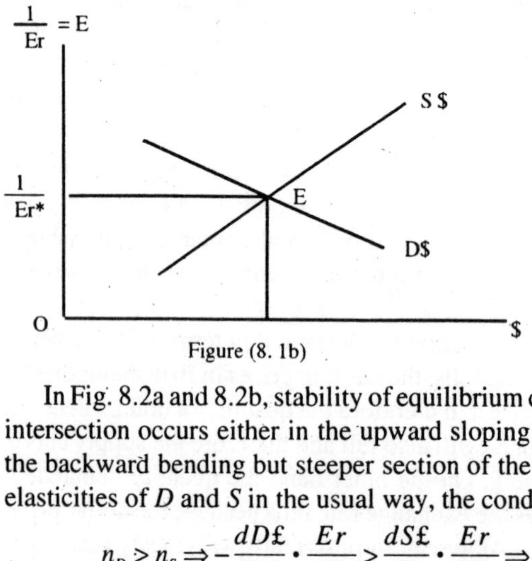


Figure (8. 1b)

In Fig. 8.2a and 8.2b, stability of equilibrium can be achieved because intersection occurs either in the upward sloping region (e.g., in *a*) or in the backward bending but steeper section of the supply curve. Defining elasticities of *D* and *S* in the usual way, the condition for stability is

$$n_D > n_S \Rightarrow -\frac{dD£}{D£} \bullet \frac{Er}{dEr} > \frac{dS£}{S£} \bullet \frac{Er}{dEr} \Rightarrow -n_D < n_S \tag{8.1}$$

In a freely floating exchange rate system currencies are left to find their own market equilibrium levels. In the real world governments seldom allow their currencies to float freely and like to manipulate exchange rates in the desired direction and this system is called managed floating. Under the Bretton Woods agreement of 1944, currencies of many countries were rigidly tied to the US dollar and up until the late sixties and early 70's the central banks of these countries acted so as to stabilise their currencies within 1 per cent of their par value. For example, the par value of the pound was $2.80 from 1949-67. The rigid system was abandoned in the early seventies. However the European monetary System (EMS) created in 1979 again aimed at stabilising the currency values of all Western European countries or members of the EEC. The EMS, it was thought, would expand trade and investment and would equalise the rates of inflation among all member countries. Arguments against joining the EMS are that the burden of adjustment would be mainly on the countries with BOP deficits; such countries, being unable to devalue under EMS, would be forced to follow deflationary monetary (and fiscal) policies which, in turn, would lead to unemployment and a lower rate of economic growth in the domestic economy.

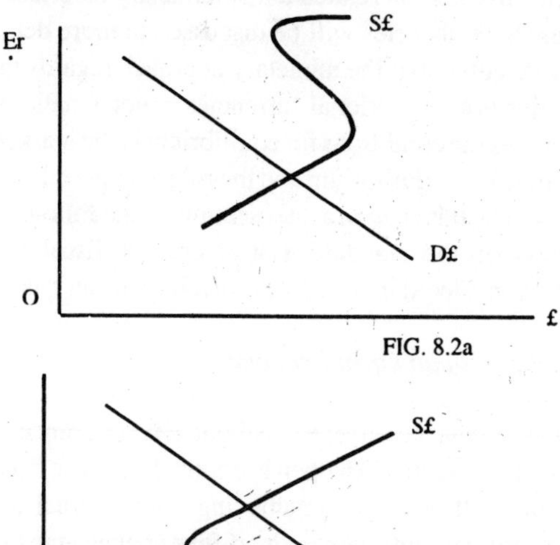


FIG. 8.2a

FIG. 8.2b

The above elements of the traditional exchange rate theory — the demand for and the supply of foreign exchange, price elasticity of such demand and supplies — identify the exchange rate with the relative price of domestic and foreign goods. This is known as the Purchasing Power Parity (PPP) doctrine.

In its absolute version the PPP theory states that the equilibrium exchange ratio equals the rate of domestic to foreign prices. In its relative version, the PPP theory relates changes in the exchange rate to changes in price ratios.[1]

Some controversy exists regarding the choice of proper price indices to be used in computing the parity. The commodity arbitrage view favours the use of traded goods' price index; the asset view emphasises the role of asset equilibrium in determining the exchange rate and advocates the use of a consumer price index; a third approach is to use the wage rate or the production costs parity.

The asset view of the exchange rate equating the purchasing power of the domestic and foreign currencies is related to the monetary theories of BOP and exchange rates. Such theories will be discussed in more detail later on. For now it may be noted that the monetary approach regards the exchange rate as the relative price of national currencies — not of national outputs and that it emphasises the conditions for equilibrium in the markets for stocks and assets, of portfolio equilibrium and the role of expectations.

Each of these issues will be taken up in a later section. In the following section, the effectiveness of the standard instruments of fiscal and monetary policies will be considered in the context of a Keynesian model.

*Monetary and Fiscal Policies in an Open Economy*

So far such policies have been considered without any reference to equilibrium in the foreign trade sector. An open economy has to use fiscal and monetary instruments with a view to achieving both internal and external balance. Policy combinations vary under different exchange rate regimes. As already pointed out many countries moved from fiscal to flexible exchange rate systems from 1973 onwards. Also there was a gradual increase in the international movement of capital. Implications of various policies also depend on the degree of capital mobility. It is customary, in the literature, to begin the analysis of the effectiveness of fiscal and monetary policies with Mundell (1962) and Fleming's (1962) contribution.

1. Frenkel, J.A. (1976), pp. 201-204.

*Mundell and Fleming*

Mundell and Fleming published the articles under consideration in the IMF Staff Papers and the two are complementary. Mundell used the internal and external balance schedules to show how monetary and fiscal policies can be combined to achieve internal stability with BOP equilibrium maintaining a fiscal exchange rate and without imposing trade controls. He argues that monetary policies should aim at external balance and fiscal policy at internal balance. If fiscal policy aimed at external balance and monetary policy at internal balance instead, the disequilibrium situation would worsen. The condition for internal balance was interpreted solely in terms of output market equilibrium, written as in (4.75i):

$$S + T + Im = I + G + X$$

Savings, taxes and imports constitute withdrawals from domestic output in real terms which must equal total injections into the domestic goods market in real terms. Assuming that saving investment equilibrium in the private sector is maintained by adjusting inventories, the relation between government budget surplus and external balance was derived as

$$T - G = X - Im \tag{8.2}$$

Mundell assumed exports and foreign policies to be exogenous. While the latter is a typical assumption for a small open economy most of the other simplifying assumption of Mundell (1962) were changed in his later contributions. Fleming (1962) extended Mundell's model to include money market equilibrium as part of internal balance and considered the relative effectiveness of monetary and fiscal policies under fixed and floating exchange rates. He used a simple Keynesian model essentially, similar to the one discussed in the next section. The minor differences between Fleming's (1962) model and the one discussed below are:

1. Fleming used a quantity theory version of the money demand equation as in (4.2)

   $$V^Y = \frac{Y}{M}$$

   where $V^Y$ is the income velocity.
2. Secondly, interest rate was taken as a function of the income velocity;

   $$r = r(V^Y), \quad r^1 > 0$$

The implications of the Mundell-Fleming model remain unchanged even if one uses the more general versions of money demand function and determines interests rate from the conditions of overall equilibrium — internal and external.

The internal equilibrium comprises money and output market equilibria given by the IS and the LM curves of an open economy and the external equilibrium consists of equilibrium in the foreign trade sector. As shown below the latter is given by what is known as the BB curve. The Mundell-Fleming model with fixed prices consists of the IS, the LM and the BB equations as shown in (8.15), (8.14) and (8.7) respectively. The economic theory underlying each of these equations is discussed in detail in the following section. A Keynesian model with variable prices will be considered in 8.2.3.

The equilibrium condition for the goods market in a small open economy was given in equation (2.1) but the export and import demand functions need to be rewritten more realistically for an open economy. Import demand depends on income and relative price of the overseas produced goods. The latter are priced in terms of respective foreign currencies and have to be expressed in terms of the domestic currency to be used as an argument in the import demand function. If $P_f$ is an index of the general price level in the rest of the world, the price of overseas produced goods in foreign currency is $P_f$ and in terms of domestic currency $E\,P_f$.

Then, the relative price of imported goods can be measured by $\frac{EP_f}{P}$ (where $P$ is the index of the general price level in the home country as used before). The ratio $\left(\frac{P}{E \cdot P_f}\right)$ measures the relative price of home produced goods and is known as the *terms of trade*. An import demand functions can be written in the general form as

$$Im = Im\left[Y, \left(\frac{E \cdot P_f}{P}\right)\right] \tag{8.3a}$$

$\frac{\partial Im}{\partial Y}$ is the marginal propensity to import and is restricted as $0 < Im_1' < 1$ and $Im_1' < C'$; the other partial derivative obeys the usual inverse relation of demand to price:

$$Im_2' < 0$$

Imports can be broadly grouped under competitive *imports* and *non-competitive imports*. The former comprise goods produced also in the domestic economy and the latter are those which are not produced in the domestic economy at all. Motor vehicles and tea are two examples of competitive and non-competitive imports respectively in the UK. Imports comprise consumption and investment goods and raw materials. While consumption demand for overseas goods depends on households' disposable income and relative price, investment demand depends on rate of interest and the demand for raw materials on the quantity of output produced in the home country. For the sake of simplicity, direct taxes and interest rate have been excluded from (8.3a). Competitive imports are likely to be more sensitive to changes in the terms of trade than the non-competitive imports.

The exports are thought of as imports by the trading partners and these will depend on their real income and the relative price. Since we have assumed a small open economy, the real income of the rest of the world is determined effectively outside this economy and, therefore, can be regarded as exogenous. So, an exports function can be written as:

$$X = X\left(\frac{E \cdot P_f}{P}\right) \tag{8.3b}$$

If relative price increases, i.e., the goods exported by the domestic economy become more attractive to the rest of the world, then exports rise implying $X' > 0$.

Excluding invisibles for the time-being the Balance of Trade (BOT) can be expressed in terms of domestic currency as:

$$BT = X \cdot P - Im \cdot E \cdot P_f \tag{8.4}$$

*The Marshall-Lerner Condition*

As in the case of the demand for the domestic good, price elasticities can play an important role in the domestic demand for overseas produced goods and in the overseas demand for the goods produced by the country under consideration. The relative price elasticities of exports and imports can influence the final effect of a change in the exchange rate on the balance of trade. For example, a devaluation of the home currency can raise BOT surplus provided the sum of export and import elasticities exceeds unity. This restriction on demand elasticities is known as the Marshall-Lerner condition. If the domestic currency, say, pound sterling is devalued, it means more pounds sterling have to be paid for the same amount of foreign currencies. So, it implies a rise in $E$ as defined above. The Marshall-Lerner condition is derived below. Choosing appropriate units of measurement, prices can be set equal to unity: $P = P_f = 1$. Differentiating (8.4) w.r.t. $E$,

$$\frac{dBT}{dE} = X' - [Im + E \cdot Im'] \tag{8.5}$$

$$\Rightarrow \frac{dBT}{dE} = \left[\frac{X'}{Im} - 1 - \frac{EIm'}{Im}\right] Im$$

The division by $Im$ was a necessary manipulation for deriving elasticities. Assuming BOT in equilibrium, i.e., $X = Im$ and using the definition of elasticities,

$$\frac{dBT}{dE} > 0 \quad \text{if} \frac{X'}{Im} - 1 - E\frac{Im'}{Im} > 0$$

ie., if $\frac{X'}{X} - 1 + E \cdot \eta Im > 0$

ie., if $\eta X + \eta Im > 1$ (8.6)

So the BOT improves if the sum of export and import elasticities exceeds unity. (8.6) is the Marshall-Lerner condition. If foreigners' demand for exports of a country are price elastic, then a devaluation raises the total expenditure on exports since the goods are cheaper in terms of the foreign currencies; if domestic demand for imports of a country are price elastic, then a devaluation reduces the total expenditure on imports since the imported goods are dearer in terms of the domestic currency than they were before.

### *The BOP and its Implications for the Money Market*

The balance of payments is the balance on the current and balance on the capital account. It can be written as

$$BP = P \cdot X - E P_f Im + Ki \tag{8.7}$$

where $Ki$ is the net capital inflow. As already pointed out net capital inflow depends on the difference between the domestic rate of interest and the rate ruling overseas, $r - r_f$. However, a small economy cannot influence the latter and considers $r_f$ as exogenous. In case of perfect capital mobility, the domestic rate is closely related to that in the rest of the world implying

$r = r_f$. If the differential $r - r_f$ rises, foreigners are encouraged to invest in the domestic economy. The net capital inflow function can be written as:

$$Ki = Ki\,(Y, r - r_f) \tag{8.8a}$$

with $Ki_1' > 0$ and $Ki_2' > 0$.

The domestic income is included on the ground that a rise in income generally encourages investment. So, the BOP function is:

$$BP = PX - E \cdot P_f I\,m + Ki\,(Y, r) \tag{8.8b}$$

From (8.7)–(8.8b), change in official reserve assets is

$$\Delta F = PX - E \cdot P_f \cdot Im + Fi \tag{8.9}$$

Putting both price indices at unity as before

$$\Delta F = X - E \cdot Im + Ki \tag{8.10}$$

Under a flexible exchange rate system $E$ is adjusted to maintain BOP equilibrium so that $\Delta F \equiv 0$ and there is no feedback from the BOP to the domestic money supply.

A surplus on the BOP will be associated with the accumulation of foreign reserves. These will be included in the assets of the Bank of England and the Bank will then increase its liabilities to the commercial banks and in turn public's current account deposits will increase; therefore, domestic money supply must also increase. In the open economy the liabilities of the Central Bank increase not only on account of Government budget deficit but also of changes in official reserve assets. Also, the Bank has to decide what proportion of the BOP surplus it must sterilise by an open market sale of bonds. Therefore, the change in the monetary base of the domestic economy is:

$$\Delta F\,(1 - s) + \gamma + \theta P\,(G - T) \tag{8.11}$$

Where $0 \le s \le 1$ is the proportion of BOP surplus sterilised, $\gamma$ any exogenous change in money supply and $\theta$ is, as before, the proportion of this nominal budget deficit financed by raising money supply. As shown in Chapter 4, any change in monetary base leads to a change in the money supply. Assuming that the non-bank sector holds a constant amount of notes and coins (implying $CU^P$ constant in equation 4.71) change in money supply:

$$\Delta M^s = w \cdot \Delta Bd \tag{8.12a}$$

where $w$ is the monetary base multiplier as derived in (4.71). Now as explained above the change in bank deposits in an open economy is given by:

$$\Delta Bd = \theta P\,(G-T)+(1-s)\Delta F+\gamma$$

$$\Rightarrow \quad \Delta M^s = w\,[\theta P\,(G-T)+(1-s)\Delta F+\gamma]$$

$$\Rightarrow \quad \frac{\Delta M^s}{P} = w\left[\theta(G-T)+(1-s)\frac{\Delta F}{P}+\frac{\gamma}{P}\right]$$

$$\Rightarrow \quad \frac{M_t^s}{P} = \frac{M_{t-1}^s + w[\theta P\,(G-T)+(1-s)\Delta F+\gamma]}{P} \tag{8.12b}$$

(8.12b) assumes an exogenous tax system and no interest payment on government bonds. The condition for equilibrium in the domestic money market of an open economy becomes:

$$L\,(Y,r) = \frac{M^s}{P} = \frac{M_{t-1}^s + [\theta p\,(G-T)+(1-s)\Delta F+\gamma]}{P} \tag{8.13}$$

Setting $\Delta F = BP$, (8.13) can be written as:

$$L\,(Y,r) = \frac{M_{t-1}^s + w\,[\theta p\,(G-T)+(1-s)BP+\gamma]}{P} \tag{8.14}$$

Equation (8.14) is, therefore, the equation to the LM curve of an open economy. This version also includes the budget constraint in a simple way. The effect of budget deficits in an open economy will be taken up in more detail later on in the context of Frenkel and Razin's model.

*The BB Curve*

In addition to the IS and the LM curves one needs also to look at the combinations of real income and interest rates in the domestic economy which will keep the foreign trade sector in equilibrium. This is given by the 'BB' curve. As income increases, import demand increases for a given relative price leading to a deficit on the current account. This, to be offset by a surplus on the capital account, $Ki$ must rise. For $Ki$ to rise, domestic interest rate must rise relative to the rates ruling abroad. The BB curve is, therefore, upward sloping in the $(Y, r)$ axes. The equilibrium in the domestic economy in goods, money and BOP holds simultaneously at the point $E$, where the IS, the LM and the BB curves intersect.

The equation to the IS curve is derived from (8.2)–(8.3b) as:

$$Y - C\,(Y-T) - I\,(r) + E\,Im\,(Y,E) - X\,(E) = G \tag{8.15}$$

assuming $P_f = P = 1$ for the sake of simplicity.

Its slope for a given rate of exchange is obtained by differentiating (8.15) w.r.t. $Y$ and solving for $\frac{dr}{dY}$:

$$1 - C' + E \cdot Im_1' - I'\frac{dr}{dY} = 0 \Rightarrow \frac{dr}{dY} = \frac{1 - C' + E \cdot I'm_1}{I'}$$

$$\Rightarrow \left(\frac{dr}{dY}\right)_{IS} < 0$$

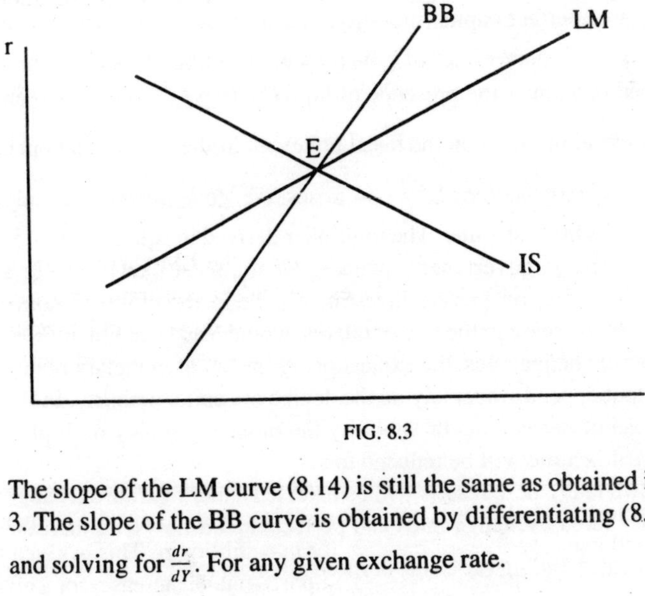


FIG. 8.3

The slope of the LM curve (8.14) is still the same as obtained in Chapter 3. The slope of the BB curve is obtained by differentiating (8.7) w.r.t. $Y$ and solving for $\frac{dr}{dY}$. For any given exchange rate.

$$-E \cdot Im_1' + Ki_1' + Ki_2'\frac{dr}{dY} = 0$$

$$\Rightarrow \frac{dr}{dY} = \frac{E \cdot Im_1' - Ki_1'}{Ki_2'} \qquad (8.16)$$

For $\left(\frac{dr}{dY}\right)$ to be positive, $E \cdot Im_1' > Ki_1'$.

The above analysis provides all the ingredients of the Mundell-Fleming (MF) model.

The model comprises equations (8.15), (8.14) and (8.7):

$$Y - C(Y - T) - I(r) + E \cdot Im(Y, E) - X(E) = G$$

$$L(Y,r)-\{M^s_{t-1}+w(1-s)\Delta F+w\theta(G-T)+\gamma w\}=0$$

$$BP-X(E)+E\cdot Im(Y,E)-Ki(Y,r)=0$$

To explain the fixed exchange rate regime, $Y$, $r$ and $BP$ are treated as endogenous variables and $G$, $\gamma$ and $E$ as exogenous policy instruments. The policy multipliers for the open economy can be derived by applying the usual comparative statics method. The Jacobian, and the multipliers are derived in the Appendix 8.A.1. As shown in the equation (8.A.3) the magnitude of the expansionary effect of fiscal policy on real output under a fixed exchange rate system depends on the degree of capital mobility. In the event of perfect capital mobility, i.e., when $Ki_2'=\infty$, there is the strongest expansionary effect of government spending on real income. For a closed economy, the presence of liquidity trap $L_2'=-\infty$ was seen to have this kind of effect on the fiscal policy multiplier, $\frac{\partial Y}{\partial G}$. For an open economy, $Ki_2'=\infty$ and/or, $L_2'=-\infty$ raises the government spending multiplier to its highest value. The multiplier derived in equation (8.A.5) shows that a rise in government spending would, most likely, lead to a crowding out effect on private investment (like in the close economy model) but the increase in the rate of interest would lead to capital inflow. Under fixed exchange rates, the expansionary impact of monetary policy on real output depends inversely on the degree of capital mobility. In the extreme case of perfect capital mobility the monetary policy multiplier effect on real income will be reduced to zero.

As shown later, these results will be reversed under flexible exchange rates. Under fixed exchange rates and perfect capital flows, an increase in government spending raises the domestic interest rate $\left(\therefore \frac{\partial r}{\partial G}>0\right)$ which leads to capital inflow and an increase in the money supply. Perfect capital mobility keeps the interest rate constant and leads to the strongest multiplier effect on real income. An increase in money supply, on the other hand, tends to lower interest rates $\left(\frac{\partial r}{\partial \gamma}<0\right)$ which leads to capital outflow or demand for foreign assets (and, therefore, for foreign currency) by the non bank public and this leads to a fall in domestic money supply gradually to its original level leading, in turn, to the impotency of monetary policy under fixed exchange rates and perfect capital mobility. This is explained in Fig. 8.4. In the case of the fiscal policy the movement is from the points $A$ to $B$ and then from $B$ to $C$. The IS curve shifts from $IS_0$ to $IS_1$

because of the rise in $G$; with interest rate above the previous equilibrium level $r^*$ capital inflow continues to raise money supply until overall equilibrium is reached at point $C$; the new level of output is $OY_3$.

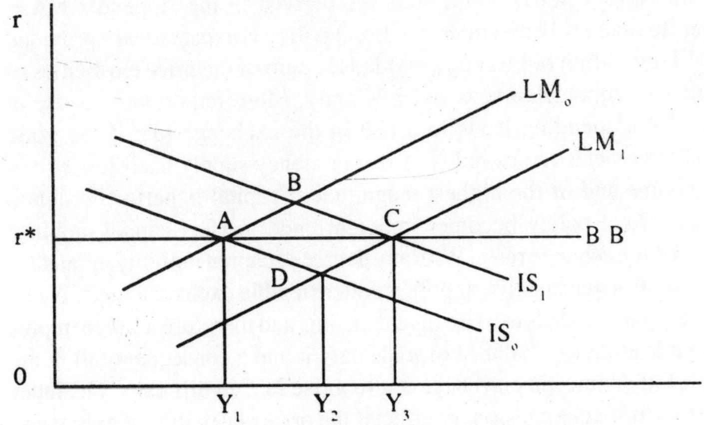


FIG. 8.4

In the case of a rise in the domestic component of the money supply, the LM curve shifts to $LM_1$ leading, initially to a rise in real income and a fall in interest rates. The latter leads to a capital outflow and an eventual fall in money supply to its original level, shifting real income back to $OY_1$ and resulting in a zero multiplier effect. For the sake of convenience, government budget diagram in the fourth quadrant has been omitted. Under less than perfect capital mobility, it is the degree of sterilisation which influences the efficacy of monetary policy under fixed exchange rates. As long as $0 < s < 1$, that is there is only partial sterilisation, monetary policy will have some effect on real output. The difference in the outcome in a closed and in an open economy model is due to the fact that money supply is assumed exogenous in the IS/LM model; and in the IS-LM model with government budget although money supply is made endogenous, its influence on balance of payments is ignored.

Under flexible exchange rates, the BOP is kept in equilibrium through fluctuations in the exchange rate. So, $BP = 0$ and $E$ is an endogenous variable in this case. To show the efficacy of fiscal and monetary policies on real income, interest rate and the exchange rate, the LM and BOP equations are rewritten as:

$$L(Y, r) - M^{s}_{t-1} - \theta w(G - T) - w\gamma = 0 \tag{8.17}$$

$$X(E) - E \cdot Im(Y, E) + Ki(Y, r) = 0 \tag{8.18}$$

The various policy multipliers are derived in the Appendix 8.A.1. Under flexible exchange rates, the fiscal policy is expansionary provided the M-L condition holds, i.e., provided the sum of the price elasticities of export and import demands exceeds unity. More importantly, a rise in government spending leads to a rise in the exchange rate if the same restriction on elasticities holds. A rise in money supply leads to a rise in real income and of the highest magnitude if capital is perfectly mobile whereas fiscal policy becomes impotent under perfect capital mobility and flexible exchange rates. With any degree of capital mobility, monetary policy is stronger than fiscal policy under flexible exchange rates. A rise in money supply leads to a rise in real income and therefore a rise in import demand leading to a balance of trade deficit and a consequent fall in the value of the domestic currency, i.e., to a rise in $E$ in this case. The latter leads to a further expansionary effect if the price elasticities of export and imports are high.

Cooper (1976) points out a number of conceptual weaknesses of the Mundell-Fleming type model discussed above:

(a) It ignores stock equilibrium and balance sheet requirements of the domestic and foreign residents and the monetary authorities. Capital movements simply change in portfolio positions of the public and monetary authorities and, therefore, such movements would stop when portfolio equilibrium was restored. In the MF flow analysis, on the other hand, a given interest rate leads to capital flows of a given magnitude for an indefinite period of time without any effect on money supply. However as Mundell (1969) has shown accommodating portfolio equilibrium and stock adjustment cannot be done without making a number of simplifying assumptions which minimise the role of stabilisation policy. Under these assumptions, monetary measures cannot influence domestic output at all under fixed exchange rates but they can influence aggregate money demand under flexible rates; fiscal policy cannot influence aggregate demand under flexible rates if capital is perfectly mobile but it can with imperfect mobility.

The class of models which adopted the flow equilibrium approach with the balance sheet requirements, suffers from "unresolved stock disequilibria".[2]

(b) The MF type model suffers from a specification error in the sense that the structural parameters of the economy are assumed to be completely unaffected by capital movements. Under a flexible exchange rate system, capital movements can create a "price effect" and a "speculative effect"[3] depending on exchange rate expectations. Per Meinich, (1976) disagrees with Cooper and argues that uncertainty in the case with flexible exchange rates can be reduced by forward exchange contracts. Besides, there is uncertainty even under a fixed exchange rate system. Under the latter system, the alternative to depreciation is depletion of international reserve assets leading, in turn, to a restrictive economic policy.

(c) The demand for money specification used in such models is too simple to account for the fact that the residents may switch to the use of foreign money to such an extent that the domestic economy loses its monetary control over aggregate demand even under a flexible exchange rate system. The demand for money function should at least have included the exchange rate as an explanatary variable.

(d) As pointed out by Frenkel and Razin (1986), the MF type of models does not take an explicit account of government budget deficits or of the private sector's response to government policies. Different time patterns of fiscal spending are shown to have different impacts in the Frenkel-Razin (FR) model. This will be discussed in 8.2.4.

(e) This type of model ignores factor price responses to exchange rate movements. Such factor price responses can lead to imported inflation. Depreciations may lead to more immediate demands for higher wages whereas wage reductions may be slow or non-existent in response to currency appreciations. In order to minimise the problem of factor price response sudden changes in the exchange rate must be avoided and a flexible exchange rate should be controlled at least to a reasonable extent by the monetary

---

2. Cooper, R.N. (1976), p. 152.
3. Cooper, R.N. (1976), p. 153.

authorities. Cooper (1976) also recommends that capital movements should be subject to direct control as "movements of liquid funds can play havoc with domestic monetary control under a fixed rate and with the exchange rate under a flexible rate" (p.162). As will be noted in the following section, 8.2.2, Myhrman (presenting his paper at the same conference as Cooper) relates such debates about domestic inflation and movements of exchange rate to the past history of exchange rate fluctuations.

### 8.2.2 **"New Theories"**

The so-called new theories of exchange rates and BOP were presented at the conference on "Flexible Exchange Rates and Stabilisation Policy" held in Stockholm in 1975. All these papers with comments and general discussion have been collected in the 1976 issue of the Scandinavian Journal of Economics. The Conference concentrated on a number of important issues (Black, 386-89):

1. The relationship between stocks and flows. Stock equilibrium of assets in various currencies determines the equilibrium exchange rate in the short-run and the flow equilibrium in the markets for traded goods determines the equilibrium exchange rate in the long run.
2. The short-run equilibrium was discussed in terms of a monetary as well as an asset analysis of exchange rates. The former concentrated on demands and supplies of different monies and the latter on the willingness to hold stocks denominated in different currencies. Mussa adopted the monetary approach and Kouri and others adopted the latter.
3. The relation between the conditions for short and long-run equilibria has also thrown considerable light on in some contributions e.g., Kouri demonstrated how the short-run analysis should converge to a long-run equilibrium related to purchasing power parity.
4. The monetary approaches not only emphasise stock equilibrium and balance sheet consistency but also the role of expectations.
5. Both the monetary and real factors were shown to be important, e.g., in Dornbusch's general equilibrium analysis. The expected

rate of inflation acts as an important link between the monetary and real sectors. Some of these models are discussed below. These are similar in a number of respects:

(a) They all make the small country assumption.
(b) The exchange rate is defined as the price per unit of foreign currency in terms of domestic currency.
(c) The commodity arbitrage version of the PPP theory is used in the linear or log-linear form implying:
$P = E \cdot P_f \ldots (8.19a) \Rightarrow \log P = \log E + \log P_f$ (8.19b)
(d) The monetary models including the role of price expectation make the expected rate of inflation a major variable in the demand for money function e.g., Frenkel and, later on, Barro (1978).
(e) In many of these models, the money market equilibrium condition is manipulated to get the price levels — home and foreign — in terms of the exchange rate, e.g., Frenkel and Dornbusch, use demand and supply equilibrium condition in the following simple way to derive the exchange rate:
$M^d / P = L(\dot{p}^e, Y, r)$ (8.20)
Dornbusch assumes $L = L(Y, r)$ and Frenkel assumes $L = L(\dot{p}^e)$ using the equilibrium condition $M^d = M^s = M$, both derive $M/P = L \Rightarrow P = M/L = E \cdot P_f$ using (8.19a).
$\Rightarrow \quad E = M/(P_f \cdot L)$ (8.21)
(8.21) is useful for deriving the effect of money supply on exchange rate in the simple way:
$\partial E / \partial M = 1/(LP_f) > 0$ (8.22)
(f) Expectations are formed by either the adaptive (Dornbusch) or by the rational expectations (Mussa, Barro) rule.
(g) The role of wealth is included in the saving and money demand functions is Myhrman's but excluded for the sake of simplicity in Barro's model.
(h) Exchange rate expectations assume important role in Mussa, Dornbusch and Barro.
(i) Most of the models assume domestic and foreign money as the only two assets.

*Myhrman*

Myhrman's "monetary impulse hypothesis" seeks to examine the two competing views:

(a) that exogenous shifts in different items on the BOP termed "real shocks" cause exchange rates to fluctuate and

(b) that such fluctuations are caused by monetary shocks or changes in the money supply — on the basis of historical evidence. His study excludes the role of price or exchange rate expectations but includes wealth in the foreign and domestic savings functions and makes money demand proportional to wealth. The equations of the model are:

$$S\,(r, Y, V) + S_f(r_f, Y_f, V_f) = 0 \tag{8.23}$$

$S_1' > 0, \quad S_2' > 0, \quad S_3' < 0$ and the same for $S_f$

$$V = M/P + K \quad \text{and} \quad V_f = M_f/P_f + K_f \tag{8.24}$$

$$M/P = V \cdot L\,(r, Y) \text{ and } M_f/P_f = V_f \cdot L_f(r_f, Y_f) \tag{8.25}$$

and $\quad P = E \cdot P_f \qquad$ (8.19a)

Equation (8.23) is the condition for global equilibrium on the current account balance. This is because Myhrman assumes zero investment (and therefore a constant capital stock) and that the government sector is in balance in both economies. On these assumptions, private saving equals current account balance:

$$X - Im = S - I + T - G = S \text{ when } \quad I = 0 \text{ and } G = T.$$

Equation (8.24) defines wealth for each economy and equation (8.25) equates money demand assumed porportional to wealth to respective money supply. These five equations and the commodity arbitrage version of PPP constitute the model. The historical evidence from Sweden in the 18th century and from England in the 19th century and in the inter-war period support Myhrman's monetary impulse hypothesis. In the short-run both the real and monetary shocks can explain the fluctuations in the exchange rate but the long-run dynamics are explained better by the monetary factors. In the long-run stationary state equilibrium actual and desired wealth are equal. The long-run real output determined by employment and capital stock in the usual way is assumed to grow at the same rate in each country. In both the long and the short-run analysis, the determination of output is dichotomised and the exchange rate is solved in terms of money and capital stocks and real output. Myhrman does not derive the multipliers in his 1976 paper but only reports that rises in money supply definitely raise the exchange rate whereas the effects of other variables on the exchange rate are uncertain (1976, p.184). Following the assumptions of Myhrman Appendix 8.A.2 shows how the money supply multiplier can be derived.

*Frenkel*

Frenkel like Mussa, Dornbusch, Barro and others includes the role of expectations and derives a simple but important relation between exchange rate and money supply and expected inflation from the demand supply equilibrium conditions in the money market. He emphasises, quite accurately for a monetary approach, the stock rather than flow demand and supply and the role of inflationary expectations. Frenkel uses the German hyperinflation of 1920-23 which was caused by monetary rather than real disturbances as the basis of his model. This is why he could ignore real factors other than the expected inflation. Manipulating the equilibrium condition in the money market, the price level for the domestic economy is obtained in terms of money supply and expected rate of inflation as shown in (8.20) and (8.21). Frenkel's money demand function is a restricted version of (8.21):

$$M^d/P = L(\dot{p}^e), \quad L' < 0 \tag{8.20$'$}$$

as the expected rate of inflation is the dominant variable in the midst of hyperinflation. Using the equilibrium condition for the money market and the PPP condition (8.19a), the Frenkel version of (8.21) is:

$$E = M/\{P_f L(\dot{p}^e)\} \tag{8.21$'$}$$

The derivation of the money supply multiplier (8.22) is further simplified by assuming $P_f = 1$; for the German economy during hyperinflation the domestic price level $P$ would be changing at a rate much faster than $P_f$, which, therefore, can be assumed fixed. Putting $P_f = 1$, (8.21)′ and (8.22) can be rewritten, respectively, as:

$$E = E(M, \dot{p}^e) \tag{8.26}$$

and $$\left(\frac{\partial E}{\partial M}\right) = \frac{1}{L} > 0 \tag{8.27}$$

More importantly one can derive a positive relation between the exchange rate and the expected rate of inflation:

$$\frac{\partial E}{\partial \dot{p}^e} = -\frac{ML'}{L^2} > 0 \quad \text{because } L' < 0 \tag{8.28}$$

The result in (8.28) contradicts with the implications of interest rate parity theory as well as with the explanation that a higher expected inflation raises the nominal rate of interest which leads to a surplus on the BOP either by reducing expenditure or by attracting foreign capital; the surplus on the BOP leads to an appreciation of the domestic currency or a lower spot exchange rate. Frenkel's theory explains the positive relationship between $E$ and $\dot{p}^e$ by emphasising the role of asset equilibrium. A rise in $\dot{p}^e$ lowers the demand for real money balances and given the nominal money stock, domestic price level has to rise; through the PPP condition and fixed foreign price level, a rise in $P$ can be achieved by a rise in $E$.

For the purpose of estimation, a long-linear form of (8.26) was used and the unobserved variable, $\dot{p}^e$ was replaced by $(1+\dot{p})$:

$$\log E = a_0 + a_1 \log M + a_2 \log(1+\dot{p}) \tag{8.27}$$

The coefficients were all statistical significant at 5 per cent level and the null hypothesis that exchange rate has unitary elasticity with money supply ($H_0 : a_1 = 1$) was accepted at the same significance level.

*Mussa*

Mussa extended the monetary framework to examine the role of stabilisation policy and to show that the problems of policy conflict existing under a system of fixed exchange rates are reduced under managed floating. Mussa considered the role of exchange rate expectations in asset demands and adopted the RE rule for the former. In his model, expectations of future returns to assets as well as those of changes in the exchange rate have an important role to play in determining the exchange rate itself. Asset holders' expectations of exchange rates depend on supplies of foreign and domestic monies, the domestic demand for money and fiscal policy. In addition to the expectations, the balance of payments and exchange rates are influenced by prices of exports and the level and fluctuations of real income. Mussa, like Myhrman and Frenkel concentrated on the reduced form equation for the demand for domestic money to which he adds the RE rule and two different sets of assumptions regarding the domestic money supply. The model comprises the following equations (8.28)–(8.30b):

$$\log M_t = a_0 \log E_t + a_1 \log \dot{E}_t^e + A_t + u_t \tag{8.28}$$

$$\dot{E}_t^e = E_t[(\log E_{t+1} - \log E_t) \mid If_t] \tag{8.29}$$

$$\log M_t = \overline{\log M_t} + u_t' \text{ with } u_t'$$

$$= \rho u_{t-1}' + v_t, \quad 0 \le \rho \le 1 \tag{8.30a}$$

$$\log M_t = \log M_{t-1} + \alpha_t + v_t \text{ with } \alpha_t = \alpha_{t-1} + \delta_t \tag{8.30b}$$

Equation (8.28) is the demand for domestic money where $\dot{E}_t^e$ is the expected rate of change of the exchange rate and $A_t$ summarises the influence of all other variables affecting the willingness to hold money. The elasticities $a_0 > 0$ and $a_1 < 0$ can be explained by the following argument: An increase in $E$ increases the domestic price of traded goods and may also increase domestic output and income and both lead to an increase in the demand for money. On the other hand an increase in $\dot{E}^e$ decreases the attractiveness of domestic money relative to foreign money and foreign assets. Equation (8.29) is the RE rule applied to the log-linear form. In the logarithmic form the rate of change can be expressed as the first difference of logs:

$$\dot{E}^e = \left(\frac{dE}{dt}\right)\frac{1}{E} = \frac{d\log E}{dt}$$

in the continuous and $\Delta \log E$ in the discrete form. The equation (8.29) concerns the RE rule already explained before. Equations given in (8.30a) constitute the rule number one for domestic money supply; that it has a fixed mean $\overline{\log M}$ and an autocorrelated disturbance. (8.30b) gives the alternative money supply rule assumed in Mussa's model: that money supply follows a random walk on levels as well as growth rates. The other error terms of the model, $u_t$, $v_t$ and $\delta_t$ are assumed to have zero expectation, constant variance and zero autocovariance. Some of the implications of the model subject to the rules (8.29) and (8.30) have been derived in the Appendix 8.A.3.1. They show that variability of the exchange rate depends on the behaviour of the money supply. The more ill behaved the money supply the more variable will be the exchange rate.

In his 1982 paper, Mussa further examined the exchange rate dynamics building on the previous models of Dornbusch, Frenkel, Kouri, Barro which will be examined later on in the present section. Mussa's 1982 model extends his previous model to include exchange rate expectations and a detailed breakdown of the output market into tradables and non-tradables. It is demonstrated that with unchanged outputs and asset stocks the current equilibrium exchange rate depends not only on the current monetary and real factors affecting absolute and relative prices but also on current expectations regarding the future behaviour of these exogenous variables. The following equations describe Mussa's 1982 model:

$$\log P = \sigma \log P_1 + (1-\sigma)(\log E + \log P_{f2}) \tag{8.31}$$

$$\log q = \log P_1 - (\log E + \log P_{f2}) \tag{8.32}$$

$$\log M = a\, rn + \log P + \log A, \quad a < 0 \tag{8.33}$$

$$rn = \Phi + rn_f \tag{8.34}$$

$$\Phi = \log E^e_{t+1} - \log E_t \tag{8.35}$$

$$X^d = \alpha\sigma(\bar{r} - r) + \beta \log(\bar{q} - \log q) \tag{8.36}$$

$$\alpha > 0, \beta > 0$$

$$r = rn - \dot{p}^e \tag{8.37}$$

$$\log E^e_{t+1} = \underset{t}{E}(\log E_{t+1}/If_t) \tag{8.38}$$

$$\dot{p}^e = \underset{t}{E}[(\log P_{t+1} - \log P_t) | If_t] \tag{8.39}$$

Equation (8.31) expresses the domestic general price level as a weighted average of the prices of non-tradables, $P_1$ and tradables $P_2$ where $0 < \sigma < 1$. Applying the logarithmic version of the PPP, (8.19b), $\log P_2 = \log E + \log P_{f2}$. Equation (8.32) explains the terms of trade in the logarithmic form. The terms of trade $q$ expressed as a relative price $P_1/P_2 \Rightarrow \log q = \log P_1 - \log P_2 = \log P_1 - (\log E + \log P_{f2})$. The money demand function includes the domestic nominal interest rate as the explanatory variable and Fisher equation (8.37) shows the definitional relation between real and nominal interest rate. Asset market equilibrium requires that domestic securities with forward cover are perfect substitutes for securities paying the world market nominal interest, $rn_f$. This forward cover, $\Phi$ or the percentage forward premium on foreign exchange is equal to the expected rate of change in the exchange rate. Equation (8.36) is a real market equation which expresses the desired excess demand for goods as a function of the excess of actual interest rate over the natural rate, $\bar{r}$, and of the excess of the actual terms of trade over the "natural" terms of trade, $\bar{q}$. If $r = \bar{r}$, $X^d = 0$ if $r < \bar{r}$, $X^d > 0$ implying an increase in the equilibrium relative price of domestic goods. If $q < \overline{q}$, $X^d > 0$. The equation (8.38) and (8.39) are the RE rules applied to the expected rates of exchange and inflation respectively in the logarithmic form. The equations (8.31)–(8.36) are manipulated to derive the equilibrium values of $P_1$, $E$ and $Q$. Asset market equilibrium requires (8.33) and (8.34). The latter yield the equilibrium price level as:

$$\log P^* = \log M - \log A - a\,(\Phi + rn_f) \qquad (8.40)$$

The equilibrium value of $\log q$ follows from the excess demand equation (8.36) and equations (8.37) and (8.34). In equilibrium, excess demand should be zero.

$$\Rightarrow \quad \log q^* = \log \overline{q} + \frac{1}{\beta}[\alpha\sigma(\overline{r} - r)]$$

$$\Rightarrow \quad \log q^* = \log \overline{q} + \frac{\alpha\sigma}{\beta}(\overline{r} - rn + \dot{p}^e)$$

$$\Rightarrow \quad \log q^* = \log \overline{q} + \frac{\alpha\sigma}{\beta}(\overline{r} - rn_f - \Phi + \dot{p}^e) \qquad (8.41)$$

The equilibrium values of $\log P_1$ and $\log E$ are obtained from (8.31), (8.32) and (8.40) and (8.41). Equation (8.31) yields

$$\log P_1^* = \frac{1}{\sigma}[\log P^* - (1-\sigma)(\log E^* + \log P_{f2})] \qquad (8.42)$$

From (8.32) $\log E^* = \log P_1^* - \log q^* - \log P_{f2}$ (8.43)

Substituting (8.43) in (8.42)

$$\log P_1^* = \frac{1}{\sigma}[\log P^* - (1-\sigma)(\log P_1^* - \log q^*)]$$

$$\Rightarrow \quad \log P_1^*\left(1 + \frac{1-\sigma}{\sigma}\right) = \frac{1}{\sigma}[\log P^* + (1-\sigma)\log \log q^*]$$

$$\Rightarrow \quad \log P_1^* = \log P^* + (1-\sigma)\log q^* \qquad (8.44)$$

Substituting (8.44) into (8.43), equilibrium exchange rate can be obtained as:

$$\log E^* = \log P^* - \sigma \log q^* - \log P_{f2} \qquad (8.45)$$

The equilibrium under RE and the consequent dynamics of Mussa's 1982 model will be discussed in the Appendix 8.A.3. The overshooting of the exchange rate in Mussa's model is different in nature than that in Dorubusch's (1976) model examined next in this section. Mussa shows that when domestic prices are sticky, the unexpected change in the actual exchange rate in response to new information about the exogenous monetary factors is shown to be greater than the unexpected change in the equilibrium exchange rate. The analysis does not restrict the source of overshooting to a permanent but unexpected change in money supply as in Dorubusch's model. If the price of the domestic goods is not sticky there is no exchange rate overshooting. The major policy implication of Mussa's present model are that government could affect both the exogenous monetary factors by affecting $\overline{\log M}$ or $\log A$ and the exogenous real factors by affecting $\bar{r}$ or $\bar{q}$. Because of the important role assigned to expectations, even a modest policy can have a significant effect on the exchange rate by altering expectations concerning future policy. As the equilibrium price level depends on money supply the effect of an unexpected change in monetary policy altering expectations of future monetary policy will be even stronger on the exchange rate because of the spill over effect of the unexpected change in the equilibrium price of domestic goods. As already pointed out, Mussa's (1982) model draws heavily on Dornbusch's (1976) exchange rate overshooting model. The following section reveals the similarities.

*Dornbusch's Exchange Rate Overshooting Model*

Dornbusch uses a general equilibrium framework by including both the real and the money markets of the home and foreign countries and by including the stock and the flow conditions of equilibrium. The short-run effects are explained by various price rigidities and expectational errors and the longer-run effects by asset market conditions like capital mobility and money market equilibrium. The following equations describe Dornbusch's model.

$$X^d(P_2/P, r, G) = 0, \quad X_1^{d'} > 0, X_2^{d'} < 0, X_3^{d'} = 1 \tag{8.46}$$

$$r = r(M/P, Y), \quad r_1' < 0, r_2' > 0 \tag{8.47}$$

$$r - \left(\frac{\bar{E} - E}{E}\right) = r_f \tag{8.48}$$

$$M/P = L(Y, r) \quad \text{and} \quad M_f/P_f = L_f(Y_f, r_f) \tag{8.20$'$}$$

$$P_2 = EP_{f2} \tag{8.19a)'$$

$$\overline{E}_t = E_t^e = \lambda E_t + (1-\lambda) E_{t-1}, \quad 0 < \lambda < 1 \tag{8.49}$$

Equation (8.46) states the condition for equilibrium in the goods market as zero excess demand. It increases with an increase in the relative price of traded goods as it shifts consumers' demand to home produced goods. $G$ is government spending on non-traded goods implying any rise in $G$ has to be fully accommodated. Unlike in Mussa (1982)'s, equation (8.46) is the excess demand function in the general form. Equation (8.47) is a derived equation for real interest rate exploiting the money demand function (8.21) and money market equilibrium condition. The interest arbitrage assumption is written in the linear form in (8.48). It explains the difference between the domestic and foreign interest rates by a forward premium equal to the excess of the forward rate, $\overline{E}$ over the current spot rate, $E$ expressed as a percentage.

Equation (8.19a)′ writes the PPP condition for traded goods. Finally equation (8.49) applies the adaptive expectation rule. The algebraic manipulation of the above basic equations yields the following relations. From (8.46), $(P_2/P)$ can be solved out in terms of interest rate and government spending:

$$P_2/P = h(r, G), \quad h_1' > 0, h_2' < 0$$

Extending the same principles to the foreign country, one gets the pair of equations

$$P_2 = P \cdot h(r, G) \quad \text{and} \quad P_{f2} = P_f h_f(r_f, G_f) \tag{8.50}$$

From (8.19a)′ and (8.50)

$$E = (P/P_f)(h/h_f) \tag{8.51}$$

Using the money market equilibrium conditions for the home and foreign countries the price levels are written as:

$$P = M/L \quad \text{and} \quad P_f = M_f/L_f \Rightarrow$$

$$E = (M/M_f)(L_f/L)(h/h_f) \tag{8.52}$$

Also (8.48) can be rewritten as:

$$\overline{E}/E = r - r_f + 1 \tag{8.48)'$$

For the short and the long-run dynamics of the model, the rates of changes in the forward and spot rates of exchange are derived from the time derivatives of (8.48)′ subject to (8.47) and assuming $r_f$ and $P$ and $Y$ constant in the short-run. Differentiating (8.48)′ subject to (8.47) ⇒

$$(\bar{E}/E) - (\bar{E}\,\dot{E}/E^2) = r_1'\dot{M}/P = \dot{M}/PL_r' \tag{8.53}$$

(8.53) can be divided through by (8.48)′ to get the following equation in rates of changes denoted by the respective small letters

$$\bar{e} - \dot{e} = \left(\frac{1}{r - r_f + 1}\right)\frac{M}{L_r'P} \tag{8.54}$$

Defining a composite elasticity term, η, (8.54) can be further simplified to:

$$\eta\,(M/P) = L_r{}'(r - r_f + 1) \tag{8.55}$$

Substituting (8.55) into (8.54) the equation in proportional rates of changes becomes:

$$\bar{e} = \dot{e} + (1/\eta)\,\dot{m} \tag{8.56}$$

Equation (8.48) or its variant (8.48)′ or the rate of change version (8.56) together with the expectation rule (8.49) can prove the overshooting incidence. In the short-run with inflexible prices and output a decrease in the domestic money supply ($\dot{m} < 0$) requires a rise in the domestic interest rate, $r$ ($r - r_f > 0$) which, in turn causes a potential capital inflow which can be stopped only if the domestic exchange rate is expected to depreciate. An expected depreciation of the domestic currency calls for an appreciation of the actual spot rate above its long run equilibrium value. The extent of overshooting depends inversely on the interest elasticity of the demand for money and the speed of adjustment of expectations as shown below. As the expected future spot rate is the same as the forward exchange rate, the expectations rule yields:

$$\bar{E}_t = E_{t-1} + \lambda(E_t - E_{t-1})$$

$$\Rightarrow \quad [(\bar{E}_t - E_{t-1})/E_{t-1}] = \lambda(E_t - E_{t-1})/E_{t-1}$$

$$\Rightarrow \quad \bar{e} = \lambda\dot{e} \tag{8.57}$$

Substituting (8.57) into (8.58)

$$(1 - \lambda)\,\dot{e} = -(1/\eta)\,\dot{m}$$

$$\Rightarrow \quad \dot{e} = -\left\{\frac{1}{\eta\,(1-\lambda)}\right\}\dot{m} \tag{8.59}$$

This differential equation can be rewritten in terms of $E$ and $M$ as:

$$(\dot{E}/E) = -\left\{\frac{1}{\eta\,(1-\lambda)}\right\}\dot{M}/M \tag{8.60}$$

Integrating (8.60) with respect to time one can obtain:

$$\log E_t = -\left(\frac{1}{\eta(1-\lambda)}\right)\log M_t + C \tag{8.61}$$

Where the constant of integration $C$ can be evaluated at equilibrium as:

$$\log E_t^* + \left\{\frac{1}{\eta(1-\lambda)}\right\}\log M_t^*$$

$\Rightarrow$ the solution for $E$ can be written as:

$$\log E - \log E^* = -\frac{1}{\eta(1-\lambda)}\{\log M - \log M^*\} \tag{8.62}$$

(8.62) excludes variables like, $Y, P$, etc., by assumption and $r$ and $r_f$ by substitution but these can be included explicitly very easily by following an alternative route in substitution. For example, by using (8.48) and the goods and money market equilibrium conditions. However, the overshooting of exchange rate above its long-run equilibrium value, $E^*$ in response to money supply is evident from (8.62). This derivation is subject to the assumption that the forward exchange rate is an accurate predictor of the future spot exchange rate. But this assumption may not always be a valid one. Among other, Stulz (1987) develops a model where the forward exchange rate is, in general, a biased predictor of the future spot exchange rate. Stulz's model will be discussed later.

### *Kouri (1976)*

Kouri goes beyond Dornbusch (1976) in his short and longer run dynamic analyses of flexible exchange rates. The role of exchange rates in a monetary model is to equilibriate the international markets for financial assets. This therefore necessitates an examination of the demand and supplies of different national monies and assets. (The stock approach is more important than the flow approach as revisions of existing portfolios in an international context are of a much larger size than minor additions to asset demands through new saving). Viewing the exchange rate as a relative price of two financial assets, Kouri links stability of exchange rates to asset substitution effects and the nature of expectations formation. The short and long-run effects of stabilisation policies depend on the nature of expectations formation. A number of simplifying assumptions are made in Kouri's model: full employment of labour, flexibility of wages, production of traded goods only and these have a fixed relative price in the world market and that domestic and foreign money are the only two assets in the economy. The layout of the model is very similar to that of the MF model. The obvious differences are the inclusion of expected rate of inflation in the demand functions — consumption, real money balances and foreign assets demand. A wealth constraint is added in the usual way — wealth is the sum of real money and foreign assets. Investment is assumed to be zero making domestic absorption equal to $C+G$. The short-run and the long-run dynamic implications of the model are shown in the Appendix 8.A.4. The results can be summarised as follows:

1. Real variables and fiscal policy in particular affect the long run demand for money and, therefore, the exchange rate cannot be determined by monetary factors alone.
2. An important difference between the fixed and flexible exchange rate regimes in the long-run is made by the expected rate of inflation and the latter can be varied independently of the rest of the world which in turn, alters money demand and therefore the stock of wealth.
3. An once and for all intervention in the foreign exchange market has no long-run effect on the real variables. A purchase of $x$ units of foreign currency by the Central Bank leads to a period of current account surplus which add up to exactly $x$ units of foreign exchange. Such intervention will, therefore, manifest itself in a proportionate increase in the exchange rate.
4. Fiscal policy can affect the long-run equilibrium position by changing the tax revenue and the rate of inflation. The effect of an increase in $\dot{p}^e$ is shown in (8.A.4).

*Barro (1978)*

Barro's model of exchange rate determination is similar in many respects to some of the models already discussed above but it has at least two important differences:

(a) it considers specific explicit sources of uncertainties, e.g., those concerning the time paths of the domestic money stock and quantity of output and of the world price level in the rational expectation framework; and
(b) the exchange rate is not determined by the BOP equilibrium condition but by the equilibrium between actual and desired or target domestic holdings of foreign money.

The stock demand for domestic money is assumed to be a function of real income and the expected relative rate of inflation. Wealth is excluded for the sake of convenience.

The log-linear form is assumed throughout. The expected relative rate of return on foreign money is accordingly given by:

$$\Phi = \log P^e_{t+1} - \log P_t - (\log P^e_{ft+1} - \log P_{ft}) \quad (8.63)$$

Barro assumes $(\log P^e_{ft+1} - \log P_{ft}) = \overline{p}f =$ constant trend growth rate of $P_f$.

From the logarithm of the PPP equation (8.19b)

$$\log P_t = \log P_{ft} + \log E_t$$

$$\Rightarrow \quad \Phi = \log E^e_{t+1} - \log E_t \quad (8.35)$$

(8.35) means that the expected rate of return on foreign money relative to domestic money is the expected depreciation of the exchange rate. The stock demand for domestic money is assumed to have unitary income elasticity:

$$\log M_t - \log P_t = a_0(\dot{p}^e_t - \dot{p}^e_{ft}) + \log Y_t \quad (8.64)$$

The expected domestic rate of inflation relative to the foreign rate can be re-expressed in terms of expected rate of exchange rate depreciation:

$$\dot{p}^e_t = \frac{\dot{P}^e}{P^e} = \Delta \log P^e \text{ in the discrete form}$$

$$\Rightarrow \quad \dot{p}^e_t - \dot{p}^e_{ft} = \log P^e_{t+1} - \log P_t - \log P^e_{ft+1} + \log P_{ft}$$

$$= \log E^e_{t+1} - \log E_t.$$

Substitution of this and (8.19b) yields

$$\log M_t - \log E_t - \log P_{ft}$$

$$= a_0(\log E^e_{t+1} - \log E_t) + \log Y_t \quad (8.65)$$

$a_0$ in (8.65) < 0. Similarly, the target demand for foreign money is $\log M^*_f$ given by (8.66) and the actual demand adjusts to the target demand each period at a speed $0 < \lambda < 1$. The desired flow of foreign money also depends on the normal rate of growth of domestic output, $g$ and it has to maintain a fixed real value. Including all these considerations, the desired flow of foreign money is given by (8.66):

$$\log M_f^* - \log P_f = b_0 + b_1(\log P_{ft+1}^e - \log P_{ft}) + \log Y_t$$

$$+ b_2(\log E_{t+1}^e - \log E_t) \quad (8.66)$$

and

$$\log M_{ft+1} - \log M_{ft} = \lambda[\log M_{ft}^* - \log M_{ft}] + g \quad (8.67)$$

$b_1 < 0$, $b_2 > 0$ and $0 < \lambda < 1$ (8.66) and (8.67) together yield

$$\log M_{ft+1} - \log M_{ft} = \lambda[b_0 + b_1(\log P_{ft+1}^e - \log P_{ft})$$

$$+ \log Y_t + b_2(\log E_{t+1}^e - \log E_t)$$

$$- (\log M_{ft} - \log P_{ft})] + (\log P_{ft+1}^e$$

$$- \log P_{ft}) + g \quad (8.68)$$

In explaining the process generating the domestic money supply Barro distinguishes between permanent and temporary random shocks, *mp* and *mt* respectively each of which is assumed to be normally and independently distributed with zero mean, constant variance, $\sigma_p^2$ and $\sigma_t^2$ respectively and zero autocovariance. The normal rate of growth of money stock is assumed to be $\overline{m} = \overline{\log M}$. These assumptions yield the money supply equation:

$$\log M_t = (\log M_{t-1} - \log mt_{t-1}) + (\log mp)_t$$

$$+ (\log mt)_t + \overline{m} \quad (8.69)$$

Actual growth of output is its normal trend growth plus a random disturbance which is again assumed to be a white noise like *mp* and *mt* implying

$$\log Y_t = gt + u_t \quad (8.70)$$

The world price level is assumed to have its growth rate given by

$$\log P_{ft} = \log P_{ft-1} + \overline{p}_f + \varepsilon_t \quad (8.71)$$

where $\varepsilon_t$ is another white noise term.

Finally the assumption of RE is added to the model consisting of (8.63)–(8.71). The determination of $E_t$, $E_{t+1}^e$ and balance of payments is discussed in the Appendix 8.A.5. The BOP is related to the proportional growth rate of domestic holdings of foreign money, i.e., to the difference: $\log M_{ft+1} - \log M_{ft}$ which can be obtained from (8.68). The solution for the expected change in the exchange rate is derived by assuming a constant normal or trend growth rate, $\overline{m}$ and a constant expected rate of inflation abroad, $(\log P^e_{ft+1} - \log P_{ft}) = \overline{p}_f$. The solution of the model as given in (8.A.88) shows that the expected change in the exchange rate remains unchanged after an increase in the current domestic money stock assuming the temporary component of shock to be fixed.

*Calvo and Rodriguez (1977)*

Their model is very similar to that of Barro and Mussa's (1982) already discussed above. But they concentrate on the real exchange rate determination assuming complete flexibility of prices (and RE and considering domestic and foreign money as the two assets) with explicit consideration of the consumption functions for traded and non-traded goods. In the short-run, the real exchange rate is shown to depend on the rate of growth of money supply but in the long-run only the real variables affect the exchange rate. The consumption of traded and non-traded goods is assumed to depend on the real exchange rate and the real value of assets. The foreign currency price of traded goods is assumed equal to unity implying that the domestic currency price of the traded good equals the nominal exchange rate. The real exchange rate is the nominal exchange rate divided by the nominal price of the non-traded goods. In this model the only way the economy can alter the level of foreign currency holdings is through an excess supply or demand for traded goods:

$$(dM_f/dt) = Y_2(er) - C_2(er, v) = F(er, v) \tag{8.72}$$

where $Y_2$ and $C_2$ are the rates of production and consumption of traded goods respectively, $er$ is the real exchange rate. $Y_2$ increases with $er$ but $C_2$ falls as $er$ increases $\Rightarrow M'_{f1} > 0$. $V$ is the real value of assets consisting of foreign and domestic monies:

$$V = (M/P_1) + er\, M_f \tag{8.73}$$

Prices are assumed completely flexible and the market for non-traded goods is always in equilibrium:

$$Y_1(er) = C_1(er, v) \tag{8.74}$$

$Y_1' < 0$ as a rise in the real exchange rate makes the production of tradables more profitable. From the above three equations (8.71)–(8.74) and the sign restrictions on the derivatives a reduced form equation for total assets can be derived:

$$V = V(er), \quad V' < 0 \tag{8.75}$$

Substituting (8.75), one can derive the following dynamic equation for the stock of foreign exchange:

$$(dM_f/dt) - H(er) \text{ where } H' = F_1' + F_2'V' > 0 \tag{8.76}$$

(8.76) constitutes one of the two dynamic equations of the CR model. The other dynamic equation is for the real exchange rate derived in the following way. The real rate of return on domestic currency holding is the negative of the domestic rate of inflation and that on foreign currency holdings is the rate of depreciation of the domestic currency minus the domestic rate of inflation. The expected difference between the two rates of return is, therefore,

$$(\dot{E}^e - \dot{p}_1) - \dot{p}_1 = \dot{E}^e$$

where $\dot{p}_1$ is the rate of change of non-traded goods price. No other country is assumed to hold small country's currency. Like Mussa, Calvo and Rodriguez assume perfect foresight and therefore equates the expected rate of change to the actual rate and writes the ratio of domestic to foreign currency demands as a function of $\dot{E}$ and then derive a reduced form equation for $\dot{E}$:

$$\frac{M/\hat{p}_1}{er\,M_f} = g(\dot{E}) \Rightarrow$$

$$\dot{E} = \Phi\left(\frac{M/P_1}{er \cdot M_f}\right) \text{with } \Phi' < 0 \tag{8.77}$$

Using the definition of the real exchange rate, $er = (E/P_1)$, the rate of change, $\dot{E} = \dot{e}r + \dot{p}_1$ where $\dot{e}r = \frac{der}{dt} \cdot \frac{1}{er}$

$$\Rightarrow \quad e\dot{r} + \dot{p}_1 = \Phi(\cdot) \tag{8.78}$$

Now the rate of inflation as shown on many occasions before (and used in the context of Barro's model) is the difference between the rates of growth of nominal and real money stocks:

$$\dot{p}_1 = \dot{m} - \mu \tag{8.79}$$

$$\Rightarrow \quad e\dot{r} = \Phi(\ldots) + \mu - \dot{m} \tag{8.80}$$

Finally the rate of change of real money stock is obtained from the equations of the model. From (8.73), the real money stock is:

$$M/P_1 = V - er \cdot M_f \tag{8.81}$$

Differentiating (8.81) w.r.t. time,

$$dM/dt \cdot \frac{1}{P_1} - \frac{MdP_1/dt}{P_1^2} = (dV/dt) - er\,dM_f/dt - M_f d\,er/dt$$

Dividing through by $M/P_1$, the rate of change of real money stock is obtained as:

$$\mu = \frac{1}{(V - er \cdot M_f)}\left[V'\frac{der}{dt} - erF - M_f\frac{der}{dt}\right]$$

$$\Rightarrow \quad \mu = \frac{er}{(V - er \cdot M_f)}[(V' - M_f)e\dot{r} - F] \tag{8.82}$$

Substitution for $\mu$ yields the final expression for the second dynamic equation of the CR model:

$$e\dot{r} = \Phi(\cdots) - \dot{m} + \left(\frac{er}{V - erM_f}\right)[(V' - M_f)e\dot{r} - F]$$

$$\Rightarrow \quad e\dot{r}\left\{1 - \frac{er\,(V' - m_f)}{V - er \cdot M_f}\right\} = \Phi - \dot{m} - \frac{er \cdot F}{V - er \cdot M_f}$$

$$\Rightarrow \quad e\dot{r} = \left(\frac{V - er \cdot M_f}{V - er \cdot V'}\right)(\Phi - \dot{m}) - \left(\frac{er}{V - er \cdot V'}\right)F \tag{8.83}$$

(8.76) and (8.83) constitute the dynamic model of Calvo and Rodriguez. From (8.83), it follows that a higher rate of monetary expansion produces an instantaneous deterioration of the local exchange rate. It also follows from the asset stock function (8.75) and the nature of the consumption functions that a higher real exchange rate means a lower stock of assets ($V' < 0$) is required for equilibrium in the home market (as $C_1$ increases with *er*). But with a given stock of foreign currency and a given initial stock of nominal money balances, the only way in which $V$ can fall is through a rise in $P_1$. A rise in the real exchange rate with a rise in the domestic price level must imply that the exchange rate will depreciate by more than the increase in the price level as a result of the monetary expansion.

Helpman and Razin (1982) point out that Calvo and Rodriguez should have considered the effects of future incomes on current spending. It is their model that we turn to in the next section.

## 8.2.3 The Microfoundations of Open Economy Models

### 8.2.3.1 *The Microfoundations of Monetarism Under a Floating Exchange Rate Regime*

In the models discussed above home and foreign economies have well defined aggregate money demand functions and the exchange rate is derived by the real supply of each currency relative to its real demand. But the links between the consumption behaviour and relative money demands have not been adequately discussed in any of these models. The supply structure of and the propensities to spend on traded and non-traded goods in the home and foreign economies have important implications for money demands and exchange rate movements.

*Helpman and Razin (HR) (1982)*

Helpman and Razin consider the effects of sectoral factors on the dynamics of the real exchange rate and show that unanticipated changes in money supply affect the real exchange rate through redistribution of wealth whereas anticipated changes in money supply have no such effects. The HR model is similar to the models discussed above in many respects. For example, it assumes that the foreign and the domestic economy produce both traded and non-traded goods; that the PPP and the interest rate parity conditions hold etc. But there are important modifications to the previous analysis as well. The model includes the bond markets and an infinite time horizon.

The representative consumer of each economy is assumed to choose an optimal infinite time pattern of consumption of traded and non-traded goods such that the discounted present value of utility is maximised subject to the budget constraint. As the model assumes an infinite planning horizon, the budget constraint consists of the discounted present value of its output plus an indebtedness term. The indebtedness is inherited from the past and cannot be altered in period $t = 0$. The foreign country's indebtedness is the negative of the home country's implying that the net value of indebtedness across countries is zero. The intertemporal allocation of spending between the traded and the non-traded goods for the domestic economy is obtained as solutions to the problem:

$$\text{Choose} \quad \{C_{1t}, C_{2t}\}_{t=0}^{\infty} \tag{8.84a}$$

such that $\sum_{t=0}^{\infty} d^t u'(C_{1t}, C_{2t})$ (8.84b)

is maximised subject to:

$$V_0 \leq \sum_{t=0}^{\infty} d_t'(P_{1t}Y_{1t} + P_{f2t}Y_{2t}) - (B_0/E_0) - B_{f0} \tag{8.84c}$$

The above optimising problem uses $d$ and $d'$ as the discounting factors for future utility and future income respectively. The foreign economy version can be written in exactly the same way with a change of subscript. The equation (8.84c) is the home country's net wealth in terms of foreign currency at the beginning of period zero. From this intertemporal allocation problem, the temporal allocation of spending can be separated in terms of an indirect utility function, which is additively separable in prices and spending, $Z$:

$$U(P_1, P_{f2}, Z) = \log Z - a_1 \log P_1 - a_2 \log P_{f2} \tag{8.85}$$

where $Z_t = P_{1t}C_{1t} + P_{f2t}C_{2t}$ (8.86)

The optimal allocation problem implied by (8.84) now means choosing $\left\{Z_t\right\}_{t=0}^{\infty}$ to maximise $\sum_{t=0}^{\infty} d^t \log Z_t$ subject to $\sum_{t=0}^{\infty} (d')^t Z_t \leq V_0$.

The solution to this problem and how the demand functions can be derived from (8.87) is shown in the Appendix 8.A.6. The demand functions are given in (8.88). Equations (8.90) are the equilibrium conditions in commodity markets of respective economies. Helpman and Razin assume that all money is used for transaction purposes. So, the demand for a country's money equals the value of the world's demand for its good. This is expressed by equations (8.89) where $M$ and $M_f$ are the money supply of the domestic and foreign economies respectively. As shown in the appendix the solutions for $Z_t$ and $Z_{ft}$ together with (8.89)–(8.91) determine the equilibrium time paths of prices, interest rates and exchange rates for given $M_t$, $M_{ft}$ and $V_0$ and $V_{f0}$. Helpman and Razin assume perfect foresight and consider monetary policies which assure positive interest rates in every country in every period. This means that neither currency will be used as a store-of-value. Future value of output is discounted, as shown in (8.92), on the basis of the interest rate parity. The HR model consists of the following equations:

$$u(C_1, C_2) = a_1 \log C_1 + a_2 \log C_2 + a_0 \tag{8.87a}$$

where $a_1, a_2 > 0$, $a_1 + a_2 = 1$ and $a_0 = -(a_1 \log a_1 + a_2 \log a_2)$.

$$u(C_{f1}, C_{f2}) = a_{f1} \log C_{f1} + a_{f2} \log C_{f2} + a_{f0} \tag{8.87b}$$

where $a_{f1}, a_{f2} > 0$, $a_{f1} + a_{f2} = 1$ and $a_{f0} = -(a_{f1} \log a_{f1} + a_{f2} \log a_{f2})$.

$$C_{1t} = a_1 Z_t / P_{1t}, \quad C_{2t} = a_2 Z_t / P_{f2t} \tag{8.88a}$$

$$C_{f1t} = a_{f1} Z_{ft} / P_{f1t}, \quad C_{f2t} = a_{f2} Z_{ft} / P_{f2t} \tag{8.88b}$$

$$P_{1t} Y_{1t} + P_{f2t} Y_{2t} = M_t / E_t \tag{8.89a}$$

$$P_{f1} Y_{f1t} + P_{f2t} Y_{f2t} = M_{ft} \tag{8.89b}$$

$$P_{1t} Y_{1t} = a_1 Z_t \tag{8.90a}$$

$$P_{f1t} Y_{f1t} = a_{f1} Z_{ft} \tag{8.90b}$$

$$P_{f2t}(Y_{2t} + Y_{f2t}) = a_2 Z_t + a_{f2} Z_{ft} \tag{8.91}$$

$$(1 + r_t) = (1 + r_{ft}) E_{t+1} / E_t \tag{8.92}$$

$$P_{f2} E = P_2 \tag{8.19a}$$

*Stulz (1987)*

It is evident from above that the HR model assumes no investment in the foreign or domestic economy. The optimisation problem of households has been considered by Stulz for the purpose of determining exchange rates and asset prices. Not only does the model deal with international investment but it also considers the case of imperfect information.

The similarities and the differences are discussed below:

1. Like Dornbusch, Mussa and others, Stulz assumes that each country in the two country model produces an internationally traded and a non-traded commodity. But the production is uncertain and the technologies change stochastically over time.
2. The households can trade a large number of financial assets but the currency of each country is held only by the households of that country. Four of the financial assets are taken to be equities. The financial markets of both countries are assumed to be extremely well developed such that households can even trade claims to future transfers.
3. Like in the HR model each household is assumed to have a logarithmic utility function but it is time additive and utility depends on the consumption of commodities and the holdings of

real balances. Households are assumed to have constant expenditure shares so that no aggregation problem arises within each country; but expenditure shares can vary across countries.

4. Households are also assumed to have the same wealth in terms of the domestic currency. A household's wealth consists of holdings of financial assets, real money balances and the current value of the future transfer payments from the government.
5. The stochastic elements of the model imply that the household will have to maximise the expected utility. Stulz formulates a continuous time model where the representative household maximises the expected life time utility from consumption and real money balances.
6. As noted in the case of the HR model, consumption demands are derived, from logarithmic utility functions, as linear functions of wealth. Likewise, Stulz derives consumption and portfolio decisions as linear functions of wealth.
7. Due to the simplifying assumptions of constant expenditure shares, constant wealth holding, no holding of foreign currency etc., the equilibrium prices of financial assets, etc. are independent of the world distribution of wealth.
8. The previous assumptions and the assumption of PPP for the traded good imply that the equilibrium nominal exchange rate depends only on expenditure shares, nominal interest rates and money supplies but not on output or wealth.
9. As in the monetary models discussed in this Chapter, the nominal exchange rate in Stulz's model increases with domestic money supply and nominal interest rate and falls as the foreign money stock increases. But unlike in the former class of models, the nominal exchange rate is independent of a direct influence of output.
10. Assuming constant returns to scale, perfect capital mobility and well developed financial and capital markets Stulz shows that the real exchange rate solely depends on the relative stocks of domestic and foreign non-traded goods. The real exchange rate, therefore, will respond to real shocks. For example if the stock of foreign non-traded goods increases whereas the stock of the domestic non-traded goods stays constant, the former will be relatively cheap implying a fall in the real value of the foreign currency and a departure from the PPP. The effect on the real exchange rate of such output shocks can be either temporary or permanent

depending on the time series properties of such shocks. Like Mussa's time-series modelling of monetary shocks to explain variation of the nominal exchange rate, Stulz discusses the time series properties of real shocks to explain overshooting of real exchange rates.

### 8.2.4 Microfoundation when Government Budget is Included

Chapter five has considered a number of closed economy models including government budget constraints on the assumption that government bonds constitute net wealth to individual asset holders. In an open economy context the international transmission of government spending and its effect on world real rates of interest have been the subject of a number of important contributions. Surveys of these models are available in Fair, Mussa (1979) and in Marston (1985). Frenkel and Razin have discussed the impact of world debt and fiscal policy on world interest rates in the context of open economy macro models in 1985 and 1986. The following is adapted from their 1986 paper.

*Frenkel and Razin*

Frenkel and Razin (FR) (1986) discuss the microfoundations in terms of a two-economy global model for the present, $t = 0$, and the future time period $t = 1, 2, \cdots \infty$. The entire future time period is consolidated into a single time period by considering the present values of future consumption, output and government budget deficits. Similar to the HR and Stulz's analyses, FR derive the aggregate consumption demand as a linear function of aggregate wealth following the analysis of inter-temporal maximisation of a logarithmic utility function. Aggregate wealth consists of the difference between human wealth and private debt. Human wealth is measured, as in the life cycle hypothesis, by the present value of future disposable incomes discounted at the *effective* rate of interest. The effective rate of interest is a function of the average market rate of interest and the probability of death which is the same for all individuals and is independent of age. There are other simplifying assumptions made to minimise the aggregation error. In addition, there is no private investment and government spending is simply assumed to be financed by taxation and bond sales. As there are both private and government debt in the model an additional subscript, $g$, is added to $B$. The total value of debt in each economy is the sum of private and government debt. Capital markets are assumed to be completely integrated such that both countries face the same market rates of interest. This feature therefore, constitutes the main channel through which fiscal policies of one country affect the rest of the world. The periods considered in the FR model are the current period denoted by the subscript zero and the future consisting of $t = 1, 2, \cdots \infty$. The two sets of equilibrium conditions for each economy specify the initial equilibrium value of wealth and that the present and future goods markets clear. These are given in the equations (8.93) and (8.94) respectively.

*The FR Model*

$$V_0 = (Y_0 - T_0) + \left(\frac{\alpha R}{1-\alpha R}\right)(Y - T) + B_{go} - B_0 \tag{8.93a}$$

$$V_{f0} = (Y_{f0} - T_{f0}) + \left(\frac{\alpha R}{1-\alpha R}\right)(Y_f - T_f) + B_{fg0} + B_0 \tag{8.93b}$$

$$(1-\alpha d)\,V_0 + (1-\alpha d_f)\,V_{f0} = Y_0 - G_0 + Y_{f0} - G_{f0} \tag{8.94a}$$

$$\left[(\alpha d V_0) + \frac{R\,(1-\alpha)(Y-T)}{(1-R)(1-\alpha R)}\right] + [\left(\alpha d_f V_{f0} + \frac{R\,(1-\alpha)(Y_f - T_f)}{(1-R)(1-\alpha R)}\right]$$

$$= \frac{R}{1-R}[Y - G + Y_f - G_f] \tag{8.94b}$$

$$(T_0 - G_0) + \frac{R}{1-R}(T - G) = B_{g0} \tag{8.95a}$$

$$(T_{f0} - G_{f0}) + \frac{R}{1-R}(T_f - G_f) = B_{fg0} \tag{8.95b}$$

$$V_t = H_t - B_{pt} \tag{8.96a}$$

$$V_{ft} = H_{ft} - B_{pft} \tag{8.96b}$$

Where $H_t$ is the discounted present value of future disposable incomes. $R$ is termed as a "constancy equivalent" interest factor (p. 569). $\alpha$ is the constant probability of death assumed equal not only within a country but also across countries. Equations (8.93a) and (8.93b) specify the initial equilibrium values of wealth for the domestic and the foreign economy respectively. (8.94a) specifies the equilibrium in the world market for goods for the current period. The sum total of current consumption and current government spending equals the total current output in the world market, $(Y_0 + Y_{f0})$. The current consumption in each economy is derived from an analysis similar to that in the HR and Stulz models. The representative consumer maximises the expected utility of lifetime consumption taking explicit account of the probability of death and subject to a budget constraint. The budget constraint requires that the value of debt at the beginning of a period plus the value of consumption be equal to the disposable income in each period. Future consumption being discounted at the rate, $d$, the current consumption is derived as $C_0 = (1 - \alpha d)\, V_0$ and $C_{f0} = (1 - \alpha d)\, V_{f0}$ as shown in the Appendix 8.A.7.

Equation (8.94b) states the global equilibrium condition for the future goods market. Future consumption demands and output in the foreign and domestic economies are derived as the discounted sum of the series of consumption and output for all future time periods. The output series is discounted using $R$, the interest constancy factor. The present and future consumption demands are derived in the Appendix 8.A.7. The equations (8.95) specify the government budget constraints for the present and the future time periods for the domestic and the foreign economies. As already implied, the budget constraint for the future is the discounted value of the budget deficit series $(T_t - G_t)$ for all the future periods $t = 1, 2, \cdots \infty$ discounted at the rate, $R$. Frenkel and Razin focus on the impact of budget deficits rather than on that of government spending. They assume that changes in budget deficits are brought about by changes in lump-sum taxes for a given path of government spending. Since government spending is assumed to remain unchanged, current tax changes must be exactly offset by future tax changes in the opposite direction. So the condition for balanced budget requires, in addition to (8.95),

$$dT_0 = -\frac{R}{1-R}\, dT \tag{8.97}$$

where $(R/1 - R) = \frac{1}{r}$ and $R = \frac{1}{1+r}$

The foreign government is assumed to follow a balanced budget policy. This assumption implies that the domestic fiscal deficits affecting the world interest rates do not cause any secondary changes in foreign fiscal policies.

The reduced form of the FR model can be derived by using the government budget equations and Walras's law. The latter can make equation (8.93a) redundant and substitution from the government budget equations reduce the FR model to the two equations (8.A.103a) and (8.A.103b) as shown in the Appendix, 8.A.7. The effects of current and future budget deficits on interest rate factor and on consumption and wealth of the foreign and domestic economies can then be derived from the reduced form of the model in the usual manner. The results derived in the Appendix, 8.A.7, show that these three sets of multipliers are highly sensitive to the nature as well as the time patterns of fiscal policies. The conclusions of the model are subject to the main assumptions of the model. The most important one being the absence of money from the consumption demand, wealth and the government budget equations. Assuming that the probability of death is less than one, the FR model is able to alter the Ricardian proposition that "budget deficits do not matter" (p. 284). An important characteristic of the FR model is that it draws a distinction between the market interest factor influencing the government budget equation and the effective interest factor that individuals use in discounting future taxes.

### 8.2.5 A Synthesis of Keynesian and Monetary Theories

In the previous sections of the present Chapter, a good many number of open economy models have been discussed. Some of these models have emphasised the importance of real factors like trade and capital flows while some have stressed the importance of monetary factors in explaining the exchange rate and BOP. In the literature the former group of models has been understandably classified as Keynesian and the latter as monetary. The nature of these models and the factors examined and analysed also demonstrate the interdependence between these two types of approaches to theories of BOP. The two groups of models can be viewed as complementary rather than rivals. The Keynesian approach emphasising variation in employment and production of traded and non-traded goods and relations among exports and imports is important in the short-run context and the monetary approach is important in the long-run context. To explain both the short and long runs one has to mingle the two approaches. Such a synthesis is provided, among others, by Frenkel, Gylfason and Halliwell, (1980) and Montiel (1986). Their contributions are discussed below. The following discussion especially that of Montiel's, being closely related to the ideas explained and explored in various sections of the present (and previous) chapter(s) also removes the need for a separate section on conclusions in this chapter.

*Frenkel, Gylfason and Helliwell*

Frenkel *et al.* provide a synthesis of the two approaches for the short-run. The basic ingredients of the short-run Keynesian model are given by the equations (8.3a)–(8.8b) yielding the reduced form equation (8.9). The basic ingredients of the short-run monetary model are given by the equations (2.30), (4.71) yielding the reduced form equation (8.14) which is the equation to the LM curve of an open economy. The long-run monetary model assumes that there is no sterilisation and therefore the BOP must influence the money supply. The short-run Keynesian models assume full sterilisation. The two approaches can be joined together and to solve for all three endogenous variables, $P$, $Y$ and $r$, the model can be closed by a simple assumption about aggregate supply of output. The short-run synthesis therefore is provided by the output market and money market equilibrium and the aggregate supply function:

$$Y = Y(P), \quad Y' > 0 \tag{8.98}$$

*Montiel*

All the equations of Montiel's open economy models have been used and/or explained before, e.g., the sectoral production functions for traded and non-traded goods are special cases of the production function (3.2), the price-mark-up equations for non-traded goods is a special case of (6.1), the asset market equations for the open economy can be explained by the arguments given in the previous section 8.2.2 and so on.

Equations (8.99a) and (8.99b) are the production functions for non-traded and traded goods respectively where labour has positive diminishing marginal productivity in each sector.

Labour receives equal money wage in each sector and a Phillips-Curve equation (c) explains the rate of wage inflation in terms of unemployment and the expected rate of inflation. Equation (c) embodies the Keynesian characteristics emphasising that employment is demand-determined in the short-run. Percentage change in money wage exceeds the expected rate of inflation except at the natural level of employment. A small country faces an infinitely elastic demand for its traded good and purchasing power parity is assumed for the traded good. Labour demand in the traded goods sector is given by real wage as explained in (e). Stickiness of aggregate money wage is ensured by making it a continuous function of time as implied by (c).

The analysis of the non-traded goods sector follows in terms of notional and effective demands along the Clower and Barro-Grossman tradition explained in 3.6.2. Output is assumed to be demand-determined in this sector and the firms are assumed to follow a variable mark-up pricing rule. While equation (g) is a special case of equation (6.1), the mark-up factor $mr_1$ is not a constant. It increases when actual demand for non-traded goods exceeds the notional supply of firms and it falls when actual demand for non-traded goods falls short of firms' notional supply. The rate of change of $mr_1$ gives the rate of change of money wage in the non-traded goods sector as implied by equation (g). The effective demand for labour in the non-traded goods sector is derived, therefore, as a function of the demand-determined output in this sector as given in (f). The usual profit maximising level of labour demand depends on the real wage in this sector. However the effect of demand changes on prices via mark-up is assumed, realistically, to be weaker than that of unemployment on wage and price changes implying the restriction on respective slopes: $f' < \dot{\omega}$. The aggregate domestic price level is a weighted average of the two prices as in (8.31) implying the rates of change equation (j). Equations (k) and (l) explain aggregate real output and total employment respectively. Equation (m) expresses the real balance of trade in terms of the traded good. Private consumption is derived from a log-linear utility function implying constant expenditure shares, $\sigma$ and $1-\sigma$, respectively of non-traded and traded goods. Total private consumption consists of those of traded and non-traded goods and interest rate is included as a separate explanatory variable.

Investment spending of the private business sector is excluded from the model and output of the non-traded good as already pointed out is demand determined as indicated in equation (p). Equation (q)–(v) follow from equations (8.31) and (i) when the real exchange rate, *er* is defined as the price of traded in terms of non-traded goods.

The short-run equilibrium of the economy can be summarised by equations that determine the level of real output $Y$, the domestic rate of inflation $\dot{p}$ and the level of output of non-traded goods, $Y_1$.

The reduced form equations of the real sector are given by (v) of (8.99) rewritten as in (8.A.110) and equations (8.A.111) and (8.A.115) in the Appendix 8.A.8 to this chapter.

The asset market equations (8.100) can be explained very easily as follows. The real demand for domestic money is a function of real income and real interest rate. Montiel assumes the domestic interest rate to be equal to the foreign rate, $r_f$ and that it is constant.

*Montiel's Model*

*The Real Sector Equations (8.99)*

$$Y_1 = Y_1(N_1) \tag{a}$$

$$Y = Y_2(N_2) \tag{b}$$

$$Y_i' > 0 \quad \text{and} \quad Y_i'' < 0, \quad i = 1, 2$$

$$\dot{w} = \dot{w}\,(N_1 + N_2 - \overline{N}) + \dot{p}^e \tag{c}$$

$$P_2 = EP_{f2} \tag{d}$$

$$\dot{w}\,(0) = 0 \quad \text{and} \quad \dot{w}' > 0$$

$$N_2 = N_2(W/P_2) \tag{e}$$

$$N_2' < 0$$

$$N_1^{ed} = N_1^{ed}(Y_1) \quad N_1^{ed} > 0 \tag{f}$$

$$P_1 = mr_1 W \tag{g}$$

$$\dot{m}r_1 = -\dot{w}_1 = f(N_1^{ed} - N_1(W/P_1)) \tag{h}$$

$$f(0) = 0, f' > 0 \text{ and } f' < \dot{w}'$$

$$\dot{p}_1 = \dot{m}r_1 + \dot{w} \tag{i}$$

$$\dot{p} = \sigma\dot{p}_1 + (1-\sigma)\,\dot{p}_2 \tag{j}$$

$$\dot{p} = \dot{p}_e \Rightarrow \text{perfect foresight}$$

$$Y = (P_1/P)\,Y_1 + (P_2/P)\,Y_2 \tag{k}$$

$$N = N_1 + N_2 \tag{l}$$

$$BT = (P_2/P)\,(Y_2 - C_2 - G_2) \tag{m}$$

$$C = C_1 + C_2 \tag{n}$$

$$C = C\,(Y - T, r_f, V_p) \tag{o}$$

$$0 < C_1' < 1, \quad C_2' < 0, \quad C_3' > 0$$

$$Y_1 = C_1 + G_1 \tag{p}$$

$$C_1 = \sigma C P_1/P \tag{q}$$

$$C_2 = (1-\sigma)\, C P_2/P \tag{r}$$

$$er = P_2/P_1 \tag{s}$$

$$er^{\sigma} = P_1/P \tag{t}$$

$$er^{1-\sigma} = P_2/P \tag{u}$$

$$Y = er^{\sigma} Y_1 + er^{1-\sigma} Y_2 \tag{v}$$

*The Asset Market Equations (8.100)*

$$M/P = L(Y, r_f) \tag{a}$$

$$V_p P = M + EF_{pf} + B_p \tag{b}$$

From (a) and (b):

$$\Rightarrow \quad EF_{pf} = V_p P - B_p - L(Y, r_f) \tag{c}$$

$$V_g P = EF_{gf} + B_g - B_p = M \tag{d}$$

$$\Rightarrow \quad BOP = E\dot{F}_{gf} = \dot{M} - \dot{B}_g + \dot{B}_p$$

$$\Rightarrow \quad BOP = P\,(L_1'\dot{Y} + L_2'\dot{r}_f) + M\dot{P} - \dot{B}_g + \dot{B}_p \tag{e}$$

$$VP = (V_p + V_g)P \tag{f}$$

$$F_f = F_{gf} + F_{pf} \tag{g}$$

$$CUr = Y + r_f EF_f - C - G \tag{h}$$

$$Sn = (\dot{P} V_p + P\dot{V}_p) = PY + r_f P\,(V_p - M/P) - PT - PC \tag{i}$$

$$S = Sn/P \tag{j}$$

Equation (b) gives total financial wealth of the private sector. The demand for foreign securities by the private sector, $F_f$, is then derived from (a) and (b). The government's net financial wealth similarly consists of foreign securities $F_{gf}$ and credit extended to the domestic sector net of all liabilities. The latter consist of total money supply and borrowing from the public. As explained in the equations (4.75) and (4.76) *BOP* can be related to changes in money supply, domestic credit etc.

Montiel uses a continuous time version of (4.76) and uses equation (e) of (8.100). Total financial wealth consists of private plus government wealth and it represents total savings of the private and government sectors as shown in the section 4.3. From similar considerations the real value of the current account is derived as in the equation (h) of (8.100).

The long-run equilibrium has to take complete account of the dynamics of the model. The dynamic equations have been derived in the Appendix 8.A.9. The main conclusions of the present model incorporating Keynesian and Monetary elements are summarised here:

(a) In the long-run the economy attains Walrasian equilibrium in the sense that full-employment prevails and all firms in the non-traded goods sector sell on their notional supply curves.
(b) The long-run constancy of real exchange rate implies that relative purchasing power parity holds in the long-run.
(c) Equilibrium of the *BOP* implies that changes in the stock of domestic credit are exactly offset by changes in the stock of foreign exchange reserves assumed to be held in the form of foreign securities. This, in turn, implies that an exchange rate devaluation will leave the *BOP* unchanged in the long-run.

Montiel combines the Keynesian approach emphasising wage-price inflexibility with the monetary approach emphasising the flow of reserves in a simple open economy model. This model is also entirely based on the ideas already explained in the various chapters of the present book.

### 8.2.6 A Note on Efficient (Foreign Exchange) Market Hypothesis and Exchange-Rate Determination

Simultaneously with the development of the monetary or asset approach to the theory of *BOP* and exchange rate determination examined in the previous sections there emerged a parallel approach towards exchange-rate determination based on the hypothesis of efficient foreign exchange markets. The efficient market hypothesis means that "economic agents act upon information available to them in such a way that the spot exchange rate always reflects all available information that could be potentially useful in developing trading rules that earn excess profits" [Caves and Feige (1980) p. 120]. This concept of efficient markets draws heavily from the theories of security market. The monetary models including rational expectations rule are obviously very close to the idea of efficient markets as the RE rule means that the economic agents use and act on all the relevant information available up until the time when expectations are being formed. But there is an important difference between the two approaches. One of the important consequences of an efficient foreign exchange market is that all monetary effects on the exchange rate will be contemporaneous whereas the monetary theories including RE lead to a systematic relationship between exchange rate and past supplies of money. An inefficient market is one in which prices respond sluggishly to new information implying that new information can be used to improve forecasts of future price movements in an inefficient market. In an efficient market, on the other hand, no new information can improve the forecasts as market prices "fully reflect" available information.

# APPENDIX TO CHAPTER 8

## 8.A.1 The Fiscal and Monetary Policy Multipliers in the MF Model:

The effect of a change in government spending is obtained by differentiating equations (8.15), (8.14) and (8.7) partially w.r.t. $G$. This yields the following system of equations.

$$J\begin{vmatrix} \dfrac{\partial Y}{\partial G} \\ \dfrac{\partial r}{\partial G} \\ \dfrac{\partial B{\cdot}P}{\partial G} \end{vmatrix} = \begin{vmatrix} 1 \\ w\theta \\ 0 \end{vmatrix} \tag{8.A.1}$$

where the jacobian, $J$ is

$$\begin{vmatrix} 1-C'(1-T')+E\cdot Im_1' & -I' & 0 \\ L_1'+w\theta T' & L_2' & -(1-s)w \\ E\cdot Im_1'-Ki_1' & -Ki_2' & 1 \end{vmatrix}$$

$$\Rightarrow \quad J=\{1-C'(1-T')+E\cdot Im_1'\}\,\{L_2'-Ki_2'w\,(1-s)\}$$

$$+I'\{L_1'+\theta wT'+w\,(1-s)(E\cdot Im_1'-Ki_1')\} \tag{8.A.2}$$

$=> J<0$ following the previous restrictions on the parameters. Applying Cramer's rule as before

$$\frac{\partial Y}{\partial G}=\frac{1}{J}\begin{vmatrix} 1 & -I' & 0 \\ w\theta & L_2' & -w\,(1-s) \\ 0 & -Ki_2' & 1 \end{vmatrix}$$

$$=\frac{1}{J}\{L_2'-w\,(1-s)\,Ki_2'+I'w\theta\} \tag{8.A.3}$$

$$\Rightarrow \quad \frac{\partial Y}{\partial G}>0 \tag{8.A.4}$$

It is important to note that in the event of perfect capital mobility, i.e., $Ki_2' = \infty$ there is the strongest expansionary effect of fiscal policy on real output regardless of liquidity trap or $L_2' = -\infty$.

Similarly,

$$\frac{\partial r}{\partial G} = \frac{1}{J}\begin{vmatrix} 1 - C'(1-T') + E \cdot Im_1' & 1 & 0 \\ L_1' + w\theta T' & w\theta & w(1-s) \\ E \cdot Im_1' - Ki_1' & 0 & 1 \end{vmatrix}$$

$$\Rightarrow \quad \frac{\partial r}{\partial G} = \frac{1}{J}[\theta w \{1 - C'(1-T) + E \cdot Im_1'\}$$

$$- \{L_1' + \theta w T' + (1-s) w (E \cdot Im_1' - Ki_1')\}] \tag{8.A.5}$$

$\frac{\partial r}{\partial G}$ is likely to be positive, i.e., a rise in government spending would lead to a crowding out effect (like in the closed economy model) since the first group of terms is $I'\theta W$ times the slope of the IS curve it is likely to be less than the second group of terms consisting of $-L_2'$ times the slope of the LM Curve, $\theta w$ times the marginal rate of tax and $w(1-s)Ki_2'$ times the slope of the BB curve.

If investment demand is less sensitive to interest rate changes than money demand to income and interest rate changes, then, given a steeper BB curve than the IS or LM, the multiplier in (8.A.5) is certain to be positive, i.e., a rise in government spending will lead to a rise in the interest rate in the fixed exchange rate regime.

The effect of monetary policy in this simple open economy model is given by the partial derivatives w.r.t. $\gamma$— the exogenous change in money supply. Differentiating (8.15), (8.14) and (8.7) w.r.t. $\gamma$ and then applying Cramer's rule.

$$\frac{\partial Y}{\partial \gamma} = \frac{1}{J}\begin{vmatrix} 0 & -I' & 0 \\ 1 & L_2' & -(1-s)w \\ 0 & -Ki_2' & 1 \end{vmatrix} \tag{8.A.6}$$

$$\Rightarrow \quad \frac{\partial Y}{\partial \gamma} = \frac{I'}{J} > 0 \tag{8.A.7a}$$

So, monetary policy is expansionary in the fixed exchange rate regime as long as investment demand is sensitive to interest rate changes.

The effect of a rise in the exogenous component of money supply on interest rate is summed up in

$$\frac{\partial r}{\partial \gamma}=\frac{1}{J}\begin{vmatrix} 1-C'(1-T')+E\cdot Im_1' & 0 & 0 \\ L_1'+w\theta T' & w & -w(1-s) \\ E\cdot Im_1'-Ki_1' & 0 & 1 \end{vmatrix}$$

$$\Rightarrow \quad \frac{\partial r}{\partial \gamma}=\frac{1}{J}w\{1-C'(1-T')+E\cdot Im_1'\} \tag{8.A.8}$$

$$\Rightarrow \quad \frac{\partial r}{\partial \gamma}<0. \tag{8.A.9}$$

$\Rightarrow$ Monetary policy like in the closed economy model has no negative effect on private investment but the expansionary effect on output is reduced by high capital mobility under fixed exchange rates. Dividing the numerators and the denominators of the respective multipliers (8.19) and (8.21a) by $Ki_2'$, it is seen that, if $Ki_2'=\infty$, then

$$\frac{\partial Y}{\partial G}=\frac{w(1-s)}{w(1-s)\{1-C'(1-T')+E\cdot Im_1'\}}$$

$$\Rightarrow \quad \frac{\partial Y}{\partial G}=\frac{1}{1-C'(1-T')+E\cdot Im_1'} \tag{8.A.3a}$$

$$\text{and}\ \frac{\partial Y}{\partial \gamma}=0 \tag{8.A.7b}$$

In other words under perfect capital mobility, fiscal policy is most expansionary and monetary policy impotent under fixed exchange rates.

Now differentiating the three equations (8.15), (8.17) and (8.18) w.r.t. $G$, the fiscal policy multipliers under flexible exchange rate system are obtained as:

$$\frac{\partial Y}{\partial G}=\frac{1}{J}\begin{vmatrix} 1 & -I' & -A \\ \theta w & L_2' & 0 \\ 0 & Ki_2' & A \end{vmatrix} \tag{8.A.10}$$

where $A=X'-E\cdot Im_2'-Im \Rightarrow (A/Im)=\eta_x+\eta_{Im}-1 \Rightarrow A>0$ if the Marshall-Lerner condition holds.

$$J = \begin{vmatrix} 1 - C'(1-T') + E \cdot Im_1 & -I' & -A \\ L_1' + \theta w T' & L_2' & 0 \\ Ki_1' - E \cdot Im_1' & Ki_2' & A \end{vmatrix}$$

$$\Rightarrow \quad J = A[L_2'\{1 - C'(1-T') + E \cdot Im_1'\} + I'(L_1' + \theta w T')]$$

$$-A\,[Ki_2'(L_1' + \theta w T') - L_2'(Ki_1' - E \cdot Im_1')] \qquad (8.A.11)$$

$\Rightarrow J < 0$ if the Marshall-Lerner condition is satisfied. Evaluating (8.A.10) the effect of a change in $G$ on real income is shown to be expansionary if the M-L condition holds:

$$\frac{\partial Y}{\partial G} = \frac{A}{J}(L_2' + \theta w I' - \theta w Ki_2') \quad \Rightarrow \qquad (8.A.10a)$$

$$\frac{\partial Y}{\partial G} > 0 \quad \text{if } A > 0 \quad \Rightarrow$$

$$\frac{\partial Y}{\partial G} > 0 \quad \text{if } \eta_x + \eta_{Im} > 1$$

More importantly, a rise in government spending leads to a rise in $E$ if the same restriction on elasticities holds. By Cramer's rule,

$$\frac{\partial E}{\partial G} = \frac{1}{J}[-\theta w Ki_2'\{1 - C'(1-T') + E \cdot Im_1'\} - I'\theta w\,(Ki_1' - E \cdot Im_1')$$

$$+ Ki_2'\{(L_1' + \theta w T') - L_2'(Ki_1' - E \cdot Im_1')\}]$$

$$\Rightarrow \quad \frac{\partial E}{\partial G} > 0 \quad \text{if } Ki_2'(L_1' + \theta w T') < \text{the sum of the other three.}$$

This restriction is likely to hold. A rise in government spending leads to a rise in income and, therefore, to a rise in imports and a deficit in the balance of trade and under flexible exchange rate system, exchange rate rises or the value of domestic currency falls as government spending rises.

The monetary policy multipliers are obtained in (8.A.12) and (8.A.13)

$$\frac{\partial Y}{\partial M} \Rightarrow \frac{\partial Y}{\partial \gamma} = \frac{1}{J}\begin{vmatrix} 0 & -I' & -A \\ \theta w & L_2' & 0 \\ 0 & Ki_2' & A \end{vmatrix}$$

$$\Rightarrow \quad \frac{\partial Y}{\partial \gamma} = \frac{A}{J}(I'\theta w - \theta w Ki_2') \qquad (8.A.12)$$

$\Rightarrow \frac{\partial Y}{\partial \gamma} > 0$ or that monetary policy has expansionary effect on real income.

$$\frac{\partial E}{\partial \gamma} = \frac{1}{J}\begin{vmatrix} 1 - C'(1 - T') + E \cdot Im_1' & -I' & 0 \\ L_1' + \theta w T' & L_2' & \theta w \\ Ki_1' - E \cdot Im_1' & Ki_2' & 0 \end{vmatrix}$$

$$\Rightarrow \quad \frac{\partial E}{\partial \gamma} = \frac{-\theta w Ki_2' - I'\theta w\,(Ki_1' - E \cdot Im_1')}{J} \tag{8.A.13}$$

$$\Rightarrow \quad \frac{\partial E}{\partial \gamma} > 0$$

Since a rise in money supply leads to a rise in real income a balance of trade deficit opens up through a rise in import demand and it leads to a fall in the value of the domestic currency i.e., to a rise in $Er$.

Looking at the relevant multipliers (8.A.10a) and (8.A.12) one can derive the effects of capital mobility on the efficacy of fiscal/monetary policy. Dividing through by $Ki_2'$, it is observed that

$$\frac{\partial Y}{\partial G} = 0 \text{ and } \frac{\partial Y}{\partial M} = \frac{\theta w}{L_1' + \theta w T'} \quad \text{if } Ki_2' = \infty \tag{8.A.14}$$

In other words, under perfect capital mobility fiscal policy is impotent and monetary policy potent under flexible exchange rates. With any degree of capital mobility, monetary policy is more potent than in the closed economy case. The increase in money supply initially leads to a fall in interest rate and a rise in output; and they both lead to a BOP deficit and a depreciation of the exchange rate. The latter leads to additional expansionary effect on output provided that ML condition holds.

### 8.A.2 The Effect of Money Supply on Exchange Rate in Myhrman's Model

Eliminating $V$ and $P_f$, the reduced form of Myhrman's model can be written as the following three equations in $r$, $P$ and $E$.

$$S\,(r, Y, M/P + K) + S_f(r_f, Y_f, M_f E/P + K_f) = 0 \tag{8.A.16}$$

$$KL\,(r, Y) + (M/P)(L - 1) = 0 \tag{8.A.17}$$

$$K_f L_f(r_f, Y_f) + (M_f E/P)(L_f - 1) = 0 \tag{8.A.18}$$

Differentiating the system of equations w.r.t. $M$, one can obtain:

$$S_1'\partial r/\partial M + S_{f3}'M_f/P\frac{\partial E}{\partial M} - \frac{\partial P}{\partial M}(S_3' + S_{f3}')(M + M_fE)/P^2 = -S_3'/P$$

(8.A.19)

$$\left(\frac{M}{P} + K\right)L_1'\frac{\partial r}{\partial M} - \frac{M}{P^2}(L-1)\frac{\partial P}{\partial M} = (1-L)/P \quad (8.A.20)$$

$$M_f/P\,(L_f - 1)\frac{\partial E}{\partial M} - (M_f/P^2)(L_f - 1)\frac{\partial P}{\partial M} = 0 \quad (8.A.21)$$

We have used small country implication such that:

$\partial r_f/\partial M = 0, \partial P_f/\partial M = 0$ etc.

Putting $\Phi = -(S_3' + s_{f3}')\left(\frac{M + M_fE}{P^2}\right)$ the Jacobian of Myhrman's model can be written as:

$$J = \begin{vmatrix} S_1' & \Phi & S_{f3}'M_f/P \\ (M/P + K)L_1' & -\frac{M}{P^2}(L-1) & 0 \\ 0 & -M_fE/P^2(L_f - 1) & (L_f - 1)M_f/P \end{vmatrix}$$

$$\Rightarrow \quad J = -S_1'(L_f - 1)M_f/P\,M/P^2(L-1) - \Phi(M/P + K)L_1'(L_f - 1)M_f/P$$
$$- S_{f3}'M_f/P\,M_fE/P^2(L_f - 1)(M/P + K)L_1' \quad (8.A.22)$$

$$\frac{\partial E}{\partial M} = \frac{1}{J}\begin{vmatrix} S_1' & \Phi & -S_3'/P \\ (M/P + K)L_1' & (L-1)(-M/P^2) & (1-L)/P \\ 0 & -M_fE/P^2(L_f - 1) & 0 \end{vmatrix}$$

(8.A.23)

⇒ The numerator of (8.A.23) can be simplified as:

$$(S_1'(1-L)/P)(M_f/P^2(L_f - 1)) + S_3'/P\,(M/P + K)L_1'M_fE/P^2(L_f - 1)$$

Dividing the numerator and the denominator of $\partial E/\partial M$ through by $1/P\,(L_f - 1)M_f/P^2$

$$\frac{\partial E}{\partial M} = \frac{S_1'(1-L) + (M/P + K)L_1'S_3'}{[(1-L)S_1' + (S_3' + S_{f3}')(M/P + K)L_1'(M + M_fE) - S_{f3}'M_fE\,(M/P + K)L_1']}$$

(8.A.24)

The denominator can be simplified as:

$$(1-L)S_1' + (S_3' + S_{f3}')(M/P + K)L_1'M + S_3'(M/P + K)L_1'M_fE$$

Dividing the numerator and the denominator by $S_1'(1-L)$, (8.A.24) can be rewritten as:

$$\frac{\partial E}{\partial M} = \frac{1 + (M/P + K)(S_3'L_1')/S_1'(1-L)}{1 + \left\{S_3'(M + M_fE) + S_{f3}'M\right\}\left\{\frac{(M/P+K)L_1'}{S_1'(1-L)}\right\}} \tag{8.A.25}$$

Given that $S_1' > 0, L_1' < 0, S_3' < 0$ and $S_{f3}' < 0$ both the numerator and the denominator of $\partial E/\partial M$ have the same sign

$$\Rightarrow \quad \partial E/\partial M > 0 \tag{8.A.26}$$

### 8.A.3.1 *The Solution of Mussa's (1976) Model*

The reduced form equation of Mussa's model is given in (8.32). This is combined with the RE assumption (8.33) and each set of assumptions regarding the money supply rule.

Substituting (8.29) into (8.28)

$$\log M_t = a_0 \log E_t + a_1 \underset{t}{E}\left[(\log E_{t+1} - \log E_t)\Big| If_t\right] + A_t + u_t$$

Now the exchange rate at time $t$, $E_t$ is known when the expectations are being formed at time $t$ about the rate of the next period. So, the RHS can be simplified as:

$$\log M_t = (a_0 - a_1)\log E_t + a_1 \underset{t}{E}\left(\log E_{t+1}\Big| If_t\right) - A_t$$

$$\Rightarrow \quad \log E_t = \left(\frac{1}{a_0 - a_1}\right)\left[\log M_t - a_1 \underset{t}{E}\left(\log E_{t+1}\Big| IF_t\right) - A_t - u_t\right]$$

(8.A.27)

As in the LSW type of models the information set has to consist of the component equations of the model. This is provided by the alternative money supply assumptions as in (8.30) and (8.31). Writing equation (8.A.27) for $t+1$,

$$\log E_{t+1} = \left(\frac{1}{a_0 - a_1}\right)\left[\log M_{t+1} - A_{t+1} - a_1 \underset{t+1}{E}(\log E_{t+2}) - u_{t+1}\right]$$

(8.A.28)

Taking expectation at time $t$

$$\underset{t}{E}\log E_{t+1}=\left(\frac{1}{a_0-a_1}\right)\underset{t}{E}\left[\log M_{t+1}-A_{t+1}-a_1\underset{t+1}{E}(\log E_{t+2})-u_{t+1}\right] \tag{8.A.29}$$

Noting that

$$\underset{t}{E}\left[\underset{t+1}{E}(\log E_{t+2})\right]=\underset{t}{E}\log E_{t+2}$$

8.A.29 can be rewritten as:

$$\underset{t}{E}\log E_{t+1}=\left(\frac{1}{a_0-a_1}\right)\underset{t}{E}\left[\log M_{t+1}-A_{t+1}-a_1\log E_{t+2}-u_{t+1}\right] \tag{8.A.30}$$

Now $\underset{t}{E}\log E_{t+2}$ can be substituted for by forwarding (8.A.30) by one period:

$$\underset{t}{E}\log E_{t+1}=\left(\frac{1}{a_0-a_1}\right)\underset{t}{E}\left[\log M_{t+1}-A_{t+1}-u_{t+1}-\left(\frac{a_1}{a_0-a_1}\right)\right.$$
$$\left.\underset{t}{E}\left\{\log M_{t+2}-A_{t+2}-u_{t+2}-a_1\log E_{t+3}\right\}\right] \tag{8.A.31}$$

Through repeated substitution (8.A.30) can be finally written as:

$$\underset{t}{E}\log E_{t+1}=\left(\frac{1}{a_0-a_1}\right)\sum_{i=1}^{\infty}\underset{t}{E}\left[\left(\log M_{t+i}-u_{t+i}-A_{t+i}\right)\right.$$
$$\left.\left(\frac{a_1}{a_0-a_1}\right)^{i-1}\right] \tag{8.A.32}$$

From the money supply scheme given by (8.30):

$$\underset{t}{E}\log M_{t+i}=\underset{t}{E}\,(\overline{\log M_{t+i}}+u'_{t+i}) \tag{8.A.33}$$

Repeated substitution into $u'_t=\rho u'_{t-1}+v_t$ yields

$$u'_t=\rho(\rho u'_{t-2}+v_{t-1})+v_t$$

$\Rightarrow\quad u'_t=\rho^2(\rho u'_{t-3}+v_{t-3})+\rho v_{t-1}+v_t$ and so on.

$$\Rightarrow\quad u'_t=\sum_{i=0}^{\infty}\rho^i v_{t-i}+\rho^i u'_{t-i}$$

$$\Rightarrow \quad u_t' = \sum_{i=0}^{\infty} \rho^i v_{t-i} + \rho^i u_{t-i}'$$

$$\Rightarrow \quad \underset{t}{E} u_t' = \underset{t}{E}\left( \sum_{i=0}^{\infty} \rho^i v_{t-i} + \rho^i u_{t-i}' \right) \tag{8.A.34}$$

Substitution of (8.A.34) into (8.A.33) yields

$$\underset{t}{E} \log M_{t+i} = \overline{\log M} + \rho^i \underset{t}{E} u_t' \tag{8.A.35}$$

Mussa assumes that the decision-making agents not only knows the stochastic process generating $\log M_t$ and $\overline{\log M}$ but also $u_t'$ which equals the difference between $\log M_t$ and the mean $\overline{\log M}$. The long-run expected value of the exchange rate is taken to be the one which is consistent with $\log M_t = \overline{\log M}$ and with $\underset{t}{E} A_{t+i} = a$ constant for all $i$, say $\overline{A}$. This long-run expected value of the exchange rate is then:

$$\overline{\log E} = \frac{1}{a_0}(\overline{\log M} - \overline{A}) \tag{8.A.36}$$

Using (8.A.36) and assuming $E(u_t) = 0$ for all $t$, (8.A.32) yields

$$\underset{t}{E} \log E_{t+1} = \overline{\log E} + \left\{ \frac{\rho}{a_0 - a_1(1-\rho)} \right\} u_t' \tag{8.A.37}$$

Substitution yields

$$\log E_t = \overline{\log E} + \left\{ \frac{1}{a_0 - a_1(1-\rho)} \right) u_t' \tag{8.A.38}$$

Subtracting (8.A.38) from (8.A.37) one finally obtains the expected rate of change in the exchange rate:

$$\dot{E}_t^e = \left\{ \frac{\rho - 1}{a_0 - a_1(1-\rho)} \right\} u_t' \tag{8.A.39}$$

The RHS of (8.A.39) can be replaced by $(1-\rho)(\overline{\log E} - \log E_t)$ as can be verified by multiplying both sides of (8.A.38) by $(1-\rho)$.

$$\dot{E}_t^e = (1-\rho)(\overline{\log E} - \log E_t) \tag{8.A.40}$$

(8.A.38) shows the bigger the value of the autocorrelation coefficient, $\rho$, the bigger will be the effects of random disturbances on the exchange rate. If $\rho = 1$, the exchange rate follows a random walk. The main implication is that the more ill behaved is the money supply the larger will be the variability of the exchange rate.

8.A.3.2 *The Dynamics of Mussa's (1982) Model*

Mussa assumes perfect foresight in deriving the expected paths of prices and the exchange rate. Perfect foresight means that the expected rate of change equals the actual rate of change ⇒ (8.35) can be written

$$\Phi = \log E^*_{t+1} - \log E^*_t = D \log E^* \tag{8.A.41}$$

letting $D$ stand for the forward difference operator. From (8.43)

$$D \log E^* = D \log P^*_1 - D \log q^* - D \log P_{f2}$$

Substituting for $\log P^*_1$ from (8.44)

$$D \log E^* = D \log P^* + (1-\sigma) D \log q^* - D \log q^* - D \log P_{f2}$$

$$\Rightarrow \quad \Phi = D \log P^* - \sigma D \log q^* - \dot{p}_{f2} \tag{8.A.42}$$

where $\dot{p}_{f2}$ is the rate of price inflation of traded goods. The general rate of price inflation is given by $D \log P^*$. Taking the forward difference of (8.31),

$$D \log P^* = \sigma D \log P^*_1 + (1-\sigma)(D \log E^* + \dot{p}_{f2}) \tag{8.A.43}$$

Substitution of (8.A.42) and (8.A.43) into (8.41) yields:

$$\log q^* = \log \bar{q} + \frac{\alpha\sigma}{\beta}(\bar{r} - rn_f - D \log P^* + \sigma D \log q^* + \dot{p}_{f2} + D \log P^*)$$

$$\Rightarrow \quad \log q^* = \log \bar{q} + \frac{\alpha\sigma}{\beta}(\bar{r} - rn_f + \dot{p}_{f2}) + \frac{\alpha\sigma^2}{\beta} D \log q^*$$

Putting $B_1 = \log \bar{q} + \frac{\alpha\sigma}{\beta}(\bar{r} - rn_f + \dot{p}_{f2})$ (8.A.44)

the difference equation for $\log q^*$ can be written as:

$$D \log q^* = \beta/\alpha\sigma^2 (\log q^* - B_1) \tag{8.A.45}$$

Similarly substituting for $\Phi$ into (8.40) a difference equation for $\log P^*$ can be obtained as:

$$\log P^* = \log M - \log A - a(rn + D \log P^* - \sigma D \log q^* - \dot{p}f_2)$$

$$\Rightarrow \quad \log P^* = B_2 - aD \log P^* + a\sigma D \log q^* \tag{8.A.46}$$

where $B_2 = \log M - \log A - a(rn - \dot{p}f_2)$ (8.A.47)

(8.A.42), (8.A.45) and (8.A.46) provide the three dynamic equations of Mussa's (1982) model which can be solved in the usual way. Before that it should be noted that the exogenous variables summarised in $B_1$ and $B_2$ are the forcing variables which are ultimately responsible for the evolution of the exchange rate, of absolute and relative prices and all the other endogenous variables. $B_1$ summarises the exogenous real factors and $B_2$ the exogenous monetary factors.

The dynamic model consisting of (8.A.42), (8.A.45) and (8.A.46) is such that $\log q^*$ can be solved from the difference equation (8.A.45) and can be substituted in (8.A.46) to obtain the dynamic path for $\log P_t^*$ and finally $\log E_t^*$ can be obtained by substituting for $\log P_t^*$ and $\log q_t^*$ in (8.A.42).

The particular solution for (8.A.45) is obtained as:

$$\log q_{t+1}^* = \log q_t^* = \log \bar{q} = B_1 \qquad (8.A.48)$$

The general solution for the homogeneous part is obtained by trying

$$\log q_t^* = m\lambda^t \Rightarrow m\lambda^{t+1} - (1 + \beta/\alpha\sigma^2) m\lambda^t = 0$$

$$\Rightarrow \quad \lambda = 1 + \beta/\alpha\sigma^2$$

where $m$ is to be evaluated at $t = 0$. The general solution is:

$$\log q_t^* = m\,(1 + \beta/\alpha\sigma^2)^t + B_t \Rightarrow m = \log q_0^* - B_1.$$

The complete solution for $\log q_t^*$ is:

$$\log q_t^* = (\log q_0^* - B_1)(1 + \beta/\alpha\sigma^2)^t + B_1 \qquad (8.A.49)$$

Proceeding in the same way, the particular solution for (8.A.46) is

$$\log \bar{P} = B_2 \qquad (8.A.50)$$

and the general solution for the homogeneous part is:

$$an\lambda^{t+1} + (1-a)n\lambda^t - a\sigma m\lambda^{t+1} + a\sigma m\lambda^t = 0$$

$$\Rightarrow \quad an\lambda + (1-a)n - a\sigma m\lambda + a\sigma m = 0$$

$$\Rightarrow \quad \lambda(an - a\sigma m) = (a-1)n - a\sigma m$$

$$\Rightarrow \quad \lambda = \frac{(a-1)n - a\sigma m}{an - a\sigma m} \qquad (8.A.51)$$

The unknown constant, $n$ is to be obtained from the initial condition as before. The general solution for $\log P_t^*$ is then

$$\log P_t^* = B_2 + n\left\{\frac{(a-1)n - a\sigma m}{an - asimgam}\right\}^t \quad (8.A.52)$$

where, $n = \log P_0^* - B_2$ (8.A.53)

and $m$ given in (8.A.49).

Finally, the equilibrium exchange rate is obtained from (8.45) by substituting the dynamic solutions for $\log P_t^*$ and $\log q_t^*$.

Expected time paths of prices, absolute and relative, and the exchange rate can be obtained by taking expectation of the respective dynamic solutions conditioned upon the information available up to the latest time point, $t$. Writing the solution for $\log E_t^*$ from (8.A.52), (8.A.49) and (8.45)

$$\log E_t^* = B_2 - \sigma B_1 - \log P_{f2} + \{(\log P_0^* - B_2) - \sigma(\log q_0^* - B_1)\}$$

$$\left(1 + \frac{\beta}{\alpha\sigma^2}\right)^t \quad (8.A.54)$$

From (8.A.54), the expected change in the equilibrium exchange rate is seen to depend on the factors influencing the expected change in the equilibrium absolute price level and on the factors influencing the expected change in the relative price level.

### 8.A.4. **The Solution of Exchange Rates in Kouri's Model**

The world price is assumed constant and equal to 1 as in (8.5) implying $P = E$ from (8.19a). Assuming investment equal to zero, the current account balance is written as:

$$B = Y - C(Y - T, V) - C \quad (8.A.55)$$

where wealth $V$ consists of domestic money and foreign assets:

$$\dot{V} = (M/P) + F \quad (8.A.56)$$

The equilibrium conditions for domestic money and foreign assets are, respectively:

$$L(\dot{p}^e, Y, V) = M/P \quad (8.A.57a)$$

and $F(\dot{p}^e, Y, V) = F$ (8.A.57b)

Because of the wealth constraint only one of (8.A.57a) and (8.A.57b) can be taken as independent. Substituting for $V$, the equilibrium condition for the asset market as a whole is rewritten as:

$$L\left(\dot{p}^e, Y, \frac{M}{P} + F\right) = \frac{M}{P} \tag{8.A.58}$$

By virtue of the assumption $P = E$ the actual and expected rates of inflation can be equated to the actual and expected rates of changes in the exchange rate:

$$\dot{p} = \dot{E}, \quad \dot{p} = \hat{e} \quad \text{and} \quad \dot{p}^e = \hat{e}^e \tag{8.A.59}$$

From the asset market equations and the wealth constraint, the solutions for $M/P$ and $V$ are:

$$\dot{(M/P)} = H(\dot{p}^e, Y, F) \tag{8.A.60}$$

$$V = V(\dot{p}, Y, F) \tag{8.A.61}$$

The restrictions on the partial derivatives of $H$ and $V$ follow from those on the demand for assets functions:

$$H_1' < 0, \quad H_2' > 0, \quad H_3' > 0 \tag{8.A.62a}$$

$$\text{and } V_1' < 0, \quad V_2' > 0, \quad V_3' > 0 \tag{8.A.62b}$$

Next a government budget constraint is added in the form:

$$G - T = m(M/P) \tag{8.A.63}$$

(8.A.63) implies that the government fixes the rate of change of nominal money supply, $(\dot{M}/M) = m$. From (8.A.63) and the equations (8.A.60), (8.A.61), the other reduced form equation is derived as:

$$BT = Y - C(Y - T, M/P + F) - T - m(M/P)$$

$$\Rightarrow \quad BT = BT(Y, T, F, \dot{p}^e, M) \tag{8.A.64}$$

The restrictions on the partial derivatives of $BT$ follow from those of the demand functions:

$$BT_1' > 0, BT_2' < 0, BT_3' < 0, BT_4' > 0, BT_5' < 0 \tag{8.A.65}$$

Finally the equilibrium condition for the foreign trade sector is added as:

$$(-Ki =) \dot{F} = BT(Y, T, F, \dot{p}^e, M) \tag{8.A.66}$$

The reduced form of Kouri's model consists of (8.A.58) and (8.A.66).

From the foreign assets demand function (8.A.57b), the planned change in foreign assets is:

$$\dot{F} = F_1' \dot{p}^e = F_2' \dot{Y} + F_3' \dot{V} \tag{8.A.67}$$

$\dot{Y} = 0$ because of the assumption of full employment.

In the stationary state $\dot{Y} = \dot{V} = 0,\ \dot{p}^e = \dot{p} = \dot{m}$; all nominal variables grow at the same rate and the stock as well as the composition of wealth are constant. The constancy of the stock and composition in turn implies that the real domestic and foreign assets are held in the desired proportions. The conditions for the steady state are given in (8.A.68) and (8.A.69).

$$L(\dot{p}^e, Y, (M/P)^* + F^*) = (M^*/P) \tag{8.A.68}$$

$$BT = 0 \Rightarrow Y = C(Y - T, (M/P)^* + F^*) + T + m\,(M/P)^* \tag{8.A.69}$$

The equations (8.A.68) and (8.A.69) imply that an once for all intervention in the foreign exchange market has no long-run effect on the real variables.

It is also clear from the layout of the model that the rate of inflation can be used as a policy instrument. The effect of a rise in the rate of inflation is obtained from the stationary-state model consisting of (8.A.68) and (8.A.69).

Differentiating with respect to $\dot{p}^e$ and then solving by Cramer's rule, the effect of a rise in the rate of inflation on the stationary state holding of foreign and domestic money can be obtained as follows:

$$L_1' + L_3'\left[\frac{\partial}{\partial \dot{p}^e}(M/P)^* + \frac{\partial F^*}{\partial \dot{p}^e}\right] = \frac{\partial}{\partial \dot{p}^e}(M/P)^*$$

$$\Rightarrow \quad (L_3' - 1)\frac{\partial}{\partial \dot{p}^e}(M/P)^* + L_3'\frac{\partial F^*}{\partial \dot{p}^e} = -L_1' \tag{8.A.70}$$

$$\text{and } C_2'\left[\frac{\partial}{\partial \dot{p}^e}(M/P)^* + \frac{\partial F^*}{\partial \dot{p}^e}\right] + \dot{p}^e\frac{\partial}{\partial \dot{p}^e}(M/P)^* = 0$$

$$\Rightarrow \quad (C_2' + \dot{p}^e)\frac{\partial}{\partial \dot{p}^e}(M/P)^* + C_2'\frac{\partial F^*}{\partial \dot{p}^e} = 0 \tag{8.A.71}$$

The Jacobian determinant from (8.A.70) and (8.A.71) is evaluated as:

$$C_2'(L_3' - 1) - L_3'(C_2' + \dot{p}^e) = -(C_2' + \dot{p}^e L_3')$$

$$\Rightarrow \quad \frac{\partial}{\partial \dot{p}^e}(M/P)^* = \frac{-C_2'L_1'}{-(C_2' + L_3'\dot{p}^e)} < 0 \quad \text{as } L_1' < 0 \tag{8.A.72}$$

$$\text{and } \frac{\partial F^*}{\partial \dot{p}^e} = \frac{L_1'(C_2' + \dot{p}^e)}{-(C_2' + L_3'\dot{p}^e)} \tag{8.A.73}$$

The sign of (8.A.73) however cannot be determined independently as (8.A.72) and (8.A.73) have to satisfy the wealth constraint.

$$\frac{\partial V^*}{\partial \dot{p}^e}=\frac{L_1'C_2'-L_1'(C_2'+\dot{p}^e)}{C_2'+L_3'\dot{p}^e}=\frac{-L_1'\dot{p}^e}{C_2'+L_3'\dot{p}^e}$$

The dynamic behaviour of the model is examined by making $\dot{p}^e$ endogenous by assuming an adaptive expectations rule given by (8.A.74) and taking simplified versions of (8.A.66) and (8.A.68). Kouri's dynamic model, therefore consists of the following equations:

$$\dot{F}=\dot{F}(\dot{p}^e, F) \tag{8.A.66)$'$(}$$

$$M/P=H(\dot{p}^e, F) \tag{8.A.68)$'$(}$$

and $$\frac{d\dot{p}^e}{dt}=\lambda(m-\dot{\mu}-\dot{p}^e) \tag{8.A.74}$$

where $\dot{\mu}$ is the proportional rate of change in real money balance and $0<\lambda<1$ is the coefficient of adaptation. Differentiation of (8.A.68) is made on the simplifying assumption of log-linearity so that the time derivative yields:

$$\dot{\mu}=H_1'\frac{d\dot{p}^e}{dt}+H_2'\dot{F} \tag{8.A.75}$$

This eliminates $\dot{\mu}$ from the model. Differentiation of (8.A.66)′ yields the dynamic equation (8.A.76).

As examined more than once before, the solution of the dynamic model (8.A.76) and (8.A.77) can be obtained as follows. Kouri however does not solve the dynamic model in his paper.

The model after substitution of (8.A.75) in (8.A.74) is:

$$\frac{d\dot{p}^e}{dt}=\lambda\left(m-H_1'\frac{d\dot{p}^e}{dt}-H_2'\dot{F}-\dot{p}^e\right)$$

$$\Rightarrow \quad \frac{d\dot{p}^e}{dt}(1+\lambda H_1')+\lambda H_2'\dot{F}+\lambda\dot{p}^e=\lambda m \tag{8.A.77}$$

and $$\frac{d\dot{F}}{dt}-\dot{F}_1'\frac{d\dot{p}^e}{dt}-\dot{F}_2'\dot{F}=0 \tag{8.A.76}$$

$$\Rightarrow \quad \begin{vmatrix}1+\lambda H_1' & 0\\ -\dot{F}_1' & 1\end{vmatrix}\begin{vmatrix}d\dot{p}^e/dt\\ d\dot{F}/dt\end{vmatrix}+\begin{vmatrix}\lambda & \lambda H_2'\\ 0 & -\dot{F}_2'\end{vmatrix}\begin{vmatrix}\dot{p}^e\\ \dot{F}\end{vmatrix}=\begin{vmatrix}\lambda m\\ 0\end{vmatrix} \tag{8.A.78}$$

For particular integrals constant solutions like $\dot{p}^e=\overline{p}$ and $\dot{F}=\overline{\dot{F}}\Rightarrow$

$$\frac{d\dot{p}^e}{dt}=\frac{d\dot{F}}{dt}=0\Rightarrow$$

$$\begin{vmatrix} \lambda & \lambda H_2' \\ 0 & -\dot{F}_2' \end{vmatrix} \begin{vmatrix} \bar{p} \\ \bar{F} \end{vmatrix} = \begin{vmatrix} \lambda m \\ 0 \end{vmatrix}$$

$$\Rightarrow \quad \lambda\bar{p} + \lambda H_2'\bar{F} = \lambda m$$

and $\dot{F}_2'\bar{F} = 0 \Rightarrow \bar{F} = 0$ and $\bar{p} = m$

The complementary solutions are tried as $\dot{p} = ae^{\gamma t}$ and $\dot{F} = be^{\gamma t}$

$$\Rightarrow \quad \begin{vmatrix} 1+\lambda H_1' & 0 \\ -\dot{F}_1' & 1 \end{vmatrix} \begin{vmatrix} a \\ b \end{vmatrix} \gamma e^{\gamma t} + \begin{vmatrix} \lambda & \lambda H_2' \\ 0 & -\dot{F}_2' \end{vmatrix} \begin{vmatrix} a \\ b \end{vmatrix} e^{\gamma t} = 0$$

As $e^{\gamma t} \neq 0$ we get the characteristic equation as:

$$\gamma \begin{vmatrix} 1+\lambda H_1' & 0 \\ -\dot{F}_1' & 1 \end{vmatrix} + \begin{vmatrix} \lambda & \lambda H_2' \\ 0 & -\dot{F}_2' \end{vmatrix} = 0$$

$$\Rightarrow \quad \begin{vmatrix} \gamma + \gamma\lambda H_1' + \lambda & \lambda H_2' \\ -\gamma \dot{F}_1' & \gamma - \dot{F}_2' \end{vmatrix} = 0$$

$$\Rightarrow \quad (\gamma - \dot{F}_2')(\gamma + \gamma\lambda H_1' + \lambda) + \gamma \dot{F}_1' \lambda H_2' = 0$$

$$\Rightarrow \quad \gamma^2 + \gamma^2 \lambda H_1' + \gamma\lambda - \dot{F}_2'\gamma - \dot{F}_2'\gamma\lambda H_1' - \lambda\dot{F}_2' + \gamma\dot{F}_1'\lambda H_2' = 0$$

$$\Rightarrow \quad \gamma^2(1+\lambda H_1') + \gamma(\lambda - \lambda H_1'\dot{F}_2' - \dot{F}_2' + \dot{F}_1'\lambda H_2') - \lambda\dot{F}_2' = 0$$

$$\Rightarrow \quad A\gamma^2 + B\gamma + C = 0 \qquad (8.A.79)$$

The roots are given by

$$\gamma_1, \gamma_2 = \frac{-B \pm \sqrt{B^2 - 4AC}}{2A}$$

Where $A = 1 + \lambda H_1'$, $B = (\lambda - \lambda H_1'\dot{F}_2' - \dot{F}_2' + \dot{F}_1'\lambda H_2')$ and $C = -\lambda\dot{F}_2'$.

The condition for stability is that $\gamma_1 < 1$, $\gamma_2 < 1$ and can be ensured by $|\gamma_1 \gamma_2| < 1$.

For real and unequal roots $B^2 - 4AC > 0 \Rightarrow B^2 > 4AC$

For real and equal roots $B^2 - 4AC = 0$

The product of roots is $\frac{C}{A}$ and stability requires

$$\frac{C}{A} < 1 \quad \Rightarrow \quad -\lambda\dot{F}_2' < 1 + \lambda H_1'$$

Now: $\dot{F}_2' < 0$ and $H_1' < 0 \Rightarrow -\lambda\dot{F}_2' > 0$ and $\lambda H_1' < 0$ as $0 < \lambda < 1 \Rightarrow$

Stability requires

$$\lambda H_1' < 1 \tag{8.A.80}$$

It can be proved easily that the stability condition in the case of complex roots, i.e., when $B^2 - 4AC < 0$ will be the same.

### 8.A.5 **The Solution of Barro's (1978) Stochastic Model**

The domestic money demand equation (8.65) yields:

$$\log E_t = \log M_t - \log P_{ft} - a_0\Phi - \log Y_t \tag{8.A.81}$$

Substituting $\Phi = \log P^e_{t+1} - \log P_t - \overline{p}_f$ into (8.A.81)

$$\log E_t = \log M_t - \log P_{ft} - a_0(\log P^e_{t+1} - \log P_t - \overline{p}_f) - \log Y_t \tag{8.A.82}$$

Substituting (8.69), (8.71) and (8.70) for $\log M_t$, $\log P_{ft}$ and $\log Y_t$ respectively, (8.A.82) can be rewritten as:

$$\begin{aligned}\log E_t = {} & (\log M_{t-1} - \log mt_{t-1}) + \log mp_t + \log mt_t \\ & + \overline{m} - (\log P_{ft-1} + \overline{p}_f + \varepsilon_t) - a_0\dot{p}^e_t \\ & + a_0\overline{p}_f - (gt + u_t)\end{aligned} \tag{8.A.83}$$

Forwarding (8.A.83) by 1 period and then taking expectation

$$\begin{aligned}\log E^e_{t+1} = {} & (\log M_t - \log mt_t + \overline{m}) - (1 - a_0)\,\overline{p}_f \\ & - a_0\dot{p}^e_{t+1} - \log P_{ft} - g\,(t+1)\end{aligned} \tag{8.A.84}$$

Expectation of all white noise terms can be assumed zero for $t + 1$.

Subtracting (8.A.83) from (8.A.84), (8.A.85) is obtained:

$$\begin{aligned}\log E^e_{t+1} - \log E_t = {} & (\log M_t - \log M_{t-1}) - (\log mt_t - \log mt_{t-1}) \\ & - \log mp_t - \log mt_t + (\log P_{ft-1} + \overline{p}_f + \varepsilon_t) \\ & + a_0\dot{p}^e_t - a_0\overline{p}_f + gt + u_t - \overline{p}_f + a_0\overline{p}_f \\ & - a_0\dot{p}^e_{t+1} - \log P_{ft} - g\,(t+1)\end{aligned} \tag{8.A.85}$$

Further substitution from (8.69) yields

$$\log E^e_{t+1} - \log E_t = (\overline{m} + \log mp_t + \log mt_t - \log mt_{t-1})$$

$$- \log mt_t + \log mt_{t-1} - \log mp_t - \log mt_t$$

$$- (\log P_{ft} - \log P_{ft-1}) - a_0(\dot{p}^e_{t+1} - \dot{p}^e_t)$$

$$- g + u_t + \varepsilon_t \qquad (8.A.86)$$

(8.A.86) can be further simplified by noting that (8.71)

$$\Rightarrow \quad \log P_{ft} - \log P_{ft-1} = \overline{p}_f + \varepsilon_t \qquad (8.A.87a)$$

By definition: $\dot{p}^e_{t+} - \dot{p}^e_t = (\log P^e_{t+} - \log P_t)$

$- (\log P^e_t - \log P_{t-1})$

where the expected growth of the domestic price level, $(\log P^e_t - \log P_{t-1})$ is nothing but the trend rate of growth given by the difference between the trend rates of growth of money supply and real output $\Rightarrow$

$$\log P^e_t - \log P_{t-1} = \overline{m} - g \qquad (8.A.87b)$$

Finally by the implications of the PPP,

$$\log P^e_{t+1} - \log P_t = \overline{p}_f - (\log E^e_{t+1} - \log E_t) \qquad (8.A.87c)$$

Accommodating (8.A.87) fully into (8.A.86) and simplifying,

$$(1 - a_0)(\log E^e_{t+1} - \log E_t) = (1 - a_0)(\overline{m} - g - \overline{p}_f) + (u_t - \log mt_t)$$

$$\Rightarrow \quad (\log E^e_{t+1} - \log E_t) = (\overline{m} - g - \overline{p}_f) + [1/(1 - a_0)]$$

$$[u_t - \log mt_t] \qquad (8.A.88)$$

### 8.A.6 **The Solution of the HR Model**

The representative consumer in the domestic economy chooses $\{Z_t\}^{\infty}_{t=0}$ such that $\sum_{t=0}^{\infty} d^t \log Z_t$ is maximised subject to the wealth constraint

$$V_0 \geq \sum_{t=0}^{\infty} d'_t Z_t$$

The Lagrangean for this optimising problem can be written as:

$$\log Z_0 + d \log Z_1 + d^2 \log z_2 + \cdots + \lambda [V_0 - Z_0 - d'_1 Z_1 - \cdots]$$

as $d'_0 = 1$ in the HR model.

The first order conditions for maximisation are:

$$\frac{1}{Z_0}-\lambda=0,\quad \frac{d}{Z_1}-\lambda d_1'=0,\quad \frac{d^2}{Z_2}-\lambda d_2'=0\quad \cdots$$

and $V_0=Z_0+d_1'Z_1+d_2'Z_2+\cdots$

From the first equation $\lambda=\frac{1}{Z_0}$

Substitution of $\lambda$ into the other equations yields:

$$Z_1=\frac{dZ_0}{d_j'},\ Z_2=\frac{d^2Z_0}{d_2'}\Rightarrow Z_t=\frac{d^t}{d_t'}Z_0$$

Substituting for $Z_1, Z_2\cdots$ into the wealth constraint

$$V_0=Z_0+dZ_0+d^2Z_0+\cdots$$

$$\Rightarrow\quad V_0=Z_0(1+d+d^2+\cdots)$$

$$\Rightarrow\quad V_0=\frac{Z_0}{1-d}$$

$$\Rightarrow\quad Z_0=V_0(1-d)$$

Substitution of $Z_0$ into the general pattern

$$Z_t=\left(\frac{d^t}{d_t'}\right)Z_0\quad\text{yields}$$

$$Z_t=(1-d)\left(\frac{d^t}{d_t'}\right)V_0,\quad t=0,1,2,\qquad(8.A.89a)$$

The foreign economy counterpart of the solution is obtained by maximising $\sum_{t=0}^{\infty} d_f^t\log Z_{ft}$ subject to the constraint

$$V_{f0}=\Sigma d_f'Z_{ft}$$

The solution will be given by:

$$Z_{ft}=(1-d_f)\left(\frac{d_f^t}{d_{ft}'V_{f0}}\right)\qquad(8.A.89b)$$

the discount factor $d_t'$, obtained next as follows. From (8.89) and (8.90)

$$a_1 Z_t + P_{f2t} Y_{2t} = M_t / E_t \tag{8.A.90a}$$

and $a_{f1} Z_{ft} + P_{f2t} Y_{f2t} = M_{ft}$ (8.A.90b)

From (8.91),

$$P_{f2t} = \frac{a_2 Z_t + a_{f2} Z_{ft}}{Y_{2t} + Y_{f2t}} \tag{8.A.91}$$

Substitution for (8.A.91) into (8.A.90) respectively yields:

$$\left\{ a_1 + \left( \frac{Y_{2t}}{Y_{2t} + Y_{f2t}} \right) a_2 \right\} Z_t = \frac{M_t}{E_t} - \frac{a_2 Y_{2t} Z_{ft}}{Y_{2t} + Y_{f2t}} \tag{8.A.91a}$$

and

$$\left\{ a_{f1} + \left( \frac{Y_{f2t}}{Y_{2t} + Y_{f2t}} \right) a_{f2} \right\} Z_{ft} = M_{ft} - \frac{a_{f2} Y_{f2t} Z_t}{Y_{2t} + Y_{f2t}} \tag{8.A.91b}$$

Writing $\alpha_t$ and $\alpha_{ft}$ for the shares of foreign traded goods in the world supply of traded goods, (8.A.91) can be rewritten as:

$$(a_1 + a_2 \alpha_t) Z_t = M_t / E_t - a_2 \alpha_t Z_{ft} \tag{8.A.92a}$$

and

$$(a_{f1} + a_{f2} \alpha_{ft}) Z_{ft} = M_{ft} - a_{f2} \alpha_{ft} Z_t \tag{8.A.92b}$$

Substitution for $Z_t$ and $Z_{ft}$ from (8.A.89) yields solutions for $d_t'$ and $d_{ft}'$ in terms of $M_t$, $M_{ft}$, $E_t$ and $d^t$ and $d_f^t$. $M_t$ and $M_{ft}$ are given and from the interest rate parity condition

$$(d_t' / d_{t+1}') = 1 + r_{ft}.$$

So the discount factors yield solution for interest rates under a few simplifying assumptions. Equilibrium prices $P_{f2t}$ and $P_{1t}$, $P_{ft}$ are obtained from (8.A.91) and (8.89) and finally the exchange rate is calculated from (8.89a) on substitution for the equilibrium prices. As evident from the nature of the component equations the exchange rate solution can be written in the form

$$E_t = (M_t / M_{ft}) F(Z_t, Z_{ft}) \tag{8.A.93}$$

Where $F(Z_t, Z_{ft})$ is a function of $Z_t$ and $Z_{ft}$ with $a_1, a_2, \alpha_t$ and $a_{f1}, a_{f2}$ and $\alpha_{ft}$ as parameters. Now $Z_t$ and $Z_{ft}$ contain $V_0$ and $V_{f0}$ respectively. $V_0$ and $V_{f0}$ contain the indebtedness terms $B_0$ and $B_{f0}$. So, while anticipated changes in monetary policy have no real effects unanticipated changes in the same can have real effects through the international indebtedness.

### 8.A.7 The Solution of the FR Model

*The Derivation of the Current and the Future Consumption Functions*

The log-linear utility function at period $t$, of an individual of age, $s$, is written as:

$$u = \sum_{i=t}^{\infty} d^{i-t} \log C_{ji}, \quad j = i - s \tag{8.A.94}$$

where $d$ is the subjective discount factor and $C_{ji}$ is the consumption of an individual of age, $s$, in period $i$. The probability as of period, $t$, that the individual will be alive in period $i$ is given by $(\alpha)^{i-t}$ where $\alpha$ is assumed less than unity. So, expected utility will be given by:

$$u_t^e = \sum_{i=t}^{\infty} (\alpha d)^{i-t} \log C_{ji} \tag{8.A.95}$$

The expected utility given in (8.A.95) is to be maximised subject to the budget constraint that the discounted present value of the series of future disposable incomes equals the discounted value of all future consumption and the value of debt at the beginning of the period. Assuming the tax rate for period $t$ to be, $a_t$, the discounted present values of consumption and disposable incomes are written, respectively, as:

$$\sum_{i=t}^{\infty} (\alpha^i a_i / \alpha^t a_t) C_{ji} = \sum_{i=t}^{\infty} A_i C_{ji}, \quad \text{say}$$

and $\sum_{i=t}^{\infty} (\alpha^i a_i / \alpha^t a_t) y'_{ji} = \sum_{i=t}^{\infty} A_i y'_{ji}, \quad \text{say}$

where $y'_{ji}$ is the income of the individual of age, $s$ at period $i$. The budget constaint of this individual can then be written as:

$$\sum_{i=t}^{\infty} A_i C_{ji} + b_{jt} = \sum_{i=t}^{\infty} A_i y'_{ji} \tag{8.A.96}$$

In FR's model, individual's wealth consists of the difference between human wealth and debt $\Rightarrow$

$$V_{jt} = \sum_{i=t}^{\infty} A_i y'_{ji} - b_{jt} \tag{8.A.97}$$

Combining (8.A.96) and (8.A.97), the budget constraint for period $t$ can be rewritten as:

$$\sum_{i=t}^{\infty} A_i C_{ji} = V_{jt} \tag{8.A.98}$$

The necessary conditions for maximisation of (8.A.95) subject to (8.A.98) are:

$$\frac{(\alpha d)^{i-t}}{C_{ji}} - \lambda A_i = 0, \quad i = t \cdots \infty \tag{8.A.99a}$$

$$\text{and } \sum_{i=t}^{\infty} A_i C_{ji} = V_{jt} \tag{8.A.99b}$$

where $\lambda$ is the undetermined Lagrange multiplier.

$$\frac{(\alpha d)^{i-t}}{A_i C_{ji.}}$$

From (8.A.99a),

$$\lambda = \frac{(\alpha d)^{i-t}}{A_i C_{ji}}, \quad i = t \cdots \infty$$

$$\Rightarrow \quad \lambda = \frac{1}{A_t C_{jt}} \quad \text{From the } t \text{ th equation.}$$

The other equations of (8.A.99a) can then be written as:

$$\frac{\alpha d}{C_{jt+1}} - \frac{A_{t+1}}{A_t C_{jt}} = 0, \frac{(\alpha d)^2}{C_{jt+2}} - \frac{A_{t+2}}{A_t C_{jt}}$$

$$\Rightarrow \quad C_{jt+1} = \frac{\alpha d \, C_{jt} A_t}{A_{t+1}}, \; C_{jt+2} = \frac{(\alpha d)^2 C_{jt} A_t}{A_{t+2}}$$

Substituting for $C_{ji}$ in (8.A.99b)

$$V_{jt} = C_{ji} A_i (1 + \alpha d + \alpha d^2 + \cdots\cdots)$$

$$\Rightarrow \quad V_{jt} = C_{ji} A_i [1/(1 - \alpha d)]$$

$$\Rightarrow \quad C_{ji} = (1 - \alpha d) V_{jt} / A_i$$

Substituting for $A_i$, consumption of period $i$ can be solved as:

$$C_{ji} = (1 - \alpha d) \left[ \frac{\alpha t a_t}{\alpha^i a_i} \right] V_{jt} \quad i = t, \cdots \infty \tag{8.A.100}$$

On a number of simplifying assumptions to get rid of aggregation errors, aggregate consumption, aggregate wealth and aggregate private debt are taken to be, respectively,

$$C_t = \sum_{j=-\infty}^{t} \alpha^{t-j} C_{jt} \tag{8.A.101a}$$

$$H_t = \sum_{i=t}^{\infty} (\alpha^i a_i / \alpha^t a_t)\, y_i \tag{8.A.101b}$$

and $$B_{pt} = \sum_{j=-\infty}^{t} (\alpha^t / \alpha^j)\, b_{jt} \tag{8.A.101c}$$

Using the definition of individual consumption function, $C_{ji}$ for $i = t$ from (8.A.100) and the definition of wealth from (8.96a) the aggregate consumption function (8.A.101a) can be rewritten as:

$$C_t = (1-\alpha d)(H_t - B_{pt}) = (1-\alpha d)\, V_t \tag{8.A.102}$$

*The Reduced Form of the FR Model*

The reduced form of the model is derived by substituting for $V_{f0}$ and $B_{fg0}$. Substituting for $V_{f0}$ from (8.93b), (8.94a) can be rewritten as:

$$(1-\alpha d)\, V_0 + (1-\alpha d_f)\left[(Y_{f0} - T_{f0}) + \frac{\alpha R}{1-\alpha R}(Y_f - T_f)\right.$$

$$\left. + B_{fg0} + B_0\right] = Y_0 - G_0 + Y_{f0} - G_{f0} \tag{8.A.103a}$$

Substituting for $B_{fg0}$ from (8.95b), (8.A.103a) can be further rewritten as:

$$(1-\alpha d)\, V_0 + (1-\alpha d_f)\left[(Y_{f0} - G_{f0}) + \frac{\alpha R}{1-\alpha R}(Y_f - T_f) + B_0\right.$$

$$\left. + \frac{R}{1-R}(T_f - G_f)\right] = Y_0 - G_0 + Y_{f0} - G_{f0} \tag{8.A.103b}$$

Similar substitution into (8.94b) yields:

$$\left[\alpha d V_0 + \frac{R(1-\alpha)(Y-T)}{(1-R)(1-\alpha R)}\right] + \left[\alpha d_f \left\{(Y_{f0} - G_{f0}) + \frac{\alpha R}{1-\alpha R}\right\}\right.$$

$$\left.(Y_f - T_f) + B_0 + \frac{R}{1-R}(T_f - G_f) + \frac{R(1-\alpha)(Y_f - T_f)}{(1-R)(1-\alpha R)}\right]$$

$$= \frac{R}{1-R}[Y - G + Y_f - G_f] \tag{8.A.103c}$$

*The Impact of Budget Deficits in the FR Model*

The effects of changes in domestic taxes on $R$, $V_0$ and $V_{f0}$ can be obtained as follows. As already noted, the model is overdetermined in $R$, $V_0$ and $V_{f0}$ and therefore, one of the equations from (8.93)–(8.94) can be dropped.

Dropping (8.94b) and substituting for $B_{g0}$ and $B_{fg0}$ from (8.95), (8.93) can be rewritten as (8.A.104):

$$V_0 - \frac{\alpha R}{1-\alpha R}(Y-T) - \frac{R}{1-R}(T-G) = Y_0 - G_0 - B_0 \tag{8.A.104a}$$

$$V_{f0} - \frac{\alpha R}{1-\alpha R}(Y_f-T_f) - \frac{R}{1-R}(T_f-G_f) = Y_{f0} - G_{f0} + B_0 \tag{8.A.104b}$$

The Jacobian of the model consisting of (8.A.104) and (8.94a) can be written as:

$$J = \begin{vmatrix} 1 & 0 & \theta_1 \\ 0 & 1 & \theta_2 \\ 1-\alpha d & 1-\alpha d_f & \theta_3 \end{vmatrix} \tag{8.A.105a}$$

Where $\theta_1, \theta_2$ and $\theta_3$ are the coefficients of $(\partial R/\partial T)$ from (8.A.104) and (8.94a) respectively:

$$\theta_1 = -\left[\frac{\alpha(Y-T)}{(1-\alpha R)^2} + \frac{T-G}{(1-R)^2}\right] \tag{8.A.105b}$$

$$\theta_2 = -\left[\frac{\alpha(Y_f-T_f)}{(1-\alpha R)^2} + \frac{(T_f-G_f)}{(1-R)^2}\right] \tag{8.A.105c}$$

$$\theta_3 = 0 \tag{8.A.105d}$$

From (8.A.105),

$$J = -\theta_2(1-\alpha d_f) - \theta_1(1-\alpha d) \tag{8.A.106}$$

Using Cramer's Rule:

$$\frac{\partial R}{\partial T} = \frac{1}{J}\begin{vmatrix} 1 & 0 & \psi_1 \\ 0 & 1 & \psi_2 \\ 1-\alpha d & 1-\alpha d_f & \psi_3 \end{vmatrix} \tag{8.A.107a}$$

Where $\psi_1 = \frac{R}{1-R} - \frac{\alpha R}{1-\alpha R} = \frac{R(1-\alpha)}{(1-R)(1-\alpha R)}$ (8.A.107b)

$\psi_2 = \psi_3 = 0$ as (8.A.104b) and (8.94a) do not contain $T$.

From (8.A.107)

$$\frac{\partial R}{\partial T} = \frac{-\psi_1(1-\alpha d)}{J} = \frac{-R(1-\alpha)(1-\alpha d)}{J\cdot(1-R)(1-\alpha R)} \tag{8.A.108}$$

Further using the budget constraint (8.97), the impact of current budget deficits can be derived as:

$$\frac{\partial R}{\partial T_0} = \frac{\partial R}{\partial T}\cdot\frac{\partial T}{\partial T_0} = \frac{\partial R}{\partial T}\left[-\frac{1-R}{R}\right]$$

$$\Rightarrow \quad \frac{\partial R}{\partial T_0} = \frac{(1-\alpha)(1-\alpha d)}{(1-\alpha R)J} \tag{8.A.109}$$

$\frac{\partial V_0}{\partial T_0}$ and $\frac{\partial V_{f0}}{\partial T_0}$ can be obtained in the same way by Cramer's Rule.

### 8.A.8 **The Reduced Form Equations of Montiel's Model**

*The Real Sector*

*Short-run Equilibrium*

Equation (v) of (8.99) is a reduced form equation to describe short-run equilibrium. It is obtained by substituting (e) into (a) and using the equations (t) and (u) into (k) of (8.99).

The steps are:

$Y_2 = Y_2[N_2(W/P_2)] = Y_2(w_2)$ say

$Y = (P_2/P)\,Y_2(w_2) + (P_1/P)\,Y_1 \Rightarrow$

$$Y = er^{\sigma}Y_1 + er^{1-\sigma}Y_2(w_2) \tag{8.A.110}$$

The equation for domestic rate of inflation is obtained by substituting (h) and (c) into (i) and then using (j) of (8.99).

The steps are:

$$\dot{p}_1 = f(\ldots) + \dot{w}(\ldots) + \dot{p} \tag{8.A.111a}$$

From (j) and (8.A.111a)

$$\Rightarrow \quad \dot{p} = \sigma f(\ldots) + \sigma\dot{w}(\ldots) + \sigma\dot{p} + (1-\sigma)\,\dot{p}_2$$

$$\Rightarrow \quad \dot{p} = \frac{\sigma}{1-\sigma}[f+\dot{w}] + \dot{p}_2 \tag{8.A.111b}$$

For the remaining endogenous variable of short-run equilibrium, equations (o), (q), (p) and (s) and (t) are used. Substitution of (o) into (q) yields

$$C_1 = \sigma P_1 / PC(Y - T, r_f, V_p) \tag{8.A.112}$$

Measuring real private financial wealth in terms of traded good,

$$V_p = (P_2/P)V_{p2} = er^{1-\sigma}V_{p2} \tag{8.A.113}$$

Substitution of (8.A.113) into (8.A.112) and substitution of the result into (p) yield:

$$Y_1 = (\sigma P_1/P)C[Y - T, r_f(P_2/P)V_{p2}] \tag{8.A.114}$$

Making use of (s) and (t) in (8.A.114) the output of non-traded goods becomes:

$$Y_1 = \sigma er^{\sigma}C[Y - T, r_f, er^{1-\sigma}V_{p2}] \tag{8.A.115}$$

The equations (8.A.110), (8.A.111) and (8.A.115) constitute the reduced form model of the real sector.

*The Monetary and Real Sectors Together: Log-run Equilibrium, The Dynamic Equations of the Model*

Substitution of (a) of (8.100) and of (o) of (8.99) into (i) of (8.100) yields:

$$\dot{P}V_p + P\dot{V}_p = P(Y - T) + r_f(V_pP) - r_fL(Y, r_f)$$
$$- PC(Y - T, r_f, V_p) \tag{8.A.116}$$

Expressing wealth in terms of traded good as in (8.A.113) and exploiting (t) and (u) of (8.99) and differentiating the result with respect to time:

$$\dot{V}_{p^2} = er^{-(1-\sigma)}[Y - T - C(Y - T, r_f, er^{1-\sigma}V_{p2})$$
$$- r_fL(Y, r_f) + (r_f - \dot{P}/P)V_p]$$
$$\Rightarrow \quad \dot{V}_{p^2} = er^{\sigma-1}[Y - T - C(\;) - r_fL(\;)$$
$$+ (r_f - \dot{p})er^{1-\sigma}V_{p2}]$$
$$\Rightarrow \quad \dot{V}_{p^2} = er^{\sigma-1}[Y - T - C(\;) - r_fL(\;)]$$
$$+ (r_f - \dot{p})V_{p2} \tag{8.A.117}$$

The dynamic equation of the real exchange rate is easily derived from the time derivative of equation(s) of (8.99) and dividing by *er* and then substituting (*j*) and finally (8.A.111b). The steps are:

$$\dot{e}r = \dot{p}_2 - \dot{p}_1 = -1/(1-\sigma)(\dot{p}-\dot{p}_2)$$

$$\Rightarrow \quad \dot{e}r = -\frac{1}{(1-\sigma)}\left[\frac{\sigma}{1-\sigma}(f+\dot{w})+\dot{p}_2-\dot{p}_2\right]$$

$$\Rightarrow \quad \dot{e}r = -\frac{1}{(1-\sigma)}[\sigma/(1-\sigma)(f+\dot{w})] \tag{8.A.118}$$

The remaining dynamic equation is for the rate of change of real wage measured in terms of traded goods. The steps are explained below:

The rate of change of the real wage of the traded goods sector is given by:

$$\frac{dw_2/dt}{w_2} \equiv \dot{w} = \dot{w} - \dot{p}_2 = \dot{w}\,(N,+N_2-\overline{N}) + \dot{p}^e - \dot{p}_2$$

from equation (c) of (8.99).

Substituting from (e), (f) and assuming perfect foresight

$$\dot{w} = \dot{w}\,[N_1^{ed}(Y_1) + N_2(w/p_2) - \overline{N}] + \dot{p} - \dot{p}_2$$

Substitution of (i) and (j) yields

$$\Rightarrow \quad \dot{w} = \dot{w}\,(\ldots) + \dot{p} - 1/(1-\sigma)(\dot{p}-\sigma\dot{p}_1)$$

$$\Rightarrow \quad \dot{w}_2 = \dot{w} + \frac{\sigma}{1-\sigma}(f+\dot{w}) - \frac{\sigma\dot{p}}{1-\sigma} \quad \text{from} \tag{8.A.118}$$

$$\Rightarrow \quad \dot{w}_2 = \frac{1}{1-\sigma}[\sigma(f-\dot{p})+\dot{w}\,(\ldots)] \tag{8.A.119}$$

(8.A.117), (8.A.118) and (8.A.119) constitute the dynamic model. Long-run equilibrium has to satisfy the conditions.

$$dV_{p_2}/dt = der/dt = dw_2/dt = 0 \tag{8.A.120}$$

The dynamic simultaneous equation model can be solved in the usual way.

# 9

# CONCLUSIONS

Macroeconomic models of static and dynamic, non-stochastic and stochastic nature have been considered in the book in detail and the distinguishing features known as classical, Keynesian, monetarist, new classical and finally new Keynesian have been highlighted. Differences between various schools of thought have been discussed mainly in terms of policy effectiveness. To deal with the latter, the comparative static method has been applied throughout. The main conclusions of the book are summarised below.

In the simple non-stochastic macro analysis of the economy involving the output and the money markets the effectiveness of policies depends on elasticities of money and investment demands. The higher (lower) the elasticity of money and inelasticity of investment demands, the stronger will be the effect of fiscal (monetary) policy in influencing real output and interest rates. The expansionary effect of monetary (fiscal) policy would be the weakest (strongest) in the extreme case of infinite elasticity of money demand and zero elasticity of investment demands in response to changes in real interest rate.

In the conventional classical analysis of the economy including aggregate demand and aggregate supply of output, the role of money supply is limited to affecting only the price level and the money wage rate in equal proportions leaving the real wage and, therefore, employment and output unchanged. The neutrality of money and the consequent dichotomy between the real and monetary sectors of the economy is due to the absence of money illusion among the suppliers of labour. The conventional Keynesian analysis changes this assumption and makes labour supply dependent on money rather than real wage. The introduction of money illusion destroys the dichotomy between real and monetary sectors and money no longer acts as a veil.

However, the relative effectiveness of fiscal and monetary policies still depends on interest-elasticities of money and investment demands.

The classical analysis alludes to a virtually non-interventionist approach to the economy as the market imbalances can be cured by price and wage flexibility. For instance unemployment can be reduced by a general wage cut. However, the conventional Keynesian analysis shows that the employment enhancing effect of a wage reduction is solely dependent on the same elasticities — viz., the interest elasticities of real demands for money and investment. The real balance effect introduced by Pigou overcomes the negating effects of interest elasticities and shows that a general wage-cut can reduce unemployment provided real consumption demand depends positively on the quantity of real money balances.

The demand and supply functions of the classical system are all homogeneous of degree zero in prices and the labour supply depending positively on real wage rate fits in with this general pattern and such behaviour of workers is rational and is consistent with constrained utility optimisation. The introduction of money illusion among workers deprives the Keynesian system of an optimising Walrasian general equilibrium framework. The conventional Keynesian three-sector model lacks the micro foundations of an optimising behaviour of workers but it is shown by the supporters of Keynesian economics to be an important recognition that markets do not always clear. Whereas the classical model is consistent with market clearing and walrasian general equilibrium Clower, Patinkin, Barro and Grossman, Leijonhufvud and Phelps derive a choice-theoretic basis and the microfoundations of a general disequilibrium analysis from Keynes's behavioural assumptions. The conventional interpretation of Keynes as given in 3.4 and 3.5 indicates the possibility of disequilibrium in the labour market due to wage rigidity but such disequilibrium was not based on choice-theoretic foundations. In other words, Barro, Grossman, Clower and others took Keynesian macroeconomics a significant step forward. The relative effectiveness of fiscal and monetary policies solely depends on elasticity of money demand and inelasticity of investment demand but only in the static, short-run Keynesian analysis ignoring the dynamics of government budget constraint and the wealth effects. An important consequence of the latter is that the short-run effects of a rise in government spending on real income are very different from those in the long-run. The monetarists show that fiscal policy is effective only when used in conjunction with monetary policy. While Friedman and other monetarists claim that monetary policy will have stronger expansionary effects and achieve stability, the supporters of Keynes, e.g., Blinder and Solow, Miller and others have derived the condition for stability when government budget is financed by selling bonds. If the marginal rate of income tax, marginal propensities to spend out of income and wealth have certain plausible values, the crowding-out effects of fiscal policy would be far outweighed by the expansionary effects on real income even in the long-run and with stability.

The effects of government budget, of the consequent crowding-out and their implications for Keynesians-monetarists' debate have been explored much further by assuming a variable capital-stock, a variable price level and unemployment. Tobin and Buiter show that the crowding out effects of fiscal policy disappear in the long run with variable capital stock and variable price level. Increase in government spending reduces both the nominal interest rate and the price level even in the midst of full-employment and the rise in real output is due to capital-deepening.

A variable price level not only has repercussions on the output market but also on the labour market. The traditional Phillips curve analysis shows a trade-off between inflation and unemployment but such trade-off cannot contain the dynamic effects of expectations of economic agents. Whether expectations are formed rationally or non-rationally, once such expectations are taken into consideration there no longer exists a trade-off between inflation and unemployment in the long-run.

The assumption of rational expectations lies at the heart of new classical economics. Economic agents use all the information available upto the time when expectations are being formed. The price level changes only when actual output is different from the expected level of output. The macro rational expectation models include stochastic variables and an important use of the latter is to distinguish between the anticipated and unanticipated changes of policy. Lucas, Sargent and Wallace, the founders of new classical macroeconomics have developed models to show that the systematic or predictable changes in money supply do not affect the real output or, the real interest rate and that the variance of the stochastic elements which form the unpredictable part only affects the variance but not the expected level of real output. The policy ineffectiveness proposition survives the inclusion of the government budget constraint, the wealth effects and interest payments on government bonds. Ineffectiveness of monetary policy reinstates the neutrality of money first encountered in classical economics. The RE assumption on its own cannot however lead to the neutrality of money as policy effectiveness can be regained even under rational expectations by including some form of wage-rigidity — a Keynesian element. Thus Fischer shows that if wage-contracts are made for longer than one period and in nominal terms activist monetary policy can affect real output and employment even under rational expectations. Phelps and Taylor use the cost of acquiring information as a reason for wages and prices being predetermined when monetary policy is introduced. Their model is structurally different from that of Fischer's but nonetheless it restores the old faith that even systematic changes in monetary policy matter for the fluctuation of output and employment, even when expectations are formed rationally. Thus Phelps and Taylor put "the old wine in a new and secure bottle".

Rising inflation has repercussions on workers' post tax real income. If the expected rate of inflation is considered exogenous and if wage-claims are made such that there is no change in the real after tax income of the workers, the value of the monetary policy multiplier is less than that in the models without inflation. This is because a higher rate of inflation creates an additional negative feedback. The first round effects of a rise in money supply are the same as in the models with no inflation viz., a lower interest rate, higher investment and, therefore, a higher income. The second round effects are however not only an offsetting rise (fall) in interest rate (real income) due to a higher demand for money but also a higher rate of inflation reducing real balances and leading, in turn, to a further offsetting rise (fall) in interest rate (real income). Under the simplifying assumptions of constant returns to scale, constant demand and supply elasticities, rational expectations do not destroy the expansionary effect of monetary policy under a progressive and elastic tax structure and if the income effect is stronger than the substitution effect. However, it should be noted that the introduction of government budget constraint in the IS-LM models including inflationary expectations does not always lead to unambiguous policy multipliers.

Monetarists not only advocate monetary policy to have a lasting effect on output and price level but also hold that inflation is exclusively a monetary phenomenon. Lowering the rate of unemployment below the natural rate calls for a continuous rise in the money stock but such attempts lead to a continuous rise in the actual rate of inflation. Fischer shows that the adaptive expectations rule is required to produce an ever accelerating rate of inflation to maintain unemployment below the natural rate. Stein has highlighted the difference between monetarists and fiscalists (or, Keynesians) in terms of the response of the rate of inflation to a change in the ratio of bonds to money. The rate of inflation in the monetarists model depends not only on the rate of unemployment and of expected inflation but also on real money stock, government spending and the debt-money ratio. The monetarists hold that the rate of inflation does not rise with government spending whereas the neo-Keynesians hold that it does. Consequently, fiscal policy is ineffective (effective) in reducing unemployment in the monetarist (Keynesian) model. Monetarists (Keynesians) consider a wide (narrow) range of assets and market interest rates. A rise in the rate of monetary expansion raises the amount of cash balances relative to other assets and agents' endeavour to adjust their portfolios finally manifests into an effect on income and spending.

Keynesian macroeconomics was also under attack from the new classical school for its lack of reliance on optimising behaviour, market clearing or on rational expectations. The new classical macroeconomics has consequently developed on the principles of continuous market clearing, rational expectation, imperfect information about some crucial current aggregate variables, a supply function depending on the gap between actual and expected price level and a natural rate hypothesis. Phelps's "islands" models show the importance of local variables specific to "islands" in influencing individual decisions — of employers' and employees'. Changes in relative prices lead to movements in real output and employment and the relative prices because of imperfect information. The new classical macroeconomics views business cycles as equilibrium phenomena.

The acclaimed superiority of the new classical to the Keynesian macroeconomics of unemployment has been put to test as the former easily lends itself to joint econometric tests of RE and NR hypotheses. However the results of such tests are not all favourable to new classical economics. A strong defence for Keynesian economics came from Blinder. He holds that Keynesian economics can explain the events of the eighties much better than NCM; the Phillips Curve with supply shocks added survives the empirical tests and Keynesian economics is consistent with RE. The theoretical foundations of Keynesian economics are provided by the recent developments of labour theories.

Alongside NCM there developed an approach in favour of Keynesian economics which was consequently named as new-Keynesian macroeconomics. Fischer and Phelps and Taylors' defense of the Keynesian tradition of wage-price stickiness was further extended and formalised by the implicit contract theory popularised by Bailey, Azariadis, Grossman and others. This theory replaced the auction-market approach of classical economics. The microfoundations of unemployment were explained by assuming that the employers are less risk-averse than the employees and that there exists a market, so to say, in labour contracts rather than in labour as such.

In open economy macroeconomics once again the distinction between Keynesian and monetarist traditions is highlighted in determining the equilibrium exchange rate and ascertaining the roles for fiscal and monetary policies in influencing the balance of payments and the equilibrium exchange rate. The relative effectiveness of various policies depends on the degree of capital mobility and the nature of the exchange rate regime. In the simple IS-LM-BB model of the Mundell-Fleming type, the higher the degree of capital mobility the stronger will be the expansionary effects of government spending on real income under a fixed exchange rate whereas the expansionary impact of monetary policy would depend inversely on the degree of capital mobility. Under perfect capital mobility and fixed exchange rates the monetary policy multiplier effect on real income will be reduced to zero. These results get reversed under flexible exchange rates. Under the latter the balance of payments is kept in equilibrium through fluctuations in the exchange rate. From 1973 onwards and till the birth of the European Monetary System, many industrialised nations moved in favour of a flexible exchange rate system. In reality exchange rates do not float freely but are "managed" by the authorities to a limited extent. Under flexible exchange rates fiscal policy is expansionary provided the sum of price elasticities of export and import demands exceeds unity. Whenever capital is mobile, monetary policy will have stronger expansionary effects than fiscal policy under flexible exchange rate regime.

The Mundell-Fleming approach was criticised on grounds of a number of weaknesses and "new theories" developed. These new theories not only emphasised the role of stock equilibrium of balance sheet requirements following the monetarists tradition but an ideal union of monetary and real factors was provided in the form of general equilibrium analysis. The short-run and the long-run equilibria were separately analysed and a monetary and asset analyses combined. The monetary analysis concentrated on the demands and supplies of different monies and the asset analysis on the willingness to hold stocks of different monies. The role of expectation was emphasised in order to link the monetary and real sector. Mussa assumed the rational expectation rule and showed that expectations of future returns to assets and of changes in the exchange rate itself are important in determining the exchange rate and that the problems of policy conflict existing under a fixed exchange rate system are reduced under managed floating. Dornbusch relied on the adaptive expectations rule for his general equilibrium model. In the short-run with inflexible prices and output, a fall in domestic money supply requires a rise in the domestic interest rate leading to a potential capital inflow which can be stopped only if the domestic exchange rate is expected to depreciate. An expected depreciation of the domestic currency calls for a rise of the actual spot rate above its long-run equilibrium value. The extent of overshooting depends inversely on the interest elasticity of the demand for money and the speed of adjustment of expectations.

Rational expectations play an important role in Barro's stochastic model and the latter ideally combines the various issues about inflation, demand for money, expectations and purchasing power parity discussed in the previous chapters of the book.

The microfoundations of open economy models explain the important links between consumption demands for traded and non-traded goods derived from utility maximisation and relative demands for domestic and foreign monies with exchange rate movements. In this context, Helpman and Razin and Stulz's contributions have been discussed. Frenkel and Razin have also included the government budget constraint in explaining the microfoundations. Government budget deficits current and future are shown to have important effects on interest rate and consumption and wealth of the foreign and domestic economics.

A number of contributions to the literature on the "New Theories" demonstrated that the fluctuations in the exchange rate cannot be explained by the Monetary factors alone. For example, Kouri in his short and longer-run dynamic analyses of exchange rates, shows that fiscal policy (or, real variables) affects the long-run demand for money and, therefore, the exchange rate. A synthesis of Keynesian and monetary theories has to look upon these two approaches as complementary rather than rivals. The Keynesian approach is important in the short-run as it emphasises variations in the employment and output of traded and non-traded goods and relative changes in exports and imports in explaining fluctuations in the exchange rates and balance of payments. The long-run dynamics of exchange rate movements are better explained by the monetary factors. One synthesis between Keynesian and monetary approaches is provided by Montiel. Montiel's analysis ties up the various issues discussed in Keynesian and monetary analyses of closed and open economies earlier on in the book. The Keynesian approach emphasising wage-price inflexibility is combined with the monetary approach emphasising the flow of reserves to explain the short and the long-run equilibria of a small open economy.

An alternative approach to the determination of the exchange rate developed in the name of the efficient market hypothesis. The monetary models including rational expectations rule are close to the idea of the efficient markets in an important respect: The efficient market hypothesis assumes that the spot exchange rate is based on all available information used by the economic agents to develop trading rules to earn maximum profits. An efficient market cannot be improved by new information as the latter is already accommodated. The efficient market theory has emanated from the theories of security market but it is in its early stage of development. Unlike the monetary models including rational expectation the efficient market theory implies that all monetary factors affect the exchange rate contemporaneously whereas the former group of models leads to a systematic relationship between exchange rate and past supplies of money.

# BIBLIOGRAPHY


Addison, J.T. and Burton, J., "Keynes's Analysis of Wages and Unemployment Revisited", *The Manchester School*, Sept. 1982.

Artis, M.J. and Lewis, M.K., "The Demand for Money in the UK, 1963-1973", *Manchester School* (MS), 1976.

———, "Money Supply and Demand", Chapter 1 in Bandyopadhya, T. and Ghatak, S. (Eds.), *Current Issues in Monetary Economics*, Barnes and Nobles, 1990.

Azariadis, C., "Implicit Contracts and Underemployment Equilibria", *JPE*, 1975.

Bailey, M.N., "Wages and Employment Under Uncertain Demand", *R E Studies*, Jan. 1974.

Barro, R. and Grossman, H.I., "A General Disequilibrium Model of Income and Employment", *American Economic Review* (AER), 1971.

Barro, R.J., "Rational Expectations and the Role of Monetary Policy", *Journal of Monetary Economics* (JME), 1976.

———, "Long-Term Contracting, Sticky Prices, and Monetary Policy" *JMoE*, 1977.

———, "A Capital Market in an Equilibrium Business Cycle Model", *Econometrica*, Sept. 1990.

———, *Money, Expectations and Business Cycles*, 1981.

———, "A Stochastic Equilibrium Model of an Open Economy Under Flexible Exchange Rates", *QJE*, February 1978.

Baumol, W.J., "The Transactions Demand for Cash : An Inventory Theoretic Approach", *Quarterly Journal of Economics* (QJE), 1952.

———, *Economic Theory and Operational Analysis*, Prentice-Hall, 1977.

Begg, D.; Fishcher, S. and Dornbusch, R., *Economics*, British Edition, McGraw Hill, 1984.

Benassy, J.P., *The Economics of Market Disequilibrium*, Academic Press, 1982.

Black, S.W., "Comment on R.N. Cooper, Monetary Theory and Policy in an Open Economy", *Scandinavian Journal of Economics* (SJE), 1976.

Blinder, A.S. and Slow, R.M., "Does Fiscal Policy Matter?", *Journal of Public Economics*, 1973.

———, "Does Fiscal Policy Still Matter? A Reply". *Journal of Monetary Economics*, April 1976.

———, *in: The Economics of Public Finance*, Brookings Institution, Washington D.C.

Blinder, A.S., "The Fall and Rise of Keynesian Economics", *Economic Record*, December 1988.

Brechling, F.P.R., "The Trade-Off Between Inflation and Unemployment", *JPE*, 1968.

Buiter, W.H. "'Crowding Out', and the Effectiveness of Fiscal Policy", *Journal of Public Economics*, 1977.

Cagan, P., "The Monetary Dynamics of Hyperinflation" in Friedman M. (ed), *Studies in the Quantity Theory of Money*, 1956, University of Chicago Press.

Calvo, G.A. and Rodriguez, C.A. "A Model of Exchange Rate Determination Under Currency Substitution and Rational Expectations, *SJE*, 1976.

Capie, F. and Roderik-Bali, "The Behaviour of Money and its Determinants in Interwar Britain", City University Business School, February, 1986.

Caves, D.W. and Feige, E.L., "Efficient Foreign Exchange Markets and the Monetary Approach to Exchange Rate Determination", *AER*.

Chen, C.H. and Steindl, F.G., "Anticipated Monetary and Fiscal Policy Effect on Output", *JME*, 1987.

Chiang, A.C., *Fundamental Methods of Mathematical Economics*, 1984.

Christ, C.F., "A Simple Macroeconomic Model with a Government Budget Constraint", *Journal of Political Economy (JPE), 1968.*

Clower, R., "The Keynesian Counter-Revolution : A Theoretical Appraisal" Reprinted in Clower, R. (ed.), *Monetary Theory*, 1969.

Coghlan, R.T., "A small monetary model of the UK economy", *Bank of England Discussion Paper, No. 3*, 1979.

Cooper, R.N., "Monetary Theory and Policy in an Open Economy", *SJE*, 1976.

Courakis, A.S., "Serial Correlation and the Bank of England's Demand for Money Function : Exercise in Measurement Without Theory", *EJ*, September, 1978.

Cuthbertson, K., *The Supply and Demand for Money*, Basil Blackwell, 1988.

Darby, M.R., "The Allocation of Transitory Income Among Consumers' Assets". *The American Economic Review* (AER), 1972.

Dennis, G.E.J., *Monetary Economics*, Longman.

Dornbusch, R., *Open Economy Macroeconomics*, New York Basic, 1980.

———, "PPP Exchange-Rate Rules and Macroeconomic Stability", *JPE*, 1982.

———, "The Theory of Flexible Exchange Rate Regimes and Macroeconomic Policy", *SJE*, 1976.

Duesenberry, J.S., *Income, Saving and the Theory of Consumer Behaviour*, HUP, 1946.

Fackler, J.S., "A Note on the Interactions among Monetary Policy, the Tax structure and Equilibrium Output". *JME*, Winter, 1982.

Fischer, S., "Long-Term Contracts Rational Expectations and the Optimal Money Supply Rule". *Journal of Political Economy* (JPE), 1977, Reprinted in Lucas, R.E. Jr. and Sargent, T. (eds), *Rational Expectations and Econometric Practice*, George Allen and Unwin, 1981.

———, "Comment on R. Dornbusch, The Theory of Flexible Exchange ... Policy", *SJE*, 1976.

———, "Comments on Tobin and Buiter" in Stein, J.L. (ed), *Monetarism*, 1976.

Fisher, I., *The Purchasing Power of Money*, New York, Macmillan, 1911.

Fleming, J.M., "Domestic Financial Policies Under Fixed and Under Floating Exchange Rates", IMF Staff Papers, 1962.

Frenkel, J.A., "A Monetary Approach to the Exchange Rate : Doctrinal Aspects and Empirical Evidence", *SJE*, 1976.

Frenkel, J.A., Gylfason, T. and Helliwell, J.F., "A Synthesis of Monetary and Keynesian Approaches to Short-run Balance of Payments Theory", *The Economic Journal* (EJ), 1980.

Frenkel, J.A. and Razin, "Fiscal Policies in the World Economy", *JPE*. 1986.

Friedman, M., *Studies in the Quantity Theory of Money*, (ed), University of Chicago Press, 1956.

———, "The Quantity Theory of Money : A Restatement" in Friedman, M. (ed) 1956.

———, *A Theory of the Consumption Function*, 1957.

———, "The Role of Monetary Policy", *AER*, 1968.

———, *The Optimum Quantity of Money, and Other Essays*, Chicago, 1969.

———, "A Theoretical Framework for Monetary Analysis", *JPE*, 1970.

———, "A Monetary Theory of National Income", *JPE*, 1971.

———, "The Nobel Lecture : Inflation and Unemployment", *JPE*, 1977.

Friedman, M. and Schwartz, A., "Money and Business Cycles", *Review of Economics and Statistics* (R E Stats.) Supplement, 1963.

Gordon, D.F., "A Neo-Classical Theory of Keynesian Unemployment", *Economic Enquiry*, December 1974.

———, "What is New-Keynesian Economics?", *Journal of Economic Literature*, Sept. 1990.

Gowland, D. *Control of Money in the United Kingdom.*

Greenaway, D. and Shaw, R., *Macroeconomics : Theory and Policy in the U.K.*

Grice, J. and Bennett, A., "Wealth and Demand for £M3 in the United Kingdom 1963-78", *MS*, 1984.

Groenwold, N., "The Effects of Fiscal Policy in a Two-Period Model", *JME*, Winter 1984.

Grossman, H.I. and Lucas, R.E. Jr., "The Macroeconomic Effects of Productive Public Expenditure", *MS*, June 1974.

Grossman, H.I., "Employment Fluctuations and the Mitigation of Risk", *Economic Enquiry*, 1979.

Grossman, J., "The Rationality of Money Supply Expectations and the Short-run Response of Interest Rates to Monetary Surprises", *Journal of Money, Credit and Banking*, 1981.

Hall, R.E., "Stochastic Implications of Life-Cycle Permanent Income Hypothesis", Reprinted in Lucas, R.E. and Sargent, T.J. (eds), 1981.

Haache, G., "The Demand for Money in the U.K. Experience Since 1971", *Bank of England Quarterly Bulletin*, Sept. 1974.

Helpman, E. and Razin, A., "Towards a Consistent Comparison of all Exchange Rate Systems", Canadian Journal of Economics, 1979.

Henderson, J.M. and Quandt, R.E., *Microeconomic Theory*, McGraw Hill, 1980.

Hicks, J.R., "Mr Keynes and the Classics : Suggested Interpretation", *Econometrica*, 1937.

———, "Is-LM — An Explanation", *Journal of Post-Keynesian Economics*, November 1980.

Hiller, B., "Rational Expectations, the Government Budget Constraint and the OptimalMoney Supply"", *Journal of Macroeconomics*, 1985.

Johnson, H.G. and Nobay, A.R. (eds), *The Current Inflation*, London, 1971.

Johnston, R.B., "A Disequilibrium Monetary Model of the U.K. Economy", *H M Treasury*, 1983.

Keynes, J.M., *The General Theory of Employment, Interest and Money*, London Macmillan, 1936.

———, "The General Theory of Employment", *QJE*, 1937.

———, "Professor Pigou on Money Wages in Relation to Unemployment", *EJ*, 1937.

Knight, F.H., *Risk, Uncertainty and Profit*, Boston, 1921.

Kogiku, A.C., Macroeconomic Models, 1968.

Kouri, P.J.K., "The Exchange Rate and the Balance of Payments in the Short-run and in the Long-run : A Monetary Approach", *SJE*, 1976.

Laidler, D., *The Demand for Money : Theories and Evidence*, 1969.

———, "The Phillips Curve, Expectations and Incomes Policy" in H.G. Johnson and Nobay, A.R. (eds), *The Current Inflation*, London New York, 1971.

Laidler, D. and Parkin, M., "The Demand for Money in the United Kingdom 1956-67". *MS*, 1970

———, "Inflation : A Survey", *EJ*, December 1975.

Laumas, G.S., "A Test of the stability of the demand for money", *Scottish Journal of Political Economy*, 1978.

Leijonhufvud, A., *On Keynesian Economics and the Economics of Keynes*, Oxford University Press, 1968.

Leontief, W., "The Fundamental Assumption of the Keynes's Monetary Theory of Unemployment", *QJE*, 1937.

———, "Postulates : Keynes's General Theory and the Classicists" in Harris, S.E. (ed.), *The New Economics — Keynes"s Influence on Theory and Public Policy*, NY, 1947.

Levacic, R. and Rebman, A., *Macroeconomics : An Introduction to Neo-Classical and Keynesian Controversies*, Macmillan, 1982.

Lipsey, R.G., "The Relationship between Unemployment and the Rate of Change — 1861-1957", a Further Analysis, *Economica*, 1960.

Lipsey, R.G. and Parkin, M.J., "Incomes Policy : A Reappraisal", *Economica*, 1970.

Lucas, R.E. Jr., "Expectations and the Neutrality of Money", *Journal of Economic Theory* (JET), 1972.

———, "Some International Evidence on Output-Inflation Trade-Offs", *AER*, 1973, 326-34.

———, "An Equilibrium Model of the Business Cycle", *JPE*, 1975.

Lucas, R.E. Jr. and Sargent, T.J. (eds.), *Rational Expectations and Econometric Practice*, 1981.

Malinvaud, E., "Wages and Unemployment", *Economic Journal* (EJ), 1982.

Mankiw, N.G., "A Quick Refresher Course in Macroeconomics", *J E Lit*, December 1990.

Mayer, T., "the Empirical Significance of the Real Balance Effect"", *QJE*, 1959.

Mayes, D., *Applications of Econometrics*, Prentice Hall, 1981.

McMahon, M.R., "An Appraisal of the New Classical Macroeconomics", *JME*, Summer 1984, p.335-46.

Meltzer, A.H., "The Demand for Money : The Evidence from the Time-Series", *JPE*, June 1963.

Miller, S.M., "Dynamic Monetary and Fiscal Policy and the Government Budget Constraint : A Growth Equilibrium", *JME*, Summer 1980.

Mishkin, J., "Does Anticipated Monetary Policy Matter? An Econometric Investigation", *JPE*, 1982, pp.22-51.

Montiel, P., "Long-run Equilibrium in a Keynesian Model of a Small Open Economy", IMF Staff Papers, 1986.

Mundell, R.A., "The Appropriate Use of Fiscal and Monetary Policy for Internal and External Stability", IMF Staff Papers, 1962.

Mussa, M., "The Exchange Rate, the Balance of Payments and Monetary and Fiscal Policy under a Regime of Controlled Floating", *SJE*, 1976, pp.229-48.

———, "A Model of Exchange Rate Dynamics", *JPE*, 1982.

Muth, J.F., "Rational Expectations and the Theory of Price Movements", *Econometrica*, 1961, pp.315-35.

Myhrman, J., "Experiences of Flexible Exchange Rates in Earlier Periods : Theories, Evidence and a New View", *SJE*, 1976.

Nash, C.R., "Two Person Cooperative Games", *Econometrica*, 1953.

Nelson, C.R., "Adjustment Lags Versus Information Versus Lags : A Test of Alternative Explanations of the Phillips Curve Phenomenon", *JMCB*, 1981.

Nickell, S., "Unemployment, A Survey", *EJ*, June 1990.

Ott, D.J. and Ott, A.F., "Budget Balance and Equilibrium Income", *Journal of Finance*, 1965.

Patinkin, D., *Money, Interest and Prices*, Harper and Row, 1956, 1965.

Perry, G.L., "The Determinants of Wage Rate Changes and the Inflation-Unemployment Trade-Off for the United States", *R E Studies*, 1964.

Per Meinich, Comment on R.N. Cooper, "Monetary Theory and Policy in an Open Economy", *SJE*, 1976.

Pesaran, M.H., "A Critique of the Proposed Tests of the Natural Rate — Rational Expectations Hypothesis", *EJ*, 1982.

Phelps, E.S., *Microeconomic Foundations of Employment and Inflation Theory*, Norton 1970.
———, "Money Wage Dynamics and Labour Market Equilibrium", *JPE*, 1968.
———, *Employment and Inflation*, Academic Press, 1979.
——— and Taylor, J.B., "Stabilising Powers of Monetary Policy Under Rational Expectations", *JPE*, 1977.
Phillips, A.W., "The Relation between Unemployment and the Rate of Change of Money Wage Rates in the U.K. '1861-1957", *Economica*, 1958.
Pigou, A.C., "The Value of Money", *QJE*, 1917.
———, *The Theory of Unemployment*, London Macmillan, 1933.
———, "Real and Money Wages in Relation to Unemployment", *EJ*, 1937.
———, "The Classical Stationary State", *EJ*, December 1943.
———, *Employment and Equilibrium*, Macmillan, London 1944.
———, *Lapses from Full Employment*, Macmillan 1944.
———, *The Veil of Money*, Macmillan 1949.
———, *Keynes's General Theory : A Retrospective View*, Macmillan 1952.
Possen, U. and Slutsky, S., "Private Public Consumption Trade-Offs and the Balanced Budget Multiplier", *QJE*, December 1980.
Rowan, D.C. and Miller, J., "The Demand for Money in the UK 1963-77", University of Southampton Discussion Paper, 1979.
Sapsford, D., *Labour Market Economics*, Allen and Unwin, 1981.
Sargent, T.J., "Rational Expectations, The Real Rate of Interest and the Natural Rate of Unemployment", Reprinted in Lucas, R.E. and Sargent, T.J. (Eds.) 1981.
——— and Wallace, N., "Rational Expectations, the Optimal Monetary Instrument and the Optimal Money Supply Rule", Reprinted in Lucas, R.E. and Sargent, T.J. (eds.) 1981.
Scarth, W.M., "Friedman's Framework for Economic Stability and the Government Budget Constraint", *The Manchester School*, 1982.
———, "Rational Expectations and the Instability of Bond Financing", *Economic Letters*, 1980.
Smith G., "The Long Run Consequences of Monetary and Fiscal Policies When the Government Budget is Not Balanced", *Journal of Public Economics*, 1979.
———, "Flexible Policies and IS-LM Dynamics", *JME*, Summer, 1980.
Stein, J.L. (ed.), *Monetarism*, North Holland, 1976.

Stulz, R.M., "An Equilibrium Model of Exchange Rates Determination and Asset Pricing with Nontraded Goods and Imperfect Information", *JPE*, 1986.

Surrey, M.J.C., *Macroeconomic Themes Oxford University Press*, 1976.

Teigen, R., "Demand and Supply Functions for Money in the United States : Some Structural Estimates", *Econometrica*, 1964.

Thornton, D.L., "The Government Budget Constraint with Endogenous Money", *JME*, Winter 1984.

Tobin, J., "The Interest Elasticity of Transactions Demand for Cash", *R E Stats.*, 1956, pp.241-47.

———, "Liquidity Preference As behaviour Towards Risk", *R E Studies*, 1958.

———, "Friedman's Theoretical Framework", *JPE*, 1972.

———, *Essays in Macroeconomics*, 1975.

———, "Inflation and Unemployment", *AER*, 1972.

——— and Buiter, W., "Long-Run Effects of Fiscal and Monetary policy On Aggregate Demand", Chapter 4 in Stein, J.L. (ed.) *Monetarism.*

Trevithick, J.A., "Inflation, the Natural unemployment Rate and the Theory of Economic Policy", *Scottish journal of Political Economy*, 1976.

———, "Money Wage Inflexibility and the Keynesian Labour Supply Function", *EJ*, 1976.

———, *Inflation : A Guide to the Crisis in Economics*, Penguin, 1977.

Turnovsky, S.J., *Macroeconomic Analysis and Stabilisation Policy*, Cambridge University Press, 1979.

———, "The Expectations Hypothesis and the Aggregate Wage Equations : Some Empirical Evidence for Canada", *Economica*, 1972.

Wicksell K., *Interest and Prices*, Cass Reprint of Economics Classics, London, 1962.

# INDEX